Muzhik
and Muscovite

Muzhik and Muscovite

Urbanization in
Late Imperial Russia

Joseph Bradley

UNIVERSITY OF CALIFORNIA PRESS
Berkeley · Los Angeles · London

University of California Press
Berkeley and Los Angeles, California
University of California Press, Ltd.
London, England
© 1985 by
The Regents of the University of California
Printed in the United States of America

1 2 3 4 5 6 7 8 9

Library of Congress Cataloging in Publication Data

Bradley, Joseph.
  Muzhik and Muscovite.

  Based on the author's doctoral thesis.
  Bibliography: p.
  Includes index.
  1. Urbanization—Russian S.F.S.R.—Moscow—History.
2. Rural-urban migration—Russian S.F.S.R.—Moscow—
History.   3. Social integration—Russian S.F.S.R.—Moscow
—History.   4. Social classes—Russian S.F.S.R.—Moscow—
History.   I. Title.
HT145.S58B73   1985   307.7′6′0947312   84-2535
ISBN 0-520-05168-8

To Ira

Contents

Illustrations

PLATES

Tables

Acknowledgments

This book could never have been completed without the generous financial support of many institutions. Grants from the International Research and Exchange Board and the Committee on Fulbright-Hays Fellowships sponsored a year of research in the Soviet Union, and employment as an editor at "Mir" Publishers permitted me to spend an additional year in Moscow. Financial support for other periods of research, writing, and manuscript preparation came also from the Russian Research Center of Harvard University, the National Endowment for the Humanities, and the Office of Research, the Word Processing Center, and the College of Arts and Sciences of the University of Tulsa.

I am grateful to the staffs of several libraries and archives. In the Soviet Union, the librarians of Reading Room Number One at the Lenin Library cheerfully trotted out unending piles of municipal publications. Very helpful also were librarians and archivists at the Leningrad Public Library, the Historical Library in Moscow, the Museum of the History and Reconstruction of Moscow, the Central State Historical Archive of the City of Moscow, and the Central State Historical Archive in Leningrad. Much of the published material I have used is available outside the Soviet Union, and I was fortunate to be able to use the research facilities of Harvard University Library, the Library of Congress, New York Public Library, Columbia University Library, and the Slavic Division of the Helsinki University Library. Finally, I am grateful to the staff of the Interlibrary Loan Office at the University of Tulsa.

I have benefited greatly from the encouragement and criticism of many individuals. Richard Pipes guided the doctoral dissertation that provided the basis for the present book. In the Soviet Union Ivan D. Koval'chenko and Aleksandr S. Nifontov gave valuable advice on sources. I am also grateful to many who read earlier versions of this work and shared their comments: Dan Brower, Tom Buckley, John Bushnell, Ben Eklof, Dan Field, Greg Freeze, Patricia Grimsted, Michael Hamm, Pat Herlihy, Ned Keenan, Kate Lynch, Brenda Meehan-Waters, Thomas Owen, Andrejs Plakans, Marc Schulkin, and Theodore Von Laue. Any shortcomings that still remain are my own responsibility.

Michael Ramirez and Suzanne Tumy have been especially helpful in computing and compiling detailed statistical material, and Susan Matula helped track down rare sources. Randy Schmidt prepared the maps and graphs, and Susan Huffman and Connie Robins have quickly and cheerfully typed the manuscript. My editors at the University of California Press—Sheila Levine, Phyllis Killen and Gladys Castor—have efficiently and meticulously transformed the manuscript into a book.

I wish to thank the editors of *Russian History* and *Russian Review* for permission to include revisions of my articles. Parts of chapter 4 appeared in a somewhat different form as "Patterns of Peasant Migration to Late Nineteenth-Century Moscow: How Much Should We Read into Literacy Rates?" *Russian History*, 6, pt. 1 (1979): 22–38; and parts of chapters 7 and 8 appeared as "The Moscow Workhouse and Municipal Welfare Reform in Russia," *Russian Review*, 41, no. 4 (October 1982): 427–44.

Photographs 1 and 7 were provided through the courtesy of the Library of Congress. The remaining photographs were provided through the courtesy of the Museum of the History and Reconstruction of Moscow.

Finally, according to table 18 of volume 7 of the terse 1970 Soviet census, between 1968 and 1970, 201,639 persons had moved to Moscow and 37,803 had left Iaroslavl' *oblast'*. One of those individuals, Irina Krivtsova, is now my wife, and I am grateful for her assistance in my research and for her understanding and support at all stages in the preparation of this book.

Abbreviations

The following abbreviations and short titles have been used in the footnotes and bibliography:

GPD 1902   *Glavneishie predvaritel'nye dannye perepisi g. Moskvy 1902 g.*

GPD 1912   *Glavneishie predvaritel'nye dannye perepisi g. Moskvy 1912 g.*

IMGD   *Izvestiia Moskovskoi gorodskoi dumy*

PM 1882   *Perepis' Moskvy 1882 g.*

PM 1902   *Perepis' Moskvy 1902 g.*

PSZ   *Polnoe sobranie zakonov Rossiiskoi imperii*

PVP   *Pervaia vseobshchaia perepis' naseleniia Rossiiskoi imperii, 1897 g.*

Sbornik statei   *Sbornik statei po voprosam, otnosiashchimsia k zhizni russkikh i inostrannykh gorodov*

SEM   *Statisticheskii ezhegodnik g. Moskvy*

SEMMG   *Statisticheskii ezhegodnik Moskvy i Moskovskoi gubernii*

SSS 1889   *Sbornik statisticheskikh svedenii o blagotvoritel'-nosti Moskvy za 1889 g.*

SSS 1901   *Sbornik spravochnykh svedenii o blagotvoritel'nosti v Moskve*

TPZ   *Torgovo-promyshlennye zavedeniia g. Moskvy v 1885–1890 gg.*

TsGAM   Tsentral'nyi gosudarstvennyi arkhiv g. Moskvy
TsGIA   Tsentral'nyi gosudarstvennyi istoricheskii arkhiv
            SSSR

Introduction

At the beginning of the twentieth century urban Russia faced "a most serious danger—a growing class of people who avoid a normal life and regular work." According to one contemporary, "the streets of Russia are swarming with . . . vagrants, paupers, idlers, parasites and hooligans." If the West "with more advanced labor and welfare legislation and a more cultured population" had a large number of persons who "avoid regular work," then what could be expected in Russia "where conditions are very favorable for the spread of a class of people having no livelihood and consequently risking nothing in their bold attacks on the lives, property, and honor of their neighbors."[1]

Written in the aftermath of the 1905 revolution, these words express the threat the empire's teeming and volatile urban and industrial areas posed to the established order. The "disorders" of 1905, more concentrated than Russia's many peasant rebellions and more protracted than any previous strike movement, demonstrated the urgency of urban social problems in what was still generally regarded as an agrarian country. Particularly volatile was Moscow, a city which had had less industrial strife than St. Petersburg or some of the smaller mill towns not far away, but which exploded in the general strike and in the December uprising of 1905. In this context, a "growing class of people who avoid a normal life and regular work" and who make "bold attacks on the lives, property, and honor of their neighbors" posed a special danger, not only to the authorities and industrialists,

---

1. V.A. Gagen, "Predstoiashchaia reforma rabotnykh domov," *IMGD*, 32, no. 6–7 (June–July 1908): 30, 32, 36.

but to the very fabric of the city and all its residents. Yet, though 1905 heightened the fear of the "elemental passions of the masses" and the sense of urgency about social problems, the underlying attitude of the educated elite toward the common people—their alleged vices, disreputable behavior, and lack of commitment to the values of modern urban industrial society—was formulated well before this fateful year in Russian politics. Because of the importance of a stable and disciplined citizenry in Russia's new urban and industrial social order, long before the barricades of 1905, the city council, the police, and the professionals were well aware of the consequences of an unhealthy urban environment.

The purpose of the present study will be to analyze the strains of Russia's urbanization and the interaction between the educated elite and the common people through a case study of late nineteenth-century Moscow, the empire's second largest city. Who composed this "growing class of people swarming the streets of Russia" and why did they appear to be avoiding "normal life and regular work"? What conditions favored their growth? How did the city's educated elite, in the title represented by "Muscovite," try to integrate the common people, in the main first- and second-generation peasant immigrants and in the title represented by "muzhik," into the modern urban industrial world and its values?[2] The thesis of this book is that specific economic, demographic, and social conditions of metropolises such as Moscow created not only unprecedented opportunity but also "streets swarming" with "people having no livelihood," hardly an encouraging sign for the development of a disciplined labor force and sober urban citizenry; that in their effort to ameliorate these deleterious conditions and transform a semipeasant labor force, reformers, like their counterparts in Europe and North America, fearful of the alleged laziness, depravity, and demoralization of the common people, tried to transform the values and habits of the city's muzhiks; and finally, that in the effort to transform the muzhik at the end of the nineteenth century, an ethos of individual and social reform evolved among urban professionals, administrators, and philanthropists.

2. Throughout this study the term "muzhik" signifies the common people or the "lower classes," not exclusively those of the peasant estate or those born in the countryside. This usage conforms to the primary meaning of the word given in Dal'. The term "Muscovite" refers to the educated elite, not necessarily to those of Moscow birth. These terms represent images rather than precise socioeconomic categories. See Vladimir Dal', *Tolkovyi slovar' zhivogo velikorusskogo iazyka* (reprinted from the 2d ed. 4 vols. Moscow, 1955), vol. 2, p. 357.

❖   ❖   ❖

The social history of late imperial Russia cannot be written without an analysis of urbanization, the building blocks of which are local studies. Since there are still too few local histories, one of the objectives of this study is to present a strong sense of place.[3] Moscow is a natural choice of study because of the abundance of statistical and descriptive material gathered by its active organs of local administration. In particular, the remarkably detailed city censuses of 1882 and 1902 and a myriad of government reports made Moscow and its hinterland the most thoroughly studied part of the empire. A living city does indeed emerge from dry municipal reports and statistics, through which the growth and development of the city as well as the texture of daily life of the muzhik may be observed. The living city emerges also from the impressionistic descriptions of contemporaries; indeed, the images so formed, far from being solely abstractions, were themselves a factor in the process of urbanization. These municipal reports and descriptions are doubly valuable because they also reveal to the historian the attitude of the municipal authorities and reformers toward the common people. Formed during periods of relative industrial calm, the attitude of Muscovite toward muzhik has a certain pristine clarity before the industrial and political strife that engulfed the city in 1905. Accordingly, this is a study not of Moscow in revolution but of the process of urbanization.

Moscow's demographic and economic dynamism also makes it a

3. Among the best of the local studies, particularly concerning St. Petersburg and Moscow, are Reginald Zelnik, *Labor and Society in Tsarist Russia: The Factory Workers of St. Petersburg, 1855–1870* (Stanford, 1971); B. N. Kazantsev, *Rabochie Moskvy i Moskovskoi gubernii v seredine XIX veka* (Moscow, 1976); M. K. Rozhkova, *Formirovanie kadrov promyshlennykh rabochikh v 60-kh-nachale 80-kh godov XIX v.: Po materialam Moskovskoi gubernii* (Moscow, 1974); Robert E. Johnson, *Peasant and Proletarian: The Working Class of Moscow in the Late Nineteenth Century* (New Brunswick, N.J., 1979), and "Peasant Migration and the Russian Working Class: Moscow at the End of the Nineteenth Century," *Slavic Review*, 35, no. 4 (December 1976): 652–64; James H. Bater, *St. Petersburg: Industrialization and Change* (Montreal, 1976), and "Transience, Residential Persistence and Mobility in Moscow and St. Petersburg, 1900–1914," *Slavic Review*, 39, no. 2 (June 1980): 239–54; Laura Engelstein, "Moscow in the 1905 Revolution: A Study in Class Conflict and Political Organization," Ph.D. dissertation (Stanford University, 1976); Diane Koenker, *Moscow Workers and the 1917 Revolution* (Princeton, 1981); Victoria Bonnell, *Roots of Rebellion: Workers' Politics and Organizations in St Petersburg and Moscow, 1900–1914* (Berkeley, 1984), and "Urban Working Class Life in Early Twentieth-Century Russia: Some Problems and Patterns," *Russian History*, 8, pt. 3 (1981): 360–78. However, with the exception of Bater's work on St. Petersburg, the study of the *city* and of *urbanization* is subordinate to the study of the working class.

natural choice of study. By the beginning of the twentieth century, its one million inhabitants made Moscow the tenth most populous of the world's cities and, among these ten, the fastest growing. In the half century preceding the outbreak of World War I, its size increased four-fold. During the period 1900–1914 Moscow's growth rate was almost 4 percent per annum, on a par with that of New York. Like New York, Moscow was a city of immigrants: almost three-quarters of the population had been born somewhere else, and two-thirds of the population were registered in the peasant estate.[4] As the heart of the Central Indus-trial Region and hub of the empire's railway network and as one of the major centers of the production, distribution, and consumption of goods and services, Moscow had a diversified economy, and its labor force was distributed in every craft and trade practiced at the end of the nineteenth century. Thus, the strains of urbanization can be examined from a broad economic and social perspective.

Important as the building blocks of a local study are, urbanization consists of much more than the growth, development, and images of cities. By definition a process of change, urbanization illustrates broader changes in society. Like a prism that scatters rays of light, urbanization as an object of study reveals a broad spectrum of prob-lems confronting a society in the process of modernization. For ex-ample, a particularly critical aspect of urbanization, as well as of broader societal change, is the transformation of a large part of the rural population into a stable urban citizenry. The immigration of larger and larger numbers of the rural population constitutes only part of this transformation. The city must integrate the common people into the ways of life and values of the modern urban and industrial world. To borrow a phrase from Gaetano Mosca, the "organized minority" must impose more disciplined economic and social orga-nization and rational value systems upon the "unorganized majority."[5]

The social history of late imperial Russia cannot be written without an analysis also of the interaction between the world of the educated elite and that of the common people, most of them peasants. The interaction of these two worlds, of course, had begun long before the second half of the nineteenth century, but the Great Reforms ushered in an era of unprecedented dynamism in Russian society and of

4. Moskovskaia gorodskaia uprava, *Sovremennoe khoziaistvo goroda Moskvy* (Moscow, 1913), 7; A. G. Rashin, *Naselenie Rossii za 100 let (1811–1913): Statisti-cheskie ocherki* (Moscow, 1956), 112, 116.

5. Quoted in T. B. Bottomore, *Elites and Society* (New York, 1964), 3, 31, 37.

increasing contact between the two worlds. Bodies of local administration and government, such as the zemstvo, as well as private organizations attracted a growing number of professionals whose duties consisted of studying the common people and formulating policy to meet their needs. Whereas the struggle of the educated elite, and in particular the professionals, against the autocracy for political and civil liberties and autonomy in local affairs, and their struggle with radical politicians for leadership of the opposition and for support among the populace, have been well documented, their struggle against the poverty and ignorance of the common people has only recently begun to receive attention.[6] In the present study I have chosen the areas of poor relief and housing reform to illustrate this struggle.[7] The effort at social and individual reform proceeded throughout the nation at a quickening pace after the 1890s. Nowhere was the urgency of social reform greater than in the two metropolises, St. Petersburg and Moscow. Here the problems posed by economic development and structural shifts, rapid population growth and increased mobility, and chaotic urban expansion urgently demanded attention at the turn of the century. These problems and the relationship between the common people, who allegedly were responsible for them, and the educated elite, who tried to

6. The political struggles of the liberals can be found in many studies, including George Fischer, *Russian Liberalism from Gentry to Intelligentsia* (Cambridge, Mass., 1958); Shmuel Galai, *The Liberation Movement in Russia, 1900–1905* (Cambridge, 1973); Richard Pipes, *Struve: Liberal on the Left, 1870–1905* (Cambridge, 1970); and William Rosenberg, *Liberals in the Russian Revolution: The Constitutional Democratic Party, 1917–1921* (Princeton, 1974). Unfortunately, studies not only of liberalism but also of the government tend to slight urban institutions and urban reforms. See, for example, N. P. Eroshkin, *Ocherki istorii gosudarstvennykh uchrezhdenii dorevoliutsionnoi Rossii* (Moscow, 1960); George L. Yaney, *The Systematization of Russian Government: Social Evolution in the Domestic Administration of Imperial Russia, 1711–1905* (Urbana, Ill., 1973); S. Frederick Starr, *Decentralization and Self-Government in Russia, 1830–1870* (Princeton, 1972). Among the urban studies available are Walter Hanchett, "Moscow in the Late Nineteenth Century: A Study in Municipal Self-Government," Ph.D. dissertation (University of Chicago, 1964); Michael Hamm, ed., *The City in Russian History* (Lexington, Ky., 1976), and "Khar'kov's Progressive Duma, 1910–1914: A Study in Russian Municipal Reform," *Slavic Review*, 40, no. 1 (March 1981): 17–36; James Bater, "Some Dimensions of Urbanization and the Response of Municipal Government: Moscow and St. Petersburg," *Russian History*, 5, pt. 2 (1978): 46–63; and Daniel Brower, "Urban Russia on the Eve of World War I: A Social Profile," *Journal of Social History*, 13, no. 3 (Spring 1980): 424–36. See also the series *Russkii gorod*, volumes of which appear irregularly, published by Moscow State University.

7. Studies of the struggle of professionals against the poverty and ignorance of the common people in the areas of public health and education include the contributions of Nancy Frieden and David Ransel in David Ransel, ed., *The Family in Imperial Russia* (Urbana, Ill., 1978); Arthur Benoit Eklof, "Spreading the Word: Primary Education and the Zemstvo in Moscow Province, 1864–1910," Ph.D. dissertation (Princeton University, 1976); and Frieden, *Russian Physicians in an Era of Reform and Revolution, 1856–1905* (Princeton, 1981).

solve them, were the essence of urbanization and will be the subjects of the following chapters.

Part One of this study will set the stage for analyzing the relationship between muzhik and Muscovite by presenting a broad survey of economic changes, population growth, and urbanization of Moscow's hinterland. This is followed by a discussion of Moscow's history, physical environment, and economy. Part Two analyzes three of the most important aspects of the muzhik's experience: immigration, employment, and the housing market. Part Three introduces Muscovites' perceptions of and attitudes toward the muzhik and traces the evolution of welfare policy from one limited to relief and repression to a more ambitious policy promising individual reform and regeneration. Parts One and Two both begin with the relationship between Moscow and its hinterland and then proceed to concentrate on the city itself; Part Three reverses this pattern somewhat by beginning with an analysis of welfare in the city and closing with a discussion of an ethos of individual reform that extended far beyond the city limits of Moscow.

PART ONE

Moscow

CHAPTER ONE

Moscow and Its Hinterland, 1861–1900

Many of the images we have of imperial Russia are of rural life: the country estates of the nobility, log cabins, peasants working in the fields, troikas streaking over a meringue-like countryside, languid summer evenings, the ozoned scent of pine forests. Occasionally a fleeting image of a city will appear—the angular facades of St. Petersburg, the gilded onion domes of Moscow—but we do not now, nor did many people then, associate old Russia with its cities, much less with urban life. Yet city growth was proceeding at a rapid pace, and by 1900 Russia was the only country except the United States to have two cities among the world's ten largest. Rapid urban growth was both a cause and an effect of important national and regional demographic, economic, and social trends, trends which provide the background for the particularly acute strains of urbanization in Moscow.

These acute strains developed in the context of tremendous overall national economic growth. Industrial growth began cautiously in the 1860s and 1870s, continued with the boom of the 1890s, and picked up again in the years before World War I. The saga of Russian industrialization—the Witte system, foreign entrepreneurship, production figures for steel and oil—is too familiar to merit repeating here. Most impressive was the rapidity of industrial growth: of 14,464 industrial establishments in operation at the beginning of the twentieth century, 85 percent were founded after 1861 and 40 percent were founded between 1891 and 1902.[1] Although Moscow and its hinterland, Rus-

1. A. G. Pogozhev, *Uchet chislennosti i sostava rabochikh v Rossii* (St. Petersburg, 1906), 4–5.

sia's oldest industrial region, did not experience such spectacular growth in the half century prior to World War I, the Moscow region remained the nation's largest and one of the most important industrial regions. The value of production of the city's industries grew from 28,428,000 rubles in 1853 to 134,299,000 rubles in 1890. By 1900 Moscow accounted for 8.6 percent of the value of European Russia's industries and 14.1 percent of the value of its domestic commerce.[2] In 1908 Moscow handled 11.8 percent of the empire's total freight, one-third of which was in transit.[3] Its share of the empire's railroad freight was greater and grew from approximately 11 percent of the empire's 83,664,000 tons in 1891–93 to more than 14 percent of 116,460,000 tons in 1897–1898.[4]

The overall importance of Russia's rapid industrial growth and economic dynamism notwithstanding, Moscow's socioeconomic conditions and rapid population growth can be better understood in the context of the agriculture and industry of its hinterland. That hinterland included Moscow province itself and seven surrounding provinces. One of the smallest provinces in European Russia (only Kaluga, Tula, Kursk, and Estonia were smaller), Moscow province was divided into thirteen counties (*uezdy*); named for their county seats (*uezdnyi gorod*), they were Bogorodsk, Bronnitsy, Dmitrov, Klin, Kolomna, Moscow, Mozhaisk, Podol'sk, Ruza, Serpukhov, Vereia, Volokolamsk, and Zvenigorod. (See map 1.) In very crude terms we could divide the province into the more industrial southeastern counties of Bogorodsk, Kolomna, Serpukhov, and Moscow itself, and the nonindustrial western counties of Ruza, Mozhaisk, Vereia, and Volokolamsk; the remaining counties fell somewhere in between, both geographically and economically. In the more industrial counties a relatively smaller portion of the land was arable than in the western counties, though more was used intensively and profitably for truck gardening and dairying. Factories had sprung up in the late eighteenth century, and by the end of the nineteenth century, several in Kolomna and Serpukhov, such as the Kolomna Machine Plant, were among the largest in the country. The inhabitants of Bogorodsk, almost one-quarter of whom were Old Believers, engaged

2. Akademiia nauk SSSR, Institut istorii, *Istoriia Moskvy*, 6 vols. (Moscow, 1952–1959), 4:73; 5:35.

3. Ibid., 5:46. The Russian measurements are 4,648,000,000 and 6,470,000,000 *poods*, respectively.

4. Ibid., 5:52; P. I. Liashchenko, *History of the National Economy of Russia*, trans. L. M. Herman (New York, 1949), 512; *Moskva: Putevoditel'* (Moscow, 1915), 220.

MAP 1. COUNTIES OF MOSCOW PROVINCE

extensively in small-scale domestic production, especially in wool and silk weaving.

Farther from Moscow, the provinces of Kaluga, Iaroslavl', Riazan', Smolensk, Tula, Tver', and Vladimir constituted the remainder of the hinterland. (See map 2.) Two provinces, Tula and Riazan', were considered by the government to be part of the Central Agricultural Region (the other provinces being Kursk, Voronezh, Orel, Tambov, and Chernigov); the remaining, along with Moscow itself as well as Kostroma and Nizhnii Novgorod, constituted the Central Industrial Region. Following the grouping made above for the counties of Moscow province, it makes sense to speak of one industrial province—Vladimir—and six semi-industrial or agricultural provinces. The names Ivanovo-Voznesensk, Shuia, and Orekhovo were synonymous with the country's textile industry. Pokrov county of Vladimir had two gigantic Morozov factories, one of which, the Nikol'skaia factory of Savva Morozov with 17,252 workers in 1894, was the largest in the country. The average factory in Vladimir employed 483, the largest figure in the region. By comparison, the average factory employed 229 workers in Tver', 224 in

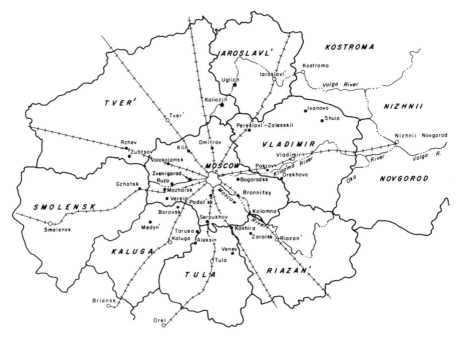

MAP 2. MOSCOW'S HINTERLAND

Moscow province, 189 in Riazan', 177 in Iaroslavl', 110 in Kaluga, 95 in Smolensk, and 75 in Tula.[5]

Accounts of late-nineteenth-century peasant life are nearly unanimous in their pessimistic portrayal of rural stagnation and agricultural decline in the Central Industrial and Central Agricultural Regions. Decades of unprecedented rural population growth had made the countryside hopelessly overcrowded. Although peasants owned approximately 50 percent of the land and almost everywhere gentry primacy in landholding was giving way to that of the peasants, the size of the peasant allotments was shrinking to such an extent that by 1900 the average allotment was less than two-thirds what it had been

5. L. N. Iasnopol'skii, ed. *Statistiko-ekonomicheskie ocherki oblastei, gubernii i gorodov Rossii* (Kiev, 1913), 264; N. A. Komarov, *Voenno-statisticheskoe opisanie Moskovskoi, Vladimirskoi i Nizhegorodskoi gubernii* (Moscow, 1895), 289; and P. A. Orlov and S. G. Budagov, eds., *Ukazatel' fabrik i zavodov Evropeiskoi Rossii*, 3d ed. (St. Petersburg, 1894), 41. For good general descriptions of the region, see V. P. Semenov (Tian-Shanskii), ed., *Rossiia: Polnoe geograficheskoe opisanie nashego otechestva*, vol. 1: *Moskovskaia promyshlennaia oblast'* (St. Petersburg, 1899); Ia. E. Vodarskii, *Promyshlennye seleniia tsentral'noi Rossii* (Moscow, 1972); and M. K. Rozhkova, *Formirovanie kadrov promyshlennykh rabochikh*.

in 1861. In Moscow province the average land allotment in 1900 was 2.5 *desiatiny* (a little less than seven acres) per male resident. An additional one and one-half acres were available as rented land. The tax arrears were greater than tax assessments for an entire year in half the districts of the province.[6] One peasant complained that

the land cut off for the peasants for their redemption was very poor in quality, the meadows were reduced by half, and it was impossible to keep the necessary livestock. Therefore, agricultural labor was very meagerly rewarded. We usually got a twofold return on rye and oat seed; a threefold return was a rare harvest. Buckwheat grew well only with fertilizer; as yet few potatoes were planted.[7]

Farming in the central Industrial Region was notoriously precarious. In the 1880s only 10.3 percent of Kostroma's village parishes had extra grain; another 27.8 percent had enough grain for the entire year, and 61.9 percent had to buy grain.[8] The situation was a little better in Moscow province, according to Sergei Semenov, a peasant from Volokolamsk and author of *Twenty-five Years in the Village,* a rare peasant memoir.[9] After a "good" year when his income from agriculture was 90 rubles, he still had to take out 60 rubles to buy food. Zemstvo studies confirm that the peasant from Moscow province used his own grain for an average of less than five months; for the rest of the year he had to buy grain.[10] "In our village," Semenov recalled at the outbreak of World War I,

hardly anyone fed himself; we made up the difference with purchases in Moscow. In the entire village, perhaps five or six households scraped by with their own reserves. As for the rest, some got by until early November (*do*

---

6. A. A. Bulgakov, *Sovremennoe peredvizhenie krest'ianstva* (St. Petersburg, 1905), 8–9, 11. See also Theodore Von Laue, "Russian Labor between Field and Factory," *California Slavic Studies,* 3 (1964): 33–38; and Geroid T. Robinson, *Rural Russia under the Old Regime* (Berkeley, 1967), 94–116.

7. S. T. Semenov, *Dvadtsat' piat' let v derevne* (Petrograd, 1915), 1. Only 32 percent of the land of the Moscow Industrial Region was arable. The average peasant household in Moscow province had 19.7 acres. See also V. P. Semenov, *Moskovskaia promyshlennaia oblast',* 125, 128–29.

8. D. N. Zhbankov, "O gorodskikh otkhozhikh zarabotkakh v Soligalicheskom uezde, Kostromskoi gubernii," *Iuridicheskii vestnik,* 9 (1890): 132.

9. Semenov also contributed to the periodical press. See, for example, "Pis'ma iz provintsii (Volokolamska)," *Novoe slovo,* 5 (1890): 5; and "Iz istorii odnoi derevni (Zapiski volokolamskogo krest'ianina)," *Russkaia mysl',* 23, no. 1 (January 1902): 20–38.

10. Moskovskaia gubernskaia zemskaia uprava, Statisticheskoe otdelenie, *Statistika dvizheniia naseleniia v Moskovskoi gubernii, 1883–97,* compiled by P. I. Kurkin (Moscow, 1902), 485–90.

Mikhailova dnia), some until Christmas, some until *maslensitsa*—and then they had to buy grain.[11]

Another 20 rubles went for other necessary expenditures (including 16 rubles for direct taxes). This left less than 10 rubles for the entire year to buy wood, kerosine and pitch, salt, grits, tea, and sugar; to pay for the priest, a big holiday, a funeral, renovations, repairs, or for replacement of inventory; and to set aside for a rainy day. Since the peasant could count on one harvest in every three being poor, there clearly were all too many "rainy days."

Yet the Semenovs were among the better-off families. Twenty percent of the registered peasant families in Moscow province had no allotment land, and 15 percent of the registered peasant families who had allotment land were not working it. The latter figure was much higher (38 percent) among registered peasant families absent at the time of the survey. Of those families with allotment land, 16 percent had no horse and 69 percent had no iron plough.[12] The women in N. A. Leikin's novel *Na zarabotkakh* (Working) frequently talk about life in the village; their conversations are full of melancholic passages such as the following:

Honey, everywhere you look there's poverty in the village. . . . Look, my brother writes from home that things are dreadful (*strast' kak u nikh plokho*): the winter crop froze and the livestock are dying. . . . Only those who have someone working in "Peter" can keep a house, and even at that, God knows, it's terribly hard. People were selling livestock all winter. The children have no milk.[13]

Despite the many tales of misery in the village, other evidence points to improvements in yields, technology, and consumption. Literacy rates were rising rapidly in the village, surely not a sign of universal gloom and doom. The Moscow region, in particular, benefited from proximity to the Moscow market, agricultural specialization such as truck gardening and dairying, a greater utilization of machines, and the help of the empire's most active zemstvo. Budget studies of Moscow province showed that 45 percent of the peasant's

11. S. T. Semenov, *Dvadtsat' piat' let*, 1. See also N. A. Leikin's *Na zarabotkakh: Roman iz zhizni chernorabochikh zhenshchin* (St. Petersburg, 1891), 255, for a strikingly similar passage.

12. Moskovskaia gubernskaia zemskaia uprava, Statisticheskoe otdelenie, *Moskovskaia guberniia po mestnomu obsledovaniiu 1898–1900*, vol. 1: *Poselennye tablitsy i pouezdnye itogi*, no. 3 (Moscow, 1904), 470–79; V. P. Semenov, *Moskovskaia promyshlennaia oblast'*, 141–42. In my calculations of horseless households, I excluded families without allotment land.

13. Leikin, *Na zarabotkakh*, 402, 420.

income still came from agriculture, the largest single source.[14] Zemstvo surveys of the small-scale, one-family peasant economy near Moscow showed that a small proportion of the families actually had abandoned agriculture or their villages altogether. In fact, farming in Moscow province was given a shot in the arm by the myriad sources of nonagricultural income that proximity to Moscow provided. Revisions of the theory of peasant impoverishment suggest that the 55 percent of the peasant's budget derived from nonagricultural sources went not to keep the household alive at the subsistence level but to meet rising standards of consumption.[15] To make ends meet at whatever level, peasants sought nonagricultural employment for part, and in many cases all, of the year, particularly in the non-black-earth zone. This had traditionally been employment in or near the village in handicrafts, in the cottage industries, and at local factories.

The Central Industrial Region, especially the eastern and southeastern counties of Moscow province and Vladimir province, was Russia's oldest manufacturing center, and silk and velvet making can be traced back to the second half of the sixteenth century. Cloth and linen mills first opened in the city under Peter I. With the coming of the railroad, Moscow and its hinterland gained competitive advantage over regions which were less favorably situated vis-à-vis the railroad lines. Thus, cloth production in Voronezh, a factory town in the early nineteenth century, as well as in Orel, Smolensk, Penza, Tambov, and Riazan', declined as a result of competition from Moscow.[16] By the 1890s the Central Industrial Region was manufacturing about 600 million rubles

14. Kurkin, *Statistika*, 486; Komarov, *Voenno-statisticheskoe opisanie*, 302; P. Maslov, *Agrarnyi vopros v Rossii*, 3d ed. (St. Petersburg, 1906), 347; A. M. Anfimov, *Krupnoe pomeshchich'e khoziaistvo Evropeiskoi Rossii* (Moscow, 1969), 113. The dependence on agriculture is even more striking inasmuch as Kurkin's figures included all peasants of the province, even those who lived in Moscow. On agricultural specialization such as dairying, see also the observations of the British consular officer. ("Report for the year 1907 on the Trade and Agriculture of the Consular District of St. Petersburg," Great Britain, *Parliamentary Papers: Diplomatic and Consular Reports: Russia*, no. 4323 [1908], 5.)

15. James Y. Simms, Jr., "The Crisis of Russian Agriculture at the End of the Nineteenth Century: A Different View," *Slavic Review*, 36, no. 3 (September 1977): 377–98, especially 385–90.

16. Moskovskaia gubernskaia zemskaia uprava, *Sbornik statisticheskikh svedenii po Moskovskoi gubernii*, 4 vols. (Moscow, 1881–1893), vol. 4, pts. 1–2: *Obshchaia svodka po sanitarnym issledovaniiam fabrichnykh zavedenii Moskovskoi gubernii za 1879–1885 gg.*, ed. F. F. Erisman and E. M. Dement'ev (Moscow, 1890–1893); Mikhail Tugan-Baranovskii, *Russkaia fabrika v proshlom i nastoiashchem*, 3d ed. (St. Petersburg, 1907), 91–92, 101, 239; E. M. Dement'ev, *Fabrika: chto ona daet naseleniiu i chto ona u nego beret*, 2d ed. (Moscow, 1897), 36–37; Bulgakov, *Sovremennoe peredvizhenie*, 28. See also Johnson, *Peasant and Proletarian*, 11–27.

worth of articles every year and employing 500,000 workers, more than a third of whom worked in factories.[17]

The most salient feature of the factories in this region had always been their ruralness. This continued to be the case even during the industrial boom of the 1890s. At the beginning of the twentieth century, 61 percent of Russia's factories and 59 percent of all factory workers were located outside towns. The proportions were even higher in the Central Industrial Region, where 65 percent of the factories and 65 percent of the workers were outside the towns.[18] "All around Moscow at distances varying from two to six hours by train," wrote one foreigner, "are great spinning, weaving and cotton-printing mills."[19] The small number of factories and factory workers in the provincial and county towns around Moscow illustrates nonurban factory location: in the city of Riazan', twenty factories employed 532 workers out of a total population of 44,552; Kaluga had sixty-two factories with 1,337 workers, less than 10 percent of that province's estimated factory workers.[20] No less an authority than Ivan Ianzhul, in discussing the difficulties he faced in his first tour as the head factory inspector of the Moscow Industrial District in 1882, noted the remoteness of industry in the region:

In spite of the fact that six railroad lines cut through Moscow province, not less than a vast majority of factories are situated away from them; many are even as far away as several dozen *versts* . . . a few railroad lines like the Nizhnii Novgorod line seem to purposely skirt industrial centers and several large factories.[21]

17. By 1909, the region employed 622,101 workers. See V. P. Semenov, *Moskovskaia promyshlennaia oblast'*, 164–66; Iasnopol'skii, *Ocherki*, 264; and Komarov, *Voenno-statisticheskoe opisanie*, 289.

18. A. Pogozhev, *Uchet*, 50; Iu. I. Seryi, "K voprosu ob osobennostiakh formirovaniia rabochikh v razlichnykh raionakh Rossii," in L. M. Ivanov, Iu. I. Kir'ianov, and Iu. I. Seryi, eds., *Rabochie Rossii v epokhu kapitalizma: Sravnitel'nyi poraionyi analiz* (Rostov-on-Don, 1972) 23–24; K. A. Pazhitnov, *Polozhenie rabochego klassa Rossii* (Moscow, 1906), 21; Thomas Stanley Fedor, *Patterns of Urban Growth in the Russian Empire during the Nineteenth Century* (Chicago, 1975), 151; Von Laue, "Russian Labor," 48. The disadvantage of these figures is, of course, the administrative definition of town which in imperial Russia excluded many factory settlements. Yet, even if these settlements were included in the category of town, a significant proportion of the factory working class worked out of Russia's urban mainstream.

19. Henry Norman, *All the Russias* (New York, 1902), 28–29. See also Moskovskaia gorodskaia uprava, *Sovremennoe khoziaistvo goroda Moskvy* (Moscow, 1913), 22.

20. *Entsiklopedicheskii slovar'*, pub. F. A. Brokgauz and I. A. Efron, 41 vols. in 82 (St. Petersburg, 1890–1904), 27:89, 95; 54:528.

21. I. I. Ianzhul, *Fabrichnyi byt moskovskoi gubernii* (St. Petersburg, 1884), xiv–xv.

The proportion of Moscow province's factory workers employed outside the city of Moscow was higher than the average for even the
Central Industrial Region and remained remarkably constant for a
sixty-five-year period that saw the emancipation of the serfs and a
great industrialization drive.[22]

The larger the enterprises the more likely they were to be located
outside the major cities. In the Central Industrial Region, 69 percent
of all factories employing more than 1,000 workers, and 72 percent of
all workers so employed, were located outside the provincial and
county towns. That it remained advantageous to operate large factories outside the major cities is affirmed by the fact that of fifteen new
establishments employing 1,000 or more workers which opened in
Moscow province during the boom years of 1910–1913, only three
opened in Moscow city.[23] The manufacturing heart of the Central
Industrial Region continued to be the factory villages outside Moscow,
and it would appear that the factory, as it had for a century, was still
coming to a rural labor force.

The rural districts of the Central Industrial Region were important
not only for their large textile factories. Even with its rapidity, emphasis on producers' goods, and concentration in plant and enterprise,
industrialization was a boon to many "preindustrial" or "nonindustrial" trades. Moscow's hinterland continued to be the location of a
lively cottage industry. At the turn of the twentieth century the Ministry of Internal Affairs estimated that four-fifths of the adult men and
one-half of the adult women were employed in local or nonlocal cottage industries.[24] From time immemorial the peasants themselves made
the things needed for the household. Then in the eighteenth and early
nineteenth centuries, the gentry began to promote peasant industry
and trade, particularly in the north, where seigneurial dues were predominantly in the form of cash. Since the amount of quitrent, or
obrok, was determined by the wealth of the serfs, the gentry had an
interest in the income of the peasant craftsman, called *kustar',* and
began to promote cottage industries.[25] Handicrafts were frequently

22. Dement'ev, *Fabrika,* 36–37; Seryi, "K voprosu," 23–24.
23. Moskovskii sovet rabochikh, krest'ianskikh, i krasnoarmeiskikh deputatov, *Statisticheskii atlas g. Moskvy i Moskovskoi gubernii* (Moscow, 1924), 3:57–58; S. I.
Antonova, *Vliianie stolypinskoi agrarnoi reformy na izmeneniia v sostave rabochego
klassa: Po materialam Moskovskoi gubernii, 1906–1913* (Moscow, 1951), 156–57;
Pogozhev, *Uchet,* 53–56; Seryi, "K voprosu," 23–24.
24. TsGIA, f. 1284, op. 194, d. 79, l. 3–4
25. Tugan-Baranovskii, *Russkaia fabrika,* 39–40.

combined with other occupations, as a German observed at the end of the eighteenth century:

Nowhere does one see such a blending of urban and rural occupations as in Russia. In Russia peasants engage not only in agriculture but even more in other trades. Very often agriculture plays a secondary role even in the peasant's labor, and manufacturing is the chief occupation, so that one finds entire villages which are populated solely by artisans.[26]

Not only were wool, worsted, linen, silk, and flax produced chiefly by the cottage industry, but cotton, beginning in the 1830s and 1840s, became one of the major branches of domestic production in the Central Industrial Region. Interestingly enough, the cottage cotton industry around Moscow arose after the penetration of the factory system. Mill owners saw that it was profitable to "put out" (razdavat') cotton yarn to villages. Moreover, the spread of factories actually fostered the spread of the domestic worker because the factory was almost the only trade school for the methods of production and new technology necessary for the small independent peasant producers. The factory also disseminated skills whenever the worker returned to the village. Furthermore, factories in Moscow and Vladimir provinces often expanded their production not by increasing the number of their factory workers but by putting out the yarn for weaving in peasant cottages and workshops.[27]

The putting-out system around Moscow developed in the 1830s and 1840s. The owner of the material or of a calico mill furnished wholesale yarn to a contractor who ran a distribution center (razdatochnaia kontora). The latter placed the yarn at the disposal of a peasant middleman (masterok) who distributed it among the workshops (svetelki) or cottages of individual workers. The middlemen themselves often owned small workshops and hired their own weavers. Such practice was particularly common in the silk industry of Bogorodsk county, since the high price of the material and the necessity for a clean product made weaving in dark and dirty peasant cottages impossible. Handwork in these small workshops was preserved longer here than in other branches of the textile industry, and as late as the 1880s most of the hired weavers in the silk industry were working in such "factories."[28]

26. Quoted in Ibid., 46.
27. Ibid., 167–68. See also Maslov, Agrarnyi vopros, 341.
28. Tugan-Baranovskii, Russkaia fabrika, 195–96. See also V. P. Semenov, Moskovskaia promyshlennaia oblast', 158–59; A. M. Pankratova, ed., Istoriko-bytovye ekspeditsii, 1949–50 (Moscow, 1953), 150–52; and E. A. Oliunina, Portnovskii promysel v Moskve i v derevniakh Moskovskoi i Riazanskoi gubernii: Materialy k istorii domashnei promyshlennosti v Rossii (Moscow, 1914), 36–37, 58–59, 66.

With the rapid spread of the cottage industries during the nineteenth century, the enterprising domestic worker could easily accumulate a modest sum and set up a small factory. By the end of the century, such peasant factory owners had a proud genealogy: their grandfathers had worked at the loom, their fathers had set up workshops, and they themselves had founded small factories.[29]

Structural changes enabled the cottage industry to cling tenaciously to its important position in the economy of the Central Industrial Region. The Moscow zemstvo observed a decrease in the number of small factories and workshops and the transfer of weaving from workshops to cottages. The fragmentation of the domestic industry actually led to an increase in the number of semi-independent craftsmen working in their own cottages. Up to the 1880s small-scale domestic weaving still predominated over factory weaving in terms of workers employed in all provinces but Moscow. The putting-out centers and workshops continued to exist side by side with the factories because of the availability of cheap peasant labor and the proximity of the Moscow market. In fact, there is reason to suggest that Moscow's huge retail market and the demand for both cheaply made goods and luxury items attracted domestic workers and craftsmen from the village.[30] An authority on the region's peasantry observed that "local cottage industry is neither growing nor declining. For many reasons the *kustar'* stops working for himself and becomes a laborer, either at a factory or at a new small workshop. The latter easily turns into a sweatshop run by a Moscow company."[31]

Nevertheless, it is a commonplace among contemporary observers and historians alike that by the end of the nineteenth century the cottage industry in its traditional form in the countryside was on the decline. In many localities, according to zemstvo reports, domestic weaving was devastated by the power loom, and the number of middlemen shrank. In many workshops handlooms piled up like junk.

---

29. Tugan-Baranovskii, *Russkaia fabrika*, 79–81, 165–66. Important studies on peasant handicrafts include V. P. Vorontsov, *Ocherki kustarnoi promyshlennosti v Rossii* (St. Petersburg, 1886), *Artel' v kustarnom promysle* (St. Petersburg, 1895), and "Znachenie kustarnykh promyslov, obshchee uslovie ikh razvitiia i mery ikh podderzhivaniia v Rossii" *S"ezd deiatelei po kustarnoi promyshlennosti* (St. Petersburg, 1902). A more recent study is P. G. Ryndziunskii, *Krest'ianskaia promyshlennost' v poreformennoi Rossii* (Moscow, 1966).

30. V. P. Semenov, *Moskovskaia promyshlennaia oblast'*, 148; Tugan-Baranovskii, *Russkaia fabrika*, 347, 360, 378; Vorontsov, *Ocherki*, 7; *Ekspeditsii*, 152; A. M. Pankratova, "Proletarizatsiia krest'ianstva i ee rol' v formirovanii promyshlennogo proletariata Rossii," *Istoricheskie zapiski*, 54 (1955): 210.

31. Bulgakov, *Sovremennoe peredvizhenie*, 9.

The prices for domestic articles fell, and peasant handicrafts (particularly textiles) found it harder to compete with factory production. The *Statistical Annual* of the Moscow zemstvo repeatedly reported the difficulty for shoemakers, cabinetmakers, weavers, and other craftsmen to find work at home.[32] The Ministry of Internal Affairs reported that in spite of state and zemstvo aid to the cottage industry, "the domestic worker's wage has gone down recently, since hand labor is being displaced by machines introduced by the larger and wealthier businessmen."[33]

The cottage industry in Moscow's hinterland was in a stage of rapid transition at the end of the nineteenth century. Modern methods of production and marketing had only just begun to penetrate the Russian village. Thus, while the cottage industries faced stiffer competition than ever before from cheap, mass-produced, and mass-marketed products, demand was greater than ever before, and the functions of the local craftsmen had not been entirely supplanted. For this reason, the increase in the numbers of workers employed nation-wide in small-scale and domestic manufacturing kept pace with that in the factories and mines. Similarly, the continued poor differentiation of the peasant economy contributed to the tenacity of the domestic industries. Virtually every yearly report on nonagricultural income in the *Statistical Annual* of the Moscow zemstvo began with the observation that the average household could subsist on its own produce for less than five months and that the remainder had to be provided by a variety of nonagricultural earnings, both local and away from home. The Russian laborer had the reputation of being a jack-of-all-trades, moving from farm to village workshop, to factory, to distant construction sites as job opportunities changed. Nowhere was this more true than in Moscow's hinterland, and the particularly variegated labor force of Moscow itself was one product.

The precarious but still essential industry in the peasant economy figured prominently in the perceptions of the strains of urbanization, particularly in Moscow. It was widely assumed that the cottage industry was declining, that this decline was a major source of poverty in the village, and that this poverty was a potential if not actual burden

---

32. See the section on nonagricultural income in Moskovskaia gubernskaia zemskaia uprava, *Statisticheskii ezhegodnik Moskovskoi gubernii* (Moscow, 1885–1913). See also Tugan-Baranovskii, *Russkaia fabrika*, 347–48; and a report of the Ministry of Internal Affairs on the cottage industry (TsGIA, f. 1284, op. 194, d. 106, l. 8).

33. TsGIA, f. 1284, op. 194, d. 79, l. 3–4.

on the city itself. In the 1880s and 1890s the government created many schemes for revitalizing the cottage industry by subsidizing local workshops, promoting vocational education, setting up craft museums, and by aiding in the procurement of raw materials and in the marketing of wares—measures that would not have been likely had the industry been flourishing.[34] The ideal of the mixed household economy and of the peasant craftsman continued to play an important role in official attitudes even if the reality was transforming.

❖   ❖   ❖

Urban development in Moscow also took place in the context of rapid national population growth. Although structural demographic changes alone could theoretically cause urbanization, in most countries urbanization is part of overall population growth. Russia was no exception. In the nineteenth century imperial Russia was Europe's most populous and one of its fastest growing countries. Its population almost doubled in the half century preceding the emancipation of the serfs in 1861 and then doubled again to almost 170 million by the time of the revolution.[35] With no absorption of populous territory and no significant foreign immigration, the population explosion was due entirely to natural growth. During the second half of the century the annual birthrate hovered around 50 births per 1,000 population; indeed, in the forty years preceding the first census of the empire in 1897, the birthrate fell below 50 per 1,000 only thirteen times and went lower than 48.8 only during wartime (1878) and famine (1892). These two years showed higher than average annual death rates, which in normal years hovered around 35 per 1,000. Consequently, the natural rate of population growth was approximately 15 per 1,000 per year, that is, roughly one million every year.[36]

A detailed examination of the reasons for this high rate of population growth falls outside the scope of this study. It appears that although a rising age of first marriage may have hinted at a coming demographic transition on selected estates even before the emancipation, peasant Russia decidedly retained its "east European type" of

34. For example, see *Pravitel'stvennoe sodeistvie kustarnoi promyshlennosti za 10 let (1888–1898)* published by the Ministry of Agriculture and State Properties (St. Petersburg, 1898).
35. Rashin, *Naselenie*, 154.
36. Ibid. See also S. A. Novosel'skii, *Voprosy demograficheskoi i sanitarnoi statistiki* (Moscow, 1958), 67–68.

demographic behavior and family structure—large family, early and almost universal marriage—throughout the nineteenth century.[37] It is also likely, as H. J. Habbakuk suggests in another context,[38] that the emancipation, by retaining the land allotment and its periodic redistribution, coupled with the system of equal inheritance and the even greater subdivisions of land by the end of the century, provided no incentive to limit family size. Hence, the notorious "land hunger" that the peasant suffered by the end of the century meant that an allotment that fed two mouths in 1860 had to feed three in 1900.[39]

As in the case of economic development, Moscow's population growth, illustrated in figure 1, can be better understood in the demographic context of its hinterland. Not all parts of the empire grew at the same rate, and it would appear, for example, that Moscow's hinterland experienced a slower rate of growth. With their populations almost doubling, Riazan' and Smolensk were the only two provinces, except Moscow itself, to approach the average national growth rates for the period 1863–1914. A rather unfavorable natural growth of the hinterland's population explains in part the lower than average growth rate. Although the number of births per marriage exceeded the Russian average in every province, and although birthrates and the proportion of women married were close to national averages, Moscow's hinterland had notably higher than average death rates. Not only the industrial provinces of Moscow and Vladimir but also Smolensk and Tula were unhealthy places to live. Particularly dismal were the high rates of infant mortality. Contributing to the high death rates was the fact that the hinterland's population density far exceeded the average for European Russia. This was particularly true not only of industrial Moscow but of agricultural Riazan' and Tula. Within Moscow province itself, the relatively sparsely settled agricultural counties of Mozhaisk, Ruza, and Vereia had the worst death and infant mortality rates. The record was particularly dismal in Ruza where almost every other infant died.[40]

    37. Peter Czap, Jr., "Marriage and the Peasant Joint Family in the Era of Serfdom," in David L. Ransel, ed., *The Family in Imperial Russia*, 114.
    38. "Family Structure and Economic Change in Nineteenth-Century Europe," *Journal of Economic History*, 15, no. 1 (1955): 1–12, and especially 5–6.
    39. Robinson, *Rural Russia*, 94.
    40. Tsentral'nyi statisticheskii komitet, *Statisticheskii vremennik Rossiiskoi imperii*, 3d ser., no. 8: *Sbornik svedenii po Rossii za 1884–85* (St. Petersburg, 1886), table 2–3; Tsentral'nyi statisticheskii komitet, *Okonchatel'no ustanovlennoe pri razrabotke perepisi nalichnoe naselenie gorodov* (St. Petersburg, 1905), 11; Kurkin, *Statistika*, 56, 97, 166, 197; Semenov, *Moskovskaia promyshlennaia oblast'*, 87; Iasnopol'skii, *Statistiko-ekonomicheskie ocherki*, 257–58; Rashin, *Naselenie*, 78–79, 180–83, 188–91, 251–52.

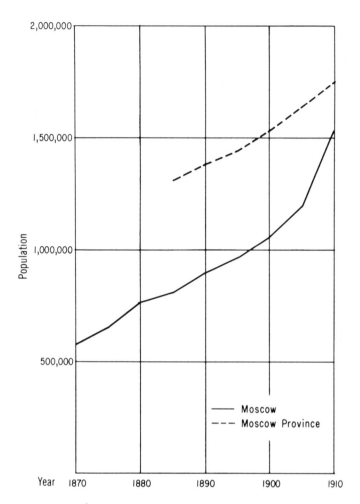

FIGURE 1. POPULATION GROWTH IN MOSCOW AND
MOSCOW PROVINCE

Source: S. A. Novosel'skii, *Voprosy demograficheskoi i sanitarnoi statistiki* (Moscow, 1958), 67–68.

The city of Moscow showed lower birth and death rates than the rest of the hinterland. However, as figure 2 shows, the rate of decrease of both births and deaths was also quite low. Particularly disturbing to the authorities was the high infant mortality and the slow drop in the death rate, from 27.1 per 1,000 population in 1870 to 24.2 forty years later. Altogether, in the half century between 1862 and 1912, the death rate dropped less than 4 per 1,000, hardly a precipitous decline. Throughout the 1870s and 1880s the death rate almost equaled the

birthrate and in one year (1871) actually exceeded it. Accompanying
the gradual drop in the death rate was a slow decline in the infant
mortality rate from an average of 360 per 1,000 in the period 1868–
1872 to 270 per 1,000 in the period 1908–1912. Yet until the end of
the 1890s, the annual number of infant deaths per 1,000 population
remained considerably over 300.[41] Moscow's performance lagged not
only behind that of major European cities but behind that of St. Petersburg, hardly a model of a healthy city: the percentage decrease in
the death rate from 1881 to 1910 was only 17.1 percent in Moscow;
it was 22.3 percent in Petersburg and 28.3 percent in Paris; all other
European cities registered decreases of at least 30 percent.[42] The
higher death rate in the old capital was generally attributed to higher
infant mortality rates and higher death rates from contagious diseases,
particularly from tuberculosis, the most lethal contagious disease of
the nineteenth century and responsible for almost half of Moscow's
deaths from contagious diseases.[43]

The rapid national population growth could have left the geographical distribution of the population unchanged if everyone had
stayed at home. Moreover, the distress in agriculture and in the cottage industries described above might have been far worse had the
peasants remained as bound to the land and the commune as the
emancipation edict of 1861 had intended. In fact, unprecedented mobility accompanied unprecedented population growth. Since a subsistence economy on land too poor to support them continued to be facts
of life, peasants sought work outside their native villages. Communal
authorities permitted departure (*otkhod*) for varying periods of time
so that the peasant could earn money to pay taxes, and more and
more peasants managed to loosen, if not break, the bonds with the
commune. At the same time, even before the Stolypin reforms some of
the legal and fiscal obstacles to peasant movement were removed:
redemption payments were reduced in 1881, the poll tax was abol-

41. P. I. Kurkin and A. A. Chertov, *Estestvennoe dvizhenie naseleniia goroda
Moskvy i Moskovskoi gubernii* (Moscow, 1927), 12–13, 23, 25; SEM, 3 (1910–11):
26–31, 39; S. A. Novosel'skii, *Voprosy demograficheskoi i sanitarnoi statistiki*, 67–68;
Sovremennoe khoziaistvo, 12–13.
    42. Kurkin and Chertov, *Estestvennoe dvizhenie*, 23–25; Z. Frankel', "Neskol'ko
dannykh o sanitarnom sostoianii Moskvy i Peterburga za 1909 g.," *Gorodskoe delo*, no. 20
(October 15, 1910): 1405–1407. For comparisons with death rates in Europe, see V. V.
Sviatlovskii, *Zhilishchnyi vopros s ekonomicheskoi tochki zreniia*, 5 vols. (St. Petersburg,
1902), 4:65; and S. K. Alaverdian, *Zhilishchnyi vopros v Moskve* (Erevan, 1961), 69.
    43. A. Berezovskii, "Zaiavlenie k voprosu o bor'be s tuberkulozom v Moskve,"
Doklady Moskovskoi gorodskoi dumy (Moscow, 1910), 6:2.

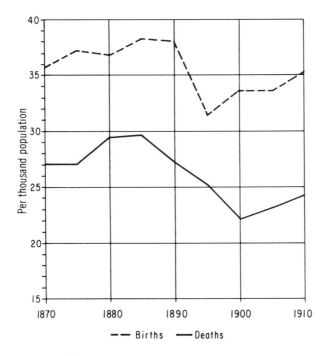

FIGURE 2. BIRTH AND DEATH RATES IN MOSCOW

Source: P. I. Kurkin and A. A. Chertov, *Estestvennoe dvizhenie naseleniia goroda Moskvy i Moskovskoi gubernii* (Moscow, 1927), 23–24.

ished in 1885, and collective responsibility was terminated in 1903.[44] By the end of the nineteenth century, the paths of peasant movement had become major thoroughfares. At the time of the 1897 census, about 18.4 million people, or nearly 15 percent of the total population of the empire, resided in a county or a city other than the one in which they were born.[45] In spite of legislative inconsistencies and remaining obstacles, one statistician was prompted to observe that the peasant's geographical mobility "is unequaled in western Europe and perhaps can be compared only with the mobility of American workers."[46]

A paradox of serfdom, migration—or let us say a certain degree of spatial mobility—had been traditionally an important feature of Rus-

44. A. A. Leont'ev, *Krest'ianskoe pravo* (St. Petersburg, 1909), 47–49.

45. Tsentral'nyi statisticheskii komitet, *Obshchii svod po imperii rezul'tatov razrabotki dannykh pervoi vseobshchei perepisi naseleniia 1897 g.* (St. Petersburg, 1905), 90–95.

46. B. P. Kadomtsev, *Professional'nyi i sotsial'nyi sostav naseleniia Evropeiskoi Rossii po dannym perepisi 1897 g.* (St. Petersburg, 1909), 67.

sian society, especially in the northern and central provinces where peasants needed outside nonagricultural earnings to pay their dues and taxes. At the beginning of the nineteenth century a German observed that

in several localities men leave agriculture almost entirely to women and themselves depart in search of earnings. . . . In summer, peasants stream into towns from all over to work as petty traders, carpenters, masons, and so forth.[47]

From distant districts serf-owners sent young peasants all the way to Moscow or Petersburg to learn a trade, since artisans in the big cities earned much more than common laborers. According to Dmitrii N. Zhbankov, the leading contemporary authority on the phenomenon of seasonal labor in northern Russia, this effort at profit maximization on the part of the serf-owners, who depended on peasant income for their livelihood, accounted for "the odd fact that inhabitants of remote counties started going to faraway capitals and engaging in trades which have absolutely no application in the village."[48]

The emancipation, a gradual loosening of the peasant's bonds to the village commune, a scarcity of local jobs, an increasing labor surplus, the availability of more seasonal city jobs in the construction and transport trades, as well as in casual labor and domestic service, and the decline of earnings in the cottage industry—all caused an increase in departures from the village, an increase reflected in the number of passports issued for temporary absence.[49] The women in Leikin's novel *Working* came to St. Petersburg every spring from Novgorod.[50] In Iaroslavl', in 1893, 130,000, or 13 percent of the total population, were working elsewhere. An estimated 1,300,000, or 14 percent of the entire rural population of Kaluga, Nizhnii Novgorod, Tver', Iaroslavl', Vladimir, and Kostroma, were away. As in many areas, more peasants engaged in migratory labor than in local trades.[51]

47. Quoted in Tugan-Baranovskii, *Russkaia fabrika*, 42.
48. Zhbankov, "O gorodskikh otkhozhikh zarabotkakh," 132, and *Bab'ia storona: Statistiko-etnograficheskii ocherk* (Kostroma, 1891), 24.
49. Rashin, *Naselenie*, 172; E. E. Kruze, *Polozhenie rabochego klassa Rossii v 1900–1914 gg.* (Leningrad, 1976), 18–45.
50. Leikin, *Na zarabotkakh*, 11.
51. *Statisticheskii ezhegodnik Moskovskoi gubernii za 1901* (Moscow, 1902), 12; Kurkin, *Statistika*, 528; V. P. Semenov, *Moskovskaia promyshlennaia oblast'*, 110, 184–85; *Ekspeditsii*, 110, 142; *Statisticheskii ezhegodnik Tverskoi gubernii za 1903 i 1904*, vyp. 2 (Tver', 1906), 42–43; L. A. Kirillov, "K voprosu o vnezemledel'cheskom otkhode krest'ianskogo naseleniia," *Trudy Imperatorskogo vol'nogo ekonomicheskogo obshchestva*, 3 (1899): 270; L. P. Vesin, "Znachenie otkhozhikh promyslov v zhizni russkogo krest'ianstva," *Delo*, 19, no. 7 (November, 1886): 137.

Such massive departures help explain the apparent slow rate of growth of many provinces around Moscow.

Decades of seasonal migratory labor gave certain townships, counties, and even provinces a reputation for specialization in certain trades. Thus Pokrov county of Vladimir was known for its carpenters, Tver' for its stone masons, Kostroma for its painters, and Iaroslavl' for its waiters and shop clerks, Mosal' county of Kaluga for its tailors, and so on.[52] In addition, migratory laborers of the same trade and from the same village, township, or county lived, worked, and traveled together in groups known as artels or, like Arina and Akulina in Leikin's *Working*, looked "for their own kind" while on the road.[53] The artel was well suited to the needs of transient, migratory peasant labor force, and according to Russian folk wisdom, "artel porridge is better" (*artel'naia kasha luchshe*) and "It's hard for one but easy for an artel" (*Trudno odnomu, da legko arteli*).[54]

Seasonal migratory labor had a strong impact on the "home villages," or, in Zhbankov's colorful terminology, back in "women's land" (*bab'ia storona*). Whereas early in the nineteenth century only the strongest and most energetic villagers (almost exclusively boys and men) left, by the end of the century entire families would temporarily leave home; rare was the peasant of Soligalich county in Kostroma, for instance, who had never spent any time in either Moscow or Petersburg. Peasant households in townships with highly developed seasonal migratory labor were wealthier, as was evidenced by the presence in such households of samovars, frequent breaks for tea served with lemon and white bread, wines, tobacco, store-bought clothes, German-cut dresses and jackets, umbrellas, mirrors, table lamps, pen and ink, higher standards of personal hygiene, watch chains, rings, accordions, new dances, and vulgar limericks (*chastushki*). Women in such households were apt to be more independent and forthright, observed Zhbankov, and both men and women could

---

52. Vesin, "Znachenie otkhozhikh promyslov," 140. In Chekhov's "Peasants" young boys from Zhukovo were always hired in Moscow as busboys or waiters. See A. P. Chekhov, *Sobranie sochinenii v vos'mi tomakh* (Moscow, 1970), 6:196–227.

53. Leikin, *Na zarabotkakh*, 5, 11, 77–78; Zhbankov, *Bab'ia storona*, 10; Kirillov, "K voprosu," 292; Ianzhul, *Fabrichnyi byt*, 80, 86, 91. *Ekspeditsii*, 118. The basic histories of the Russian *artel'* are N. Kalachov, *Arteli v drevnei i nyneshnei Rossii* (St. Petersburg, 1864); V. P. Vorontsov, *Artel'nye nachinaniia russkogo obshchestva* (St. Petersburg, 1895), and *Artel' v kustarnom promysle* (St. Petersburg, 1895); A. Isaev, *Arteli v Rossii* (Iaroslavl', 1881); and *Sbornik materialov ob arteli v Rossii*, 3 vols. (St. Petersburg, 1873–1875).

54. Vladimir Dal', *Russkie narodnye poslovitsy i pogovorki* (Moscow, 1957), 13.

break away from the "tyranny of their fathers and the commune."[55] Greater independence of younger members contributed to the demise of the large partriarchal family and more household divisions or, as the saying went, "Marry today, leave tomorrow" (*Segodnia zhenitsia, a zavtra otdelitsia*).[56]

Migratory labor in particular and increased mobility in general had important structural consequences. Most noticeable was the gender imbalance. Women constituted 54 percent of the Central Industrial Region, and the northwestern counties of Kostroma as well as parts of Vladimir and Iaroslavl' were called "women's land" because so many of the men over the age of twelve were away and because women headed a disproportionate share of households. In fact, in four villages of Soligalich county in Kostroma, 50–75 percent of the adult men were gone during the summer, leaving the burden of farming to the women and children and the aged.[57] This explains other social and demographic peculiarities. For example, seasonal migratory labor was generally correlated with higher literacy rates but, because of the greater opportunity cost, with lower school attendance.[58]

The major destination of these seasonal migratory laborers, of course, was Moscow itself, and subsequent chapters will examine in greater detail the dynamics of peasant immigration and settlement in the city. Suffice it to say here that Moscow grew in the context of an entire region where migratory labor, protracted absences from home, age and gender imbalances in the population, family dislocations, and the "bifurcated household," in Robert Johnson's words, were facts of life.[59] Consequently, when the authorities and social reformers, acutely aware of these problems, attributed to them many of the city's social ills, they were judging not just alleged urban pathologies but a regional economic and social system.

The industrial expansion and spread of the factory system grafted onto a base of widespread cottage industry, population growth, and mobility, and the spread of seasonal migratory labor all contributed to

55. Zhbankov, *Bab'ia storona*, 66–69, and "O gorodskikh otkhozhikh zarabotkakh," 134–35; Kirillov, "K voprosu," 260–69, 291; A. Peshekhonov, "Krest'iane i rabochie v ikh vzaimnykh otnosheniiakh," *Russkoe bogatstvo*, 8 (August 1898), 181–83, 191–93.

56. V. P. Semenov, *Moskovskaia promyshlennaia oblast'*, 104.

57. Ibid., 89; *Sbornik svedenii po Rossii za 1884–85*, 2–8; *Nalichnoe naselenie gorodov*, 4:11, 5:14; *PVP*, 24, pt. 2: *Moskovskaia guberniia* (St. Petersburg, 1904), xxv; Zhbankov, "O gorodskikh otkhozhikh zarabotkakh," 131; Kurkin, *Statistika*, 4, 10, 14.

58. Zhbankov, "O gorodskikh otkhozhikh zarabotkakh," 141, and *Bab'ia storona*, 94–100; Kurkin, *Statistika*, 526–29.

59. *Peasant and Proletarian*, 56–61.

a rapidly growing working class. At the time of emancipation an industrial working class was just beginning to appear. In 1860 Russia had less than 4 million wage laborers of all categories and less than 2 million employed in manufacturing out of a population of 74 million. Thus slightly more than one out of every twenty was a wage laborer. By the eve of World War I European Russia had between 17 and 22 million wage laborers (of whom 6–7 million were in manufacturing) out of a total population of 120 million.[60] Since the class of urban artisans that was important in the formation of the working class in the West, particularly in the most skilled trades, played a minor role in Russia, the major source of recruitment for the working class throughout the entire nineteenth century was the peasantry. As might be expected, the peasantry made a distinctive imprint on the fabric of the Russian working class, and nowhere was this more true than in Moscow and its hinterland. So distinctive was the imprint that a century ago a lively debate, focused chiefly on the conditions in Moscow's hinterland, emerged concerning the nature of the "peasant-worker." Whether the "peasant-worker" was more "peasant" or more "worker," by what stages the peasant evolved into an industrial worker, and whether this evolution was irreversible and passed on to succeeding generations, were issues that took on an almost Darwinian tone in the 1880s and 1890s.[61] Foreigners such as Gerhart von Schulze-Gävernitz, a German authority on Russian manufacturing who contributed an influential stage theory of this "evolution," joined Russian sanitary physicians, factory inspectors, economists, and revolutionary politicians in this debate.[62]

60. Rashin, *Naselenie*, 87, and *Formirovanie rabochego klassa Rossii* (Moscow, 1958), 172.

61. Dement'ev, *Fabrika*, 44, 46; Vorontsov, *Ocherki*, 1–43, 49, and *Sotsial'noe preobrazovanie Rossii* (Moscow, 1906), 63–64. See also Arthur P. Mendel, *Dilemmas of Progress in Tsarist Russia: Legal Marxism and Legal Populism* (Cambridge, Mass., 1961), 104–29.

62. Gerhart von Schulze-Gävernitz, *Krupnoe proizvodstvo v Rossii*, trans. B. V. Avilov (Moscow, 1899), 93–110. Schulze-Gävernitz's stage theory of the evolution of the Russian working class and his recognition of the importance of the continued ties to the land clearly influenced Tugan-Baranovskii. In the first edition of his study of the Russian factory, published in 1898, Tugan-Baranovskii referred to the "curtailment of the ties to the land" (pp. 415–17), whereas in the third edition, published in 1907, he refers to the "significance of the ties with the land" (pp. 341–44). See also I. I. Ianzhul, *Iz vospominanii i perepiski fabrichnogo inspektora pervogo prizyva* (St. Petersburg, 1907), 4–5, 160; Ia. T. Mikhailovskii, "Zarabotnaia plata i prodolzhitel'nost' rabochego vremeni na fabrikakh i zavodov," in Ministerstvo finansov, *Fabrichno-zavodskaia promyshlennost' i torgovlia Rossii* (St. Petersburg, 1893), 274; G. V. Plekhanov, "Nashi raznoglasiia," in *Sochineniia G. V. Plekhanova* (Geneva, 1905), 1:318–29, 353–79, 385–432; N. Gimmer, "K kharakteristike Rossiiskogo proletariata," *Sovremennik*, 4 (April 1913), 328; A. Peshekhonov, "Krest'iane i rabochie," 178–80; and V. I. Lenin, *Polnoe sobranie sochinenii*, 5th ed. (Moscow, 1967), 3:547, 600–1; 24:278.

Our understanding of the process of the formation of the working
class is complicated by the fact that, as was suggested above, much
industry was concentrated in factory villages and in peasant workshops far from the city. Consequently, not just one monolithic industrial working class evolved at the end of the nineteenth century, but
several varieties of workers. First, generation after generation of domestic or factory workers from industrial regions such as Bogorodsk
county found employment close to home and had little occasion to
seek work in Moscow or in any other large city; closely tied with their
native villages, this was a truly rural working class. On the other
hand, peasants from agricultural counties such as Ruza with few opportunities for nonagricultural employment fled villages, never to return except for perfunctory visits for passport renewals, and their
rural bonds were quickly broken.[63] A third type of worker comprised
the sons and daughters of workers, who were frequently city-born or
city-raised and had opportunities to enter apprenticeship at an early
age and move into skilled jobs. This type most nearly approached a
truly urban working class.[64] A fourth type of worker regularly moved
back and forth between factory (or city) and native village. These
workers and their "bifurcated" families were able to nourish roots in
both factory (or urban) and rural milieux.[65] Finally, a fifth variety of

63. These are the two types of workers studied by M. K. Rozhkova. See "Fabrichnaia promyshlennost' i promysly krest'ian v 60-70kh godakh XIX v." in L. M. Ivanov,
ed. *Problemy sotsial'no-ekonomicheskoi istorii Rossii* (Moscow, 1971), 195–217; and
Formirovanie kadrov promyshlennykh rabochikh. See my review of this book in *Kritika*,
14, no. 2 (Spring 1978) 106–20.
64. L. M. Ivanov, "Preemstvennost' fabrichno-zavodskogo truda i formirovanie
proletariata v Rossii," in *Rabochii klass i rabochee dvizhenie v Rossii, 1861–1917*
(Moscow, 1966), 58–140, but especially, pp. 96, 120; "O soslovno-klassovoi strukture
gorodov kapitalisticheskoi Rossii," in *Problemy sotsial'no-ekonomicheskoi istorii Rossii*, 312–40; and "Vozniknovenie rabochego klassa," in *Istoriia rabochego klassa Rossii, 1861–1900 gg.* (Moscow, 1972), 9–60. See also his earlier "K voprosu o formirovanii promyshlennogo proletariata v Rossii," *Istoriia SSSR*, no. 4, (1958), 27–51, and
"Sostoianie i zadachi izucheniia istorii proletariata v Rossii," *Voprosy istorii*, no. 3
(1960), 50–76. See also V. I. Romashova, "Formirovanie promyshlennogo proletariata
Moskvy 60-e-I polovina 80-kh gg. XIX v." (unpublished candidate dissertation, Moscow, 1963), 10, and "Obrazovanie postoiannykh kadrov rabochikh v poreformennoi
promyshlennosti Moskvy," in *Rabochii klass i rabochee dvizhenie v Rossii*, 152–62;
and Iu. I. Kir'ianov, "Ob oblike rabochego klassa Rossii," in L. M. Ivanov, ed., *Rossiiskii proletariat: Oblik, bor'ba, gegemoniia* (Moscow, 1970), 100–40.
65. This typology of the working class has been developed by Johnson, *Peasant and
Proletarian*. In general, Western scholars have emphasized the peasant side of the "peasant-worker." See in particular Von Laue, "Russian Labor between Field and Factory,"
3:41, and "Russian Peasants in the Factory, 1892–1904," *Journal of Economic History*,
21 (March 1961): 61–80; Alexander Gerschenkron, "Agrarian Policies and Industrialization in Russia," *Cambridge Economic History*, 2d ed., vol. 6, pt. 2 (Cambridge, 1966),

worker migrated from place to place, wherever jobs beckoned, and had roots neither in Moscow nor in the village. This contingent of migrant workers, as will be shown, loomed particularly large in the eyes of the authorities and urban social reformers.[66]

Given the poorly differentiated peasant economy, more than one of these ideal types may have been embodied in an individual worker or in a worker's family. Although histories of the Russian working class have used the metaphor of stages of evolution, commonly culminating in the skilled urban factory worker, recent research suggests that independent paths of development more accurately described the varieties of workers. Many of the region's industrial workers were not city residents, and many of the urban immigrants were nonindustrial laborers in the construction and transport trades, domestic service, retailing, and in clerical and artisanal jobs. Parallel to the growth of the Russian working class and more important for this study was the equally rapid growth of the nation's urban population.

❖   ❖   ❖

In 1860 Russia's urban population was estimated at slightly under six million. By the eve of World War I, this had tripled: one of every eight citizens of the empire lived in a city.[67] During the nineteenth century Russia's urban population grew twice as fast as did the entire population, and the rate of growth of the largest cities exceeded that of all cities. By 1897, 44 out of 865 cities had 53 percent of the entire urban population, compared with only 27 percent in 1863.[68] The booming southern steel or oil towns had the highest rates of growth: in the fourteen years from 1883 to 1897 the population of Ekaterinoslav and Baku tripled.[69]

Natural growth alone could never have accounted for the nation's

---

706–800. Although earlier Soviet studies minimized the influence of peasant traditions on the working class, more recent studies have acknowledged the complexities of the "proletarianization" of the peasantry. See Pankratova, "Proletarizatsiia krest'ianstva," 212–32; Rashin, *Formirovanie,* 302–578; Romashova, *Formirovanie,* 10; and Kir'ianov, "Ob oblike," 121.

66. This type of worker has received no attention from scholars. See below, chapters 5, 7, 8.

67. Rashin, *Naselenie,* 99.

68. Ibid., 87, 107; Liashchenko, *History,* 420.

69. Liashchenko, *History,* 504; David Hooson, "The Growth of Cities in Pre-Soviet Russia," in R. P. Beckinsdale and J. M. Houston, eds., *Urbanization and Its Problems: Essays in Honour of E. W. Gilbert* (Oxford, 1970), 260.

rapid urbanization. Cities all over the country were swelled by immigrants, many of whom had come long distances. In the southern industrial town of Ekaterinoslav converged "from the far corners of the Russian empire thousands of people who rode or walked here with their sack (*kotomka*) over their shoulders for a crust of bread (*v poiskakh kuska khleba*)."[70] Indeed, according to Stanley Fedor, migrants who tried to make a living in the cities were more likely to migrate to another province and to a large city than to a small town in their own province.[71] In addition, industrial and urban growth did not coincide. Only approximately half of the total population that was engaged in manufacturing lived in cities. Even though industry attracted many immigrants, employment in other branches of the economy, especially commerce and transport, were, according to Fedor, equally if not more attractive to immigrants.[72]

Despite rapid national urbanization, Moscow's hinterland exhibited surprisingly little regional urbanization. None of Moscow's adjacent provinces and only four counties of Moscow province exceeded the average proportion of urban dwellers in European Russia. Equally noteworthy, the proportion of urban dwellers in Moscow's hinterland increased very slowly or even declined. Admittedly, the "urban" residents do not include residents of various factory villages and settlements not officially listed as towns. For example, settlements such as Sergievskii *posad* in Dmitrov county and Pavlovskii *posad* in Bogorodsk county had nearly 10,000 inhabitants. Nevertheless, it is unlikely that the addition of such "nonurban" settlements would have altered the picture significantly.[73]

A metropolis such as Moscow benefited immensely from such national and regional trends. At the end of the nineteenth century, natural growth accounted for only roughly one-fifth of Moscow's annual growth,[74] but its diversified economy beckoned immigrants from beyond the borders of Moscow province. The absence of big cities and

70. Mikhail Shatrov, *Gorod na trekh kholmakh: kniga o starom Ekaterinoslave* (Dnepropetrovsk, 1969), 145.

71. Fedor, *Patterns*, 118.

72. Ibid., 120–21; *Obshchii svod*, 2:256–325. For two approaches to the issue of the attraction of manufacturing jobs for immigrants see Richard H. Rowland, "Urban In-migration in Late Nineteenth-Century Russia"; Robert A. Lewis and Richard Rowland, "Urbanization in Russia and the USSR, 1897–1970"; and Roger L. Thiede, "Industry and Urbanization in New Russia from 1860 to 1910," all in Michael F. Hamm, ed., *The City in Russian History*.

73. *Sbornik svedenii za 1884–85*, 2–8; *Obshchii svod*, 1: pt. 2, 6–7; *PVP*, 24:42–45, 58–59.

74. *Sovremennoe khoziaistvo*, 14.

the rather lethargic pace of urbanization nearby enhanced Moscow as a destination point for waves of peasants. Its growth rate far outpaced that of neighboring towns: in 1862 approximately one out of every four persons in the province lived in the city; in 1912 it was one out of two.[75] Almost three-quarters of a population of one million had been born elsewhere, and half of these had been born outside Moscow province. By 1914, one of every ten urban dwellers in Russia lived in Moscow.[76] As any porter at one of Moscow's nine railway stations could have observed, the old capital was a natural stopping place for a population on the road. The number of inns and transient housing units, let alone the benches in the railroad stations in winter and countless makeshift sleeping quarters in summer, suggest that Moscow was but a transit point for many. In the 1890s the city's railway stations annually handled six million arriving and departing passengers. A glance at a railway map of European Russia in 1900 illustrates a very important fact: the traveler who needed to go from one provincial capital to the next (in a circular movement around Moscow) would have found direct rail service only from Tula to Kaluga. Any other journey (say Tver' to Smolensk or Kaluga to Riazan') would in all probability have been completed through Moscow. Road coverage—and we must remember that spring and fall were peak migrating periods—was no better.[77]

The patterns of Russia's economic growth and population mobility created an urban population, especially in the metropolises, with a distinctive social and demographic profile. Most striking was the number of city dwellers of the peasant estate. Roughly two-thirds of the population of both St. Petersburg and Moscow were peasants. Imperial Russia was permeated with hierarchies of rank, privilege, and status that had the force of law (an entire volume, for example of the Code of Laws was devoted to *sostoianie*, or "station"), and the estate group (*soslovie*) to which one belonged was of considerable importance. Moreover, in much of the contemporary literature on the city's social problems, estate groupings were commonly used to stand for social divisions. The estate categories provide a very crude

75. Kurkin and Chertov, *Estestvennoe dvizhenie,* 23; B. M. Kabuzan, *Izmeneniia v razmeshchenii naseleniia Rossii v XVIII-pervoi polovine XIX v.* (Moscow, 1971), 167.

76. Kadomtsev, *Sostav,* 73; Rashin, *Naselenie,* 111, 133.

77. See *Sovremennoe khoziaistvo,* 22, for figures on rail traffic. For rail maps ca. 1900, see *Entsiklopedicheskii slovar',* 27a:360; and the supplemental map in *Moskovskaia promyshlennaia oblast'.* Direct rail coverage today has been extended only to link Vladimir and Riazan'. See *Skhema zheleznykh dorog SSSR* (1973).

division of the population into "privileged" and "nonprivileged," "elite" and "commoners," or, in the idiom I have chosen, "Muscovite and muzhik." Titled and nontitled gentry, honored citizens, merchants, and foreigners, by and large, composed the elite, while townsmen (*meshchane*) and peasants composed the common people. It is striking that the city should have contained such a large proportion of the "nonprivileged" groups, that this proportion was increasing (from 82.8 percent in 1882 to 86.9 percent in 1902), and that statistically this increase, and even the overall increase in the city's population, was almost entirely attributable to the increase in the number of peasants. As the census compilers laconically noted in 1902, "The influx of immigrants is turning Moscow more and more into a peasant city."[78]

.Immigration and rapid growth produced a distinctive gender ratio and age structure in Russia's cities. As the major destinations for a migratory labor force that, as will be recalled, left a disproportionate share of women behind, the metropolises had a preponderance of men. In 1897, for every 1,000 men in St. Petersburg and Moscow, there were, respectively, 826 and 755 women.[79] At the end of the nineteenth century, the proportion of men in Moscow was almost 10 percent higher than in any other European capital, all of which had an excess of women.[80] Throughout the nineteenth century (and indeed throughout its history prior to the 1920s) Moscow had more men than women. This gap between the number of men and women steadily narrowed from 700 women per 1,000 men in 1871 to 839 per 1,000 forty years later. The gap narrowed among the peasants as well: in 1871 there were only 394 peasant women per 1,000 peasant men. The proportion of females increased steadily, however, until by 1902 it was 650 per 1,000.[81] The influx of peasants was also reflected in the age structure of Moscow's population. Like other rapidly growing cities in the nineteenth century, Moscow was characterized by a swelling in the productive age groups and a relative absence of young and old family members. Of the major European capitals, Moscow had the smallest proportion in the age groups under five and over

78. *GPD 1902*, IV:22; *PM 1882*, II, pt.2, 31–32; *PM 1902*, I, 1, i, 11–13.
79. *PVP*, 24:xii; *Obshchii svod*, 1:6–15.
80. *Sovremennoe khoziaistvo*, 10; A. F. Weber, *The Growth of Cities in the Nineteenth Century* (Ithaca, N.Y., 1965), 286.
81. Moskovskii stolichnyi i gubernskii komitet, *Statisticheskie svedeniia o zhiteliakh goroda Moskvy po perepisi 12 dekabria 1871 g.* (Moscow, 1874), 68; *PM 1882*, II:8–9; *PM 1902*, I, 1, iii, 137–38.

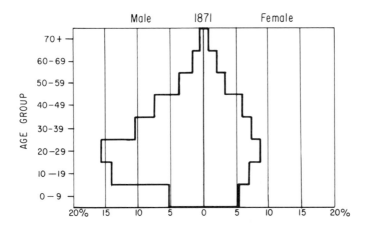

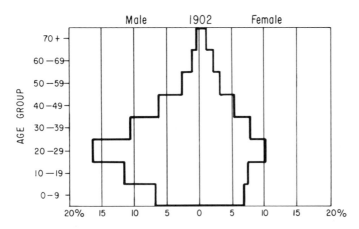

FIGURE 3. AGE STRUCTURE OF MOSCOW'S
POPULATION
Numbers along horizontal axis represent the per-
centage of the total population.

Source: *Statisticheskie svedeniia*, 14–15; *PM 1902*, I, 1, i, 4.

sixty, and the largest proportion of those from fifteen to sixty.[82] (See
figure 3.)

The rapid growth of the city, the great proportion of immigrants,
most of whom were peasants, the imbalances in gender and in age

82. *Statisticheskie svedeniia*, 14–15; *PM 1882*, II, 1–2; *PVP*, 24, i, 8–9; 24a, pt. 2,
xiii; *PM 1902*, I, 1, i, 4; Moskovskaia gorodskaia uprava, *Sbornik ocherkov po gorodu
Moskve* (Moscow, 1897), 4.

structure—these were only the beginning of the problems facing Russia's largest cities at the end of the nineteenth century. An agrarian country was beginning to urbanize, and human and productive resources were in the process of shifting to the city. Since the process had just begun, growth pains were felt everywhere, especially in the metropolises. Cities were faced with concentrated social problems; yet, like most agrarian countries, Russia had a brief and weak tradition of city government. Severely tested by rapid urban growth were Russia's organs of municipal self-government.

Statutes of 1870 and 1892 provided the legal basis for municipal self-government for the period under review. After 1870 cities were governed by a policy-making council (*duma*) and an executive board (*uprava*); the mayor, elected by the city council to a four-year term, presided over both bodies. The franchise was restricted by a two-year residence requirement and by property qualifications. The latter were broad enough, however, to give the franchise to "any male, even a peasant, who . . . owned real estate subject to municipal taxes or who had paid any other city taxes or fees, including those amounting to as little as a ruble or two for a license to set up a stall in a street market."[83] In Moscow, for example, the electorate in 1884 numbered 18,000, that is, 2 percent of the population. By raising the property qualifications to ownership of real estate valued at least at 3,000 rubles or a substantial business, the 1892 statute restricted the franchise in Moscow to 6,000 persons, considerably less than 1 percent of the population. Perhaps even more disturbing to the proponents of municipal self-government, less than one-quarter of those having the franchise in Moscow actually voted.[84] In spite of this voter apathy, Moscow had the reputation of having Russia's most active municipal government. Compared with St. Petersburg, Moscow was less in the shadow of a central government suspicious of too much local autonomy, and was administered by civic-minded industrialists, businessmen, and philanthropists interested in technological innovations in city services.[85] Nevertheless, even Moscow could not deal adequately with the problems of its citizens.

To begin with, like other Russian municipalities, Moscow faced a

83. Walter Hanchett, "Tsarist Statutory Regulation of Municipal Government in the Nineteenth Century," in Hamm, ed., *The City*, 99–100; *Istoriia Moskvy*, 4: 494–95, 512.

84. Hanchett, "Tsarist Statutory Regulation," 111; I. F. Gornostaev and Ia. M. Bugoslavskii, *Putevoditel' po Moskve i ee okrestnostiam* (Moscow, 1903), 296–97.

85. James Bater, "Some Dimensions of Urbanization," 46–63.

chronic shortage of funds, a situation exacerbated by the overall backwardness of the country. Taxing powers were limited by the city statutes, and as late as 1901 Moscow's governor-general rather disingenu-
ously noted that the city still did not have its own income and had to
rely on loans to cover not only expenses but also the budget deficit.[86]
The major sources of the municipality's income were property taxes,
taxes on businesses, profits from municipal enterprises such as the city
bakery, stockyards, and the streetcar, rents from city property, and
various licensing fees and indirect taxes such as the hospital tax and a
fee for passports and residence permits.[87] In addition, some contemporaries charged that the city council, composed largely of property
owners, failed to tax real estate even to the limits made possible by the
municipal statute, but instead charged high prices for municipal
services.[88] Since the state did not provide enough cheap credit, the city
was forced to negotiate costly foreign loans.[89] It was perhaps inevit-
able that deficits should build up: despite increased revenues from the
city's streetcars, during the period 1904–1913 Moscow's deficit averaged almost 1 million rubles annually and reached 2.75 million rubles
in 1913.[90]

Municipal expenditures fell into nine major categories: health, education, welfare, public works, obligatory expenditures, maintenance of
city property, operating expenses of municipal enterprises, operating
expenses of the city government, and interest and debt payments.
Figure 4 shows Moscow's expenditures in 1894 and 1913. Since the
revenues of the city's enterprises such as the bakery, pawnshop, and
the streetcar system exceeded the expenses, this category did not count
as a net expenditure from the city treasury. The category obligatory
expenditures included the police, gendarmes, the quartering of troops,
maintenance of prisons, and other expenses over which the municipality had no control and which amounted to a subsidy to the state.
These expenditures were illustrative of state interference in city affairs
and indeed consumed one-quarter of Moscow's budget in 1894. How-

86. TsGIA, f. 1284, op. 194, d. 128, l. 4.

87. *Sbornik ocherkov*, 7, 29–30; V. G. Mikhailovskii, *Materialy k voprosu ob usilenii sredstv goroda Moskvy* (Moscow, 1911), 60; Moskovskoe gorodskoe obshche-stvennoe upravlenie, *Deiatel'nost' Moskovskoi gorodskoi upravy za 1913–1916 gg.* (Moscow, 1916), 4.

88. *Sbornik ocherkov*, 26–27; L. M. Kleinbort, *Istoriia bezrabotitsy v Rossii, 1857–1919 gg.* (Moscow, 1925), 43.

89. Michael Hamm, "The Breakdown of Urban Modernization: A Prelude to the Revolutions of 1917," in Hamm, ed., *The City*, 184.

90. *Gorodskoe delo*, 3 (February 1, 1914), 166.

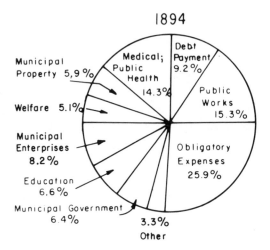

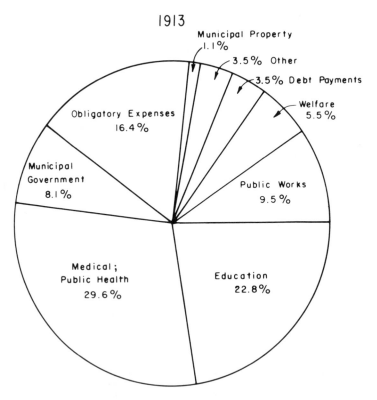

FIGURE 4. MUNICIPAL EXPENDITURES, 1894–1913
Total expenditures in 1894 and 1913 reached
8,784,000 and 22,666,000 rubles, respectively.

Source: *Sbornik ocherkov*, 138–39; *Deiatel'nost' Moskovskogo gorodskogo obshche-stvennogo upravleniia v 1913–16 gg.* (Moscow, 1916), 11.

ever, these obligatory expenses consumed a smaller, and decreasing, proportion of Moscow's budget than that of medium-sized towns.[91]

Russia's largest cities spent the largest proportion of their budgets on health, education, and welfare. St. Petersburg, Moscow, Odessa, Warsaw, and Riga spent 53 percent of all municipal expenditures on welfare in 1901.[92] In Moscow, for example, expenditures in health, education, and welfare increased from one-quarter of the budget in 1894 to almost three-fifths by 1913.[93] Elementary schools and hospitals received the lion's share of these expenses, and as a result expenditures on welfare were modest. Of 762 cities surveyed in 1907, 249 spent no money on welfare, and another 101 spent less than 1,000 rubles; only 211 cities spent more than 100 rubles. For reference, the cost of maintaining a small public almshouse was at least 300 rubles per year.[94] The transfer of several welfare institutions to municipal management in 1888 increased the amount spent on welfare in Moscow from 51,308 rubles in 1881 to 244,432 ten years later and again to 1,200,000 in 1913; nevertheless, the proportion of the total municipal budget devoted to welfare barely increased.[95] Private donations to specific charitable institutions somewhat compensated for the modest amount of municipal expenditures, but the city lacked discretionary powers over these funds.[96] Moscow easily ranked first among Russian cities in welfare expenditures, but its 1 ruble per capita did not compare it favorably with the 3.5 rubles per capita spent in Berlin.[97]

On balance, by the beginning of the twentieth century Moscow's city council had come far since the statute of 1870. Municipal expenditures increased eightfold in the forty years prior to World War I, and total expenditures outpaced population growth such that per capita expenditures tripled to 12 rubles in 1900. This may have still lagged behind Berlin's spending of 30 rubles per person,[98] but given Russia's backwardness and the fiscal constraints imposed on municipalities by the imperial government, as well as the latter's mistrust of local auton-

91. *Sbornik ocherkov*, 138–39; Hamm, "Breakdown," 184.
92. Sobstvennaia Ego Imperatorskogo Velichestva kantseliariia po uchrezhdeniiam Imperatritsy Marii, *Blagotvoritel'nost' v Rossii*, 2 vols. (St. Petersburg, 1907), 1:137–38.
93. *Sbornik ocherkov*, 95, 138.
94. *Blagotvoritel'nost' v Rossii*, 1:134–35.
95. *Sbornik ocherkov*, 42; *Deiatel'nost' Moskovskoi gorodskoi upravy za 1913–1916*, 11.
96. *Sbornik ocherkov*, 34–38, 42, 112–13; *SSS 1889*, xi.
97. S"ezd po obshchestvennomu prizreniiu, sozvannyi Ministerstvom vnutrennikh del, *Trudy* (Petrograd, 1914), 457.
98. Gornostaev, *Putevoditel' po Moskve*, 300; *Deiatel'nost' Moskovskoi gorodskoi upravy za 1913–16*, 4–11.

omy, this is not an entirely fair comparison. Even the mayor of Paris, visiting in 1911, was impressed with public works projects.[99] Moscow was considered the leader of Russian cities, and by the beginning of the twentieth century its increasingly civic-minded businessmen and professionals were more progressive than the officials of the central government in their vision of municipal improvement and reform.[100]

Nevertheless, for many reasons the municipality's resources were strained by Russia's rapid urbanization. Despite the considerable expenditures on health, for example, the city remained an unhealthy place to live, and natural growth continued to account for less than one-quarter of the city's total population growth, a proportion smaller than that of any other major city of the time. Clearly, the presence of an immigrant, often transient, unskilled, and casually employed laboring population in Russia's largest cities exacerbated basic problems of urban growth. Like other urban centers of Europe and America, Moscow was beset by shortages of low-cost housing, welfare, and cheap transportation. The large numbers of unemployed and seasonally or casually employed immigrants seriously overloaded the embryonic system of municipal employment bureaus, vocational training, and poor relief. As one student of the problem has stated, "fiscal realities were an important cause of the deterioration of the urban environment that characterized the period 1892–1917."[101] In addition, centuries of serfdom, the long absence of municipal self-government, and the mentality of the archaic estate system fostered an attitude among city authorities that existing facilities were not intended for the rural population of the empire. Perhaps most important, the values and ways of life of the common people provided a barrier which made social reform that much more difficult. Before addressing these issues, it is necessary to present a more complete picture of the city itself—the patterns of its history, its physical and human environment, and the images it projected; and, in the subsequent chapter, its economy at the close of the nineteenth century.

99. TsGIA, f. 1284, op. 194, d. 106, l. 8.

100. G. Iaroslavskii, "Gorodskoe samoupravlenie Moskvy," in I. E. Zabelin, ed., *Moskva v ee proshlom i nastoiashchem,* 12 vols. (Moscow, 1910–12), 12:18; Robert Thurston, "Urban Problems and Local Government in Late Imperial Russia: Moscow 1906–14," Ph.D. dissertation (University of Michigan, 1980), 364–65.

101. Hamm, "Breakdown," 186, 197. See also Bater, "Some Dimensions of Urbanization," 60–63.

CHAPTER TWO

Moscow: The History and the Environment

By the beginning of the twentieth century, Moscow was the tenth most populous of the world's cities. Its population of one million was only slightly less than St. Petersburg's, two-thirds of Vienna's, one-half of Berlin's, two-fifths of Paris's, and one-quarter of London's. Moscow was the fastest growing of all these cities: in the half century preceding the outbreak of World War I, its size increased fourfold. During the period 1900–1914 its growth rate was 50 percent higher than that prevailing in Petersburg and on a par with that of New York. Two-thirds of the population consisted of peasants, and almost three-quarters of the population of all estates had been born somewhere else.[1]

In addition to the size of the population, the enormity of the city was striking to contemporaries. By the 1880s the area of more or less continuous urban settlement extended beyond the Kamer-Kollezhskii rampart (*val*), the city boundaries, into many suburban settlements and villages. Sprawled in the shape of an ellipse over an area of almost sixty-five square *versts* (approximately forty-three square miles), Moscow extended eight miles from the suburbs of Sparrow Hills in the southwest to Preobrazhenskoe in the northeast. Its area was slightly larger than that of Berlin and almost equal to that of Paris. As described in an 1868 guidebook, "Moscow is so huge and complex, its streets and lanes are so ingeniously intertwined in every which way,

---

1. *Sovremennoe khoziaistvo*, 7; Rashin, *Naselenie*, 112, 116.

that the first few days of his stay, the newcomer is hopelessly lost in this incredible enormity."[2]

The city was covered by 5,600 acres of built-up land, 2,300 acres of yards and gardens, 3,100 acres of truck gardens, 2,930 acres of vacant land, 1,095 acres of rivers and ponds, 505 acres of squares, 1,950 acres of streets, and was divided into 17 wards (*chasti*) and 40 precincts (*uchastki*).[3] The newcomer was informed that his or her movement around the city would be facilitated by 934 streets, 10 quais, 81 squares, 14 boulevards, and 12 bridges. If the newcomer was Russian Orthodox—and 95 percent were—he or she could choose from 326 churches, including 7 cathedrals, 18 monasteries, 223 parish churches, and 20 chapels.[4] It is unlikely that the Russian newcomer in 1868, unless he or she had been to Petersburg or abroad, had ever seen so many palaces (5), state and public buildings (513), factories (550), shops (6,423), public baths (35), taverns (1,664), wine cellars (253), inns (603), hospitals (23), almshouses (27), or sentry boxes (431).[5] By 1904 the city claimed 1,424 streets, 94 squares, 24 cemeteries, 973 educational institutions, 94 hospitals, 201 pharmacies, 17 hotels, 161 boarding houses, 166 soup kitchens (*kharchevni*), 522 taverns, 316 beer halls, 19 theaters, 1 circus, 9 museums, and 13 newspapers.[6] (See maps 3 and 4.)

Such would have been a bird's-eye view of Moscow at the end of the nineteenth century. At this point a brief sketch of the history and physical environment of the city will help to place certain economic and social problems in the context of the growth of the city itself. The historical and geographical background that follows will enhance an understanding not only of the social forces at work at the end of the nineteenth century but also, given the dearth of English-language and high-quality Russian studies of Moscow, of the development of the present-day Soviet capital.

THE "FIRST CAPITAL"

Founded in 1147 by the Suzdal' prince Iurii Dolgorukii, Moscow was initially no more than one of several outposts defending the western borders of the Suzdal' "lands." Yet the citadel, or *kreml'*, on a high

2. M. P. Zakharov, *Putevoditel' po Moskve*, 3d ed. (Moscow, 1868), 3.
3. Ibid., 1–3.
4. Ibid., 1–3.
5. Ibid., 5–6, 9–10.
6. Gornostaev, *Putevoditel'*, 11.

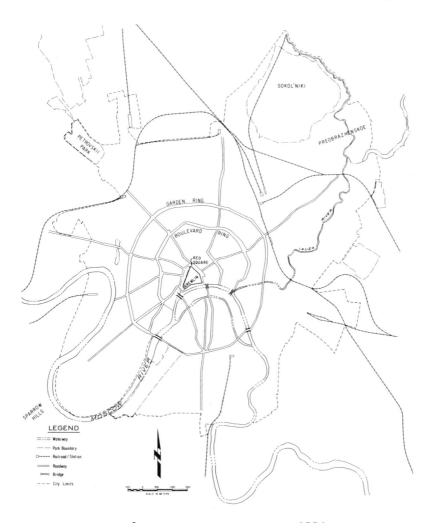

MAP 3. OVERVIEW OF MOSCOW IN 1894

bank at the confluence of the Moscow and Neglinnaia rivers, occupied
a strategic location for the commerce and defense of northeastern Rus'.[7]
After the collapse of the water routes "from the Varangians to the
Greeks" along the Dnepr through Kiev, two other important international trading networks connecting Europe and Asia developed: a water
route along the Volga from Novgorod and the Baltic, and an overland
route to the Volga from central Europe via Smolensk and Vladimir. The
princes of Moscow were conveniently situated to control these trade

7. *Istoriia Moskvy,* 1:18–20.

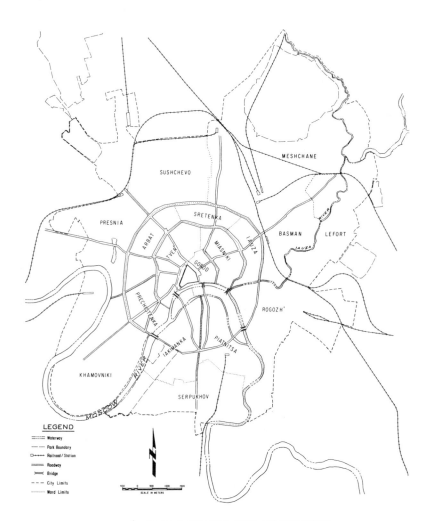

MAP 4. WARDS OF THE CITY OF MOSCOW

routes and collect duties from the surrounding peasants.[8] Moreover, behind the buffer zone of the Riazan' and Nizhnii Novgorod princedoms, Moscow suffered relatively less from the raids of the Golden Horde in the thirteenth and fourteenth centuries.[9] Its steadily increasing population of wholesalers and retailers—dealers who commanded agricultural products from the south, fish from the lower Volga, hides from

8. M. Gol'denberg and B. Gol'denberg, *Planirovka zhilogo kvartala Moskvy XVII, XVIII, XIX vv.* (Moscow and Leningrad, 1935), 9–10.
9. *Istoriia Moskvy,* 1:24. See also Hooson, "Growth of Cities," 269.

Kazan', furs and forest products from the north and east, metal products from Tula and Velikii Ustiug, linens from Tver', Kostroma, Vologda, and Iaroslavl'[10]—as well as of craftsmen, princes, boyars, ecclesiastical and monastic officials and their servitors, provided the economic and social base for a strong and vital city. As a result, in a period of two centuries Moscow developed from a frontier outpost to a major administrative center, a hub of commerce and transport, and a center of production. The city was to retain this significance, and one of the recurring images of late nineteenth-century Moscow is of its importance as a hub of commerce and transport: as the saying went, "All roads lead to Moscow."

The roads leading to Moscow centuries ago carried not only goods but also people: the impression of rapid, uncontrolled, and unprecedented population growth and peasant migration is another recurring image of late-nineteenth-century Moscow which had antecedents in the distant past. The first written reference to Moscow illustrates the importance of immigration. According to the Ipat'evskaia chronicle for the year 6655 (1147), the Suzdal' prince Iurii Dolgorukii invited his ally Sviatoslav Ol'govich to come to Moscow: "Pridi ko mne, brate, v Moskov."[11] Later, the grand princes, boyars, and clergy brought with them their retinue, and a mixture of runaway peasants and slaves, artisans and traders, collectively known as the common people (*chernye liudi*, literally, the "dark people") lived near the Kremlin. Although tax-paying, the common people, unlike the retinue of the princes, boyars, and clergy, enjoyed personal freedom, in much the same way that peasant farmers still did.[12] As early as the fifteenth century, Moscow was attracting skilled craftsmen from towns such as Novgorod, Pskov, Smolensk, Ustiug, Iaroslavl', and Tver'. Such was the magnetic field of Moscow that V. O. Kliuchevskii noted that by the sixteenth century Moscow had become a center of various regional dialects.[13]

In the absence of any population data, the growth of the medieval city is usually estimated by its expanding city boundaries and the extent of new construction. Moscow's city limits (in those days its fortifications) spread outward like bark around a tree. The first stone

10. V. O. Kliuchevskii, *Kurs russkoi istorii*, 5 vols. (Moscow, 1956–1958), 2:5–27; Komarov, *Voenno-statisticheskoe opisanie*, 327; *Istoriia Moskvy*, 1:26–28.
11. Quoted in M. Kovalenskii, ed., *Moskva v istorii i v literature* (Moscow, 1916), 7; and in N. A. Skvortsov, *Arkheologiia i topografiia Moskvy* (Moscow, 1913), 78.
12. *Istoriia Moskvy*, 1:37–40.
13. Kliuchevskii, *Kurs*, 1:299; *Istoriia Moskvy*, 1:90–92.

wall of the Kremlin was built in 1367 and was replaced in the years 1485–1495 during the reign of Ivan III by the red brick wall which still stands. The sixteenth century witnessed the building of the stone walls around Kitai-gorod, the "Walled Town," a trading quarter just east of the Kremlin (1534–1538), Belyi Gorod (1585–1593), and a wooden wall around the Zemlianoi gorod (1591–1592), which was later replaced by an earthen rampart.[14] The last fortification was beyond the present-day Garden Ring and approximately two miles from the Kremlin. (See map 5.)

Population estimates in those days were frequently laconic but tantalizing passages in the chronicles or estimates given to foreign visitors by their hosts. Thus, the great fire of 1390 allegedly wiped out "thousands of households," and Baron Sigismund von Herberstein recorded that, according to his hosts, Moscow had 41,500 houses in 1517.[15] Giles Fletcher considered Moscow bigger than sixteenth-century London.[16] The famine of 1601–1603 during the reign of Boris Godunov wiped out an estimated 120,000 inhabitants of the city, according to one contemporary; in three "state burial grounds, 127,000 bodies were buried."[17] In addition to these impressionistic counts, in the seventeenth century the Muscovite bureaucracy frequently provided population estimates (usually surveys of households) for tax purposes.[18] Taken individually, all these estimates leave much room for error; taken together, however, they suggest that just before the Time of Troubles and again during the "recovery and restoration" of the 1630s, the population of the city exceeded

14. Gol'denberg, *Planirovka*, 11, 30; V. A. Nikol'skii, *Staraia Moskva: Istoriko-kul'turnyi putevoditel'* (Moscow, 1924), 114–15; P. V. Sytin, *Katalog-putevoditel' po Moskovskomu kommunal'nomu muzeiu* (Moscow, 1929), 31. The interested visitor can still see two parts of the Kitai-gorod walls behind the Metropole and Rossiia hotels.

15. Baron Sigismund von Herberstein, *Notes upon Russia*, Hakluyt Society ed., 2 vols. (London, 1852), 2:5. It is unclear whether the Baron meant houses or households, and the figure, not coming from any document, seems exaggerated. See V. Snegirev, *Moskovskie slobody* (Moscow, 1947), 12; M. M. Bogoslovskii, "Sostav moskovskogo naseleniia v XVI–XVII vv.," in Zabelin, *Moskva*, 3:44; and *Istoriia Moskvy*, 1:37.

16. Giles Fletcher, *Of the Russe Commonwealth*, in Lloyd E. Berry and Robert O. Crummey, eds., *Rude and Barbarous Kingdom: Russia in the Accounts of Sixteenth-Century English Voyagers* (Madison, Wis., 1968), 124.

17. Bogoslovskii, "Sostav," 45. According to Avraamii Palitsyn, "The famine during Boris Godunov's reign raged with such force that in Moscow alone more than 120,000 perished."

18. The most widely cited seventeenth-century inventory, the *rospisnoi spisok* of 1638, was primarily a count of those able and armed to defend the city. See *Istoriia Moskvy*, 1:449.

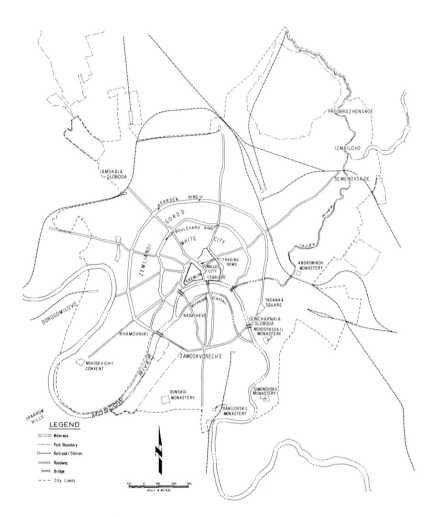

MAP 5. GROWTH AND SETTLEMENT OF MOSCOW

100,000 and may have come close to 200,000 by mid-seventeenth
century, which would have made Moscow one of Europe's largest
cities. The next two hundred years, however, were years of stagnation and very slow growth. The population at the time of the first
census of males ("Revision") in 1719 was between 100,000 and
150,000. Two estimates of the 1780s—what was probably the first
study of the city as such and Shchekatov's *Dictionary*—counted
188,654 and 216,953, respectively. The 300,000 mark was reached

in the 1830s, and by the eve of the emancipation of the serfs the city contained approximately 350,000 people.[19]

It is noteworthy that Moscow should have grown during the most tumultuous period in the nation's history before the twentieth century. When the ravages of the reign of Ivan the Terrible and of the Time of Troubles as well as the spread of the bureaucracy and serfdom drove peasants to "flee from the center" to the southern and eastern borderlands, the net population estimates suggest that Moscow at the very least held its own and may even have grown considerably.[20] "Flight to Moscow" as well as flight from the villages of central Muscovy were both brought about by the expansion of the Muscovite state and its service and military apparatus. Although the period covered by this book knows no such traumatic events as the Time of Troubles, "flight" to Moscow (and also to Petersburg) accompanied colonization of open lands such as Siberia at the end of the nineteenth century in much the same way. The image of Moscow as a refuge from village hardship recurs again and again. The observation of an 1897 collection of articles on the city was typical. "In days of old Moscow abounded with the poor and homeless . . . seeking a livelihood in the wealthy capital."[21]

Flight to Moscow in the sixteenth and seventeenth centuries was a long-term and even permanent escape from the political, social, and economic turmoil of the countryside. As a result, the city's population grew. Quieter times of the eighteenth and early nineteenth centuries obviated the need for such escape, resulting in slower population growth. More important perhaps, the apogee of serfdom from the mid-seventeenth to the mid-nineteenth century, in part a response to such flight, made further long-term flight more difficult. Short-term moves, however, not only were possible, but were encouraged by serf owners. If as a 1787 description of towns and counties in Moscow province claimed, 100,000–150,000 peasants who were in the city only during the winter season were not counted in the eighteenth-century popula-

19. The major eighteenth-century published sources on the city are A. F. Shchekatov, *Slovar' geograficheskii Rossiiskogo gosudarstva* (Moscow, 1805); *Sostoianie Stolichnogo goroda Moskvy 1785 g.* (Moscow, 1785); and *Istoricheskoe i topograficheskoe opisanie gorodov moskovskoi gubernii s ikh uezdami* (Moscow, 1787). See also *GPD 1912*, 38; Snegirev, *Moskovskie slobody*, 42; Bogoslovskii, "Sostav," 54; and Gol'denberg, *Planirovka*, 70.

20. S. F. Platonov, *The Time of Troubles: A Historical Study of the Internal Crisis and Social Struggle in Sixteenth- and Seventeenth-Century Muscovy*, trans. John T. Alexander (Lawrence, Kans., 1970), 27–30.

21. *Sbornik ocherkov*, 1.

tion estimates, it is possible that the observed slowdown in Moscow's growth may have been misleading.[22] Likewise, the existence of a fringe of temporary residents outside a core of permanent inhabitants, a pervasive characteristic of nineteenth-century Moscow, had long been a feature of the city.

Population growth and immigration and the importance of the city as a center of commerce, production, transport, administration, and consumption not only suggest constant themes which recur whether one is studying seventeenth-, nineteenth-, or twentieth-century Moscow, but also determined the composition of its labor force. Several population estimates and secondary studies point to the large number of laborers producing and distributing what the elite (and the state) was consuming. According to the 1634 inventory rolls of households compiled for tax purposes, approximately two-thirds of the population consisted of laborers, tradesmen, household or court serfs, soldiers, and their dependents.[23] According to estimates based on the population of the 1780s, approximately three-quarters of the population were laborers.[24] By 1900, 80–85 percent of Moscow's population consisted of laborers and their dependents. Thus over a period of three centuries, Moscow had a consistently large, and gradually increasing, proportion of laborers.

The court itself employed a large number of servitors and craftsmen, and in medieval Moscow, as in Soviet Moscow, the state was the biggest employer. In the seventeenth century, the provisions office (*kormovoi dvor*), for instance, hired 150 cooks, dishwashers, water carriers, and inspectors for the daily preparation of 3,000 dishes for the tsar, his family, servitors, officials, and guests. An estimated 100 barrels of wine and 400–500 barrels of beer and mead were consumed on an ordinary day, and five times more on holidays; for this, over 100 were employed. Over 300 servitors held various jobs connected with the court stables.[25] Foreign dignitaries were duly impressed. The Austrian ambassador von Mayerberg was not untypical when he noted in the seventeenth century that "in Moscow there is such a

22. Quoted in *Istoriia Moskvy*, 2:306.
23. Ibid., 1:450. Although it is true, as Max Weber stated, that medieval Moscow "represented a place where rents from possessions in land, slaves and office income were consumed," this is a one-sided view of Moscow's function and overlooks the importance of production and distribution. See Max Weber, *The City*, trans. and ed. Don Martindale and Gertrude Neuwirth (New York, 1958), 200.
24. Gol'denberg, *Planirovka*, 70.
25. Bogoslovskii, "Sostav," 46–47.

plentitude of everything necessary in life, both necessities and luxuries, and purchasable at a reasonable price, that it has no reason to be envious of any other country in the world."[26]

Entire settlements of potters, gold- and silversmiths, jewelers, tailors, armorers, and carpenters filled orders for the court and the elite. Certain settlements, such as the tsar's weavers of Kadashevo and Khamovniki, later to become important industrial districts, and the tsar's potters (near present-day Taganka Square), enjoyed privileges, such as duty-free or duty-reduced trade and customs-free transit of goods into the city and exemption from state taxes and duties (*tiaglo*) levied on the "free" settlements.[27] Other important settlements belonged to the church, monasteries, and private landowners. Many settlements were inhabited by servitors on contract to the state, such as the musketeers, cannoneers, and postmen, who had multiple occupations. In return for their military and municipal services, the musketeers were allowed to engage in small-scale manufacturing and trade free of customs duties, paid and provided with cloth for their uniforms, granted immunity from taxes, and given the right to make duty-free wine and beer on big holidays.[28] The postmen, by contrast, were not as privileged and, from their quarters on the outskirts of the city, doubled as farmers. So important was farming to the postmen that in the eighteenth century their complaints against the spreading suburban estates of the gentry focused on the encroachment of pasturage for their livestock.[29] (See map 5.)

Registration in associations or settlements of craftsmen and tradesmen fulfilled state objectives. Townsmen, whether in nominally "free" associations or in associations belonging to the court, nobility, or church, were required to serve in one way or another; for the right of household ownership the artisan paid duties or made wares, and the musketeer served in the garrison or the police.[30] It followed that membership in such associations and the privileges that came with it were conditional upon service: for instance, an artisan's household could not be freely alienated. Furthermore, service obligations took prece-

26. Quoted in Snegirev, *Moskovskie slobody*, 46.

27. Ibid., 63–64. See also *Istoriia Moskvy*, 1:470; Bogoslovskii, "Sostav," 47; and A. L. Iakobson, *Tkatskie slobody i sela v XVII v.* (Moscow and Leningrad, 1934), 64.

28. Snegirev, *Moskovskie slobody*, 44; Arthur Voyce, *Moscow and the Roots of Russian Culture* (Norman, Okla., 1964), 50.

29. N. A. Geinike et al., *Po Moskve: Progulki po Moskve i ee khudozhestvennym i prosvetitel'nym uchrezdeniiam* (Moscow, 1917), 291.

30. Snegirev, *Moskovskie slobody*, 28–29; Gol'denberg, *Planirovka*, 57.

dence over occupation and residence in classifying the tax-paying population. That is, one was registered with the association where one paid taxes; this might or might not have coincided with one's craft or residence.[31]

These associations and settlements of taxpayers declined in the eighteenth century. Settlements registered fewer and fewer households and had a smaller and smaller proportion of the city's population.[32] The 1795 population of the leather-workers' settlement south of the Moscow River was only 39 percent of its 1725 level; more and more leather-workers were living outside their settlement.[33] The transfer of the capital to St. Petersburg, the increasing importance of textile manufacturing and seasonal labor of serfs, the substitution by the city statutes of 1785 of an all-city government for the associational government, and the demands of a greatly expanding state apparatus, constantly modeling itself after European states, spelled the end of the distinctive craft settlements.

Despite the end of *sloboda* Moscow in name, the city continued to be a center of small-scale manufacture, crafts, and trade. Despite the small role Russian historians have given the cities and their artisan population in the economic and social development of the nation, there are important aspects of late-nineteenth-century Moscow that are impossible to explain without recognizing its importance as a center of production, particularly of artisan production. It is true, however, that craft production and the craftsmen themselves, as well as tradesmen and wholesale merchants, never attained the independence from the state that characterized their counterparts in western Europe. As the preceding discussion has shown, the craftsmen and tradesmen of medieval Moscow, in spite of their impressive numbers, had to serve the state in some form. Even when the service state declined in the second half of the eighteenth century, no fertile soil existed for an independent, self-reliant, urban artisan culture, and transient serf laborers earning money to pay quitrents to their owners could not fill the void.

31. E. A. Zviagintsev, " 'Kozhevniki' i ikh posadskoe naselenie v XVIII v.," in *Staraia Moskva: Trudy obshchestva izucheniia moskovskoi oblasti,* no. 5: *Stat'i po istorii Moskvy v XVII–XIX vv.* (Moscow, 1929), 114. See also J. Michael Hittle, *The Service City: State and Townsmen in Russia, 1600–1800* (Cambridge, Mass., 1979), 29–31.

32. Gol'denberg, *Planirovka,* 27; Snegirev, *Moskovskie slobody,* 12, 42, 148–49; Bogoslovskii, "Sostav," 54; *Istoriia Moskvy,* 2:56, 310–11.

33. Zviagintsev, " 'Kozhevniki'," 109–26.

SETTLEMENT PATTERNS

Moscow's history—not only the history of Muscovy and its grand princes, tsars, boyars, and metropolitans, which has been well documented elsewhere,[34] but its population growth, immigration, economic functions, and labor force—figured strongly in the images of the city at the end of the nineteenth century. Even more strongly, if only because more visible, figured the artifacts of urban growth. The city's commercial importance and scattered craft settlements had left behind a hodgepodge neighborhood development and an atmosphere of untempered disorganization, particularly striking to the foreign visitor (especially, no doubt, to those whose first stop in Russia had been Petersburg).

The city grew in concentric rings around its citadel and the adjacent trading quarters in the "Walled City." The three main streets leading away from the Kremlin through the Walled City—Nikol'skaia, Il'inka, Varvarka—were the earliest commercial thoroughfares. Starting at the walls of the Kremlin itself in Red Square and between the above three streets ran rows of shops and stalls, later called the Trading Rows (Torgovye riady), now called the State Shopping Mall (GUM). The scruffiest of the stalls, ironically, were located in Red Square itself—ironically because the present-day authorities have imparted to the area outside the Kremlin walls a shrine-like atmosphere that it never had under the tsars. Behind the Trading Rows was a lowland (*podol*) along the Moscow River; this area was also known as the Zariad'e and is now known as the Rossiia Hotel.[35]

By the end of the eighteenth century the area of urban settlement extended in a radius of two to three miles from the Kremlin to the Garden Ring (Sadovoe Kol'tso). A district named Gorod (literally, "the City") and known for its warehouses, shops, stores, and the stock exchange, constituted the Walled City. The other central wards were Tver', Miasniki (literally, "the butchers"), Iauza, Sretenka, Arbat, and Prechistenka ("the cleanest"). This was Moscow's nerve center—its government offices and institutions, stores, and best residences. As the 1868 guidebook put it, the center "is the major place for the life and business of the city. Here are the cathedrals, monasteries, palaces, luxurious homes, shops and stores, educational institutions and places

---

34. In addition to the Soviet *Istoriia Moskvy*, see I. E. Zabelin, *Istoriia goroda Moskvy* (Moscow, 1902), and P. Lopatin, *Moskva, ocherki po istorii velikogo goroda* (Moscow, 1959).

35. G. G. Antipin, *Zariad'e* (Moscow, 1973), 7–15.

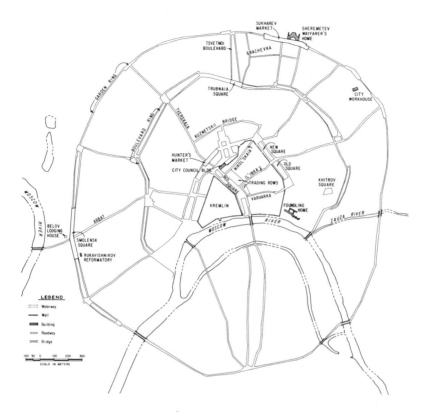

MAP 6. CENTRAL MOSCOW

of entertainment, and beautiful streets such as the ever bustling Tver-skaia, aristocratic Prechistenka and fashionable Blacksmith's Bridge (Kuznetskii most) with its enticing French and Russian signs."[36] (See map 6.)

By the second half of the nineteenth century a central business district consisting of the "City," Tver', and Miasniki wards could be distinguished from the more residential wards of Arbat, Prechistenka, Sretenka, and Iauza. Within the central business district itself, the City and Miasniki were becoming the centers of Moscow's wholesale, banking, and insurance business. As warehouses and offices began to replace living quarters, parts of this district began to lose population, though only the City showed a net loss from 1882 to 1912.[37] Tver', on

36. Zakharov, *Putevoditel'*, 11.
37. *GPD 1912*, 8.

the other hand, was becoming the retailing center with fashionable stores "with enticing signs."

Throughout the centuries, Moscow's elite had resided in different parts of the center, and as a result no single exclusive district developed. At first the lesser princes, boyars, service gentry, and officials lived within the fortified "White City," the first concentric ring outside the Kremlin and the Walled City and north of the Moscow River. In the seventeenth century greater security and, later, the residential preferences of Peter I meant that the elite more and more settled outside the White City. Early in the eighteenth century the gentry settled along the eastern arteries connecting the Kremlin, the foreign settlement, the Preobrazhenskii, Izmailovskii, and Semenovskii regiments, and the residence of Peter I. In the second half of the eighteenth century Tverskaia (now Gorky Street), the road to Petersburg via the town of Tver', became both the most important artery and the location of government offices and, later, fashionable French shops. At the same time the neighborhoods of Arbat and Prechistenka southwest of the Kremlin became the "gentry nests," which they remained until the end of the nineteenth century.[38] By the beginning of the twentieth century the gentry nests were increasingly populated by professionals and businessmen, such as Morozov, Shchukin, and Riabushinskii.[39] The 1917 guidebook described the quiet Arbat neighborhood where the United States ambassador now resides:

The illustrious Russian gentry has scattered long ago. The gentry nests are empty. The property owners along Starokoniushennyi street—all the generals, captains and lieutenants of the guards—were long ago laid to rest somewhere in the old cemetery in Donskoi Monastery. . . . Strolling through aristocratic Moscow we become nostalgic about a past that's gone forever.[40]

The classical-style mansions with gardens and private chapels of Arbat and Prechistenka gave parts of central Moscow a bucolic atmosphere. To one Englishman the side streets were

the prettiest and most quiet and retired little country retreats one can imagine. They are quite unique in their repose and neatness and their entire absence of the noise and turmoil of a great city. . . . A few yards farther on we turn down what might be a lane in a country village. On either hand are small cottages, with windows looking out on the street, but there is no doorway. To each of

38. Gol'denberg, *Planirovka*, 66–68; A. Martynov, *Nazvanie moskovskikh ulits i pereulkov* (Moscow, 1888), 1, 7.

39. Geinike, *Po Moskve*, 329; Gornostaev, *Putevoditel'*, 82; Gol'denberg, *Planirovka*, 129.

40. Geinike, *Po Moskve*, 342.

them is a large gateway opening into a green and grassy court and garden. As we walk by, the gate being half open, perhaps, we look in and witness a quiet scene of the country. There are trees, two or three small laburnums or acacias and a flower bed, and cocks and hens are walking about on a grass plot; there is perhaps a cow and a stable and a coach-house. . . . Women are seated on a verandah or on the steps leading down into the garden and children are at play. It is a sunny spot, fresh, green and bright and quiet as if fifty miles from Moscow.[41]

Anyone who is familiar with Polenov's painting A Moscow Courtyard, or who has sat on a park bench on Gogol' Boulevard, let alone on a quiet side street one hundred years later, will know the feeling.

Despite their languid atmosphere, even the residential, "nice" parts of town were not devoid of manufacturing activity or of run-down neighborhoods. The Arbat and Prechistenka wards each had over four hundred manufacturing establishments, most of them small workshops, in the late 1880s; this expressed an increase over the number counted in 1870.[42] In 1902 almost 2,000 factory workers (1,140 of them at the Butkov woolen mill alone) were employed in the riverfront precinct of Prechistenka; this was the largest number of factory workers living in any central ward and more than in several outer precincts. The shanties of stevedores along the river and the decrepit apartments housing laborers and artisans which would prompt one investigator at the turn of the twentieth century to declare that "these people live in unbearable hygienic conditions and often in disgusting moral conditions" were located in Prechistenka.[43] The city's worst skid row, Khitrov market, a subject that will merit more extensive treatment in chapter 7, was located in the central Miasniki ward. On the near north side in the neighborhood of Tsvetnoi Boulevard and Trubnaia Square was Moscow's "red light" district. Not far away was a rookery of narrow streets called the Grachevka. According to the writers Levitov and Voronov:

From time immemorial this has been a tomb for the poor, a huge grave stuffed with living corpses, devoured by poverty, perversion and other plagues of hapless humanity. Russian versions of Les Misérables can be found only here

41. G. T. Lowth, Around the Kremlin (London, 1868), 14–16. See also I. A. Slonov, Iz zhizni torgovoi Moskvy (Moscow, 1914), 48; G. Vasilich, "Ulitsy i liudi," in Zabelin, Moskva, 12:4–5. A print of Polenov's A Moscow Courtyard may be found in Gosudarstvennaia Tret'iakovskaia gallereia (Moscow, 1971), no. 40.

42. Moskovskaia gorodskaia uprava, Vedomosti nakhodiashchikhsia v Moskve torgovykh i promyshlennykh zavedenii (Moscow, 1873), passim; TPZ, Appendix, p. 2; and Orlov and Budagov, Ukazatel', passim.

43. Quoted in Sviatlovskii, Zhilishchnyi vopros, 4:41.

at Grachevka because nowhere else is there such a striking aggregation of abominable, stupefying conditions.[44] [See map 6.]

Beyond the Garden Ring lay the city's outskirts, "the other side of the tracks," as the words *za sadovoe* expressed it. As early as the seventeenth century, craft and manufacturing settlements surrounded the central districts outside the Garden Ring along the major trading arteries and water basins. Scattered throughout the city and clustered around the best defended points outside the fortifications, and closely connected to the central markets in the Walled City and to the outlying markets at the city's gates, but separated from each other by vast expanses of truck gardens and meadows, these settlements facilitated a mingling of commercial and artisan households with those of the princes, boyars, and the garrison. The resulting haphazard growth and decentralization was also brought about by the self-contained nature of some of the settlements. With most craftsmen living and working under the same roof, with each settlement having its patron saint and church, priest, almshouse, communal well, and bathhouse, each settlement resembled a small village.[45] Commercial contact was easily made with other nearby "settlement-villages" and with the "market town" of the Walled City. Closely packed wooden houses and shanties (*khibarki*) housed artisans, lower officials, and the *vshivye* (literally, "louse-infested"), or ragged. Frequent fires required rapid house construction, giving another name to the area: *skorodom*.[46] Outside the city's jurisdiction until the mid-eighteenth century, the area beyond the Garden Ring retained its reputation throughout the nineteenth century as an area the respectable Muscovite would want to avoid.

Yet by 1900 two-thirds of the city's inhabitants lived "on the other side of the tracks." Ten of the city's seventeen wards lay beyond the Garden Ring: Presnia and Khamovniki to the west, Sushchevo and Meshchane to the north, Lefort, Basman, and Rogozh' to the east, and Iakiman, Piatnitsa, and Serpukhov to the south. Beyond the municipal boundaries, the largest suburban settlements were Mar'ia's Grove, Mar'ia's Sloboda, Krest, Bogorodskoe, Cherkizovo, Blagusha, Novaia Stroika, Butyrki, and Dorogomilovo. (See map 7.) In addition to these

44. M. A. Voronov and A. I. Levitov, *Moskovskie nory i trushchoby* (St. Petersburg, 1866), 66. See also Vladimir Giliarovskii, *Izbrannoe*, 2 vols. (Kuibyshev, 1965), 2: *Moskva i Moskvichi*, 87–99, 141–54.

45. Gol'denberg, *Planirovka*, 29, 58–60.

46. Ibid., 118–19. See also Geinike, *Po Moskve*, 261, 289, 293; and E. Zviagintsev, "Vozniknovenie proletarskikh okrain v Moskve," *Istoriia proletariata SSSR*, 2 (1935): 230–44.

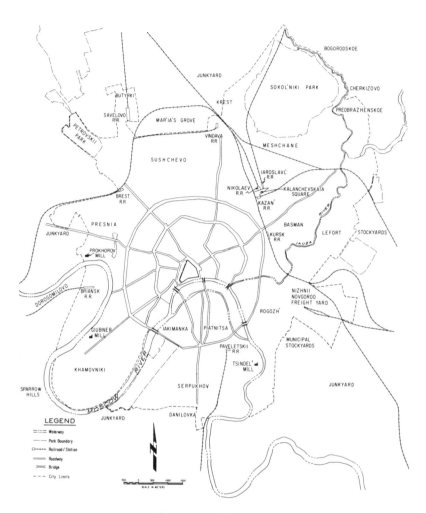

MAP 7. MOSCOW'S OUTSKIRTS

suburbs, all having a distinctly lower-class atmosphere, there were three well-to-do suburbs whose restaurants, parks, and cottages attracted the elite: Sokol'niki, a large park and summer resort area northeast of the city; Petrovskii Park, on the way to Petersburg, whose risqué restaurant, Yar, was the scene of Rasputin's highly publicized displays in 1915; and Sparrow Hills, now the grounds of Moscow University.

These outer districts contained the city's largest factories and mills (and, in 1902, 93 percent of the city's factory workers).[47] Some precincts such as Piatnitsa 2 had entire blocks occupied by a single factory. Ivanov Street was dominated by the Bakhrushin mill; on Gustianikov and Derbenov streets everything was the Tsindel' calico-printing mill. One was aware

only of factory buildings with their tall smokestacks, and huge iron-barred windows and with their incessant earth-shaking droning and knocking of machines. In several places the streets are covered with coal dust. The narrow lanes are more like deep dark corridors between tall factory buildings. And when the droning buzzer goes off at mealtime, crowds of workers pour out of the factory gates for dinner.[48]

Huge textile mills, such as the Prokhorov calico-printing mill which employed 4,000 workers at the turn of the century, dominated the western districts of Khamovniki and Presnia.[49] The other major factory wards were in the Serpukhov ward and along the Iauza River. The Iauza River in particular was considered an eyesore:

Under bushy willows meanders the dirty Iauza, dyed all colors of the rainbow by industrial discharge. Along its banks are factories surrounded by vast tracks of wasteland and truck gardens. On the inclines leading down to the river one can almost always see tramps: here they rest, sleep, mend their clothes, and so on. This is the other side of the tracks (iznanka goroda).[50]

The outer municipal districts also contained all nine of the city's railroad stations, as well as its freight and lumber yards. In a clockwise direction from the oldest station, these were the Nikolaev (now Leningrad), Iaroslavl', Kazan', Kursk, Paveletsk, Briansk (now Kiev), Brest (now Belorusskii), Savelovo, and Vindava (now Riga) stations. To these one could add the Nizhnii Novgorod freight station on the eastern edge of town. A circular railroad connected all nine lines. In 1902 the annual amount of incoming and outgoing freight was five million tons.[51] Understandably, the neighborhoods around the railroad stations were among the most congested in the city, and so they re-

47. *TPZ*, 46–48. See also *Sovremennoe khoziaistvo*, 11. Additional descriptive material on the city's districts may be found in any of the books by P. V. Sytin. See, for example, *Iz istorii moskovskikh ulits* (Moscow, 1958); *Otkuda proizoshli nazvaniia ulits Moskvy* (Moscow, 1959); and *Proshloe Moskvy v nazvaniiakh ulits* (Moscow, 1948).
48. D. A. Zharinov and N. M. Nikol'skii, *Byloe vokrug nas* (Moscow, 1922), 180.
49. *PM 1902*, III, 3, 170–215; Geinike, *Po Moskve*, 331–32.
50. Geinike, *Po Moskve*, 290.
51. *Sovremennoe khoziaistvo*, 22. For the period 1901–1904, years of economic slowdown, the city imported an average of 1.2 million tons of firewood, 200,000 tons of coal, and 470,000 tons of oil, in addition to large amounts of building materials and grain.

main to this day. This was especially true of Kalanchevskaia (now
Komsomol'skaia) Square, just northeast of the Garden Ring where the
Nikolaev, Iaroslavl', and Kazan' stations converged. As we shall see
later, reformers at the end of the nineteenth century placed these
neighborhoods high on the list of those areas of the city demanding
immediate ameliorative measures.

Despite the existence of modern-looking factories and railroad stations, perhaps the most pervasive physical attribute of these outer
districts was their overall backward-looking character: vast tracts of
undeveloped land, grinding village-like poverty, wooden shacks, and
village ways. Contemporaries were struck not only by the railroad
station square but by the dark, unpaved streets on which limped the
ragged, the barefoot, and the beggars; not only by the factory dormitories but by the shanties devoid of running water and sewers; and
not only by the fashionable suburban restaurants and cottages but by
the sleazy taverns, inns, and teahouses. A 1917 guidebook described
one neighborhood just beyond Taganka Square on the southeast side,
called Shviva Knoll and settled by ragged, poverty-stricken peasants.
Approaching Taganka Square, "ever more frequently one sees
ragged, barefooted and mendicant figures, who are testimony to the
proximity of Moscow's poorest quarters."[52] Not far away was the
Rogozh' district where resided "mainly artisans, small tradesmen and
unskilled laborers; in many places it reminds one of a provincial city
with its wooden houses, bad and dusty streets and solitude."[53] Similar neighborhoods were easily found in the northern districts of Sushchevo and Meshchane and the suburbs of Mar'ia's Grove and Krest,
among the fastest growing districts in the entire city.[54] To the well-
heeled Muscovites, these outskirts were the edge of human civilization, "untouched by kerosine lamps, pavement and police patrols."[55]
In a south-side working-class suburb such as Danilovka, "along with
the ordinary poor, which is even more ignorant here than that inside
the city limits, are nestled many wild and frequently criminal paupers who bring up children in their own image."[56] The village-like
character of the outer districts contrasted with the more modern
appearance of the center to present two conflicting images of the city

52. Geinike, *Po Moskve*, 297.
53. Gornostaev, *Putevoditel'*, 85. See also the 1868 *Putevoditel'*, 12–13.
54. *GPD 1912*, 10–11.
55. E. D. Maksimov, *Proiskhozhdenie nishchenstva i mery bor'by s nim* (St. Petersburg, 1901), 70.
56. Ibid., 72.

to contemporaries: a big village, and a modern, Europeanized metropolis.

"EUROPEAN CITY" OR "BIG VILLAGE"?

If ever a city expressed the character and peculiarities of its inhabitants, that city is Moscow, the "heart of Russia" in which the Russian "wide nature" (*shirokaia dusha*) is abundantly obvious. The character, life and tendencies of the people are seen in much greater purity here than in St. Petersburg and are much less influenced by Western Europe, though even Moscow is rapidly becoming modernized of late years.[57]

The trite references to Russian character and to the differences between Moscow and St. Petersburg aside, the Baedecker guidebook pointed to an important feature of Moscow. The city was rapidly becoming a modern metropolis, even in the eyes of Europeans. At the same time, it had not lost its old character and old ways. Moscow conveyed the image of a bustling, modern European city, on the one hand, and of a scruffy, backward, semi-Asiatic big village, on the other.

Upon first sight of Moscow, the ordinary Russian was impressed with modernity. The worker Semen Kanatchikov recalled later that he had been struck first by the stores, whose number seemed to exceed the number of houses or people.[58] The businessman Ivan Slonov remembered:

After quiet little Kolomna, I was struck by Moscow's size, its huge and brightly lit buildings, its heavy traffic and the clattering of many carriages. . . . At every step I would stop and stare at people in fancy clothes and at the pretty horses harnessed to the carriages. But most of all I was interested in the import (*kolonial'nye*) stores and in the candy stores and their pretty displays of various delicacies that I had never seen before.[59]

According to the 1868 guidebook:

Moscow was adorned with heavenly cathedrals, royal palaces, aristocratic mansions, thousands of homes, innumerable shops and stores and laced with boulevards and gardens. Made into the focal point of the domestic commerce and industry of an immense empire, the products of its factories are sent not only all over the empire but even abroad.[60]

57. Karl Baedeker, *Russia with Teheran, Port Arthur, and Peking* (London, 1914), 277.
   58. Semen Kanatchikov, *Iz istorii moego bytiia* (Moscow and Leningrad, 1929), 8.
   59. Slonov, *Iz zhizni*, 38.
   60. Zakharov, *Putevoditel'*, 6–7.

Moscow not only fit the image of a capital city or metropolis, it was also becoming more modern. The 1903 guidebook summarized the far-reaching changes the city as a whole had undergone:

Moscow has been transformed completely from a big village with an aristocratic tint to a huge, crowded commercial and industrial city (whose population is more than half peasant), adorned with museums, galleries, clinics, hospitals, charitable and educational institutions.[61]

Not only had Moscow been "transformed," but in this author's view the physical artifacts of modernity had changed from the "heavenly cathedrals, royal palaces, aristocratic mansions [and] . . . innumerable shops and stores" that had impressed the author of the 1868 guidebook to "museums, galleries, clinics, hospitals, charitable and educational institutions." A "civic" Moscow had been added to the earlier ecclesiastical, commercial, and "private" Moscow.

Many downtown taverns (*traktiry*) were losing their old Russian atmosphere and becoming Europeanized restaurants.[62] Slonov observed in 1914 that the life of businessmen in the Walled City had changed completely, that now fancy and expensive merchandise and display windows were everywhere, and that Moscow had become a European city.[63] The appearance of the businessmen themselves had changed, for

the cap and old-fashioned top hat have been replaced by the bowler hat, the long frockcoat has given way to the morning jacket (*vizitka*), and instead of high leather boots we see American spats, instead of bushy beards we see clean-shaven faces or European trims.[64]

Another observer noted the appearance of concepts such as chic and fashion, allegedly alien to Muscovites in the past, whose dress and customs had been regulated by tradition. "Fashion" inevitably came with urban civilization, and in some Darwinian process, it was already driving traditional Russian dress and customs to the outskirts.[65]

One might expect the Russians themselves to have been impressed; even foreigners, however, noted the rapid modernization of the city. The specialty and luxury stores impressed many foreign visitors:

61. Gornostaev, *Putevoditel'*, 36.
62. Vasilich, "Ulitsy i liudi," 10.
63. Slonov, *Iz zhizni*, 96, 238–39.
64. Geinike, *Po Moskve*, 307.
65. Vasilich, "Ulitsy i liudi," 7.

Here shop windows are full of the inventions of Western civilization, easy
chairs, jardinieres, statuettes, china, cravats, silk stockings, parasols, photographs of French actresses and ballet girls, yellow-covered French novels, and
the last number of *Vie Parisienne* and *Journal Amusant*.[66]

Curtis Guild wrote in the 1890s:

Moscow is fast becoming a great centre of manufacturing and a commercial
and business city with a railroad system affording the means for the reception
of material and the distribution of products, so that ere long the semi-barbaric
architecture and the flavor of Eastern life which it now possesses will gradually give way to the advance of European ideas and more pronounced features
of modern civilization.[67]

Despite the obvious modernization, the "flavor of Eastern life"
persisted. Opposed to the images of advancement and modernization
were those of backwardness. When earlier patterns of sprawling settlement were complemented by the contemporary physical environment
of wooden houses, unpaved streets, and livestock on the outskirts, the
composite impression of foreigners and Muscovites alike was that of
an "overgrown village," symbolic of the city's backwardness and the
most recurrent image of late-nineteenth-century Moscow. (To this day
Moscow is sometimes thought of as a big village, and indeed many
Russians—and especially native Muscovites—who, upon learning the
subject of my research, immediately responded: "Moscow! Ah, the big
village!")

The components of this image included the condescension of the
Westernized elite, the casual observation of Moscow's crooked streets,
wooden houses, bucolic side streets, quaint outdoor markets, and
sprawling development, and the interaction with social groups more
often associated with provincial life. The sobriquet "the big village"
was implanted by the Petersburg elite at the end of the eighteenth
century, and the remarks of Catherine II illustrate this attitude:

The city is so big that it takes days just to get around to see people on
business. . . . Besides, the people have never had anything but the manifestations of fanaticism, such as miracle-working icons on every corner, churches,
priests, monasteries, pilgrims, beggars, thieves, useless domestics at home. And
what homes! What filth! They are so huge, but their courtyards are filthy
swamps.[68]

66. Theodore Child, "Holy Moscow," in Theodore Child et al., *The Tsar and His
People* (New York, 1891), 282.
67. Curtis Guild, *Britons and Muscovites* (Boston, 1888), 176.
68. Quoted in M. Kovalenskii, *Moskva v istorii*, 166–67.

Condescension of the gentry toward Russia's merchants, as well as the humble origins and ways of life of many of the latter themselves, combined to give the city's merchant districts a reputation for backwardness. Moscow's oldest and most central merchant district was just across the river (Zamoskvorech'e) from the Kremlin. The typical home—with its greenery, gardens, high wooden fences, and even adjoining warehouses—reeked of provincialism to the gentry elite. The image imparted by the 1868 guidebook—that the south side was totally unlike a capital city, that it lacked life and movement and more closely resembled a provincial capital or even a good county seat—was unchanged almost fifty years later when it was still a "dreadful, provincial, godforsaken place."[69] Even more "provincial and godforsaken" were the east-side merchant neighborhoods of Lefort-Preobrazhenskoe and Rogozhskoe, centers of Old Believer communities readmitted to Moscow under Catherine the Great.

The middling merchants and lower townsmen, in the main Old Believers, stubbornly observe ancient traditions and resist Europeanization. The most conservative part of Moscow is Lefort and Rogozh', especially the quiet streets of the Taganka neighborhood. . . . They talk about today's Moscow as if about something distant and alien.[70]

Moscow's sprawling, unorganized settlement and growth (a striking contrast to that of St. Petersburg), as well as its many one-story wooden buildings, suggested provincial Russia to many contemporaries. One foreigner noted a vastness and an emptiness and speculated that Moscow was "built in expectation of some multitudinous future population, rather than to meet present wants."[71] Anatole Leroy-Beaulieu's generalizations about Russian towns also apply well to Moscow:

Instead of standing their houses closely side by side, instead of heaping tier on tier up to the sky, like the old cities of France, Italy and Germany, and thus forming a little world entirely distinct from the country, brimming with only men and men's works, Russian towns stretch and sprawl out into fields into which they merge leaving between the houses and public buildings acres of wasteland that can never be filled or enlivened. To the traveler arriving from Europe, they appear as something huge, deserted, unfinished; they often seem to be their own suburbs and the foreigner expects to enter the city when he is just leaving it behind him. To him they are so many overgrown villages and in

69. Zakharov, *Putevoditel'*, 12; Gornostaev, *Putevoditel'*, 84; Geinike, *Po Moskve*, 305, 320.
70. G. Vasilich, "Moskva, 1850–1910 g.," in Zabelin, *Moskva*, 11:20.
71. Child, "Holy Moscow," 249; Vasilich, "Ulitsy i liudi," 4–5.

fact there is less difference here than anywhere else, between village and town, as regards the manner of building and living.[72]

Moscow's streets and its public transport, though one of the best systems in the empire, nevertheless suggested backwardness. Slonov felt that Moscow's

most distinctive mark was its pavement.... Paved with huge cobblestones, always muddy or dusty, ... and with huge potholes in the winter, the streets were Moscow's Egyptian torture.[73]

Such streets were presumably even more torturous at night: many streets were not lighted, and what little light there was, was usually turned off after eleven or during evenings when, irrespective of cloud cover, the calendar indicated a full moon.[74] One foreigner was irritated by the "multitude of unpoetical and noisy horse cars that tear along the streets at a furious gallop with a perpetual and generally inopportune tinkling of bells."[75] The same foreigner was amused by the city's nonmechanized public transport:

The omnibus with its motley load of male and female passengers, its long-haired, brown and shapeless driver, its horses with tangled manes sweeping to the ground ... and ponderous, gaily painted dougas arching over their shoulders, is one of the most grotesque and quaint features of street life in Moscow.[76]

A Russian observed that the Belgian-built horse trams (*konka*) preserved a Muscovite slowness and patriarchal style on many main streets. It was freezing in the winter, and passengers stamped their feet to keep warm; extra horses were needed to go up the slightest incline. Passengers joked about the speed, and according to one Moscow wag, "with a transfer ticket you can get on in winter and get off in summer."[77]

The city's many open-air markets and the persistence of unorganized, informal forms of retailing, such as street peddling and market stalls, also reinforced Moscow's backward image. Furthermore, most of these markets, such as the stalls ringing Red Square and the bazaar-like Trading Rows, were in the heart of the city. Market districts like this were magnets not only for potential customers but also for street hawkers, itinerant repairmen, craftsmen, wandering holy men, and

72. Anatole Leroy-Beaulieu, *The Empire of the Tsars and the Russians*, trans. Zenaide A. Ragozin, 3 vols. (New York and London, 1905), 1:323.
73. Slonov, *Iz zhizni*, 48.
74. Mikhailovskii, *Materialy*, 2–11; Giliarovskii, *Moskva i Moskvichi*, 88.
75. Child, "Holy Moscow," 250.
76. Ibid.
77. Vasilich, "Ulitsy i liudi," 5.

beggars. After having spent years as an errand boy scurrying about in Red Square and the Trading Rows to solicit customers, Slonov described this maze of wholesale and retail commerce as a dark, damp, stuffy, noisy "Asiatic caravan" of shops where the atmosphere was familial and patriarchal and where sellers and buyers alike sat around drinking tea for hours on end, and where the customer was offered a festive atmosphere and cheap goods.[78] Likewise, a festive atmosphere characterized the Palm Sunday bazaar on Red Square well into the twentieth century:

Under the bright spring sun, this crowded marketplace presents a beautiful and vibrant picture of old Moscow. The Palm Sunday bazaar is interesting because it has not changed in the least; today it is exactly like it was fifty years ago.[79]

Besides the bucolic inner side streets and sleazy village-like outskirts, the colorful market areas and the sprawling disorderly development, one more striking feature prompted contemporaries to call Moscow a big village: the ubiquitousness of peasants. It will be remembered that two-thirds of the population in 1902 were registered in the peasant estate, that is, 700,000 peasants. Their presence was a matter of grave concern to authorities, and we will be returning to that presence again and again. Here it might be appropriate to examine the impression this made on contemporaries.

One Englishman cautioned the unfamiliar traveler:

The shock heads of matted hair and full, unkempt beard (growing up to their very eyes) of the peasants combined with the low foreheads and often brutish countenances, gave some of them the appearance of huge Skye terriers rather than human beings. In cheap bazaars and at crowded church services, sheepskin-clad individuals should be given a wide berth by the tourist, as close contact is by no means pleasant.[80]

Peasants were observed everywhere: carting loads of wood into town, selling wares, looking for work with their fellow villagers, and praying at the thousands of shrines and icons, such as the Iberian Virgin ("nowhere are the manifestations of religious feeling more conspicuous than in the streets of Moscow").[81] Upon entering or departing the city, a traveler's first and last impressions were of the peasants. Initial contact with Moscow life was likely to have been with one of the

78. Slonov, *Iz zhizni*, 121–68.
79. Ibid., 188–92. See also Vasilich, "Moskva," 21.
80. Guild, *Britons and Muscovites*, 149.
81. Child, "Holy Moscow," 277.

city's 15,000 surly cabmen (almost exclusively peasants), often a risky venture, as an 1878 Russian handbook pointed out. A newcomer's inquiries concerning the residence or whereabouts of a friend or relative were likely to have been addressed to one of 15,000 building superintendents (*dvorniki,* literally, yardmen), also almost exclusively peasants.[82] One traveler's last glance at the city reminded him of the peasant presence:

The belfries were then silent; the gilded cupolas were lost in the gloom of night; but all around the inner city before each modest shrine and over every gate, high up in the air, a lamp or lantern glimmered mysteriously against the darkly looming mass of wall or tower, and the mujiks, as they passed, saluted the holy images, crossed themselves and bowed low and then pursued their way, peaceful and resigned, neither contented nor discontented, but continuing indifferently in the traditions of their fathers and forefathers.[83]

The mingling of peasants with other social groups in the very heart of the city's business district was a common theme in the observations of foreigners:

Here may be seen an amusing mixture of trades and mercantile types. A motley crowd of Jewish and Russian vendors, mujiks, women with bright-colored kerchiefs over their heads, street hawkers, beggars, priests in long black flowing robes and nondescript hats, and now and again a chimney sweep wearing a stove-pipe hat.[84]

An Easter service in the Kremlin also illustrated to one American traveler the mingling of peasants with other social groups:

Hither come both poor and rich and meet and mingle in their supplications. . . . Pilgrims from distant parts of an immense empire, weary and footsore, mud-bespattered and travel-stained from their long journeys . . . high-booted, fur-robed merchants from the interior . . . and groups of peasants clad in dirty sheepskins with marveling honest eyes looking hungrily from masses of blonde clay-colored hair and whiskers which cover their faces, stand listlessly about, their packs upon their shoulders and their sorry-looking appearance contrasting strangely with the pomp and glory of the golden banners which ornament the church's walls.[85]

Along with the large number of peasants came distinctive ways of life and traditions, usually associated more with the village than with a

82. *GPD 1902,* VI, 13. There are many colorful descriptions of the cabmen and building superintendents. See Slonov, *Iz zhizni,* 38, 152; *Nastol'no-spravochnaia adresnaia kniga goroda Moskvy* (Moscow, 1878), 14–15; John A. Logan, *In Joyful Russia* (New York, 1891), 76–78.

83. Guild, *Britons and Muscovites,* 287–88.

84. Child, "Holy Moscow," 266–70.

85. W. C. Edgar, *The Russian Famine* (Minneapolis, 1893), 40.

metropolis of one million. Even Russian peasants themselves were aware of their distinctive dress and habits. Semen Kanatchikov remembered his own appearance upon arrival in Moscow: "Awkward, sluggish, with long bowl-cut hair, in heavy boots, I was a typical villager."[86] Skilled workers called him a dull hick (*seraia derevenshchina*). An Englishman familiar with India observed that peasants in the streets gave Moscow an Asian atmosphere:

To see those big burly fellows, with their sunburnt faces and fur caps and sheepskin coats, you are irresistibly reminded of . . . Northern India. You notice such common traits. Russian peasants do not walk alongside one another and talk, as do ordinary Europeans: they walk one behind the other and talk over their shoulders to the man behind, just as natives in India do.[87]

Peasant traditions were most easily observed in the outer wards beyond the Garden Ring. On the Seventh Thursday after Easter, for instance, one could still observe the feast of Semik in Mar'ia's Grove where "for a long time Muscovites were afraid to walk."[88] The handsome twelve-volume compendium prepared by the doyen of historians of the city, I. E. Zabelin, in 1910 admitted that

many types and professions which were curious relics of old Moscow . . . can still be found in the outskirts and off the beaten path where people are about twenty to thirty years behind the center and still live in one- and two-story houses and don't have paved roads, electricity, sewerage, running water, gas, and don't read newspapers.[89]

Indeed, to the majority of the population living beyond the Garden Ring and poorly supplied, if supplied at all, with water, the water carrier was hardly a "curious relic" but a vital necessity:

Even before daybreak they appear on their carts, groaning with the strain of barrels, inching toward the water pumps, raising the noise and swearing levels, generously pouring out the water and trying to get around in the impossible mire; they then finally begin to make the rounds of their customers. Approaching the houses while everyone is still sleeping, the water carrier starts a most frightful banging, wakes the servants, rattles the barrels around, and hurries off to make the rounds of all customers before the city's day begins.[90]

Like the water carrier, wandering artisans, street hawkers and peddlers, and handymen performed vital municipal services, did retail and

86. Kanatchikov, *Iz istorii*, 10.
87. G. Dobson, *Russia* (London, 1913), 167–68.
88. Gornostaev, *Putevoditel'*, 85; Zakharov, *Putevoditel'*, 12–13.
89. Vasilich, "Ulitsy i liudi," 14. See also Slonov, *Iz zhizni*, 96; and Martynov, *Nazvaniia*, 2.
90. Vasilich, "Ulitsy i liudi," 14.

repair work, provided the inhabitants with cheap popular books, like those about Nate Pinkerton, Nick Carter, and Sherlock Holmes, and acted as the local newspaper.[91]

Guidebooks catering to the more substantial visitor from St. Petersburg or Europe gave the impression that the city was, after all, really like European cities except for some quaint things such as bazaars which made it that much better a tourist attraction anyway. A certain amount of nostalgia for the lingering remnants of bygone eras crept into much contemporary writing about Moscow, and many writers no doubt welcomed enclaves of provincial-like solitude. Moreover, any metropolis is a city of contrasts, and many contemporaries were invigorated by Moscow's blend of huge modern buildings and log cabins, European-looking avenues and unpaved side streets, fancy stores and Asian-style open-air markets, businesslike European behavior and shoving crowds, and the cries of dumpling and kvass vendors.

❖   ❖   ❖

The images of European city and of big village suggest a duality in the city's development, population, and social and economic organization. Large-scale, impersonal, and formal forms of organization had only incompletely replaced small-scale organizations and informal ways of life. The authors of a compendium on municipal administration widely used by historians of the city observed in 1913:

Moscow has notably changed in appearance: New, multistoried buildings are going up where once stood wooden homes with gardens and overgrown yards; gardens disappear and courtyards become smaller. And these properties have plumbing and sewer lines, buildings have electricity and telephones, indoor toilets and gas stoves. Naturally all of this is available for those who can pay a handsome price for an apartment. The mass of the propertyless population of course lives as it always has.[92]

The significance of these images lies beyond their descriptive value. To Muscovites proud of the advancement of their city at the end of the nineteenth century, the continued backwardness of the city was all the more unacceptable. Despite Moscow's long prominence, never had the gap between promise and reality been greater. Educated Russians and the more reflective of the foreign visitors expressed (usually indirectly) a fear that the culture and values of the village were still too

91. Ibid., 15.
92. *Sovremennoe khoziaistvo*, 18.

remote from those of the city. At worst, the village might overrun the city, should the latter not be successful in imparting order, discipline, and progress to the disorder, laziness, and backwardness of the former. Leroy-Beaulieu observed the preponderance of peasants in the cities, and one detects a touch of trepidation between the lines:

> Setting aside the highest class, trained to foreign discipline, the bulk of the city people, by tastes and bringing up, by intellect and custom, is very near still to the rural population. In these cities, frequently built all in a lump and already populous, peasants reside in great numbers and their manners are half rural still. There is no bourgeoisie in the French acceptance of the word, nor an urban plebs comparable to the working population of large French cities and suburbs.[93]

By the turn of the twentieth century Moscow gradually began to lose its image of a big village. Every year the "civic" Moscow of museums, hospitals, and schools became more prominent. But the Europeanization of the city was not uniform: it was most noticeable among the elite and in the center of the city. The bulk of the population preserved many rustic ways and changed much more slowly. The city continued to be a residential and occupational mixture of booming trade and manufacture and quaint bazaars and tinkerers, bustling streets and quiet country lanes, crowded railway stations and mud-spattered droshkies, a cosmopolitan elite and sheepskinned "brutes."

93. Leroy-Beaulieu, *Empire*, 1:328–29, 337.

CHAPTER THREE

The Economy of the Metropolis

The descriptions of Moscow at the turn of the twentieth century cited in chapter 2 seem to be paradoxical: Russia's second largest city, the booming railway hub, and eighth largest city in the world was both a modern metropolis and an overgrown village. The specialty and luxury stores in the central business district sold silk stockings, parasols, and photographs of French actresses. According to British consular reports, electric lighting was rapidly superseding gas in the mills, typewriters (preferably Remingtons) were being universally adopted, and bicycling was becoming a popular pastime despite the bad roads.[1] At the same time two-thirds of the population lived "off the beaten path" in one-story wooden shacks devoid of gas and running water, let alone electricity, typewriters, bicycles, or parasols.

What contemporaries were noticing, of course, was an economic, social, and cultural dualism, a phenomenon occurring elsewhere in Europe and most sharply expressed in the cities, particularly in the metropolises. To the casual observer the metropolis displayed a striking contrast of economic organization and of cultures, as well as the more visible architectural contrasts. Petersburg or Moscow, Paris or London, Europe's metropolises all exhibited features of such a dualism as large-scale and impersonal economic and social organization coexisted with the small-scale and personal.

The coexistence of the large-scale and impersonal with the small-

1. "Report for the Year 1898 on the Trade and Agriculture of the Consular District of St. Petersburg," Great Britain, *Parliamentary Papers: Diplomatic and Consular Reports*, no. 2343 (1899), 54.

scale and personal economic organizations permeated every aspect of economic life in Moscow and explain many of the features of the city just described. Furthermore, the duality contributed to the great diversity of the city's economy. Virtually every imaginable product of the time was either produced or distributed in Moscow, and produced or distributed in virtually every imaginable way. To the great concern of reformers and the authorities, this diversity increased the attraction of the metropolis for a labor force from distant provinces. Although this labor force was not always prepared for or capable of adapting to the large-scale and more formal forms of economic and social organization such as the factory (and indeed such organizations could not absorb all of the city's laborers), the immigrant labor force was capable of creating or entering into a myriad of informal associations in the metropolis. This diversity and duality of the metropolitan economy will be best examined through an analysis of the structure of the city's economic base, of the coexistence of old and new forms of organization in all sectors of the economy, and of the long-term trends in operation at the turn of the twentieth century.

STRUCTURE OF THE ECONOMY

A sense of the large number of businesses in Moscow may be gained from an examination of figure 5. The city censuses recorded the total number of proprietors (*khoziaeva*) in manufacturing and commerce. Assuming that the total number of owners gives a rough approximation of the total number of businesses, by 1912, for example, more than 100,000 persons, or roughly 1 of every 12 city dwellers, operated some manufacturing or commercial business. In all censuses the total number of proprietors included employers as well as the self-employed; the latter operated extremely small concerns in the basements, garrets, and open-air markets of the city, and their inclusion may give an inflated sense of the total number of businesses in the city. The manufacturing and commercial censuses, by contrast, counted only the number of businesses employing two or more persons. With a population of approximately 900,000 at the time of the last of these censuses in 1890, there was one business for every 36 residents. While the population censuses give inflated estimates of the number of Moscow's businesses, the manufacturing and commercial census, by excluding all establishments not employing at least two workers, give deflated estimates. The resulting range is indeed great: whereas the 1890 manufacturing and commercial census counted 29,058 "businesses," the 1902 population census counted 72,521 "owners."[2] Although the actual number of businesses could have fallen anywhere in this range, for the purposes of this chapter the number of employers (38,007 in 1902) will serve as a rough approximation for the number of businesses.

To get around the difficulties of determining the city's economic activity as measured by the number of owners or businesses, the structure of the economy may be determined also by the size of the labor force employed in the various branches of production, distribution, and services. The results are shown in table 1 for 1882 and 1902.[3] Although the manufacturing sector contained less than half the number of businesses, it employed a larger proportion of the labor force than did any other single sector. However, all other sectors of the economy taken together employed more than did manufacturing. The services sector, including domestic service, casual labor, the professions, and public and private institutions, employed almost as many as did manufacturing. No other evidence could demonstrate better the sectoral diversity of the metropolitan economy.

The large groupings of industrial and commercial operations concealed a great variety of individual concerns, both large and small, modern and traditional, and a brief survey of the various branches of manufacturing, distribution, and services will highlight this variety.[4] I shall start with the major nontextile branches of manufacturing. The chemical industry, consisting of 138 establishments in 1902, employing more than 6,000 persons, included the production of chemicals and pharmaceuticals, paints, dyes and ink, and bristles. Also included in this branch of production by the census compilers were 37 sewerage and purification plants and 13 refuse companies. Needless to say, most of the latter were located on the outskirts; a particularly malodorous neighborhood must have been the third precinct of Rogozh' with 22 sewerage and purification plants. Although not as prominent

2. *TPZ*, 1, 20; *PM 1902*, I, 2, i, 2–7. The 1910 commercial census counted 30,504 owners. See *Sovremennoe khoziaistvo*, 20. The manufacturing and commercial censuses included only industrial establishments employing two or more workers. Thus all the single producers, artisan-proprietors, and establishments with only one worker were not included. In addition, the figures given for the number of workers include only those workers living at the establishment. Thus, while the manufacturing and commercial censuses present a more thorough picture of business in the city than do the many listings of factories, they are less complete than the population censuses in recording ownership and employment.

3. *PM 1882*, II, 131–34; *PM 1902*, I, 2, i, 116–97.

4. The following is based on the number of owners and wage laborers as listed by sector in *PM 1902*, I, 2, i, 116–97.

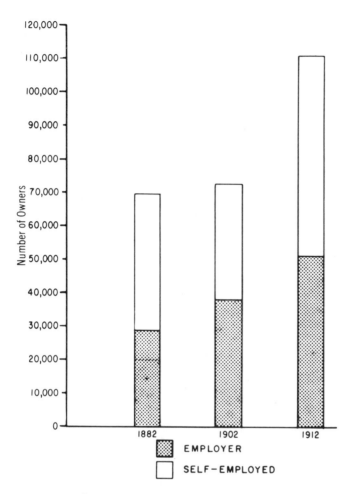

FIGURE 5. BUSINESS GROWTH IN MOSCOW

Source: *PM 1882*, II, pt. 2, 131–34; pt. 3, 101–340; *PM 1902*, I, 2, i, 116–97; *SEMMG*, 68–73.

in Moscow as in Petersburg, the chemical industry was the city's newest and one of its fastest growing. Because of its newness and also because its products were generally not made for direct retail sales, the chemical industry employed a greater than average proportion of its labor force in factory production. The most prominent chemical factories were the Brokar, with 451 workers, the Zhako, with 950 workers, the Keler, with 394 workers, the Moscow Rubber Plant in the suburb of Bogorodskoe, which employed 831 workers,

TABLE 1   STRUCTURE OF THE ECONOMY

Branch of the Economy	1882			1902				
	Owners	Labor Force Number	Percent	Employers	Other Owners[a]	Total Owners	Labor Force Number	Percent
Extractive industries[b]	2,318	5,993	1.1	1,481	608	2,089	7,169	1.0
Metalworking	1,929	19,632	3.7	466	52	518	27,145	3.6
Machine-tool	900	10,001	1.9	138	29	167	13,126	1.7
Chemical[c]	348	4,344	0.8	1,100	1,028	2,128	6,526	0.9
Textiles	5,174	58,053	10.8	443	145	588	67,028	8.9
Paper							8,071	1.1
Leather	1,403	9,931	1.9	515	275	790	9,025	1.2
Wood	2,823	14,934	2.8	1,451	680	2,131	19,923	2.7
Food	2,134	17,353	3.2	554	108	662	27,809	3.7
Clothing	17,337	65,362	12.2	7,401	11,264	18,665	80,526	10.7
Printing and industrial arts	862	7,603	1.4	722	573	1,295	15,011	2.0
Utilities				305	203	508	10,099	1.3
Unspecified	95	1,626	0.3	194	529	723	2,023	0.3
Total manufacturing	37,276	214,772	39.9	15,715	16,079	31,794	293,481	38.9
Construction	1,905	11,232	2.1	1,382	677	2,059	16,853	2.2

Retail sales	17,228	50,347	9.3	7,646	11,415	19,061	92,133	12.2
Finance, credit, insurance		2,621	0.4	233	2,913	3,146	13,740	1.9
Lodgings, restaurants	3,225	18,926	3.5	5,617	2,609	8,226	50,198	6.7
All commerce	20,453	71,894	13.4	13,486	16,937	30,423	156,071	20.7
Transport, communications	12,144	34,924	6.5	2,485	5,760	8,245	62,734	8.3
Domestic service, casual labor[d]		90,704	16.9				33,744	4.5
Institutional service, professions		58,460	10.9				132,049	17.5
All services		149,164	27.8				165,793	22.0
Miscellaneous[e]		56,084	10.4				60,294	8.0
Total self-supporting	69,923	538,072		33,068	39,453	72,521	755,226	

Source: *PM 1882*, II, pt. 2, 131–34; *PM 1902*, I, 2, i, 116–97.
[a]Includes owners employing members of their own family, and the self-employed.
[b]Includes agriculture, forestry, fishing, mining, and minerals.
[c]Includes animal and plant by-products.
[d]In 1902, servants employed in manufacturing or retailing were listed in those sectors; in 1882, all servants were listed together.
[e]Includes rentiers, persons supported by relatives or by institutions, the unemployed.

the Ralle, which employed 500 workers, and the Siu, which employed 195 workers.[5]

Printing and industrial arts consisted of 722 establishments with a total labor force of 15,011. Unlike most branches of manufacturing, which were concentrated in the outer wards, lithography, typography, engraving, icon-painting, and other industrial arts were concentrated in the central wards of the city.[6] The paper and leather industries had 443 and 515 establishments, and labor forces of approximately 8,000 and 9,000 persons. Although the industry was scattered throughout the city, the three wards on the south side of the river, traditionally the location of the leather industry, had the greatest concentration. These branches of production included a wide variety of establishments: wallpaper, cartridge, box, envelope, and carton manufacture; binderies; mattress and drapery manufacture; and the manufacture of various leather goods. The wood industries, with almost 1,500 establishments and 14,934 workers in 1902, had the third largest number of establishments and the fifth largest labor force. Included under this rubric by the census compilers were lumberyards, cabinet- and furniture-making, barrel- and basketmaking, woodcutting, brush- and comb-making, as well as the carving of toys and other wood products. More than one-third of the establishments were cabinetmaking shops; like other subgroups of the industry, cabinetmaking was scattered around the city with a slight concentration in the northern Sushchevo ward.

With 1,481 establishments and a labor force of 27,145, the metal industry was the fourth largest employer in the city. The metal industry consisted of many small workshops, most concentrated in the outer wards. Only one-third of the labor force was employed in factory production. In this sense the metal industry was similar to the paper, leather, and wood industries, all of which were characterized by small units of production. Workshops of metalsmiths, blacksmiths, jewelers, and fitters, as well as iron foundries, were the most important subdivisions within the industry. Closely related to the metal industry was the machine-tool industry, whose 466 establishments employed a labor force of 13,126, almost two-thirds of whom were

5. Orlov and Budagov, *Ukazatel'*, 167–87.

6. The best contemporary study of the printing trades is A. Svavitskii and V. Sher, *Ocherk polozheniia rabochikh pechatnogo dela v Moskve* (St Petersburg, 1909). See also Victoria E. Bonnell, *Roots of Rebellion: Workers' Politics and Organizations in St Petersburg and Moscow, 1900–1914* (Berkeley, 1984), chap. 1, passim.

employed in factories. This branch of production included machine-building, carriage and wheel manufacture, and the production of watches and of musical and scientific instruments. The combined metal and machine-tool industries were the city's largest nontextile branch of manufacturing and included some of Moscow's most prominent factories: Bromley, Nabgol'ts, Gustav List, Guzhon, Zhako, and the Westinghouse Dinamo plant.[7]

With 554 establishments and a labor force of 27,809 in 1902, more than half of whom were employed in a factory, food processing was the third largest industrial employer in the city. This industry included flour mills, bakeries, confectioners and sugar refineries, breweries and distilleries. The food industry was one of the most rapidly growing branches of the economy, and candies and jams, such as Abrikosov jam, were famous throughout the country.

The last two of the major branches of manufacturing were by far the largest. More than 67,000 made their living in the textile industry, while 80,000 were engaged in the clothing trades. The manufacture of cloth constituted the textile industry proper; the most important divisions were weaving and calico-printing. The factory system dominated the industry; the 54,794 who worked in textile factories in 1902 constituted almost half of the city's entire factory labor force.[8] This dominance was particularly noted in the cotton industry, though much less so in the wool and silk industries. Located on the outskirts, especially in the Lefort, Serpukhov, Khamovniki, Presnia, Piatnitsa, and Rogozh' wards, the largest cotton mills combined many operations, including spinning, weaving, printing, and dyeing.[9] Most prominent on Moscow's industrial landscape were the Prokhorov, Tsindel', and Guibner mills. On the other hand, the clothing industry, that is, the production of apparel, footwear, and the like for the retail market, was dominated by small-scale production. Unlike wholesale textile production, the workshops of tailors, seamstresses, and shoemakers were located in the central wards, especially in Tver', Sretenka, and Miasniki, as well as in the outer northern wards of Meshchane and Sushchevo. These two industries illustrate the coexistence of small-scale and large-scale forms of economic organization in the metropolis and will merit further discussion below. First, however, it is necessary to complete this

7. *Istoriia Moskvy*, 5:35.
8. *PM 1902*, I, 2, i, 116–59; *GPD 1902*, VI:66.
9. Moskovskaia gorodskaia uprava, Statisticheskii otdel, *Trudy*, 4 vols. (Moscow, 1882–83), 2: *Promyshlennye i torgovye zavedeniia Moskvy za 1879*, 17.

survey of the structure of Moscow's economy by turning to the non-manufacturing branches: construction, commerce, transport and communications, and services.

The construction industry employed a labor force of more than 16,000 in 1902. Most numerous were small firms of painters, plasterers, and carpenters; other branches of the industry were stone-masonry, stove fitting, street pavement, and pipe laying. Estimates of the number of businesses and the total number employed in construction are more problematical than for the preceding manufacturing industries because the construction industry was highly seasonal and the censuses, taken in the winter, did not record the summertime maximum number of workers. An undetermined number of "firms" consisted of gangs of laborers known as artels, which were in town only during the construction season. In addition, the industry was highly stratified between a skilled core of carpenters, masons, plumbers, and electricians and an unskilled, casual fringe doing the heavy tasks of hauling and digging on construction sites; while the former group numbered 13,645 in 1902, the number in the latter group is impossible to determine.[10] Although the phenomenon of casual labor will be discussed in greater detail in chapter 5, here suffice it to say that the construction industry, though booming at the end of the nineteenth century, provided very erratic employment opportunities. As a result, construction workers, especially the unskilled laborers, who appeared to have no steady jobs or place of employment, were objects of great concern to reformers.

The commercial sector of the economy consisted of three major subdivisions: banking, finance, and insurance; the lodging and restaurant business; and wholesale and retail sales. Banking, finance, and insurance was the smallest subdivision, having a labor force of only 13,740 in 1902. Next in size was the lodging and restaurant business, employing 50,198 in 5,617 establishments. This subdivision included the operation of hotels, inns, furnished rooms, and lodging houses and the operation of eating and drinking establishments. The latter group included the notorious Russian tavern (*traktir*), an establishment combining food, drink, and entertainment, usually in a series of connecting rooms. Although contemporary accounts frequently mentioned the sleaziness of taverns in the outer districts, these establishments were scattered throughout the city. The 1890 commercial census recorded

10. *PM 1902*, I, 2, i, 116–97.

603 taverns; although the second Rogozh' precinct had 43 and the second Sushchevo precinct had 35, the small central Gorod ward had 17, and the first and second Tver' precincts had 21 and 22, respectively. Traditionally the favorite eating and drinking places of the city's merchants, the taverns in recent years had become the major source of entertainment for manual laborers and persons holding lower-level sales-clerical positions.[11] Of more concern to the authorities, as the economist A. P. Chuprov pointed out, was

the tremendous growth of the tavern trade in Moscow [which] provides the only means for the large accumulation of working people without families and who in the absence of other means of shelter, find themselves refuge in the inns and drinking parlors.[12]

Wholesale and retail trade constituted the largest subdivision of commerce in Moscow; in 1902 more than 92,000 received their livelihood in more than 7,500 shops and stores (or more than 19,000 if all the self-employed shopkeepers and vendors were included). Moscow's lively retail trade was the object of amazement to Russians and foreigners alike, and not without reason: 21 percent of Moscow's population in 1902 engaged in commerce, a larger proportion than in Petersburg or Odessa and, indeed, exceeded only by that of Paris among major European cities.[13] Although gigantic cotton mills loomed large on Moscow's industrial landscape, trading operations usually remained small in size. The large number of stores, as has been noted, struck the worker-memoirist Semen Kanatchikov. His father, accompanying him to Moscow, added, "Mother-Moscow feeds all of Russia. Our shopkeepers also come here for merchandise."[14] A standard economic survey written in 1895 stated that the annual Nizhnii Novgorod fair was only a temporary extension of Moscow's commercial activity.[15] For a long time, Moscow had been the depot and distribution center for a large hinterland consisting of the Central Industrial Region and for the entire Russian empire. Raw cotton, wool, silk, and other materials were distributed to the region's factories and village

11. *TPZ*, 6–25; *PM 1902*, I, 2, i, 162–63; *Sputnik Moskvicha* (Moscow, 1890), 157; Slonov, *Iz zhizni*, 140–41; *Ushedshaia Moskva* (Moscow, 1964), 147–48; Vasilich, "Ulitsy i liudi," 10; Child, "Holy Moscow," 264–70; L. N. Tolstoi, "Tak chto zhe nam delat'?" in *Polnoe sobranie sochinenii*, 24 vols. (Moscow, 1913), 13:30; Giliarovskii, *Moskva i Moskvichi*, 307–36.
12. A. I. Chuprov, *Kharakteristika Moskvy po perepisi 1882 g.* (Moscow, 1884), 39.
13. *PM 1902*, I, 2, i, 160–73; *GPD 1902*, VI:76
14. Kanatchikov, *Iz istorii*, 8.
15. Komarov, *Voenno-statisticheskoe opisanie*, 276–77.

workshops, only a small proportion of which were located in Moscow itself. Finished goods from the most modern factories in the empire, as well as from dank peasant workshops, were distributed via Moscow. At the end of the nineteenth century a British consular official noted Moscow's commercial importance:

Moscow is not only the centre of the vast tea trade of Russia but is also a great warehouse in which are collected various imported and homemade goods destined for the Far East, Siberia, Turkestan and Persia. It has also become a halfway house for all travellers to Eastern Siberia and the want of proper hotel accommodation is already being felt. Every day new business premises are opened and picturesque old buildings are fast being replaced by large modern edifices. . . . The population has risen to over 1,000,000 and I think this important business centre, the real commercial capital of Russia, deserves more attention from British manufacturers and capitalists than they at present bestow upon it.[16]

Traditionally, Moscow's major trading area had been Red Square and the Trading Rows. As late as the 1870s and 1880s, according to Slonov, the rest of the city had virtually no stores except for bakeries, produce, and tobacco shops, and the only place to shop was the Trading Rows.[17] Considering that the author spent these years at the Trading Rows, he may have overstated his case. Still, a recent study of trade in Moscow showed that in the 1880s almost 80 percent of the wholesale and retail sales came from the Gorod, Tver', and Miasniki wards. Although the trading network extended and strengthened in the outer districts, the center retained its predominance in the following decades.[18] The side streets of neighborhoods in Arbat and Prechistenka, for example, were so quiet and placid in large part because stores were not permitted.[19]

The two remaining major sectors of the city's economy were transport and communications, and services. The former provided a livelihood for 62,734 at 8,245 establishments in 1902. The major subdivisions were postal, telegraph and telephone service, the railroads, streetcars, and carting and hauling (izvoz). The railroads, which employed more than 26,000, provided the metropolis with its essential raw materials and fuel: firewood (an average of 1.2 million tons annu-

16. "Report for the Year 1898," 54.
17. Slonov, Iz zhizni, 125.
18. Robert Gohstand, "The Internal Geography of Trade in Moscow from the Mid-Nineteenth Century to World War I," Ph.D. dissertation (University of California, Berkeley, 1973), 691. See also his "The Shaping of Moscow by Nineteenth-Century Trade" in Hamm, The City, 160–81.
19. Geinike, Po Moskve, 328.

ally from 1901 to 1905), coal, oil, building materials, and grain. In 1893, for example, 4.2 million tons of freight and 6 million passengers entered and left the city.[20] The labor force employed on the railroads was divided between the more skilled machinists in the shops and the unskilled crews employed along the lines.

Another 27,000 were employed in carting and hauling. However, like the census figures for the number of construction workers, the figure for the number of persons employed in the carrying trades is likely to be low. According to municipal tax assessments, there were more than 40,000 drivers and teamsters (*legkovye* and *lomovye izvozchiki*) operating in the city.[21] With their long coats, leather belts, high boots and caps, and with their reckless driving and surly attitude toward their passengers, the cabdrivers were a prominent and colorful feature of Moscow's street landscape.[22]

Finally, the services sector of the economy provided employment for 170,023 in 1902. This sector was sharply divided into two distinct subgroups: domestic service and day labor, on the one hand, and professional and institutional service, on the other. The former employed 90,199, and the latter employed 79,824. The major categories of professional and institutional service were in government offices, the military, prisons and police, legal service and the courts, charity, health care, the church, education, science and the arts, and sports and entertainment. The remainder of the population, not employed in any of the above sectors of the economy, were classified as rentiers, supported in institutions, unemployed, or dependents.

Although the above survey has treated the economy as static, in fact there were important structural shifts at the end of the nineteenth century. While trends pertaining to firm and factory size will be discussed below, some broad structural shifts may be noted here. Table 1 compares the structure of the economy in terms of the labor force employed in 1882 and 1902. Although the labor force in manufacturing increased by approximately 35 percent, the proportion of the total labor force employed in manufacturing dropped one percentage point. If servants were removed from the manufacturing sector, the decrease would be even greater. Although all major branches of manufacturing employed more in 1902 than in 1882, relative losses were notable in

20. Komarov, *Voenno-statisticheskoe opisanie*, 328–29; *Sovremennoe khoziaistvo*, 38.
21. *Sbornik ocherkov*, 24–25.
22. *Nastol'no-spravochnaia adresnaia kniga*, 14; *Sputnik Moskvicha*, 152.

textiles and in the clothing industry. The largest relative gain occurred in the food industry. Such structural shifts reflected the gradual diversification of manufacturing: textiles and clothing, industries which had for so long occupied such a prominent position, by 1902 employed only 50 percent of the labor force in manufacturing.

All other major branches of the economy showed relative as well as absolute gains. Most noticeable were commerce and transport and communications. The numbers employed in retail and wholesale sales, as well as those in transport and communications, almost doubled; the number employed in the provision of lodgings, food, and drink almost tripled. The metropolitan economy was widely diversified with a lively retail trade and a service sector alongside a strong manufacturing base. Although the highly mechanized factory giants attracted a large share of the labor force, a concomitant expansion of small-scale manufacture of consumer goods and the enlargement of the market and of the monied economy multiplied employment opportunities in construction, trade, transport, services, and the professions. In addition, in many areas of the economy, functional specialization was just beginning to make inroads. Many industrial and commercial activities, for example, continued to be conducted on the premises of the producer or the merchant. Although by the end of the nineteenth century a distinct central business district had formed, most retail sales of essential commodities to the common people were unspecialized and widely dispersed throughout the city in open-air markets and undertaken by peddlers and street vendors. As a result, as Victoria Bonnell has pointed out recently, the immediate work environment was most frequently a small workshop, a shop within a larger factory, or a store, and the division of labor and impersonal, formal relationships were still relatively new.[23] In short, despite, or even because of, rapid economic growth, the small units continued to exist alongside the large.

OLD AND NEW IN COMMERCE AND INDUSTRY

Moscow preserved many age-old organizational forms and ways of conducting business, not only because of the stage of development of the Russian economy as a whole, which of course mitigated against the complete penetration of modern, large-scale, impersonal commercial organizations, but also because certain small-scale, personal forms

23. Bonnell, *Roots of Rebellion*, 20–36, 60–64.

of commerce were ideally suited to the bustling metropolis. Small businesses could supply and distribute goods and services cheaply and effectively, particularly given that the small number of large commercial and service organizations could not meet the demand.

The difference between the shop and the store illustrated the difference between old and new in retailing. The names alone suggest a contrast between the Russian *lavka* (shop) and the French *magazin* (store). According to one contemporary, the new stores beckoned customers with bright signs and advertisements, a luxurious interior decor, fancy display windows, and a variety of merchandise.

The old simple sign, usually black with gold letters, which merely gave information rather than trying to attract attention, is being replaced by clamorous and colorful advertisements. Pressing against store windows, hanging above the sidewalks, on the empty walls of tall buildings and on the roofs, these new kinds of signs give the street a noisy and talkative appearance. Bright colors that strike the eye and involuntarily attract attention, ingenious figures and amusing inscriptions are visible everywhere.[24]

The store functioned as a rational business: specialization and division of labor, fixed prices, and impersonal transactions.[25] By the beginning of the twentieth century, the store was the dominant form of retailing in most of the central business district. It symbolized Moscow's modernization and the disappearance of the old "good-heartedness, sociability, beloved disorder, and freedom: life has become disciplined and riveted to the pace of the machine."[26]

Contemporaries with nostalgia for the "beloved disorder" of the past must have taken pleasure in the preservation of the shops, the bazaars and open-air markets, and other traditional and less disciplined forms of retailing. Best known for their sociability and disorder were the merchants of the Trading Rows, threatened somewhat but by no means replaced by the fancier stores.

With their hair cut straight across the neck, as if the barber had placed a basin over their heads to guide his scissors, with their ample beards spreading over their bosoms, clad in long, dark-colored coats or caftans, tall boots and cap with visor, they sit gravely in their shops playing draughts or drinking tea, while their clerks walk up and down in front praying passers with obsequious bows and voluble "pajals" (if you please) to enter and buy. . . . The abacus and glass of tea are indispensible accessories of Russian commerce; even in the largest and most progressive banks, for instance, you will see on the desks

24. Vasilich, "Ulitsy i liudi," 6.
25. Ibid., 6–7.
26. Ibid.

beside each clerk his abacus and in front of him his glass of tea which he sips from time to time. When a merchant has a deal with another merchant he invites him to accompany him to the traktir or restaurant, where he orders a pair of teapots (*pari tchaiou*), consisting of a large teapot full of hot water and a smaller teapot with tea in it.[27]

Another traveler made a similar observation:

Then, again, just as in India nothing in the way of buying or selling can be effected without shouting, gesticulating, chaffering, so here if a peasant goes to buy anything for himself or his wife, he is seized by the employees of various shops, whose business it is to stand about the shop doors and secure anybody who looks like a customer, is nearly torn into pieces by the representatives of various firms and is finally dragged into a shop, where the methods of bargaining, etc., are purely Oriental.[28]

A Moscow businessman himself confirmed the fact that the shopkeepers of the Trading Rows "spent most of their time in the taverns" and left their shops to their assistants or even unattended.[29]

Although the seeming lackadaisical attitude toward business of the merchants and shopkeepers of the Trading Rows did not approach the ideal of rationality, precision, discipline, and impersonal calculations of the modern world, these shops were nevertheless more or less permanent fixtures with overhead, sources of supply, and reputations to protect. Not so the many other forms of retail organization that dotted the metropolis. An undetermined but significant share of Moscow's retailing took place at bazaars, open-air markets, and stalls along busy streets. Some open-air sales were conducted by representatives of larger organizations. The medium and small clothing stores, for example, also sold cheaper and lower-quality merchandise at the Sunday Smolensk and Sukharev markets. Moscow was the major center for the retail sale of ready-made clothing, or, as one study phrased it, "Moscow clothes a significant portion of the Russian population," and such practices were a necessity to meet increasing peasant demand and increasing yet still limited purchasing power.[30] Similarly, many of the city's food wholesalers set up shops at the Hunter's market (Okhotny riad). (These food wholesalers must have been, or attracted, Moscow's "hard hats," for this city block, situated

27. Child, "Holy Moscow," 261.
28. Dobson, *Russia*, 168.
29. Slonov, *Iz zhizni*, 165.
30. E. Bergman, "Poslednie perepisi Peterburga i Moskvy," *IMGD*, 11, no. 6–7 (1887): 99; Oliunina, *Portnovskii promysel*, 20–21, 42.

close to the university, was on more than one occasion the scene of beatings of student demonstrators.)[31]

Other open-air sales and street vending were conducted by tradesmen hawking a more limited number of wares. Two of the busiest open-air Sunday markets were at Smolensk Square and at the Sukharev water tower on the Garden Ring. Both specialized in used and stolen merchandise and in antiques from impoverished gentry families. Both also featured food vendors whose trays doubled as boards for roulette when the police were not around.[32] The largest open-air market stretched along the walls of the old Walled City on what was known as Old Square and New Square.

Every day from morning till night a most colorful and dirty crowd pushes and shoves. . . . The very essence of the flea market [literally, "shoving market" (tolkuchii rynok)] lies in this dirty, unshaven, tattered, hideous crowd moving back and forth. Any poor man who can't spend more than a ruble for a jacket or half a ruble for a pair of pants, or who needs an old cap for a few kopeks, can go to the flea market and immediately find everything. Because of this, rubbish worn only by lower orders of Muscovites, and rags and garbage that make you sick to look at, are brought here and sold.[33]

An American observed that this flea market was,

from dawn till dusk, in fair weather, filled with eager traders who come here to buy or sell or barter. The second-hand goods are generally so well used up that they may be placed on dirty cobblestones without receiving further injury. . . . Only a few of the traffickers have stands of any kind for the exhibition of their wares. The use of these is reserved for more aristocratic merchants, who occupy sheltered places alongside the ancient wall. . . . It is among the multitude who spread dilapidated treasures on the ground that the most amusing incidents are to be noted by the inquisitive stranger.[34]

Street vendors hawked a variety of articles and extended retailing networks to the poorer outskirts of the city. According to Slonov, "they carry food in large baskets all over the city and yell not only during the day but also at night."[35] This annoyance notwithstanding,

31. Giliarovskii, *Moskva i Moskvichi*, 155–65. For a description of an altercation in 1887, see Thomas C. Owen, *Capitalism and Politics in Russia: A Social History of the Moscow Merchants, 1855–1905* (Cambridge, 1981), 101–2; for one in the 1880s, see Slonov, *Iz zhizni*, 199; for one during the Revolution of 1905, see Laura Engelstein, "Moscow and the 1905 Revolution: A Study in Class Conflict and Political Organization," Ph.D. dissertation (Stanford University, 1976), 192.

32. Vasilich, "Ulitsy i liudi," 8–9; Geinike, *Po Moskve*, 239; Slonov, *Iz zhizni*, 126, 200; Giliarovskii, *Moskva i Moskvichi*, 52–71.

33. A. Golitsynskii, *Ulichnye tipy* (Moscow, 1860), 43–45. See also Slonov, *Iz zhizni*, 126, and Giliarovskii, *Moskva i Moskvichi*, 72–81.

34. John Bell Bouton, *Roundabout to Moscow* (New York, 1887), 303.

35. Slonov, *Iz zhizni*, 53.

the street vendors, according to another observer, provided an essential function: "Since residents of the city are not able to conduct their affairs in a strictly rational (*planomerno*) way, they tend to chase around; this explains the abundance of traders and vendors who fill up the city's streets."[36]

All this should not suggest that retailing in Moscow resembled that of a village fair, although that metaphor did occur to many European visitors. As was indicated in the previous chapter, some specialty and luxury stores, catering to the gentry and merchant elite and frequently owned by first- or second-generation foreigners, had sprung up on Tver' Street and Kuznetskii Bridge. Yet, the trends toward modern organization and large-scale retailing were blunted. James Bater's summary of retailing in Petersburg is even more applicable to Moscow, where

specialized shops, centrally located or otherwise, took a supporting role when it came to the vast volume of transactions done in scruffy cellars, within evil-smelling sheds along side streets, at refuse-ridden market stalls, or over the trays carried by pestilential peasant tradesmen.[37]

The contrast between the large and the small in retailing was paralleled by a similar contrast in manufacturing. In most of the major branches of production surveyed above the factory existed alongside smaller and more informal organizational forms such as artisanal and domestic production. As figure 6 shows, the proportion of the labor force employed in factory production varied considerably from industry to industry. The newest industry, chemicals, had virtually no artisanal producers and had almost exclusively factory production. The textile industry, as has already been noted, exhibited a predominance of factory production; likewise, in the food, printing, and machine-tool industries, more than 50 percent of the labor force was engaged in factory production. On the other hand, in the metal, leather, wood, paper, and clothing industries, the great majority of the labor force was engaged in nonfactory forms of production. The textile and clothing industries illustrate best this coexistence of large- and small-scale forms of industrial organization in the metropolis.

Of 63,214 persons employed in the textile industry in 1902, 54,794 worked in factories. Forty percent of the city's factories were textile mills, which in turn employed half of the total factory labor force. By 1913 two-thirds of all textile workers were concentrated at twenty-six mills employing more than 500 workers each. In 1900, eight textile

36. Vasilich, "Ulitsy i liudi," 10.
37. Bater, *St. Petersburg,* 268.

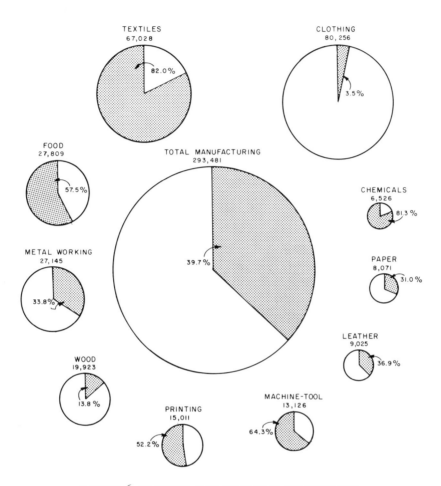

FIGURE 6. FACTORY AND ARTISANAL PRODUCTION,
1902
For each sector of manufacturing, the absolute
figure represents the total number employed, and
the shaded area and the corresponding percentage
represents the proportion employed in factories.

Source: *PM 1902,* I, 2, i, 116–59.

mills employed more than 1,000 workers each, or 40 percent of all
workers in the industry.[38] Most prominent on Moscow's industrial
landscape were the Prokhorov, Tsindel', and Guibner mills, each employing more than 1,000 workers at the turn of the century and providing housing and many paternalistic amenities. The Prokhorov mill,

38. *Istoriia Moskvy,* 5:31, 209.

situated along the Moscow River in the Presnia ward, is a case in point. Founded in 1799, by 1890 it was Russia's nineteenth largest factory with a value of production of five million rubles and a workforce of 1,230. By 1900 the work force had quadrupled, and by 1914 8,000 workers operated 45,000 spindles, 1,500 looms, and 40 cotton-printing machines.[39] Such mills, with gigantic rooms specializing in various stages of cloth-making and powered by central machines, approximated Andrew Ure's ideal of the rational mechanized factory universe.[40] At the beginning of the twentieth century, Prokhorov operated four day schools, a Sunday school, dormitories for single and married workers, and a clinic with twenty-two beds and an attending physician. As the manufacturers themselves frequently pointed out, the largest factories were better able to adopt safety measures, as well as to provide medical and cultural services, than were the smaller factories or domestic industries.[41]

Despite the existence of such huge and prominent factories, Moscow was characterized by small-scale manufacturing.[42] In 1900 Moscow had approximately 15,000 artisanal establishments, 4,000 more than in St. Petersburg.[43] While Moscow's largest factories, with the exception of the food and printing industries, made goods primarily for the wholesale market, consumer goods were made in small-scale establishments. The belongings of most city residents, as well as of the peasants who came to the city to buy and sell, were crudely produced by a myriad of small producers who arranged for the sale of merchandise or services within a very circumscribed area.

The clothing industry provides both an illustration of small-scale

39. TsGIA, f. 20, op. 12, d. 125, ll. 145–78, and d. 125a, ll. 443–62. See also Orlov and Budagov, *Ukazatel'*, ix. The basic company histories are Prokhorovskaia trekhgornaia manufaktura, *Materialy k istorii, 1799–1915* (Moscow, 1916), and *Istoriko-statisticheskii ocherk* (Moscow, 1900); and *Dvadtsatipiatiletie Tovarishchestva sittsenabivnoi manufaktury E. Tsindel' v Moskve, 1874–1899: Istoriko-statisticheskii ocherk* (Moscow, 1899). See also P. M. Shestakov, *Rabochie na manufakture T-va Tsindel' v Moskve* (Moscow, 1900).

40. In addition to the sources cited above, see Andrew Ure, *The Philosophy of Manufactures*, 3d ed. (London, 1835; reprinted New York, 1969), 13–20.

41. Other scholars have already examined various aspects of factory life in Moscow in more detail, and there is no need to duplicate their efforts. See Johnson, *Peasant and Proletarian*; Laura Engelstein, *Moscow, 1905: Working-class Organization and Political Conflict* (Stanford, 1982); Bonnell, *Roots of Rebellion*; and Diane Koenker, *Moscow Workers and the 1917 Revolution* (Princeton, 1981).

42. This point has been made by many other historians. See V. F. Kut'ev, "Dokumental'nye materialy moskovskikh gosudarstvennykh arkhivov po istorii rabochego klassa goroda Moskvy v 90-e gody XIX V.," candidate's dissertation (Moscow, 1955), 46; Koenker, *Moscow Workers*, 22; and Bonnell, *Roots of Rebellion*, 24.

43. Ministerstvo torgovli i promyshlennosti, Otdel torgovli, *Remeslenniki i remeslennoe upravlenie v Rossii* (Petrograd, 1916), 35.

manufacturing and a contrast to the textile industry. It operated in
similar fashion to the cottage industry in the villages, that is, clothes
were either made in workshops run by merchant middlemen or sub-
contracted to the garrets or basements of individual producers, who in
turn worked alone, with family members or with one or two hired
workers or apprentices. Of approximately 77,000 employed in the
clothing trades (more than half of whom were women), 75,000 were
employed in small-scale production units having fewer than 15
workers.[44] Unlike wholesale textile production, which was concentrated in the outer wards, the clothing industry was scattered all over
the city, from Tver', Sretenka, and Miasniki in the center to the northeastern suburb of Cherkizovo where almost every house was a "weaving shop containing a few looms."[45]

A detailed study of Moscow tailors in 1914 has left us with a
glimpse of this branch of domestic industry. Although the city had
almost 35,000 tailors, the seasonality of work meant that the difference between the maximum and minimum numbers of workers varied
from 40 percent to 60 percent. Two six-week "seasons" were particularly heavy: May through August and November through February for
the wholesale trade, and August through December and February
through May for the retail trade.[46] At the beginning of the twentieth
century, Moscow had already become a center for ready-made dresses.
The best tailor shops ordered expensive dresses from Paris and hung
them in the shops as models; the best seamstresses went abroad twice
a year. The medium and small shops filled orders by copying from
fashion journals. Because of the increasing demand for ready-made
clothes (and the ability of clothing stores to provide fine fashions),
the existence of distant and impersonal markets, and a leveling of tastes
and consumption patterns, the independent tailor had a harder and
harder time meeting the competition from larger establishments. Professional training was becoming less significant, as was evidenced by
the fact that a two-to-three-year apprenticeship had replaced the older
five-to-seven-year period.[47]

The sweating system enabled many of the city's tailors and seamstresses not only to withstand the competition from larger establishments but to thrive in the metropolis. The sweating system in the

---

44. *PM 1902*, I, 2, i, 131, 153; *GPD 1902*, VI:62–63.

45. "Otchet sanitarnykh vrachei Lefortovskoi chasti," *IMGD*, 3:no. 13–15 (June 1,
1879): 24.

46. Oliunina, *Portnovskii promysel*, 35–36, 166–67.

47. Ibid., 3–4, 24, 170–71. See also M. I. Pokrovskaia, "Remeslennitsy," *Zhenskii
vestnik*, 9, no. 11 (November, 1913): 247–48.

clothing trades was an attempt to adapt to the seasonal nature of production and demand as well as to changing fashions while reducing overhead to a minimum. This gave the small-scale entrepreneur the ability to expand or contract production at little cost to himself according to Moscow's large but erratic market for inexpensive, ready-made apparel. Moreover, far away from the Factory Inspectorate, the sweated industries were one answer to competition from the many village factories and workshops of the Central Industrial Region.[48] At a time when only 6 percent of Moscow's factory hands worked longer than eleven hours per day, one-third of 3,000 tailors surveyed in 1914 worked fourteen hours per day, and another one-quarter worked longer; the smaller the workshop, the longer the day.[49] Although the demand was great for labor in the artisanal and sweated industries, the erratic nature of the market, and consequently of employment, made labor particularly prone to periods of unemployment. Consequently, artisans and sweated workers repeatedly appeared in disproportion to their total numbers in studies of slum housing, welfare services, and so on. These features of the sweating system in particular and of small-scale industry in general were sources of great concern to reformers at the end of the nineteenth century.

The compilers of the 1902 census predicted that because of the diverse needs of large cities and the increased demand for consumers' goods such as clothing and footwear, the importance of the sweat system and domestic industries would increase. Allowing for the imprecision of the word "importance," this and similar assertions can be evaluated by turning to an analysis of the trends in the economy.

TRENDS IN THE METROPOLITAN ECONOMY

So far I have examined the structure of Moscow's economy as if it had been static. It is equally important to try to determine the trends operating in the city's economy in the last decades of the old regime. Insofar as these trends can be identified, they can be compared with those operating in the Russian economy as a whole, and thus, the func-

48. Oliunina, *Portnovskii promysel*, 6–9. See also Gareth Stedman Jones, *Outcast London: A Study in the Relationship between Classes in Victorian Society* (Oxford, 1971), 19–32.

49. *GPD 1902*, VI:14; Oliunina, *Portnovskii promysel*, 6–9; Iu. I. Kir'ianov, *Zhiznennyi uroven' rabochikh Rossii konets XIX-nachalo XX v.* (Moscow, 1979), 63.

tion of the metropolitan economy can be seen more clearly. Three broad trends in the Russian economy have attracted the attention of contemporary observers and scholars from Schulze-Gävernitz to Alexander Gerschenkron.[50] Commonly associated with the alleged "advantages of backwardness," they are the bigness and concentration of plant and enterprise, the rapid spread of the factory system and the concomitant expansion of the factory working class, and the steady modernization of the economy, largely under the influence of government entrepreneurship through the Ministry of Finance. How were these trends expressed in Moscow and how did they affect the problems faced by the muzhik and the relationship between muzhik and Muscovite?

Let us start by examining the trends in size of enterprise. Unfortunately, there is no series of city directories long, complete, and consistent enough to calculate changes in firm size. Surveys of the city's manufacturing and retailing establishments in the 1870s and 1880s provide numbers of businesses; however, no such series exists for a later period. These surveys, as was already noted, listed only businesses employing two or more persons, providing a deflated sense of the total number of businesses. We are left again with the city census, which, although it was not a manufacturing or commercial census, may still indicate trends. The total number of owners will give an approximation of the maximum number of enterprises, large and small, and a comparison of the number of employers with the number of employees will give a rough approximation of the size of enterprise.

The number of owners (*khoziaeva*) of all types increased slightly from 69,923 in 1882 to 72,521 in 1902, and then more rapidly to 110,129 in 1912, as was shown in figure 5. However, these figures conceal differences in the types of owners. The self-employed (*khoziaeva-odinochki*, literally, single proprietors) actually declined in number from 1882 to 1902; the number of proprietors employing only members of their own family remained virtually unchanged; and the number of owners employing salaried or wage personnel increased markedly. The increase of this last group almost kept up with the increase in the self-supporting population as a whole. The increase in the number of employers was very modest in manufacturing, where the total number of businesses actually declined. It was in manufacturing that the decrease in the numbers of self-employed from 1882 to

50. Gerhardt von Schulze-Gävernitz, *Krupnoe proizvodstvo*, 1–79; Alexander Gerschenkron, *Economic Backwardness in Historical Perspective* (Cambridge, Mass., 1962), 124–30.

1902 was most striking; 5,600 fewer small producers were able to succeed in the metropolitan economy in 1902 than twenty years earlier. The self-employed in retailing and services were not hit as hard as their counterparts in manufacturing; this, coupled with a striking 62 percent increase in the numbers of employers, caused an overall increase in the number of businesses in this sector of the economy of almost 20 percent.

This sluggish growth in the number of owners at a time of rapid overall population growth suggests business consolidations and larger firms during the period 1882–1902. Indeed, in both manufacturing and retailing, the proportion of the self-supporting population classified as owners declined while the number of employees and wage laborers per owner increased. The most dramatic change was the decline in the proportion of all owners to the total population engaged in manufacturing and retailing. This change, however, is not so dramatic when the self-employed are factored out, and indeed the striking feature about the average number of employees and wage laborers per employer is their moderate increase over a twenty-year period of rapid economic growth.[51]

The uneven economic growth of the three decades prior to World War I was reflected in the number of businesses in the metropolis. The downturn in the national economy beginning in 1900, and the scarcity and high cost of credit, made it more difficult for marginal businesses to survive. This was reflected in the 1902 census by the drop in the number of self-employed and the very sluggish growth in the total number of employers. Statistically, this appears as a marked increase in the concentration of ownership. The second economic boom beginning in 1908, more balanced than the railroad and steel boom of the 1890s, made it easier for Moscow's marginal businesses to survive (or to be established). The improvement in the metropolitan economy over 1902 was reflected in the 1912 census, which recorded an increase not only in all businessmen but especially in the self-employed, whose numbers jumped by more than 70 percent. With the number of owners increasing at a faster rate than the labor force as a whole, the number of salaried employees and wage laborers per owner actually declined from 5.0 in 1902 to 4.5 in 1912. Statistically, this appears as

51. The number of employees and wage laborers per employer rose from 9.2 to 10.8 from 1882 to 1902 and then declined to 9.7 in 1912. (*PM 1882*, II, pt. 2, 131–34; pt. 3, 101–340; *PM 1902*, I, 2, i, 116–97; *SEMMG*, 68–73.)

a reversal in the process of consolidation of ownership. Of course, with war just over the horizon, the little evidence at hand does not make it possible to determine whether the long-term process of consolidation of ownership, such a striking feature of Russian industrialization, had experienced only a temporary setback or a permanent reversal, but in good years the metropolitan economy, if not the national, was more than hospitable to small businesses.

Although there was a trend (albeit moderate) toward concentration of *ownership,* production and distribution could have become even more concentrated if owners had been closing down smaller and less profitable operations, or less concentrated if owners had been spreading production or distribution among a great number of operations. What can be said about bigness in plant and store? Given the greater availability of the data concerning factories, how were the national trends toward concentration in factory production displayed in the metropolitan economy?

To begin with, it must be emphasized that smaller factories were a more prominent feature of the city's economy than of either the provincial or national economies, and a higher proportion of Moscow's factory workers were employed in small factories than was the case of the province. Likewise, a lower proportion of workers were employed in the largest factories in Moscow than in either the province or the nation as a whole.[52]

Various surveys of manufacturing and retailing in the city conducted by the Ministry of Finance and by the municipality will help us establish changes in factory size over time in Moscow. The number of factories increased at a slightly faster rate than the number of factory workers, such that the number of workers employed at the average factory actually decreased.[53] Although inconclusive, data on factory

52. E. M. Dement'ev, *Vrachebnaia pomoshch' fabrichno-zavodskim rabochim v 1907 g.* (St. Petersburg, 1909), 2, 11–12, 39, 48–49; V. A. Kondrat'ev and V. I. Nevzorov, *Iz istorii fabrik i zavodov Moskvy i Moskovskoi gubernii (Konets XVIII-nachalo XX vv.): Obzor dokumentov* (Moscow, 1968), 142; Antonova, *Vliianie stolypinskoi reformy,* 140–41.

53. An early estimate (1879) gave 396 factories employing 65,949 workers, for an average of 166 workers per factory. There were 96,746 workers at 785 factories, or 123 workers per factory in 1902. For listings from 1906 to 1913, there were annual averages of 944 factories, 135,936 workers, or 144 workers per factory. Unfortunately, there is no series of data over time calculated by the same office or using the same definition of factory. For example, the 1902 city census counted 111,718 factory workers. Three surveys taken in the same year (1907) counted 525, 738, and 854 factories. The most that can be argued from these unsatisfactory data is that there was no trend toward

size suggest that at some point at the end of the nineteenth century, the trend toward bigness of plant and concentration of more and more workers in factories, such a striking feature of Russian industrialization, may have been arrested, at least in Moscow. What, however, can be said about the spread of the factory system and the growth of the factory working class? A reduction in the average size of factories could conceal an explosion in the size of medium-sized or even small factories and a concomitant explosion in the size of the factory working class. In fact, the number both of factories and of factory workers was on the rise, and insofar as the factory played an important social and, increasingly, political role in the city, such an explosion might be much more significant than a change in factory size.

From the mid-1880s to the eve of World War I, the total number of manufacturing establishments was remarkably constant at just under 10,000. The number of factories showed more fluctuation, dropping during the two decades after 1885 before climbing again during the boom years of 1908–1913. In 1885, 11 percent of all manufacturing establishments were factories; twenty-five years later this proportion had dropped to 9.4 percent.[54] Given the sketchiness and inconsistencies of the data, the most that can be said is that the factory was not displacing other forms of production and that the number of factories remained a small, and possibly declining, percentage of Moscow's manufacturing establishments. Of course, the factory did make more of an impact in the number of workers employed, and there can be no doubt that the absolute number of factory workers grew impressively. While the proportion of wage laborers increased noticeably from 1882 to 1902, the increase in factory workers as a proportion of all wage laborers was not particularly impressive. The 1912 census, taken in the middle of the prewar boom, showed a more rapid increase in the number of factory workers as a proportion of all wage laborers, as well as important structural changes within the labor force, which will be discussed in

---

concentration in plant and quite possibly a uniform or even declining number of workers per plant. TsGAM, f. 46, op. 14, d. 1212, ll. 55–56; TsGIA, f. 20, op. 12, d. 300, ll. 1–33. TsGIA, f. 1290, op. 5, d. 195, ll. 1–15; *Promyshlennye i torgovye zavedeniia*, 4:42–43; Pogozhev, *Uchet*, 94–95; *TPZ*, 42–43; *SEM za 1913/14*, 158–59; *Sovremennoe khoziaistvo*, 21; *PM 1902*, I, 2, i, 116–97. For more on the inconsistencies in the estimates of workers and of factories, see Pogozhev, *Uchet*, 17–18 and Bonnell, *Roots of Rebellion*, 20–23.

54. See sources cited in note 53 above.

chapter 5.[55] Although more and more of the laboring population was earning its daily bread in factories, the increase was not striking, and a majority of the city's wage laborers as well as of its industrial workers continued to be employed in nonfactory settings.

So far I have been assuming that the sketchy data are reasonably reliable and consistent over time and that, for instance, the definitions of "factory" and "factory worker" did not change with every survey. What if, however, within each survey there was a gross misrepresentation of certain types of businesses or certain groups of the labor force? In fact, the methods of gathering many of the data present a serious problem. Every year the Commercial Police (Torgovaia politsiia) made a list of all retailing and manufacturing establishments before issuing permits. To calculate the tax levied on factories, the Commercial Police checked the number of workers at factories and mills. Likewise, the number of workers in artisanal establishments was also checked because the commercial taxes depended upon the number employed. However, for establishments in commerce and transport where the size of the tax did not depend on the number of workers, the number of workers was not checked closely, and if they appeared on the lists of the Commercial Police it was almost accidental. As a result, the number of wage laborers in commerce recorded in the surveys of the 1870s and 1880s was seriously incomplete. Particularly underrepresented were draymen (3,207 were on the 1879 list, although 30,769 carrying permits were issued); peddlers were not on the list at all, although 5,078 permits were issued; only 110 workers in all the taverns and 20 in all public baths were listed; and an absurd figure of 236 workers was listed at the city's 10,701 stores and shops. By comparison, the 1882 census recorded more than 8,000 draymen (still, less than one-quarter of the carrying permits issued), 7,836 workers in taverns, 3,883 peddlers, and altogether 13,442 wage laborers engaged in retailing.[56] The numbers given for wage laborers in the commerce and transport sector of the economy may have been far less than the actual numbers. If so, factory workers may have been an even smaller proportion of the total number of wage laborers.

55. During the thirty-year period 1882–1912, the number of wage laborers as a percentage of the entire labor force increased from 32.9 to 38.4 while the number of factory workers as a percentage of all wage laborers increased from 33.3 to 41.0. (*PM 1882*, II, pt. 2, 131–34; *TPZ*, pt. 2, 35–44; *PM 1902*, I, 2, i, 116–97; *SEMMG*, 68–73.)

56. *Promyshlennye i torgovye zavedeniia*, 4:1–2. *PM 1882*, II, table 18. The problems in distinguishing between factory and artisanal establishments are also discussed in *Remeslenniki i remeslennoe upravlenie*, 2–3, and in Bonnell, *Roots of Rebellion*, 20–21.

Many contemporaries continued to regard Moscow as a center of small-scale production. Was this impression accurate? What trends were operating among the small production units? The records of the Moscow Artisan Association (Remeslennoe obshchestvo) show that from 1900 to 1910, the number of master artisans, journeymen, and apprentices registered in the Artisan Association declined from 51,581 to 33,309. During the same period, however, the total number of artisanal establishments employing wage labor increased by almost 500, from 14,535 to 14,974.[57] Although modest, such an increase at a time of rapid economic growth would seem to suggest the continual economic viability of the small producer with a small number of hired hands.[58] In fact, of Moscow's 14,974 registered artisan workshops employing hired labor in 1910, the great majority, 13,451, employed two to four workers. Interestingly, of Petersburg's 11,033 workshops, a smaller number, 8,199, employed two to four workers.[59]

It must be pointed out that the above figures pertain only to the craftsmen registered in the Artisan Association. Just as the census category "guild artisans" (tsekhovye) registered only a small percentage of the city's total artisans, the Artisan Association likewise registered only a fraction of the total number of practicing artisans.[60] Indeed, swelled by the number of peasant craftsmen in the city, listings compiled by the Central Statistical Committee in 1904 and 1909 of all the artisans in the cities and settlements (posady) of Moscow province counted over 200,000 master artisans, journeymen, and apprentices in the city of Moscow.[61] Almost 90 percent of all the province's artisans counted in these surveys were located in the *city* of Moscow. Since the province increasingly depended on the city for much of its consumer goods, such as clothing, artisans and journeymen, no less than factory laborers, were attracted by employment opportunities in the city. Although the factory was squeezing the cottage industry in the production of yarn and cloth, the factory was not making such inroads in the production of goods for the retail market. In fact, proximity to wholesale supplies and the retail market made the metropolis the most attractive shelter for the village domestic worker, drenched by the storms of industrialization.

57. *Remeslenniki i remeslennoe upravlenie*, 32, 48–49.
58. Note, for instance, the rapid growth in the number of self-employed from 1902 to 1912, shown in figure 5.
59. *Remeslenniki i remeslennoe upravlenie*, 46–48.
60. Ibid., 32.
61. TsGIA, f. 1290, op. 5, d. 256, ll. 39–44; TsGIA, f. 1290, op. 5, d. 195, ll. 1–15; and TsGIA, f. 1284, op. 194, d. 106, l. 8.

This was particularly true of certain rapidly growing industries, such as the clothing trades where, according to Oliunina, "the large clothing establishments are not driving out the small."[62]

All of these data are no more than suggestive. But they do raise the possibility that the factory system was spreading very slowly vis-à-vis other forms of business activity by the beginning of the twentieth century. Factories continued, naturally, to be prominent on Moscow's industrial landscape, and factory workers continued to be prominent in the city's labor force. Yet sometime at the end of the nineteenth century this prominence appears to have peaked, creating an equilibrium between the factory and other forms of production in the city. The impression of contemporaries that Moscow was a city of small-scale production continued to be valid at the beginning of the twentieth century and even beyond 1917 to the civil war and the early years of the New Economic Policy. Since throughout our period, nearly 90 percent of the city's manufacturing establishments employed 16 or fewer workers, the factory system and other forms of large-scale manufacturing clearly were not driving the small producer out of business.[63] A similar situation prevailed in commerce. Although larger financial institutions and larger stores catering to wider markets were opening in Moscow, the petty tradesman, vendor, and shopkeeper continued to thrive. The number of employees per employer in commerce increased by only 1.7, from 6.5 in 1882 to 8.2 in 1902.[64]

Despite the national trends toward bigness and concentration of enterprise, Moscow's economy continued to retain a variety of organizational forms from modern store and gigantic factory to street vending and sweated apparel manufacture. The richness in the structure of the metropolitan economy suggests that the steady modernization of Russia received a specific coloration in Moscow in the form of a dual economy. At the apex stood large-scale institutions of banking, credit, and insurance and industrial magnates who controlled textile empires from Samarkand to St. Petersburg. Here there was increasing concentration in plant and enterprise, with fewer (and increasingly corporate) owners and more wage and salaried employees. Although the state directed this economy somewhat less in Moscow than it did in Petersburg or in the newer industrial centers in the south, the large-scale industry was nevertheless sensitive to state needs and policies. At

62. Oliunina, *Portnovskii promysel,* 4–6.
63. *TPZ,* 42–43.
64. *PM 1882,* II, pt.1, 131–34; pt.2, 101–340; *PM 1902,* I, 2, i, 116–97.

the same time there thrived the institutions of sweated outwork, barter, haggle, and street vending and peasant entrepreneurs who controlled the carrying and hauling trades from Tver' to Tula. The large-scale, formal economic organization made the small-scale, informal organizations even more significant; the large textile mills even created the sweated clothing industry. Thus, one of the most important effects of the industrial revolution and rapid economic growth was the reinforcement of Moscow's importance as a center of small-scale production and of commerce and services.

The "two economies," to the degree that such an abstraction existed, had considerable interaction. Increased wealth and greater consumption at the apex of urban society of course necessitated increased production and distribution of consumer goods, often custom-made or luxury items. The increased usage of money and greater purchasing power at the lower economic levels also hastened the growth of small-scale producers and retailers of ready-made articles, who catered to a vast internal market of peasants in and nearby the city. As the national market grew, as large factories and the railroad penetrated even deeper into the countryside, and as capitalism appeared to be giving the traditional peasant economy in the village a mortal blow, the small-scale, informal economic organizations were still vital in the largest cities, and, paradoxically, the metropolis was ideally suited to sustain them.

One cannot help noticing a similarity between Moscow's economy in 1900 and its economy today. In the past decade American economists and journalists, as well as Soviet émigrés, have exposed the "second" or "unofficial" or "parallel" economy, an alternative in the production and (chiefly) distribution of goods and services which exists alongside, or underneath, the official, planned, state-directed economy.[65] The retail and services sector of this second economy is far more developed in Moscow, the largest market in the country, than in provincial towns. Barter, payment in kind or favors, vending outside regular stores, "self-employment," small units of distribution, now as well as then, have been important features of the second economy. Pilfering then—hoboes, for example, working as day laborers in the freight yards pilfered food, tobacco, and wood and sold

---

65. Recently, a veritable cottage industry of studies on the Soviet second economy has sprung up. See, for example, Hedrick Smith, *The Russians* (New York, 1976), 106–34; Gregory Grossman, "The 'Second Economy' of the USSR," *Problems of Communism*, 26, no. 5 (September–October 1977): 17–32; Dimitrii K. Simes, "The Soviet

it—anticipated the pilfering of "socialist property" today.[66] Now, as then, the "official" or "modern" economy depends on the "second" economy to satisfy needs that the former cannot. From time to time today's authorities launch a campaign against the parallel economy— satirical cartoons, an exposé in *Sovetskaia Rossiia*, a trial of a black marketeer—but it is clear that very little is done.

Then, as now, the authorities and reformers were concerned with the city's second economy and the persistence of undisciplined ways that it implied. Greater visibility alone made Moscow's informal economy an object of concern. Except for periods of labor strife, the largest factories, far from the center and terra incognita for most Muscovites, were removed from the public eye; the open-air markets were not. Although the latter may have been colorful, they and other seemingly casual and lackadaisical forms of production and distribution suggested disorganization, disorder, the absence of socialization into the ways of modern industry, erratic patterns of production and distribution, volatile markets. To make matters worse, it seemed that the gap between the two economies was growing; to put it another way, the more European-looking the stores on Tverskaia became and the more technologically advanced the large factories became, the more the street vendors and domestic producers stuck out. This might have been more tolerable to concerned Muscovites had it not been for the fact that the smaller and informal businesses continued to employ a significant proportion of the labor force. That Muscovites perceived this labor force to be impermeable to the forces of modernization and immune to effects to change its values and habits will be a theme to which I shall return in Part Three. At this point in the study, however, it is necessary to take a closer look at the experience of the muzhik in the city.

Parallel Market," *Survey*, 21, no. 3 (Summer 1975): 42–53; Konstantin Simis, *USSR: The Corrupt Society* (New York, 1982). Naturally, because of ideological objections to private enterprise, more of the "second economy" today is illegal than was the case a hundred years ago.

66. Studies of the second economy in Russia a hundred years ago are harder to find. See Vladimir Ovtsyn, "K istorii i statistike gorodskogo proletariata v Rossii," *Russkaia mysl'*, 12, no. 5 (May 1891): 72; and the sketches of Giliarovskii, such as *Moskva i Moskvichi* and *Trushchobnye liudi* (Moscow, 1957).

PART TWO

Muzhik in Moscow

CHAPTER FOUR

The Immigration Experience

Moscow was a city of immigrants. At the end of the nineteenth century, almost three-fourths of the city's population had been born elsewhere. This proportion was remarkably constant, having been 74 percent in 1882, 72 percent in 1902, and 71 percent in 1912. Large proportions of the city's elite—two-thirds of the merchants, almost half of the honored citizens, and more than three-fifths of the gentry—could not have called Moscow their home town. Naturally, the peasants were the most important immigrant group: in 1902, 84 percent of the city's peasants (and 87 percent of the men) had been born elsewhere.[1] Moreover, the majority of the labor force had been born outside the city. To a certain degree, this reflects the preponderance of immigrants in the population as a whole; in 1902, 76.9 percent of the male population was nonnative. Yet the city's total population included dependents, which displayed a disproportionate representation of natives. When the dependents are removed from the calculations, we find that a mere 12.2 percent of the *entire* male labor force was Moscow-born, 87.8 percent having been born elsewhere.[2] This by itself is a remarkable set of figures. Stated differently, seven of every eight men in the city's work force had entered the city at some point just prior to or during their working years.

This immigrant population looms much larger when we realize that the census measured a mobile population frozen at only one brief moment; in any given year, let alone during the period between cen-

1. PM 1882, II, pt.1, 66–77; PM 1902, I, 1, i, 2–4, 12–13; SEMMG, 68–74.
2. PM 1902, I, 3, i, table II.

suses, the number of persons *at one time or another* in the labor force
was much larger. On January 31, 1902, for example, the census
counted 781,067 immigrants out of a population of slightly more than
one million.[3] This figure, of course, represents the net migration, that
is, those who had moved in all previous years to the city and stayed
long enough to be counted on January 31. Those who had moved to
the city but who had escaped being recorded by the census takers, had
died, or had left were not counted. The censal figure for the number of
residents in the city less than one year (though in itself also a net
figure) is the closest approximation of the total number of immigrants
in one year. The two census years 1882 and 1902 show a remarkable
consistency in the number—slightly more than 100,000—of arrivals
during the preceding year.[4] Considering that an undetermined number
of additional immigrants entered the city but did not remain through
the entire year, or were highly transient in their living habits upon
arrival and were therefore not counted, 100,000–150,000 immigrants
may have come to Moscow every year during the last two decades of
the nineteenth century. To put it differently, during this twenty-year
period, 2 to 3 million immigrants, more than the entire population of
Riazan' province, at one time or another were in the city's labor
force.[5]

The reasons for coming to Moscow (or leaving, for that matter) put
far more "on the road" than the net migration figures, large as they
are, would indicate. Given the large numbers "on the road" and given
that such a large proportion of Moscow's population was born elsewhere, the phenomenon of immigration was one of the most impor-

3. *PM 1902*, I, 1, i, 11.

4. *PM 1882*, II, pt.2, 31–34; *PM 1902*, I, 2, i, 8–11. These estimates are gross, and
possibly conservative, approximations at best. For example, according to the 1882
census, still residing in the city were 80,078 persons who arrived in 1881 and an
additional 20,452 who arrived in 1882. The census was taken on January 24. If the
figures for immigrants for the first three weeks of 1882, not a peak migrating season,
were projected for the entire year, then a whopping 300,000 may have entered the city.
Assuming that 1881 and 1882 were similar migrating years, this would question the
reliability of using the number of immigrants who arrived in 1881 and remained to be
counted in 1882 as a substitute for the total number of immigrants in that year: 80,000
may have stayed through the year, but 220,000 may have left. This undercounting in my
estimates may be compensated by overcounting elsewhere. (See note 5.)

5. A different difficulty presents itself in any attempt to estimate the total number of
immigrants over a period—such as a decade or an intercensal period—longer than one
year. An immigrant could have made multiple entries into the city and, owing to the
ambiguity in the concept "length of residence" used by the census takers, have been
included more than once in my estimate of the two–three million immigrants for the
period 1882–1902.

tant life experiences of the city's muzhiks. For the most peripatetic, migration was a way of life: given the transience of residence and reverse migration to be analyzed below, immigration was not a once-in-a-lifetime experience. Immigrants brought with them specific experiences and backgrounds—birthplace, ties with home, previous urban experience, skills and occupational experience, and education—as well as the values, attitudes, and ways of life shaped by these experiences. In view of the unprecedented numbers of immigrants seeking a livelihood in Moscow, the ways of life and experiences of the new arrivals had a profound effect on the degree of their integration into the milieu of a booming metropolis. For example, placement, and particularly initial placement, in the labor force was affected by many aspects of the immigrant's background and experiences. The authorities and reformers were not only acutely aware of the problems brought by immigration, but made many assumptions concerning the nature and ways of life of the city's newest arrivals. An assessment of the experiences of the muzhik in Moscow must begin with an assessment of the type of person attracted to Moscow and then consider the differences among the immigrants as well as between those who left home and those who stayed behind. Accordingly, many aspects of the muzhik's life in the city, as well as the perceptions of that life on the part of Muscovites, will be illuminated by an analysis of the immigration experience.

BIRTHPLACE AND TIES
WITH THE VILLAGE

Throughout the nineteenth century, peasants in Moscow's hinterland had sought supplemental income off the farm, frequently in Moscow itself. The bulk of the city's population was born in the provinces of Moscow, Iaroslavl', Kaluga, Riazan', Smolensk, Tula, Tver', and Vladimir. Although most of Moscow's immigrants came from these eight provinces, the distribution was far from even. As might be expected, the greatest number came from Moscow province itself: in 1882 one-third of the city's immigrants had been born in Moscow province. In the same year 14 percent of the population registered outside Moscow was residing in the city of Moscow. The four counties sending the greatest number of immigrants—Bronnitsy, Podol'sk, Serpukhov, and Moscow—sent twice as many as the county sending the smallest number, Bogorodsk. An even greater range prevailed among the surround-

ing provinces, where Tula and Riazan' provided three times as many
immigrants as Vladimir and four times as many as Iaroslavl'.[6] Proximity to Moscow in part accounted for the distribution. Within each
province almost all of the districts which had markedly higher migration rates than average for the province bordered Moscow province:
these were Borovsk, Medyn', and Tarusa in Kaluga; Gzhatsk and
Viaz'ma in Smolensk; Zubtsov, Kaliazin, and Korcheva in Tver'; Alek-
sandrosvk, Pereslavl'-Zalesskii, and Pokrov in Vladimir; Zaraisk in
Riazan'; and Aleksinsk, Venev, and Kashira in Tula. (Zaraisk and
Kashira are in fact now within the boundaries of Moscow *oblast'*.) (See
map 2.)

Of course, the total population of the respective counties and provinces influenced the numbers of persons migrating to Moscow: we
might expect more populous (and especially more densely populated)
areas to send more people to the city. On the whole this turns out to be
true. Among the provinces ringing Moscow, the most densely settled
(though not necessarily the most populous) tended also to be best represented in the city's population. Tula and Riazan' happened to be two of
the most densely populated provinces in the empire; indeed, the latter,
along with Smolensk, almost doubled its population density from 1863
to 1914.[7] (One reason for the population density was the continued
high birthrates: Tula had the highest number of births per marriage,
and Riazan' had the highest overall birthrate in European Russia.)[8]
Moscow, Tula, Riazan', and Kaluga, ranked in order of their population densities, sent the largest number of people as well as the largest
proportion of their total populations to the city of Moscow. Indeed, 7
and 6 percent of the entire population of Tula and Kaluga, respectively,
migrated to Moscow.[9] Such a statistical correlation of population density and migration to Moscow did not prevail, however, for the counties
of Moscow province itself. Here, the sparsely settled and more distant
western counties, while sending smaller numbers of people to Moscow,
sent large *proportions* of their population. Thus the 15,207 immigrants
from Ruza residing in Moscow in 1902 constituted 27.5 percent of that

---

6. *PM 1882*, II, pt.1, 67–70.
7. *PVP*, 24:69–97; and table 9 in volumes 6, 15, 35, 40, 43, 44; *PM 1902*, I, 2, i,
28–45; *Sbornik svedenii po Rossii*, 2–8; Rashin, *Naselenie*, 77–80; V. P. Semenov,
Rossiia, 2: *Srednerusskaia chernozemnaia oblast'* (St. Petersburg, 1902), 158.
8. Rashin, *Naselenie*, 77–80, 180–83; Tsentral'nyi statisticheskii komitet, *Statistiki
Rossiiskoi imperii*, 18: *Dvizhenie naseleniia v Evropeiskoi Rossii za 1886–90 gg.* (St.
Petersburg, 1892), 9–13.
9. *PM 1902*, I, 2, i, 28–45; *Obshchii svod*, 1:2–3.

county's 1897 population. By contrast, Bogorodsk, though a county larger, more densely populated, and closer to Moscow, sent the fewest immigrants.[10] The population of the more industrial counties and provinces around Moscow, such as Bogorodsk and Vladimir, having more employment opportunities nearer home, had less reason to migrate to Moscow, while persons from more agricultural areas, such as Riazan', Tula, Kaluga, Smolensk, Ruza, or Mozhaisk, were more likely to seek a living in Moscow.

While peasants in the hinterland sought supplemental income in Moscow, most retained some form of tie with their native village, or *rodina*, in the suggestive usage of the time. Although by the beginning of the twentieth century, more and more peasants were severing these ties, this was not a process that could take place overnight. Consequently, individual or familial, as well as legal, economic, and social, ties with the village remained an important part of the immigration experience.

After the emancipation of the serfs the peasant was referred to in the law as belonging to the former tax-paying estate or having a rural station (*sel'skoe sostoianie*). Membership in the peasant commune, the virtually mandatory reception of allotment land, arrears, and collective responsibility characterized this rural station, and the passport system and residence permit enforced it. Issued (and renewed) only in the local township office, the passport, valid for the entire empire, and the identification card (*svidetel'stvo*), valid only within thirty *versts* (approximately thirty kilometers) of the place of registration, were essential in obtaining work outside the peasant's own township.[11] It is true, of course, that several changes in the laws governing the peasant began to ease restrictions on movements in the 1880s. In the 1880s and 1890s, approximately 54 percent of the population of working age of Moscow province received some kind of passport.[12] With the

10. *PM 1902*, I, 2, i, 28–45; Kurkin, *Statistika*, 37, 43, 56–57, 69, 97, 166, 197, 346.

11. "Vidy na zhitel'stvo, vydannye krest'ianskomu naseleniiu moskovskoi gubernii v 1880 i 1885 gg.," *Statisticheskii ezhegodnik Moskovskoi gubernii za 1886*, 1–2; Romashova, "Obrazovanie," 156.

12. "Vidy na zhitel'stvo," 7, 11; Bulgakov, *Peredvizhenie*, 4, 7. The number of passports issued does not correspond precisely to the number living elsewhere. Since one person could get several temporary *vidy* during one year, the number of passports was greater than the number of persons holding them. However, since the starting and ending period was often flexible, extensions were not always recorded, vagrants were not counted, and family members were counted under one passport, the number of persons living elsewhere would be greater than the number of passports issued. The authors of the study felt that the two discrepancies virtually cancelled each other out.

abolition of the soul tax and the reduction of redemption payments, the peasant's fiscal burden was eased. In 1885 the Ministry of Internal Affairs allowed Moscow's peasants residing away from their place of registration to change their passports through the factory owner (if they were factory workers) and local police. This removed one of the obstructions that kept peasants from moving into industry.[13] Nevertheless, the peasant was still subject to the collective will and disciplinary powers of the commune, special courts, and administrative organs, as well as to nonfiscal obligations from which all other classes were freed. Despite the easing of passport regulations, there was no such thing as an indefinite passport: when the passport expired, peasants had to apply for a new one, even if they did not have to return to their place of registration to do so.[14] Consequently, most passports were issued for one year or less, and increases in the issuance of long-term passports were offset by a simultaneous increase in the issuance of identification cards, valid for only short-distance moves.[15] Presumably, many more peasants came to Moscow for short-term visits than the number of passports or identification cards issued would indicate. The police complained frequently of the number of peasants residing illegally in the city; furthermore, such peasants were not deterred by severe punishment.

What about leaving the peasant estate altogether? Until the Stolypin reforms, the obstacles to a peasant's permanently leaving the village association were almost insurmountable. Peasants wanting to leave the commune needed the consent of the commune in the form of a discharge (*uvol'nitel'noe svidetel'stvo*). According to the conditions of the discharge, the applicant owning or claiming allotment land had to renounce the land or the claim in writing. The association then had to consent to take the land; this required a resolution of the village assembly. There could be no arrears on the part of the peasant family, and all taxes had to be paid. The *volost'* office could have no record of personal debts; the peasant could not be facing trial. The peasant could not leave the association with responsibility of minors, the aged, or the infirm. Finally, the peasant had to receive parental consent.[16]

    13. Romashova, "Obrazovanie," 156; Gerschenkron, "Agrarian Policies," 768–83.
    14. Bulgakov, *Peredvizhenie*, 5. See also N. M. Korkunov, *Russkoe gosudarstvennoe pravo* (St. Petersburg, 1893), pt. 1:262.
    15. "Vidy na zhitel'stvo," 6, 8–11, 13–15.
    16. Bulgakov, *Peredvizhenie*, 21; Vasil'ev, "Ob osobennostiakh," 14. (Any resemblance between these regulations and those governing the issuance of exit visas in the Soviet Union today is purely coincidental.)

So complicated was this procedure that although a peasant migrant weighed down by the ties to the village might have been prone to become a legal member of another estate, in Moscow province the total number of peasant heads of households who changed their estate during the decade 1894–1903 was only 1.4 percent of those registered as *absent* from their place of registration, that is, of those presumably most predisposed to changing their status. An average of only one out of every 2,000 peasants annually changed into the *meshchanstvo*, the most accessible estate for the peasantry. The numbers of peasants who acquired merchant, clergy, or honorary citizen status were even more miniscule.[17]

Thus the peasant who wanted (or needed) to work elsewhere, whether in another village, a mill town, or the city, retained his peasant status and traveled on a passport. He had to be careful not to be away too long, lest his passport expire or he have a hard time getting back his allotment land. The village association often excluded peasants who were unlikely to return from the periodic reapportionment and often levied an "absentee tax" (*guliatskii obrok*) on members, called idlers (*guliaki*) who were working elsewhere. As the author of a study of peasant mobility observed, "if the absence is temporary and if the peasant periodically returns and has his allotment and family in the village, there are no major changes either in his way of life or legal status."[18]

Retention of allotment and family in the village suggests two other bonds holding the peasant working in Moscow to his place of birth. P. A. Shestakov noted that only 9 percent of the peasant-workers at the Tsindel' mill in Moscow were landless and appropriately concluded that "the great majority of workers are peasants who are at the same time landowners."[19] It must be added that of these landless peasant workers, three-quarters were former household serfs and never did have an allotment, and one-half still owned a cottage or some other property in the village. According to surveys of the Moscow zemstvo, only 11 percent of the total population was registered as absent at the time of the survey, and of the "absent" households, 85 percent still owned their own cottage in the village.[20] Several surveys

17. Bulgakov, *Peredvizhenie*, 4, 22, 25–27, 34, 55–56.
18. Ibid., 4, 7.
19. P. Shestakov, "Materialy dlia kharakteristiki fabrichnykh rabochikh v Moskve," *Russkaia mysl'*, 21, no. 1 (January 1900): 161.
20. Bulgakov, *Peredvizhenie*, 12, 15–16; *Moskovskaia guberniia po mestnomu obsledovaniiu*, 1:470–79.

indicated that although the peasant did not know exactly how much land he had or where it was, he did know exactly how many head of livestock he owned.[21] Of course, peasants retained land not only because of a rational calculation of economic gain or loss but because of inertia or as a form of security; as Zhbankov observed, "you may not have a lot of fun in the village, but at least you could call the food and shelter your own."[22] Land in the village could be a burden to the peasant in the city, and one zemstvo investigator in Vladimir province observed that for an urban factory worker, the ideal was to get rid of one's land so as not to have to pay taxes.[23] Whether land in the village was a form of security or a burden depended largely on the position of the peasant in the city, which, in turn, depended largely on his job. According to the worker P. Timofeev, the common laborer (*chernorabochii*) coming to the city, even with his wife, was in an "ambiguous position." The awareness that he was not a skilled worker (*masterovoi*) or the fact that he could be laid off any minute made him want to hang onto the village. On the other hand, Timofeev claimed, most skilled workers felt that "for them the village is just an obstacle" and that "there's no gain in the village, only loss."[24]

If a peasant held onto his allotment, he himself, his family, or hired hands had to work it. Surveys of the Moscow zemstvo showed that only 5 percent of the registered peasant families actually present were not farming their own land. Of the 1,213 Tsindel' workers who had an allotment, 945 (77.9 percent) farmed it with their families and 88 (7.3 percent) hired laborers.[25] In addition, peasants, either collectively or individually, were buying and renting nonallotment land or farming alien land as sharecroppers; 13 percent of Tsindel' workers thereby maintained limited ties with the village.[26] Consequently, although the landless element was clearly present near Moscow, it would be unwise to exaggerate its proportions or the extent to which it no longer engaged in agriculture.[27]

Many peasants themselves went home in the summer to work in the fields, and this fact was frequently used by statisticians to gauge

---

21. Shestakov, "Materialy," 158, 161.

22. Zhbankov, "O gorodskikh otkhozhikh zarabotkakh," 141–42.

23. Quoted in Ivanov, "Preemstvennost'," 116.

24. P. Timofeev, "Ocherki zavodskoi zhizni," *Russkoe bogatstvo*, no. 9 (September 1905): 21, 24–25.

25. Bulgakov, *Peredvizhenie*, 12, 15–16.

26. Shestakov, *Rabochie*, 26, 35.

27. Bulgakov, *Peredvizhenie*, 12, 15–16.

the strength of the peasant's bonds to the village. This was particularly true of peasant laborers in small and unmechanized manufacturing establishments, unskilled day laborers, and seasonal laborers who were generally not at the workbench the year round. One Soviet historian has noted:

The small manufacturing and retailing establishments with their primitive, pre-steam technology or without it all, not in year-round operation, and with traditional patriarchal productive relations, could in no way completely divorce the peasant from the land and force him to irrevocably break all ties with the village.[28]

Interruption of Moscow residence was less likely for factory workers. P. Peskov and E. Dement'ev, two sanitary physicians of the Moscow zemstvo, observed in the 1880s that only 14 percent of the workers left the factory for summer work.[29] Almost two decades later, according to Shestakov, only 13 percent of the peasant workers left the Tsindel' mill in the summer.[30] Nevertheless, many large factories, although in year-round operation, cut back production in summer, changed from two shifts to one, or, as the following curious description indicates, put out work in the villages:

For a long time, up to the beginning of the twentieth century, many Moscow workers preserved their ties with the village and remained half peasants. Each spring at the beginning of the agricultural season they abandoned their workbenches and streamed back to the villages. At the same time the textile industrialists, as always, passed out yarn for winding in the surrounding villages. At the factory gates in the workers' quarters, one could see the crowds of peasant women who had come laden with great bundles of thick spools of yarn.[31]

Semenov's "Makarka's Adventures" shows that it was frequently easier to get a Moscow factory job in the summer, presumably because many workers had left; consequently, many new laborers came to the city after Easter.[32] This seasonal migration pattern was also characteristic of the construction and transport trades.

Shestakov stated that "presently a great majority of workers are not only landowners but farmers, since they engage in farming, if not

28. Kut'ev, "Dokumental'nye materialy," 32.

29. Dement'ev, *Fabrika*, 44, 46; P. A. Peskov, *Sanitarnoe issledovanie fabrik po obrabotke voloknistykh veshchestv* (Moscow, 1882), 141. The study was originally published in the *Trudy Komissii, uchrezhdennoi moskovskim gen.-gub. kn. V.A. Dolgorukovym dlia osmotra fabrik i zavodov v Moskve*, vyp. 1 (Moscow, 1882).

30. Shestakov, *Rabochie*, 39.

31. S. V. Bakhrushin, *Maloletnie nishchie i brodiagi v Moskve* (Moscow, 1913), 23.

32. S. T. Semenov, "Iz zhizni Makarki," *V rodnoi derevne* (Moscow, 1962), 428, 437.

themselves personally, then their own families."[33] The existence of some, if not all, family members back in the village was another important bond between the city peasant and the village. So pervasive was the phenomenon that statisticians in the 1870s explained the more rapid growth of Berlin (compared with Moscow) by the fact that German workers brought their families with them to the city whereas the Russian worker left his family behind in the village.[34] Schulze-Gävernitz, the German authority on Russian manufacturing, argued that this phenomenon characterized the second of four stages in the formation of a Europeanized labor force and that in the 1880s and 1890s most central Russian factory workers were in this stage.[35] If 83 percent of the Tsindel' mill operatives owned land and tilled the soil, and if only 13 percent actually returned themselves to the village, then, although the question was not put in so many words, a large number must have left family—frequently young children and the elderly—behind. More than half of Oliunina's tailors, for example, had families in the village.[36] Surprisingly, 31 percent of Moscow's printers surveyed by Svavitskii and Sher in 1907 left their entire family back in the village. Fifty percent of this skilled and relatively urbanized group periodically sent money home, a sign of village ties that one runs across repeatedly in statistical, autobiographical, and fictional accounts of Russian labor in this period.[37] Thus, 67 percent of the single workers and 42 percent of the married workers in S. N. Prokopovich's budget study of Petersburg sent money home. Although one might expect that a larger budget would be indicative of a more "urban" worker, or a worker with more of his family living with him, the bigger the budget, the larger the sum sent home (both in absolute and in relative terms).[38] It is unclear whether such figures reflect *actual* money sent or *intentions*: city workers frequently complained that they could not send money home, and dependents in the village complained (more frequently)

    33. Shestakov, *Rabochie*, 75. Russia was not unique in this regard. See David H. Pinkney, *Napoleon III and the Rebuilding of Paris* (Princeton, 1958), 157.
    34. *Promyshlennye i torgovye zavedeniia* 4:5–6.
    35. Schulze-Gävernitz, *Krupnoe proizvodstvo*, 126–32.
    36. Oliunina, *Portnovskii promysel*, 174–76.
    37. Svavitskii and Sher, *Ocherk*, 6, 9. It would be a mistake to generalize, as Ivanov does, from these data that a large proportion of urban workers had families with them. The printers were Moscow's most skilled workers, had the longest residency in the city, and had the highest proportion of Moscow-born. (See Ivanov, "Preemstvennost'," 111.) See also Leikin, *Na zarabotkakh*, 12.
    38. S. N. Prokopovich, *Biudzhety peterburgskikh rabochikh* (St. Petersburg, 1909), 35–36.

that they had not received money.[39] Even a British consular officer could observe in 1906 that "owing to famine most of the men had to send every kopek they can spare to their homes in the country. Thus their material position is worse than before."[40] One tailor complained to Oliunina that "you send all you have to the village and leave for yourself only the bare necessities; that's why you aren't fully clothed, why you don't observe 'Mondays' and don't drink."[41] Despite this financial burden, wives and other family members living in the villages enabled the peasant to take makeshift living arrangements in the city— in crowded lodging houses, as a boarder with another family, or with a group of fellow villagers—a fact of great concern to reformers.[42]

Family in the village meant frequent visits home during the holidays and summer months. According to one study of peasant mobility, "in exchange for those pouring in from the village, there is a wave from the cities."[43] Approximately two-thirds of the tailors surveyed by Oliunina went back to the village three to five times a year for visits of one week to six months.[44] As large a factory as the Gustav List machine plant was closed for a week at Christmas in the 1890s. Such vacation periods, according to Kanatchikov, were also the times for medical inspection, particularly for venereal disease.[45] Several reports on the December uprising noted the dissipation of the strike movement and the exodus of workers to the villages, especially as Christmas approached.[46] The writer Sergei Semenov described one friend, Timofei Ivanovich, about thirty years old:

He spent his winters as a journeyman in Moscow and came to the village [in Volokolamsk county] in summer, harnessed himself up to the peasant yoke, and worked side by side with others until the fall.[47]

Semenov's own career is interesting in this regard. His long-dreamed-of first chance at working in Moscow came when he was eleven years old.

39. Leikin, *Na zarabotkakh*, 199; Zhbankov, *Bab'ia storona*, 3.
40. "Report for the Year 1906 on the Trade and Agriculture of the Consular District of St. Petersburg," *Parliamentary Papers*, no. 3797 (1906), 4.
41. Oliunina, *Portnovskii promysel*, 240–41.
42. For a description of a similar phenomenon in Paris half a century earlier, see Louis Chevalier, *Laboring Classes and Dangerous Classes in Paris during the First Half of the Nineteenth Century*, trans. Frank Jellinek (New York, 1973), 430.
43. Bulgakov, *Peredvizhenie*, 6.
44. Oliunina, *Portnovskii promysel*, 174–76.
45. Kanatchikov, *Iz istorii*, 44.
46. Engelstein, "Moscow and the 1905 Revolution: A Study in Class Conflict and Political Organization," Ph.D. dissertation (Stanford University, 1976), 368–69.
47. S. T. Semenov, *Dvadtsat' piat' let*, 170–71.

I was sent to a Moscow ribbon factory. The first year I worked there until sowing time, when I was summoned home to help with the housework. Afterwards I went back to Moscow to the same factory and stayed there all winter until Easter. At Easter I again went home.[48]

From age thirteen to eighteen (this was in the 1880s), he held a series of temporary jobs all over Russia, from Petersburg, to Poltava, back to Moscow, to Ekaterinoslav, to Belgorod (in Kursk province), and back again to Moscow.

Such trips home were financially burdensome. A worker told Timofeev that when he returned to the village he had to dress well,

or else they'll say—you live in the city but dress worse than a beggar. Here [in the city] I can somehow manage but you really have to show off in the village. You have to take presents for everyone: a dress for your mother, a sweater for your wife, a scarf for your mother-in-law, shoes for the children. And then, considering you've come all the way from the city, everybody will wait for a chance to get a drink from you, and in general clean you out, because everybody knows that no one comes to the village broke."[49]

In addition to the need to visit family or to renew passports, there were four other rather specific reasons for the peasant to return—temporarily and in some cases permanently—to the native village: old age, marriage, economic hardship in the city, and improvements in village life. The elderly, disabled, ill, and infirm often returned to their village homes and families for good.

Often such persons, having lived all their life in the city, if old-age or disability or pressing need forces them, return to the village and claim their rights in the association, in spite of the fact that they never had allotment land.[50]

Zhbankov's study of "women's land" showed that despite extensive city experience, migrant laborers—well-off and poor peasants alike—married only village girls. Although it is unclear whether these village brides were of the same villages as their grooms or were from other villages and therefore possibly were met and courted in the city, the key criterion apparently was that "city" girls were unfit for farming.[51] Zemstvo surveys attributed the return to the village also to industrial

48. Ibid., 6–7.
49. Timofeev, "Ocherki," 22.
50. Bulgakov, *Peredvizhenie*, 6. Kurkin's figures for the death rate in Moscow province show that although Moscow had relatively high death rates for most age groups, it had relatively low rates for ages seventy and above, suggesting that many old people left the city. (*Statistika*, 300–1.) The same phenomenon has been observed in Paris. See Pinkney, *Napoleon III*, 153.
51. Zhbankov, "O gorodskikh otkhozhikh zarabotkakh," 142. See Chekhov's "Peasants" for an example of failure-induced return to the village.

contraction and a shortage of city jobs. One zemstvo statistician noted that in 1885

many who lost their jobs and who wandered in vain around Moscow and other industrial centers for several weeks looking everywhere for work, "went through" (*proeli*) their clothing and boots and came back to the village half-dressed, almost barefoot and living on handouts (*pitaias' Khristovym imenem*). . . . The influx of former factory workers into the village is so great that a real struggle goes on for land in many places.[52]

If a "real struggle" ensued for land, it would appear that though the peasant may have lost land, he had not relinquished his claim or his intentions of returning to the village and that the return move was conceived as relatively long-term.

Not only industrial depression but also improvements in the village motivated peasants to leave the city. The introduction of flax production in Volokolamsk in the late 1880s brought hope (and returning peasants) to the village. According to Semenov:

My appearance in the village from Moscow wasn't unique. After several good years everyone felt that one could profitably be a peasant; for some these advantages were so enticing that they stopped living in Moscow before I did and went back to the village. . . . Indeed, many living at factories or at some small cheap places left their jobs and returned home. Those who could no longer live in the village stayed in Moscow; they had either left for good or had found well-paying jobs, such as clerks or vendors, or were self-employed. There were, to be sure, factory workers, but they were mainly the crippled.[53]

It would appear that factory workers maintained more ties with the village than did the self-employed, clerks, or vendors; this observation will merit closer examination in the next chapter. Even for factory workers readjustment in the village was not always easy, as Semenov observed:

Having grown accustomed to sitting at their workbenches, they had dropped out of village life and its interests and work, and if at home they had to sow, reap or thrash, they looked as if the job made them sick. That's why in the

52. Kurkin, *Statistika*, 502–3. Tugan-Baranovskii cites the same zemstvo statistical yearbooks and notes that "many factory workers having grown completely unaccustomed to agriculture, returned to the village and took up the plow" (*Fabrika*, 258). This contradicts his view that since such a high proportion of workers had fathers who worked at the factory, reverse migration from factory to village was rare. "If the peasant ended up at the factory, he certainly will stay there. And not only he but his children are 'thrown into the factory cauldron' (*vyvarivaiutsia v fabrichnom kotle*). The land loses its power over him and he is transformed from a farmer (*zemel'nyi sobstvennik*) into a proletarian" (p. 340).

53. S. T. Semenov, *Dvadtsat' piat' let*, 12.

village, it became a saying that if someone works badly, he was told right away "You work like a factory worker" or "You're a factory worker!"[54]

Other factors, however, enabled returning peasants to overcome these difficulties and, like the army veterans who became village school-teachers, to assume leadership roles in the village. Prosperous return-ing peasants bought up property with city earnings and outfitted their cottages with city-bought furniture.[55] Semenov himself was part of the small but growing peasant intelligentsia that had been exposed to the city and then acquired some land and returned to the village.

Such migration patterns were partly responsible for perhaps the most striking sign of familial ties with the village: village birth itself. Despite the fact that only 13 percent of the mill hands at Tsindel' returned for summer field work, 94 percent had been born in the village. One could argue that these data are taken from two genera-tions and that more detailed questioning might have shown that the workers in the mill the year around were choosing to have *their* chil-dren born in the city. In view of the fact that more than 50 percent of the Tsindel' mill hands had fathers who were also factory workers,[56] and the fact that rural birth of Moscow factory workers stayed at remarkably high and, more important, constant percentages, it is unlikely that such habits were changing rapidly.

Nor did they need to. The high proportion of "factory fathers" and low incidence of urban birth was permitted by, among other things, the practice of *zemliachestvo*, recently discussed by Robert Johnson. This informal association of fellow villagers ensured that many sons could easily enter industrial occupations despite rural or distant birth. Such networks of fellow villagers (called *zemliaki*) were important not only among seasonal migratory laborers but among apparently more stable factory occupations and were an important link between city and countryside. As one statistician observed, in words that would be familiar to any American historian: "It's enough just for one villager to come to the city before this pioneer drags along his fellow villagers and helps them get set up. For this reason we have frequently seen apartments inhabited by people of the same village."[57]

54. Ibid., 12–13.
55. Ibid., 118–20, 150–51.
56. Shestakov, *Rabochie*, 24.
57. M. and O., "Tsifry i fakty iz perepisi Sankt-Peterburga v 1900 g." *Russkaia mysl'*, 23, no. 2 (February 1902): 72–92. On the phenomenon of *zemliachestvo*, see Johnson, *Peasant and Proletarian*, 67–79. On analogous phenomena, such as the *com-pagnonnage* in Paris, see Chevalier, *Laboring Classes*, 426–27, and A. Girard et al., "Geographical Mobility and Urban Concentration in France: A Study in the Provinces," in Clifford J. Jansen, *Readings in the Sociology of Migration* (Oxford, 1970), 219.

Such widespread ties with the village of peasants living and working in the city did not escape the notice of contemporary observers and
generated strong opinions. Although the opinions of Muscovites concerning the beneficial or undesirable effects of such ties may be more
appropriately considered in Part Three, a view of a peasant-worker
himself might be of interest here. Semen Kanatchikov felt that peasant
patternmakers in particular stood out:

They wore boots with boot legs, calico shirts and belts; they had "bowl"
haircuts and their beards were rarely touched by a barber. Every payday, they
immediately sent part of their money to the village. They lived all crowded
together, foully, stingily, denying themselves all the time just so they could
save more money for the village. They would wait for a chance to bum a drink
(*na darmovshchinku*). On holidays they would go to mass and to visit their
fellow villagers (*zemliaki*) to talk about grain, their land, the harvest and the
livestock. Whenever they couldn't get back to the village, they'd have visits
from the "little women"—fat, broadchested wives wearing linen shirts and
bright red calico skirts. On holidays they'd go to the tavern to live it up
(*ugoshchat'sia*) and listen to the phonograph (*slushat' mashinu*).[58]

City workers did not like these "coarse devils" (*serye cherty*) and took
every opportunity to make fun of them. Coming from a worker of
peasant origins himself, such observations are very suggestive of the
attitudes toward the ties between city and village; if a worker had such
a condescending attitude toward peasants with close village ties, one
can imagine the attitude among better-heeled Muscovites.

URBAN, EDUCATIONAL, AND
OCCUPATIONAL BACKGROUND

To Kanatchikov, such "coarse devils" had limited horizons and
were unprepared for, or slow to adopt, city ways. This was the impression of many Muscovites as well. In Moscow, as in other metropolises, it was easy for the educated to poke fun at the immigrant
from far-off quarters. A writer of sketches of Moscow street life in the
1860s condescendingly observed:

For instance the dear rustic (*muzhichek*) who has just arrived in Moscow for
the first time, especially from some distant steppe province, sticks out because
of his busy, nervous, and even frightened appearance, and particularly because
of his incredible naiveté. Here you have a wild animal that has just stumbled
into a place inhabited by humans. His innate shrewdness, if you like, hasn't
disappeared, but he is so perplexed by everything around him—the noise, the

58. Kanatchikov, *Iz istorii*, 18.

crowds, the traffic, the unfamiliar impressions—that at first he can't function properly.[59]

Though these sketches were written in an amusing vein, by the end of the century, the torrent of immigrants, whether from "the steppe" or not, was not at all amusing to reformers.

Various ties to the village such as those just discussed were in part responsible for this alleged "incredible naiveté." There were other aspects of the immigration experience that influenced the immigrant's horizons and prepared him or her for city life. In addition, other aspects of the immigration experience account for differences between those who left the villages and those who stayed behind, as well as among the immigrants themselves. Three such factors were the immigrants' urban, educational, and occupational backgrounds. It might be assumed, as most modernization studies do, that the greater the previous experience living in any city, the greater the amount of education and the more employment outside agriculture, the greater the likelihood of leaving home and the better the preparation for urban society. In turn, the better the preparation for the city, the greater the likelihood for the formation of a solid, self-reliant urban citizenry, a preoccupation of reformers. What was the nature of the urban, educational, and occupational backgrounds of the immigrants, and how well were they prepared for urban society? Were they the "coarse devils" or "wild animals" as alleged by some observers?

Let us first examine the urban background of the city's immigrants. To begin with, contemporaries had the impression that immigrants to Moscow, as well as to the other major urban magnet, St. Petersburg, were traveling greater and greater distances. Writing about Petersburg, the well-known criminologist Dmitrii Dril' commented that "in recent years there has been an exodus of workers from provinces one thousand kilometers away."[60] According to one zemstvo doctor, laborers from Riazan', Tula, and Kaluga were referred to as having "come from the steppe."[61] In fact, as data from the 1882 census demonstrate, a smaller proportion of immigrants were coming from Moscow province itself, and a greater proportion were coming from the adjacent provinces. Among these immigrants a smaller proportion were coming from the more urbanized and industrial provinces of Vladimir and

59. Golitsynskii, *Ulichnye tipy*, 23.
60. Dmitrii A. Dril', *Brodiazhestvo i nishchenstvo i mery bor'by s nimi* (St. Petersburg, 1899), 18.
61. Dement'ev, *Fabrika*, 11–13, 22, 31–32. See also Shestakov, *Rabochie*, 35.

Iaroslavl', and a greater proportion were coming from agricultural provinces such as Riazan'.[62] As chapter 1 has already indicated, despite rural overpopulation Moscow's hinterland was not marked by rapid urbanization, and most provinces had proportions of urban dwellers which were below the national averages.

Unfortunately, census data show province or county of birth, not place of previous residence before movement into Moscow. In addition, the figures do not distinguish rural from urban birthplace.[63] To obtain urban experience before arrival in Moscow, a peasant could have spent time in a nearby factory town, the county seat or capital of his native province, or in a factory town or county seat in Moscow province. That is, the Iaroslavl' peasant might have stopped off in Dmitrov, or the Kaluga peasant in Vereia, before moving on to Moscow. Although 57 percent of Moscow's peasants in 1897 were born in a different province, only 39 percent of the peasant population of Moscow province as a whole were born in other provinces. Clearly, the figure 39 percent was inflated by the city of Moscow; indeed, only 9 percent of the rural population was born outside the province. Bogorodsk was the only county other than Moscow itself which had more persons present at the time of the 1897 census than were actually registered, indicating a net surplus of immigrants. Even the industrial districts of Kolomna and Serpukhov had a net "loss" of their registered population; and their proportion of immigrants from other provinces was somewhat inflated by their proximity (just across the Oka River) to Riazan' and Tula.[64] Since the rural population included the residents of the factory villages and towns not officially classified as "urban," it does not appear that "rural" industry attracted a sizeable immigrant population.

It might be supposed that provincial capitals and county seats were more likely intermediary points of residence, or "intervening opportunities," between farm and Moscow.[65] Such cities could have provided

62. *PM 1882*, II, pt. 2, 32.

63. *PVP*, 24:69–97; and table 9 in volumes 6, 15, 25, 40, 43, 44; *PM 1902*, I, 2, i, 28–45; *Sbornik svedenii po Rossii*, 2–8.

64. Kurkin, *Statistika*, 4–5, 10, 14; Vasil'ev, "Ob osobennostiakh," 4–5. From 60 to 98 percent of the labor force of the Central Industrial Region (excluding the labor force of Moscow and its suburbs) was recruited from the local population.

65. The theory of "intervening opportunities" formulated by S. Stouffer in 1940 states that the number of persons going a given distance is directly proportional to the number of opportunities at that distance and inversely proportional to the number of intervening opportunities. See C. J. Jansen, "Migration: A Sociological Problem," in Jansen, *Readings*, 10–11.

a variety of employment opportunities, particularly in commerce and services, and a degree of urban experience not available in the village. Yet, only 4 percent of the population of Moscow province, for example, lived in towns other than Moscow.[66] Although some towns, such as Kolomna and Serpukhov, attracted immigrants, many towns, as one American visitor at the turn of the century described it, were far from bustling:

Gaps and open spaces, often in the middle of town, are frequently left unoccupied for no apparent reason. The shops are small and dark, but if there is rarely any display of articles offered for sale, to catch the eye of the passerby, this is compensated for in a larger measure by the painted sign-boards [because of illiteracy—J.B.]. . . . Should the local town happen to be upon a railway, the station would probably be in striking contrast to all other buildings. . . . [However, the railway was often situated several miles from town.] In this case a new town frequently springs up around it, but generally conveys to the visitor the same idea of being merely a temporary makeshift, waiting for something better to turn up, as is given by nearly all little towns in rural districts. . . . Cut off thus from the outer world, life in country districts . . . resembles that on board ship in mid-ocean. . . . [One can experience] a complete immunity from the worries and distractions of the outside world by a three-month's residence in a rural district in Russia.[67]

The local economies and the historical settlement patterns of county seats and provincial capitals—first, servitors, followed by artisans and merchants, the garrison, and finally suburban settlements with their peasant population (a configuration which remained virtually unchanged at the end of the nineteenth century)—did not provide enough employment opportunities to attract large numbers of peasant immigrants.[68] In addition, Moscow, like metropolises that provide urban needs of a vast hinterland, was a magnet for the rural population, or, to change the metaphor, its radio signals were so powerful as to drown out weaker local stations.[69] Many contemporaries and authori-

---

66. *PVP*, 24:xii.
67. Francis Palmer, *Russian Life in Town and Country* (London, 1901), 129–30, 136–37.
68. *PVP*, 24:xxix.
69. According to Ravenstein's "laws of migration," internal migration proceeds by short-distance stages from farm to small town to medium-sized city to metropolis. Stouffer's theory was intended, in part, to modify this "law." The experience of Moscow would seem to fit Stouffer's model better than Ravenstein's. For comparison, see Adna F. Weber, *The Growth of Cities in the Nineteenth Century* (Ithaca, N.Y., 1965), 257–70; G. Poucher, "The Growing Population of Paris: Regional Origin, Social Composition, Attitudes and Motivation," and I. B. Taeuber, "Family, Migration and Industrialization in Japan," in Jansen, *Readings*, 203–53 and 367–83 respectively; Peter Knights, *The Plain People of Boston: A Study in City Growth, 1830–1860* (New York, 1971), 35; and David Ward, *Cities and Immigrants* (New York, 1971), 4.

ties on peasant migration in particular sensed this phenomenon even if precise data were lacking. Writing in 1875, V. I. Chaslavskii noted that most of the carpenters, plasterers, stonemasons, painters, building superintendents, nurses, and tavern keepers of the non-black-earth provinces headed toward Petersburg or Moscow.[70] Ninety percent of the migratory laborers of Uglich county, Iaroslavl' province, were registered as having left for Moscow or Petersburg.[71] Although this may have been an extreme case, other counties also recorded that their migratory laborers went "mainly" to Moscow or to the "two capitals." Writing at the end of the century, L. A. Kirillov observed that long-distance migration to the urban areas, especially to the capital cities, predominated over the older village-to-village pattern of migration.[72] A study of migratory labor by the Moscow zemstvo found that 27 percent of the peasants leaving their native village went somewhere else in the same county, 8 percent went to another county, 5 percent went to another province, and fully 60 percent went to Moscow.[73] Even among the most skilled artisans, less than 20 percent of Moscow's printers had worked in any town other than Moscow.[74]

In summary, let us review the possibilities of actual residence for the Smolensk or Mozhaisk peasant who was not in his or her county of registration at the time of the 1897 census. First, he could have been doing seasonal agricultural work elsewhere. However, since the census was taken in the month of January and since nonlocal agricultural labor was not extensively practiced in the Moscow region, it is unlikely that this was the explanation. Second, he could have been engaged in local trades or employed in a local village factory. However, the figures apply to the entire county of registration and thus presumably include those working in the county seats or local factories. Third, he could have been engaged in seasonal trades or employed in a village factory in another county or province (but not Moscow). Although the likelihood of this alternative is much harder to estimate, the previous discussion casts doubts on the degree to

70. V. I. Chaslavskii, "Zemledel'cheskie otkhozhie promysly v sviazi s pereseleniem krest'ian," in V. Bezobrazov, ed., *Sbornik gosudarstvennykh znanii* (St. Petersburg, 1875), 2:182.

71. "Uglich," *Entsiklopedicheskii slovar'*, 68:494.

72. Kirillov, "K voprosu," 294–95.

73. M. B., "Otkhod krest'ianskogo naseleniia na zarabotki," *Izvestiia Moskovskoi zemskoi upravy*, 3 (1911): 20. See also the section on nonagricultural earnings in the statistical annual of the Moscow zemstvo which contains repeated references to Moscow as the destination of migrant laborers.

74. Svavitskii and Sher, *Ocherk*, 6, 11.

which small towns or village factories recruited immigrant peasants. The last alternative for the Smolensk or Mozhaisk peasant was the most likely: employment in Moscow itself. As of January 1882 about one-seventh of Moscow province's county population resided in the old capital.[75] The peculiarities of Russian development—the lack of job opportunities in the small towns, the sheer magnitude of peasant immigrants, and the many job opportunities in the metropolis—suggest that peasants headed to the world's tenth largest city with little urban experience under their belts.

One final word of caution needs to be said. Although the evidence suggests that peasants had little urban background, this is true only of their experiences before the *first* trip to Moscow. Given the large number of peasants on the road and the frequent number of trips to the city, Moscow itself, paradoxically, provided the urban background for returning peasants. To put it differently, in a certain sense peasants did migrate to Moscow in stages—the stages being Moscow itself.

Educational background was another important part of the immigration experience. It is possible that educational background was a factor determining employment opportunities and perhaps, as the discussion below will clarify, the decision to migrate to Moscow.[76] Unfortunately, the census data do not permit us to determine educational background—years and type of schooling, number of grades completed—as such, but we can determine the literacy of the immigrant population. Although literacy may be a convenient substitute for education in judging the skills of the immigrant population (and, given that not everyone acquired literacy through formal schooling, perhaps a better indicator of skills), great caution must be exercised in using the census figures. The census was by no means a literacy test: literacy was defined by the 1897 census as the ability to read. Read *what*, was never indicated, unfortunately. The instructions to the census takers stated that each person enumerated "should answer yes or no to the question, could he read in any language."[77] Thus it is quite likely that

75. *PM 1882*, II, pt.2, 226–27.

76. On the positive correlation of education/literacy and migration, see Alex Inkeles and David Smith, *Becoming Modern* (Cambridge, Mass., 1974), 15–35, 166–67, 354–56; and Barbara Anderson, "Who Chose the Cities? Migrants to Moscow and St. Petersburg Cities in the Late Nineteenth Century," in Donald Lee, ed., *Population Patterns in the Past* (New York, 1977), 277–95. For a refutation of the correlation of literacy and modern attitudes in a different context, see Kenneth A. Lockridge, *Literacy in Colonial New England* (New York, 1974); and Harvey Graff, *The Literacy Myth* (New York, 1979).

77. *Statisticheskie svedeniia o zhitel'iakh*, xix; *PVP*, pt. 2, xxii–xxv.

the literacy rates are inflated or at least reflect a wide range of conceptions of what the ability to read actually meant. Moreover, the census aggregates merely measure a person's literacy at the time *of the census*. There is no way for the historian to demonstrate when, where, or how literacy was acquired, regrettable because of the opportunities to acquire literacy after migration to Moscow.[78]

There can be no doubt that great strides were being made in the area of literacy at the end of the nineteenth century. Education and industrial skills were spreading rapidly in late-nineteenth-century Russia: the large commercial and manufacturing centers, as well as the imperial army, demanded more literate laborers and recruits, and the network of zemstvo and primary schools, as well as factory and vocational schools, was expanding to meet this demand. Two studies of Moscow province taken thirty years apart show that the laboring population was rapidly becoming literate. While barely one-quarter of Moscow province's workers surveyed in 1882 were literate, more than three-quarters were literate thirty years later.[79] The rapid spread of literacy is an uncontested fact. What is unclear is the effect of literacy on the migration experience: what were the differences in literacy between city and countryside, and did educational background (or literacy) promote or facilitate movement to the city? Were Moscow's immigrants, to put it more bluntly, the best and the brightest?

Contemporaries themselves were divided on this question. Moscow zemstvo correspondents, as well as Tugan-Baranovskii, contended that "whoever is more active, enterprising, able, and generally better armed for the struggle with the more complex conditions of city life" will end up abandoning the village, leaving the "dullards" (*serye*) behind.[80] On the other hand, Moscow's census compilers felt that the city was not receiving the most literate contingent from the village:

Unskilled workers, many categories of factory workers, domestic servants and certain other jobs which are the specialties of the immigrants in fact have a high percentage of illiterates. . . . On the contrary, the village annually sends

78. I. M. Bogdanov, *Gramotnost' i obrazovanie v dorevoliutsionnoi Rossii i v SSSR* (Moscow, 1964), 54–56.

79. E. N. Andreev, *Rabota maloletnikh v Rossii i Evrope* (St. Petersburg, 1884), 216; I. M. Koz'minykh-Lanin, *Gramotnost' i zarabotki fabrichno-zavodskikh rabochikh moskovskoi gubernii* (Moscow, 1912), 1–6; *Sbornik statisticheskikh svedenii po Moskovskoi gubernii*, vol. 3, no. 3; F. F. Erisman, *Sanitarnoe issledovanie fabrichnykh zavedenii Moskovskogo uezda Moskovskoi gubernii*, pts. 1–2 (Moscow, 1882), 1:216.

80. Tugan-Baranovskii, *Russkaia fabrika*, 389–90; S. N. Prokopovich, *Mestnye liudi o nuzhdakh Rossii* (St. Petersburg, 1904), 219.

hundreds of thousands of uneducated, truly ignorant persons who form the main contingent of illiterates in our cities.[81]

To begin with, since literacy rates were far higher in Moscow than in the province or in Russia as a whole,[82] it would appear that the city's immigrants were considerably more literate than their brethren who remained at home. The overall literacy rates, of course, conceal great differences between men and women and between young and old; moreover, since both the process of rural–urban migration and the acquisition of literacy are characteristics of the young, the literacy rates in Moscow were inflated owing to its high proportion of young males. In fact, literacy levels of young rural men (as well as of young men of the peasant estate) lagged only slightly behind those of their urban counterparts.[83] When P. Timofeev wrote that "now all apprentices come to the [urban] factory literate,"[84] he might well have added that even most young peasants who did *not* come to the factory were likewise literate. Similarly, a study of the clothing trades concluded that "no great difference in the degree of literacy" existed between urban and rural tailors.[85] Although overall literacy rates give a large "statistical" edge to the capital cities, the edge of Moscow was reduced to a few percentage points (see figure 7) when the capital's peasant males aged ten to thirty are compared with their rural counterparts. It would appear that immigrants from Moscow province were the best and the brightest because they were the youngest; of these, a cross section moved to Moscow.

It must be remembered that little more than a quarter of Moscow's immigrant population came from this province. Since more than half came from the seven provinces surrounding Moscow, it would be advisable to examine the literacy rates in these provinces as well.[86] When we examine these literacy rates, a slightly different picture emerges. Whereas 77 percent of the rural peasant males aged ten to nineteen of Moscow province were literate, only the highly literate province of Iaroslavl' exceeded the levels reached in Moscow province, and the provinces of Riazan', Tula, Kaluga, and Smolensk were noticeably not only below these levels but below the average for Euro-

81. GPD 1902, V: Gramotnost' naseleniia goroda Moskvy (Moscow, 1905), 16–17.
82. PVP, 24:12–14, 62–63; 24, pt. 2, 12–14; Bogdanov, Gramotnost', 38.
83. PVP, 24:12–14, 60–97; PVP, 24a, pt. 2, 12–14, 26–57.
84. P. Timofeev, "Zavodskie budni," Russkoe bogatstvo, no. 9 (September 1903), 183.
85. Oliunina, Portnovskii promysel, 188.
86. PM 1902, I, 1, ii, 28–45; PVP, 24:60–97.

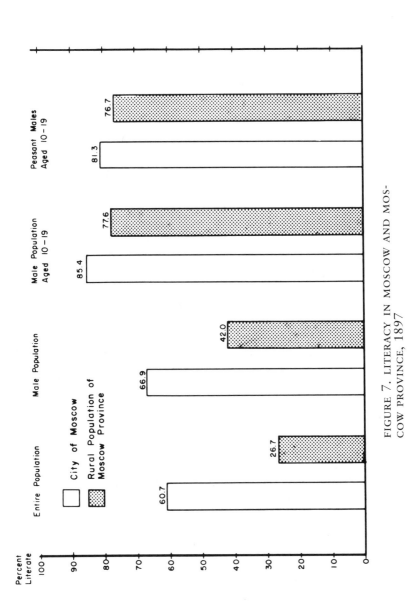

FIGURE 7. LITERACY IN MOSCOW AND MOS-
COW PROVINCE, 1897

Source: *PVP*, 24:12–14, 60–97; 24a, pt. 2, 12–14, 26–57.

pean Russia. It thus appears that more of a literacy gap existed between the old capital and the rural hinterlands farther away. Such a gap should not be too surprising: modest as public education was in Moscow province, it was considerably more widespread than in the more rural provinces of Tula, Riazan', Smolensk, and Kaluga.[87] These comparisons are all the more intriguing if we consider that the largest proportion of Moscow's peasants came from the lower literacy provinces of Tula, Riazan', Smolensk, and Kaluga.

The levels of literacy in the village varied markedly from county to county within each province. Indeed, ever since the studies of the Kostroma zemstvo in the 1890s, contemporaries and historians alike have generally accepted the correlation of higher literacy and a higher incidence of seasonal migratory labor. Dmitrii Zhbankov observed that while literacy among all Kostroma recruits in 1880 was 35.8 percent, it was 55.9 percent among recruits from counties of considerable migratory labor. Likewise, marriage registers of such counties showed higher than average literacy rates for girls. The fact that a boy who wanted to be a clerk or an errand boy needed to be literate forced his parents to be concerned about his learning the three R's. The need to correspond with family members in the big cities also had a positive effect on literacy in the villages.[88]

A close examination of literacy rates of the counties supplying a disproportionate share of Moscow's young peasant men reveals two distinct patterns. Within Moscow province itself, those counties which sent more than 20 percent of their male peasant populations—the markedly rural counties of Vereia, Mozhaisk, and Ruza on the western edge of the province and the semirural counties of Podol'sk and Zvenigorod closer to Moscow—all had lower than average literacy rates for peasant men aged ten to thirty. In addition, the province's nonfarming households (presumably containing many migrant laborers) had lower literacy levels than did farming households.[89] In the

---

87. *PVP*, table 9 in volumes 6, 15, 35, 40, 43, 44, 50. The average literacy rate in European Russia for both sexes in 1897 was 30 percent; that for Tula was 27 percent, Riazan', 27 percent, Kaluga, 26 percent, and Smolensk, 23 percent. (Bogdanov, *Gramotnost'*, 58–60.) The "youth factor" was important outside Moscow province as well: while 47 percent of some 3,000 workers in Tver' province surveyed in 1895 were literate, 77 percent of the boys aged 12–15 had acquired this skill. See V. N. Stanchinskii, "Gramotnost' rabochikh na nekotorykh zavedeniiakh Tverskoi gubernii," Vserossiiskii torgovo-promyshlennyi s"ezd 1896 g. v Nizhnem-Novgorode, *Trudy*, 6, vyp. 11 (St. Petersburg, 1897), 232–33.

88. Zhbankov, "O gorodskikh otkhozhikh zarabotkakh," 144.

89. *PVP*, 24:60–97; *PM 1902*, I, 2, i, 28–45; *Moskovskaia guberniia po mestnomu obsledovaniiu*, IV, pt.1, 105.

neighboring provinces the opposite pattern prevailed. With only a few exceptions, the counties which sent the largest proportion of their male peasants to Moscow had literacy rates that were higher than average for the given province, although lower than the average prevailing in Moscow province.[90]

Literacy levels in Moscow and in the countryside should still be compared with great caution even when sex, age, and social origin are taken into account. The factor of the acquisition of literacy is still unaccounted for. It is impossible to estimate how many of Moscow's young literate peasant men actually acquired their literacy after arrival in the city. The opportunities and the necessity for learning how to read were greater in the city for some elements in the population, and young peasant boys and men could have learned (or might have been forced to learn) this skill more quickly in the old capital than in their home village. The compilers of the 1902 census argued that, on the basis of school enrollments for the years 1898 to 1902, virtually all the illiterate boys of school age born outside the capital became literate in Moscow.[91] In the face of high dropout and truancy rates, one could question the equation of school enrollments with literacy.[92]

One also has to take into account the pride the compilers clearly felt in the advances made in municipal education. However, it is likely that the exaggerations in the acquisition of literacy by young newcomers through the municipal school system were offset by gains in literacy outside the school system and not surveyed by the census compilers. Such sources of literacy included parish schools, factory, vocational, and Sunday schools, as well as the workplace itself and the training as an apprentice or errand boy. Zemstvo surveys at the end of the nineteenth century showed that as many as half of those who could read acquired this skill outside the public school system. Zhbankov observed that many illiterate children from Kostroma who worked for a time in Petersburg returned having acquired literacy either from fellow apprentices or from their employers.[93] In fact, among boys aged 10–14 and 15–19, literacy rates increased with each additional year of residence in the city; while 85.8 percent of boys

90. PVP, vols. 6, 15, 25, 40, 43, 44—table 9 in each volume; PM 1902, I, 2, i, 28–45.

91. GPD 1902, V:18–21.

92. Eklof, "Spreading the Word," 191–223. See also Patrick L. Allston, Education and the State in Tsarist Russia (Stanford, 1969), 123–29, and Carlo M. Cipolla, Literacy and Development in the West (Baltimore, 1969), 32–33.

93. Zhbankov, "O gorodskikh otkhozhikh zarabotkakh," 145.

aged 10–14 residing less than two years in Moscow were literate, 95.1 percent of the boys of this age group who had already lived at least six years in the city were literate. The increase was even more dramatic among girls: almost 90 percent of the girls aged 10–14 and resident at least six years in the city were literate.[94] These opportunities outside the school were most important for the young peasant men in the age groups I have been examining, for the apprenticeship and initial experience on the job likely to impart the ability to read was experienced between the ages of 10 and 30 in most cases.

To summarize, literacy rates were generally high in Moscow province itself, especially among young males, and except for those from the western agricultural counties, immigrants reflected this feature. High also were literacy rates in certain counties of Vladimir, Tver', and Iaroslavl' with long traditions of urban-rural contact, as well as the counties of the remaining provinces that bordered Moscow province. However, the number of immigrants from the northern provinces was smaller in number and declining in proportion as more and more peasants were coming from Tula, Smolensk, Kaluga, and Riazan', provinces with lower than average literacy rates. Therefore, the concept of a "brain drain" of the more capable and literate peasantry to the cities which intensified the considerable disequilibrium between town and country and between literate city workers and illiterate villagers is too simplistic for the complex reality of urbanization.[95] Both as a magnet for the enterprising seeking opportunity and as a refuge for the down-and-out, Moscow attracted whatever the village had to offer, regardless of the level of literacy or educational background.

Educational background and literacy mattered to the authorities and reformers (and hence were noted by the census compilers) because these characteristics were frequently associated with occupational background. While many contemporaries assumed that the most skilled, like the most literate, were attracted to the city, others regarded the city as a mecca for the unskilled. Although a comparison of

94. *PM 1902*, I, 1, i, 14–19.

95. Equally simplistic is the argument that "modern attitudes" (measured by higher literacy of either the migrant himself or the migrant's region of origin) were a more decisive factor than the attraction of greater employment opportunities in the cities in causing rural–urban movement. See Gregory Guroff and S. Frederick Starr, "A Note on Urban Literacy in Russia, 1890–1914," *Jahrbücher für Geschichte Osteuropas*, 19, no. 4 (December 1971): 523–26, 529–30; and Anderson, "Who Chose the Cities?" 277–95. For a more extensive discussion, see my "Patterns of Peasant Migration to Late Nineteenth-Century Moscow: How Much Should We Read into Literacy Rates?" *Russian History*, 6, pt.1 (1979): 22–38.

the Moscow-born and the immigrants on the basis of a detailed occupational breakdown must wait until the following chapter, a few general points may be made here.

It will be recalled that many skilled factory workers of Moscow's hinterland, having local employment, did not need to move to Moscow; more likely than the factory worker to leave the village, as the census compilers pointed out, were unskilled laborers, domestic servants, and laborers in the construction and transport trades. As one Soviet historian has acknowledged:

The heads of absentee households [in the village] in the main engaged in trades not connected with the factory. A minority of the population leaving the village went off to the factory. . . . The majority of peasants became wage laborers in retail establishments, the construction industry, in forestry, in agriculture, in personal service, and in many other trades; in addition they applied their labor in various artisan trades or became part of the petite bourgeoisie— proprietors of taverns, inns, shops, truck gardens or other commercial establishments.[96]

Although certain counties in the hinterland had had long traditions of migratory labor, a given county by no means always sent its most skilled laborers to Moscow. The destinations of various laborers from Rzhev county, Tver' province, provides a suggestive example. Carpenters left chiefly for Petersburg and Novgorod provinces; sawyers left for the Volga and Dvina; spinners and hemp strippers went to the town of Rzhev; and unskilled laborers went to Petersburg and Moscow. The attraction of Moscow for common laborers is illustrated in the local reports of many other counties, including Korchev and Zubstov in Tver', Borov in Kaluga, Liubim in Iaroslavl', and Galich in Kostroma.[97]

In both bad times and good, occupational background may have meant less than a willingness to leave the village in shaping the composition of Moscow's immigrants. Tugan-Baranovskii contended that "the prospect of becoming a waiter, a shop assistant or a coachman seems positively enticing compared with the hard lot of the farmer burdened by intolerable payments. . . . It would be difficult to depict more vividly the city's power of attraction and the causes impelling the muzhik to flee from his native village to an alien and strange town."[98]

96. Rozhkova, Formirovanie, 27, 45, 48–49; Kurkin, Statistika, 10.
97. Entsiklopedicheskii slovar', "Borovsk," 7:432; "Galich," 14:922; "Zubtsov," 14:707; "Korcheva," 31:357; "Rzhev," 52:673.
98. Tugan-Baranovskii, Russkaia fabrika, 391.

According to one of the few peasant memoirs we have, such was the situation after the emancipation, when

all the strong, healthy and able fled the village for Moscow and got jobs wherever they could—some at the factory, others as domestics. Others turned into real entrepreneurs—the carrying trades, street vending, etc. All left—men, women, boys. . . . We eagerly awaited the time when we would be old enough to be fit for something in Moscow and when we could leave our native village and move there.[99]

Presumably in times of rapid economic expansion "all the enterprising left the village," and whatever their occupational background, "got jobs wherever they could."

A willingness to leave the village when opportunity beckoned was responsible for the large number of peasants who, regardless of occupational background, made frequent moves in and out of the city. The following example is typical of contemporary peasant "career patterns":

Andrei Petrovich Baidulin [born in Riazan' province in 1880] left for Moscow at the age of sixteen and became a driver in a sanitary brigade. Three years later he left for Kashira, where he worked for three years at a brick factory. After getting married in the village, he again returned to Moscow, where he worked for three years at a brick factory and six years in a truck garden. He then moved to Petersburg, where he worked successively as a coachman, superintendent, and porter at the Moscow railroad station.[100]

New workers who sought factory jobs in the spring to replace workers who left for home often had never worked at the factory or even in the same industry. One of the resulting banes of management, according to Schulze-Gävernitz, was the constant need to train workers.[101]

Reformers and the authorities feared that too many peasants with "undesirable" backgrounds were flocking to the city. This theme will merit more extensive discussion in Part Three. A few examples here, however, will be pertinent. The village, it was claimed, disgorged its paupers and ne'er-do-wells onto the roads leading to the great cities. Such was the image, literally, created by a report of one of imperial Russia's welfare agencies: "The Moscow-Petersburg highway is constantly crowded with travelers and drifters, either going to the capital for work or returning . . . often penniless, barefoot, tattered and

99. S. T. Semenov, *Dvadtsat' piat' let*, 5–6. See also Bulgakov, *Sovremennoe peredvizhenie*, 2.
100. *Ekspeditsii*, 147.
101. Schulze-Gävernitz, *Krupnoe proizvodstvo*, 116.

hungry."[102] The unemployed, the argument ran, were particularly prone to migration simply to find any sort of work. Most migrant laborers, such as those at Petersburg's Nikol'skii labor market in the novel *Working,* believed that there were always jobs in the big city.[103] In a study of pauperism in 1891, D. A. Linev claimed that the village unemployed streamed to the cities and in so doing made a telling observation concerning the relationship between village and city in Russia. Laborers looking for jobs

in some areas go to "Peter," in others to Moscow or Kiev. In a word, the village relies on the city not to defend its trampled rights but to fill its stomachs. The village, from time immemorial the producer, the provider of all the products of the land for the city, itself everywhere turns to the city for bread with empty hands, a hungry stomach and . . . with hope.[104]

This was particularly true after the 1892 famine. The Moscow zemstvo went so far as to consider public works projects to keep the city from being overburdened by unemployed peasants.[105] The situation was hardly improved fifteen years later, according to a British consular officer:

Although Moscow province is not one of the famine districts, being industrial and not agricultural, still the effects of the famine are felt here also. One of these is an influx of half-starved peasants who have come to find work or simply to beg in the streets. A result of this influx is an outbreak of typhus. . . . It is noteworthy that these cases are nearly all amongst the very poorest classes, and especially recent arrivals from the famine district.[106]

A proposal for a public shelter observed that even in normal years common laborers came to the city looking for work in the middle of the winter when grain was running out in the village.[107] As a census taker in the city's lodging houses in 1882, the novelist Tolstoi observed at firsthand the immigrants who were living off the city (*kormit'sia v gorode*). The writer was astounded by the number of rural paupers who looked to the city for survival:

---

102. Popechitel'stvo o trudovoi pomoshchi, *Sbornik svedenii po sostoiashchemu . . . popechitel'stvu o domakh trudoliubiia i rabotnykh domakh* (St. Petersburg, 1901), 105–6.

103. Leikin, *Na zarabotkakh,* 81. See also Maksimov, *Proiskhozhdenie nishchenstva,* 28.

104. D. A. Linev, *Prichiny russkogo nishchenstva i neobkhodimye protiv nikh mery* (St. Petersburg, 1891), 11–12, 31.

105. TsGAM, f. 16, op. 125, d. 313.

106. "Report for the Year 1906 on the Trade and Agriculture of the Consular District of St. Petersburg," no. 3797, 5.

107. "Priiut dlia chernorabochikh," *Russkaia mysl',* 3, no. 2 (February 1882):105.

Without exception they say that they have come here from the villages to subsist, that Moscow doesn't sow or reap and yet lives well, and that in Moscow they can get the kind of money needed in the village for grain, for shelter, for a horse, for the basic necessities.[108]

"Populous and fertile is Moscow" (*Moskva liudna i khlebna*) goes a Russian folk saying, and knowing the Russian village, it is not hard to see why.[109]

Not all those who came to the city with outstretched hands had honorable intentions, according to a 1900 study of poverty. The residents of entire villages, such as Shuvalovo in Vereia county, allegedly engaged in begging as a side-occupation and every spring headed to Moscow and posed as monks collecting money for Mount Athos or for cripples. "Upon their return home, the villagers of Shuvalovo have their wedding feasts and get roaring drunk."[110] Other studies confirmed that Vereia and the rural districts west of Moscow which sent the greatest number of peasants to the city also sent a disproportionate number of paupers.[111] Likewise, 1,500 registered beggars annually left Rzhev county, Tver' province, for Moscow and the Trinity-Sergius Monastery.[112] The old capital's network of municipal and private facilities of poor relief and the ample opportunities for begging on the steps of its cathedrals, churches, monasteries, convents, and shrines could never have been matched by Vereia or Vladimir, Rzhev or Riazan'.

Other immigrants drifted into the city just for relief from stifling village life, and of course the drifter figured prominently in the rogues' gallery of social reformers everywhere. One of the wards of the Moscow Workhouse in S. Podiachev's novella *Mytarstvo* (The Ordeal) tries to explain why he came to the city:

I don't even know myself! I oughtn't to have left home. . . . It's just my wicked nature, that's all! Things somehow soon bore me. For example, my wife is beautiful, kind, wonderful. I can't tell you how much I love her. We'd been married a total of three years, and you know, frankly, I left home mainly because of her. . . . My mother, a former serf, is already over seventy. I'm a *meshchanin* registered in Zvenigorod, about fifty versts from the landlord. There's a vegetable garden and a meadow. We've a cow, a horse, chickens, in short everything except money. But we can manage. I told my mother: "How

108. Tolstoi, "Tak chto zhe nam delat'?" 57.
109. Dal', *Russkie narodnye poslovitsy*, 127.
110. A. A. Levenstim, *Professional'noe nishchenstvo, ego prichiny i formy: Bytovye ocherki* (St. Petersburg, 1900), 78–79.
111. L. D. Raevskii, "K voprosu o nishchenstve v Moskve," *IMGD*, 34, no. 1 (January 1910):1–12.
112. "Rzhev," *Entsiklopedicheskii slovar'*, 52:673.

am I going to stay here all winter with nothing to do but sit on the stove with you? I'll get a job and come back in the spring when I'm ready." "You don't need a job at all," my mother said; "you just want to have a good time and get drunk. Oh, all right, get going, and God be with you."[113]

Peasant budget studies of the 1920s suggest that occupational and educational experience created the following immigration pattern: persons of average skill levels and educational backgrounds as well as of average farming abilities tended to stay in agriculture, whereas both the well-off, highly skilled, and motivated, on the one hand, and the poor, unskilled, and ne'er-do-wells, on the other, left for the cities.[114] To put it another way, the cities attracted not only the adventuresome entrepreneurs and highly skilled workers and technicians, many with extensive experience in nonagricultural trades and migratory labor, but also the common laborers and the dullards. This explains the fact that while reformers nervously pointed to the immigration of the poor and the failures and the seeming drifting of unskilled laborers, the overall high literacy rates suggested that most immigrants were not deficient in literacy or skills. Given the large number of peasant immigrants and the lack of intervening opportunities, the immigrants' skills and literacy were acquired in the main at home or while pursuing local trades rather than in another town.

The economic, social, and demographic characteristics of Moscow's hinterland discussed in chapter 1, as well as the continuing ties with the village and the urban, educational, and occupational backgrounds of the immigrants just examined, played an important role in the immigration experience. The village background was doubly significant because the experience of immigration was rarely a onetime experience but was, like the usage of the imperfective aspect, often troubling to students of the Russian language, "repeated action." All of these factors had a statistical effect on the city's population, particularly on its labor force, to be summarized in the concluding section.

A STATISTICAL PROFILE
OF THE IMMIGRANTS

When analyzing the characteristics of the immigrant population, one is faced at the outset with a serious problem. Given the unavail-

113. S. P. Podiachev, "Mytarstvo," *Izbrannoe* (Moscow, 1955), 50–51.
114. Pitrim Sorokin, Carle C. Zimmerman, and Charles Galpin, *A Systematic Source Book in Rural Sociology*, 3 vols. (Minneapolis, 1932), 3:494–98, 509.

ability of unpublished materials, particularly passport records and city residence permits, one is forced here, as in many other areas, to use the aggregates of the published census. These record information about the immigrants at the time of the census, not at the moment of the entry into the city. Thus, although many census tables conveniently separate the immigrants from the Moscow-born, the former category already had some years of residence in Moscow. If one considers that in 1902 the average length of residence in Moscow exceeded five years, then a peasant could have changed his legal status to townsman (*meshchanin*), a bachelor could have married, an illiterate could have learned to read, and a ditchdigger could have become a factory worker. In fact, the only characteristics that were not subject to change were place of birth and, barring the discovery by a Russian Foucault of kinky practices among the Moscow populace, sex. Wherever the census compilations permit, I shall consider the immigrant who had resided less than one year in the city to represent best the immigrants at moment of entry.[115]

Moscow's immigrant labor force was predominantly male. For every 1,000 male immigrants in 1882 there were 625 female immigrants. The proportion among the entire population was 737 women for every 1,000 men. Although the proportion of women was growing slowly, it is striking that twenty years later there were still only 677 immigrant women for every 1,000 immigrant men.[116] A boy's or a man's opportunities for migration were particularly noticeable in the group aged ten to twenty-nine, which had approximately twice as many men as women.[117] Moscow had a young population and, as might be expected, this was particularly true of its immigrants. Figure 8 shows the age structure of immigrants at the time of arrival. In 1882 the median age of the immigrants was just under twenty-five; twenty years later the median age had dropped to twenty-two.[118] Thus the migration stream not only was youthful, it was getting even younger. The largest numbers of immigrants were entering the Moscow labor market at an age of early entry onto the labor market. In addition, the

115. Two tables of the 1902 census did subdivide the immigrant population according to the number of years resident in Moscow. Those resident less than one year come the closest to the abstraction "the immigrant at moment of entry." Unfortunately, age, gender, and estate group are the only characteristics we can learn about such immigrants. (See *PM 1902*, I, 1, i, 6–8, 11.)
116. *PM 1882*, II, pt. 2, 1, 41; *PM 1902*, I, 1, i, 6–8.
117. *PM 1882*, II, pt. 1, 50.
118. *PM 1882*, II, pt. 1, 51–52; *PM 1902*, I, 1, i, 6–8.

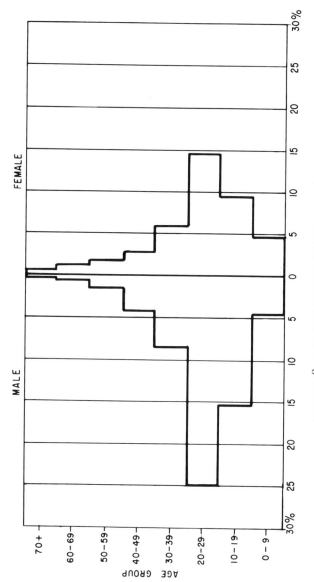

FIGURE 8. AGE STRUCTURE OF IMMIGRANTS
AT MOMENT OF ENTRY INTO MOSCOW, 1902
The closest censal category to immigrants at
the moment of entry into Moscow is of
those who had resided in the city less than
one year. The numbers along the horizontal
axis represent the percentage of the total
immigrant population of 115,000.

Source: *PM 1902*, I, 1, i, 6–8.

increased proportion of immigrants under age four suggests that more
children too young to become apprentices were coming to the cities
with their parents. Knowing the median age of all immigrants and also
for those immigrants resident less than one year allows us to estimate
the median length of residence of the immigrant population. Table 2
shows the results for men and women in 1882 and 1902. The immigrant population was by no means exclusively transient, or to put it
differently, for each person who had lived in the city less than one
year, almost three had been resident ten or more years. Yet there is no
evidence of increasing persistence of residence: if anything, just the
opposite, a fact that alarmed reformers, as later chapters will show.

It has already been established that although women were coming to the city in increasing numbers, males still decidedly predominated among the immigrant population, and that the immigrants
were youthful and becoming even younger. Was the city more
attractive to the single or to the married immigrant? The immigrant
population, and males in particular, was far more likely than the
native-born to be married. It would certainly be incorrect to think
of hordes of men without families descending on Moscow from the
countryside, although this image was prominent in the eyes of reformers. Among the immigrants, men were far more likely than
women to be married. It is, of course, conceivable that the men
who came to the city either brought their wives with them or married Muscovite girls soon after arrival. A closer look at the data,
however, shows that this was far from possible. If one were to assume for a moment that all 131,607 married immigrant women
plus the 7,717 excess married Muscovite women were married to
immigrant men, there still would have been 118,000 "extra" married immigrant men whose wives were, presumably, back in the
villages.[119] Since it is highly unlikely that all immigrant women
were married to other immigrant residents in Moscow, the figure
118,000 is no doubt conservative: it is likely that half of the married immigrant men had their wives living elsewhere.

Yet the image of married men coming to Moscow and leaving their
wives and families behind is oversimplified. Males resident less than
one year in the city had a smaller proportion married than had all
immigrant males. Just the opposite was true for women. Although

---

119. *PM 1902*, I, 1, i, 9–10. For the sake of argument, I assume that all native men
married native women. The remainder of the native women thereby "available" for
native men constitutes the "excess."

TABLE 2   PERSISTENCE OF IMMIGRANTS' RESIDENCE IN MOSCOW

Years Resident in Moscow	1882		1902	
	Immigrants	Percent	Immigrants	Percent
1 or less	83,502	15.2	115,290	14.6
1–2	37,906	6.9	53,416	6.7
2–3	36,258	6.6	56,715	7.2
3–4	29,665	5.4	47,816	6.1
4–5	20,876	3.8	37,086	4.7
5–6	20,876	3.8	41,239	5.2
6–7	21,425	3.9	30,090	3.8
7–8	16,481	3.0	26,677	3.4
8–9	13,734	2.5	25,897	3.3
9–10	19,777	3.6	14,950	1.9
0–10	320,824	58.4	449,176	56.9
11–15	—	—	122,350	15.4
16–20	—	—	76,755	9.6
21–25	—	—	41,195	5.2
26–30	—	—	41,402	5.2
31+	—	—	53,494	6.8
11 or more	228,533	41.6	335,196	42.4
Not known	—	—	6,227	0.8
All immigrants	549,357	100.0	790,599	100.0

Source: *PM 1882*, II, pt. 1, 49–50; *PM 1902*, I, 1, i, 8.
Note: Half the immigrants had resided in Moscow eight years or less in 1882; half had resided seven years or less in 1902.

among all immigrants a far higher proportion of men than of women were married, among the immigrants at the moment of entry into Moscow, the women had a higher proportion of married.[120] It would seem that men had more opportunities for marriage after arrival in the city than women had. Robert Johnson has argued that the bifurcated peasant household actually promoted marriage such that immigrant peasants working in the city had higher marriage rates than either

120. *GPD 1902*, IV:8–10.

city-born workers or peasants who stayed home.[121] It is likely that the extra cash or capital amassed in the city allowed immigrants to return to the village for marriage; such behavior would produce lower marriage rates among men who had just arrived in the city and higher marriage rates among all immigrant men. Although more and more single women were entering the city, the overall custom of the married woman to join her husband continued to prevail. That 21.5 percent of all immigrant women were widows suggests that a funeral was almost as likely for the married woman as was a wedding for the single girl during their Moscow sojourns.

So large was the immigrant population that no part of the city was unaware of the immigrant experience. In fact, in 1902 only one precinct, Iakimanka 2, had a proportion of immigrants under two-thirds. As table 3 shows, one precinct, Gorod, and four suburban settlements were more than 80 percent immigrant. Several central commercial precincts had higher proportions of immigrants than many outer factory districts. However, the striking characteristic of these figures is their uniformity. Similarly uniform was the length of residence of the immigrants in the various precincts of the city. The three precincts that did have more than 40 percent of the most recent arrivals—Khamovniki 1, Lefort 3, and Serpukhov 2—also had the city's three major barracks. Furthermore, this uniformity held for both 1882 and 1902.[122] Thus there was no marked tendency for immigrants, either at moment of entry or later during their sojourn in the city, to congregate in distinctly "immigrant" neighborhoods.

A combination of tradition, connections, the attraction of certain places of employment, and simple geographical proximity governed individual settlement decisions. Moscow was a large and sprawling city, and it might be assumed that, all other things being equal, immigrants would reside on that side of town closest to their native village. In many cases this was exactly what happened. The highest proportion of immigrants from the eastern county of Bogorodsk ended up in the east-side wards of Rogozh' and Lefort; the highest proportion of immigrants from the western county of Zvenigorod ended up in the west- and northwest-side wards of Sushchevo, Presnia, and Khamovniki; the highest proportion of immigrants from the

---

121. Johnson, "Family Relations and the Rural-Urban Nexus: Patterns in the Hinterland of Moscow, 1880–1900," in Ransel, ed., *The Family*, 267–72.
122. *PM 1902*, I, 1, iii, 109–11.

TABLE 3   IMMIGRANTS AND PRECINCT OF RESIDENCE, 1902

Precinct		Total Population	Immigrants	Percent Immigrants
Gorod		18,231	15,280	83.8
Tver'	1	16,612	11,927	71.8
	2	29,295	22,757	77.7
	3	17,753	13,946	78.6
Miasniki	1	19,337	15,261	78.9
	2	14,062	10,686	76.0
	3	21,676	15,847	73.1
Prechistenka	1	22,044	15,191	68.9
	2	20,563	14,482	70.4
Arbat	1	19,411	13,834	71.3
	2	21,974	15,800	71.9
Sretenka	1	22,409	16,581	74.0
	2	26,866	19,694	73.3
Iauza	1	14,677	10,426	71.0
	2	18,187	13,264	72.9
Khamovniki	1	33,165	25,887	78.1
	2	34,031	24,518	72.0
Presnia	1	27,911	19,914	71.3
	2	24,065	16,510	68.6
	3	29,219	19,667	67.3
Sushchevo	1	43,331	30,121	69.5
	2	31,286	23,897	76.4
	3	43,148	30,081	69.7
Meshchane	1	29,739	21,930	73.7
	2	19,475	13,925	71.5
	3	46,088	31,351	68.0
	4	26,531	19,144	72.1
Basman	1	24,776	17,792	71.8
	2	20,634	15,065	73.0
Lefort	1	41,491	29,242	70.5
	2	19,375	15,136	78.1
	3	19,484	14,697	75.4
Rogozh'	1	22,596	15,982	70.7
	2	48,020	32,901	68.5
	3	42,463	31,181	73.4

TABLE 3 (*continued*)

Precinct		Total Population	Immigrants	Percent Immigrants
Iakimanka	1	24,380	17,259	70.8
	2	30,316	19,859	65.5
Piatnitsa	1	29,028	20,596	71.0
	2	39,015	29,161	74.7
Serpukhov	1	10,372	7,044	67.9
	2	29,318	22,295	76.0
Suburb				
Mar'ina roshcha		21,951	16,151	73.6
Krestovskaia sloboda		3,142	2,414	76.8
Cherkizovo		11,876	7,830	65.9
Blagusha		8,618	6,671	77.4
Alekseevskaia sloboda		4,096	2,923	71.4
Novaia Andronovka		3,302	2,580	78.1
Khokhlovka		1,543	1,151	74.6
Simonovskaia sloboda		1,934	1,567	81.0
Nizhnekotlovskiia		9,268	7,564	81.6
Vorob'evy gory		2,185	1,252	57.3
Dorogomilovo		4,532	3,737	82.5
Za Trekhgornoi zastavoi		4,479	3,526	78.7
Khodynskoe pole		2,912	2,766	95.0
Petrovsko-Razumovskoe		2,475	1,651	66.7

Source: *PM 1902*, I, 1, 3, 106–108, 143–45.

northern county of Klin ended up in the north-side wards of Sushchevo and Meshchane.[123] Such a correlation of county of origin and ward of settlement did not always prevail. Immigrants from the two western counties of Volokolamsk and Mozhaisk, for example, settled in Presnia in notably different proportions and in Lefort in higher proportions than expected. Kinship or village ties, such as *zemliachestvo*, or the simple power of attraction of the myriad of mills in Lefort to an immigrant with no relatives or connections, accounted for such varieties of settlement. Finally, traditional occupa-

123. *PM 1882*, II, pt.2, 214–15, 220–31; *PM 1902*, I, 3, i, table II.

tion patterns explain in part the distribution of immigrants from a particular county or province. Immigrants from Iaroslavl', for example, were overrepresented in commercial occupations and accordingly settled in large numbers in the Tver' ward.

The foregoing has summarized the most readily measurable characteristics of the immigrant population as a whole. The "typical" immigrant of 1900 was a male born in one of the counties of Moscow or of the contiguous provinces (such as Tula or Riazan'), was one of two to three million who had come to the city during the preceding two decades, was married, was aged twenty-one or twenty-two, and was slightly more literate than his more sedentary fellow villagers and slightly less literate than his Moscow-born peers. Immigrants were drawn to the city by the need for income, by the opportunity to escape village burdens and routines, and by the presence of kin and fellow villagers. They settled wherever family or contacts offered them a place to stay or a place to work, or wherever job opportunities beckoned, but not in any distinctive immigrant ghettos.

The immigration experience was of profound importance for the city's population. The great majority of an adult population of one million were immigrants, and a large number of these retained family or other important connections with their place of birth. Many newcomers themselves were transient and not only immigrated more than once but experienced coming and going almost constantly—if they themselves were not coming and going, then surely a husband, wife, brother, uncle, or child was. Furthermore, in the hinterland Moscow was perceived as both a refuge and a land of opportunity. The result was a two-track immigration pattern of the enterprising, literate, and skilled along with the down-and-out and itinerant common laborers. The former group was in a better position to take advantage of the opportunities of the metropolis; the second group was more vulnerable to the erratic nature of the job and housing markets and was an object of concern to the authorities and reformers. With the exception of dependents and of the vagabonds and paupers who so caught the eye of the authorities and reformers, newcomers immediately upon entry in the city cast their lot with natives on the labor force. Their placement on the labor force is one of several issues to be examined in the following chapter.

CHAPTER FIVE

The Labor Force

On arrival in the city, or on reaching adolescence for most natives, the muzhik entered a rapidly expanding and increasingly diversified labor force. Placement on the labor force was arguably the single most important factor determining the muzhik's experience in the city. In turn, placement depended on many factors, including the structure of the labor force at any one time, changes in this stucture, and individual career responses to these changes. Despite the importance of Russia's urban labor force and recent studies of labor and the workaday world, there has been, surprisingly, no systematic analysis of the structure of the labor force, let alone of individual placement and occupational changes.[1] This chapter will examine the major divisions of the labor force and structural changes over time, the influence of immigration on placement in the labor force, individual occupational changes, and upward and downward occupational mobility.

1. See Zelnik, *Labor and Society,* and "Russian Bebels: An Introduction to the Memoirs of Semen Kanatchikov and Matvei Fisher," *Russian Review,* 35, no. 3 (July 1976): 249–89, and no. 4 (October 1976): 417–47; Koenker, *Moscow Workers;* Engelstein, *Moscow, 1905;* Johnson, *Peasant and Proletarian;* Bater, "Transience," and *St. Petersburg;* Bonnell, *Roots of Rebellion,* and "Urban Working Class Life in early Twentieth-Century Russia: Some Problems and Patterns," *Russian History,* 8, pt. 3 (1981): 360–78; Brower, "Urban Russia on the Eve of World War I," and "Labor Violence in Russia in the Late Nineteenth Century," *Slavic Review,* 41, no. 3 (Fall 1982): 417–31; and the comments by Robert Johnson, Ronald Suny, and Diane Koenker. Three recent Soviet studies of Russian labor are E. E. Kruze, *Polozhenie rabochego klassa Rossii v 1900–1914 gg.* (Leningrad, 1976); and *Usloviia truda i byta rabochego klassa Rossii v 1900–1914 godakh* (Leningrad, 1981); and Iu. I. Kir'ianov, *Zhiznennyi uroven' rabochikh Rossii* (Moscow, 1979); see also my review of the latter in *Kritika,* 17, no. 2 (Summer 1981): 87–103.

STRUCTURE OF THE LABOR FORCE

One immediately notices the large size of Moscow's work force relative to the entire population. Moscow, like Petersburg but unlike other European metropolises at the time, had a high and virtually unchanging proportion of self-supporting (sometimes called "active") persons. The proportion of the total population in the labor force declined by only six percentage points from 1882 to 1912: from 71 to 65 percent. Most of this decline, however, occurred from 1902 to 1912, and the better years after 1909 were more favorable for the support of dependents in the city. Indeed, while the entire labor force increased by 41 percent during this decade, the number of dependents increased by 68 percent.[2] These proportions do conceal sharp differences between men and women. In 1912 more than three-fourths of the total male population was in the labor force. The number of female dependents was customarily more than double the number of male dependents. Notably, the 1912 census recorded for the first time that more women were dependent than were in the labor force.[3] The continued large proportion of active persons reflects the particular stage of industrialization of the Russian economy, the demand for a dynamic metropolitan work force, and the large proportion of peasant immigrants unable to support or house dependents, an object of concern to the authorities and reformers.

The census compilers grouped the labor force into several broad categories reflecting the terms of employment. As table 4 illustrates, the main categories were owner, salaried employee, and wage laborer. An amalgam of many disparate subgroups, this categorization was meant to reflect the differences among owners (*khoziaeva*), salaried employees (*sluzhashchie*), and wage laborers (*rabochie*) employed in manufacturing, construction, commerce, and transport; those employed in personal and professional service were grouped separately. The owners included employers of wage labor, employers of members of their own family, and the single proprietors (*khoziaeva-odinochki*).

2. *GPD 1902*, VI:3; *SEMMG*, 68–73. At the turn of the century 69.1 percent of Moscow's population was "active"; by comparison the proportion in St. Petersburg was 66.2 percent, in Paris, 62.0 percent, in Vienna, 55.1 percent.
3. See note 2 above.

TABLE 4   MAJOR POSITIONS OF LABOR FORCE

Terms of employment	1882 Labor Force		1902 Labor Force		1912 Labor Force	
	Number	Percent	Number	Percent	Number	Percent
Owners, proprietors (khoziaeva)	69,923	13.0	72,521	9.6	110,129	10.5
Salaried employees (sluzhashchie)	20,022	3.7	57,431	7.6	92,375	8.8
Wage laborers (rabochie)	176,969	32.9	305,050	40.4	403,322	38.4
Apprentices (ucheniki)[a]	35,348	6.6	45,651	6.0	57,296	5.5
Domestic servants (prisluga)[b]	73,385	13.6	78,728	10.4	99,074	9.4
Other self-supporting[c]	162,425	30.2	188,721	25.0	289,067	27.5
Total self-supporting population	538,072	100.0	755,226	100.0	1,051,263	100.0
Dependents[d]	215,397	28.6	337,134	30.9	565,152	35.0
Total population	753,469		1,092,360		1,616,415	

Source: PM 1882, pt. 2, 101–340; PM 1902, I, 2, i, 116–97; SEMMG, 68–73.
[a] In 1902 and 1912 includes family members working for the head of the business
(pomogaiushchie v promysle chleny sem'i).
[b] In 1882 does not include the occupation of building superintendent (dvornik).
[c] Includes professionals, employees of public and private institutions, clergy, rentiers,
and pensioners, those receiving institutional or family support, day laborers, the unemployed.
[d] Figure represents dependents as percentage of total population.

It is unclear how rigorously these distinctions were made, and although the employers of family members could be regarded as an intermediate group between the other two, I have frequently grouped them with the single proprietors in a category "self-employed." The categories salaried employees and wage laborer were both subdivided according to branch of the economy: manufacturing, transport, and commerce. The first of these subdivisions was in turn divided into factory employment and employment in other forms of manufacturing; the third was in turn divided into employment in the real estate, housing, and restaurant business and in retailing and finance.

While the entire labor force almost doubled from 1882 to 1912, the number of owners of all categories increased by only 63 percent. As we have seen, this growth was much more rapid during the years 1902–1912 than during the years 1882–1902. The overall percentage increase also conceals differences between employers and the self-employed; whereas the former grew steadily from 1882 to 1912, the latter actually declined in number from 1882 to 1902 and then increased dramatically by 1912. Likewise, the overall percentage increase conceals sectoral differences. From 1882 to 1902 manufacturing experienced a striking decline in the number of self-employed and only a modest increase in the number of employers. In retailing and services, on the other hand, the self-employed were less hard hit, and the number of employers increased by 62 percent. (Sectoral data are not available for 1912.)

The greatest relative gain during these three decades came among the salaried employees. The share of the group in the labor force increased from 3.7 percent in 1882 to 8.8 percent in 1912 as its numbers increased by 350 percent. Such an increase is all the more noteworthy considering that these figures represent only salaried employees working in the manufacturing and commercial sectors of the economy; those employees of government or private institutions were grouped in the category personal and professional service and were excluded from these figures.

Wage laborers clearly constituted the largest category of self-supporting persons: from 176,969 in 1882, this group more than doubled in size during the next thirty years, a rate of increase greater than that of the labor force as a whole. At the turn of the century wage laborers constituted 40 percent of the labor force, a jump from 33 percent twenty years earlier. However, this proportion may have peaked sometime around 1902; by 1912 wage laborers constituted 38 percent

TABLE 5 TERMS OF EMPLOYMENT AND GENDER

Terms of Employment	1882				1902				1912			
	Men	Women	Total	Percent Men	Men	Women	Total	Percent Men	Men	Women	Total	Percent Men
Employers	22,133	6,533	28,666	77.2	24,799	8,269	33,068	75.0	32,600	11,263	44,223	73.7
Proprietors with family labor	—	—	—	—	3,556	1,384	4,940	72.0	5,047	1,748	6,795	74.3
Self-employed	27,115	14,142	41,257	65.7	22,186	12,327	34,513	64.3	33,622	25,489	59,111	56.9
All owners	49,248	20,675	69,923	70.4	50,541	21,980	72,521	69.7	71,269	38,860	110,129	64.7
Employees, factory	4,958	1,244	6,202	79.9	7,153	323	7,476	95.7	—	—	—	—
Employees, other manufacturing					3,014	319	3,333	90.4	—	—	—	—
Employees, transport	559	3	562	99.5	10,427	1,354	11,781	88.5	—	—	—	—
Employees, lodging and restaurant	1,247	80	1,327	94.0	2,979	210	3,189	93.4	—	—	—	—
Employees, retailing	11,435	496	11,931	95.8	29,662	1,990	31,652	93.7	—	—	—	—
All employees	18,199	1,823	20,022	90.9	53,235	4,196	57,431	92.7	81,541	10,834	92,375	88.3
Factory workers	114,703	26,629	153,263	74.8	78,056	29,725	107,781	72.4	115,189	49,995	165,184	69.7
Workers, other manufacturing					82,550	24,551	107,101	77.1	97,294	29,549	126,843	76.7

	Male	Female	Total	%	Male	Female	Total	%	Male	Female	Total	%
Workers, transport	9,056	8	9,064	99.9	37,227	452	37,679	98.8	⎫			
Workers, lodging and restaurant	12,166	965	13,131	92.7	29,711	1,936	31,647	96.1	⎬ 106,083	5,212	111,295	95.3
Workers, retailing	13,301	141	13,442	99.0	19,688	1,154	20,842	94.5	⎭			
All workers	149,226	27,743	176,969	84.3	247,232	57,818	305,050	81.0	318,566	84,756	403,322	79.0
Family members working for head of household	—	—	—	—	8,488	4,507	12,995	65.3	9,377	6,260	15,637	60.0
Apprentices	27,864	7,484	35,348	78.8	24,724	7,932	32,656	75.7	30,827	10,832	41,659	74.0
Domestic servants	27,017	58,400	85,417	31.6	7,965	70,763	78,728	10.1	6,761	92,313	99,074	6.8
Day laborers	2,679	2,608	5,287	50.7	6,212	2,706	8,918	69.7	8,811	3,586	10,751	82.0
Unemployed	—	—	—	—	11,755	6,326	18,081	65.0	19,720	9,692	29,412	67.0
Other self-supporting	94,248	50,858	145,106	65.0	96,064	72,782	168,846	56.9	139,755	109,149	248,904	56.1
Total self-supporting	368,481	169,591	538,072	68.5	506,216	249,010	755,226	67.0	684,981	366,282	1,051,263	65.2
Dependents	63,966	151,431	215,397	29.7	106,787	230,347	337,134	31.7	191,421	373,731	565,152	33.9
Total population	432,447	321,022	733,469	59.0	613,003	479,357	1,092,360	56.1	876,402	740,013	1,616,415	59.0

Source: *PM 1882*, II, pt. 2, 101–340; *PM 1902*, 1, 2, i, 116–97; *SEMMG*, 68–73.

of the labor force.[4] As table 5 shows, three rather distinct groups of wage laborers emerge from the censuses: factory hands, concentrated in the textile industry; workers in small-scale workshops and artisanal establishments; and laborers in construction, transport, and retailing. Although the total number of wage laborers increased at a faster rate than that for the labor force as a whole, this increase was not uniform for all kinds of wage laborers. Factory workers, for example, increased by 150 percent from 1882 to 1912 and even increased by more than 50 percent in the decade 1902–1912, a time when all wage laborers increased by only 33 percent.[5]

As a result of the differing rates of growth, the structure of the labor force shifted from 1882 to 1912. This overall shift was the net result of changes from 1882 to 1902 and again from 1902 to 1912, as well as of smaller annual changes not reflected in the census. By 1912 the labor force contained relatively more salaried employees and wage laborers (and in particular factory workers) and relatively fewer owners, apprentices, and persons employed in personal and professional service. However, during the period 1882–1902 the increase in wage laborers and the decrease in owners was particularly noticeable. During the second period, these trends reversed themselves: owners enjoyed a slight relative increase, and wage laborers experienced a slight relative decrease. Both salaried employees and persons employed in personal and professional service experienced constant increases and decreases, respectively.

Of the three census years, the national and local economies were healthiest in 1912. The expansion of business enterprise from 1902 to 1912 was reflected in both the absolute and the relative increase in the number of owners, and especially of the self-employed; the increasing sophistication and diversification of the economy was reflected in the increase in the number of salaried employees. The relative decline during this decade in the number of wage laborers would seem unexpected. This decline paralleled a slight decline in the proportion of newcomers in the labor force as a whole, and it is likely that expanding opportunities in the village may have kept some potential wage laborers home. At the same time, the expanding metropolitan economy provided more opportunity for the marginal producer or proprietor. Indeed, the category single proprietor experienced a greater than average increase. However, since the increase in the number of factory

4. *PM 1882*, II, pt. 2, 101–340; *PM 1902*, I, 2, i, 116–59; *SEMMG*, 68–73.
5. See note 4 above.

workers exceeded the average, and the number of workers in other manufacturing establishments was less than average, it is not likely that the expansion of small enterprises took place in manufacturing. Since smaller than average gains occurred among wage laborers in transportation and commerce, it is likely that these sectors demonstrated the greatest opportunity for the marginal businessman.

Placement and structural shifts such as those just described were not uniform for men and women, as table 5 shows. At the top, among owners women were found in proportion to their total representation in the labor force. This was largely due to their relatively better representation among the single proprietors and self-employed, though one-quarter of even the employers were women. Women were most poorly represented among the salaried employees, almost 90 percent of whom were men. Women actually lost ground to men from 1882 to 1902, then gained ground during the decade 1902–1912. The category wage laborer included a slightly higher, and increasing, proportion of women than did the category salaried employees. By 1912 one in five wage laborers was female. Of all forms of wage labor, the factory in general, and the textile mills in particular, hired the largest number of women, and by 1912 almost one in three factory workers was female. Not surprisingly, transport employed a miniscule proportion of women; also miniscule were the number of women wage laborers in retailing and in the lodging and restaurant business. Domestic service was the largest single employer of women. In 1912 almost twice as many women were employed in domestic service as in the factories; even the total number of female wage laborers did not exceed the number of female domestic servants. More noteworthy, domestic service was becoming an almost exclusively female job: whereas in 1882 less than 70 percent of all domestic servants had been women, by 1912, 93 percent were women. Such increasing gender stratification at the lower levels of manual labor offset the slight gains women were experiencing at the top, particularly in ownership positions.

Gender differences in the labor force are displayed even more sharply when marital status is taken into account. Whereas more than four of every five male owners were married, only one in three female owners was married. The difference was even greater among salaried employees: only 723 of 4,191 female employees were married. The highest proportion of married women was found among wage laborers, particularly among factory workers, nearly half of whom were married. The great excess of widows over widowers provides a partial explanation for the higher proportion of unmarried women. However, the fact that the proportion of married women consistently lagged behind the proportion of married men even in the group aged twenty-five to forty suggests that widowhood was not the only factor. Increasing opportunities allowed more and more single women to find spots in the labor force.[6]

That women were able to enter the labor force most easily in low-skilled occupations, such as domestic service, is confirmed by data on the terms of employment and literacy, as is shown in table 6. The category having the smallest proportion of women, salaried employees, also had the highest literacy rates—a phenomenal 98.3 percent for the group as a whole. At the other end of the scale, only 31.7 percent of all domestics (and only 27 percent of female domestics) were literate. The literacy rate for all owners—69.5 percent—was not notably high and conceals a sharp difference within the group between employers, 80 percent of whom were literate, and the self-employed, barely 60 percent of whom were literate. Likewise, the literacy rate for all wage laborers conceals sharp differences. Surprisingly, of the major subgroups, factory workers had the lowest literacy rates; wage laborers in retailing were twice as likely to know how to read or write as were their factory brethren. In all categories where the proportion of women was near or above average (domestics, factory workers, self-employed, for example), the literacy rates were markedly lower than in those occupations (employers, salaried employees, wage laborers in retailing, for example) with below average proportions of women.

As the literacy rates show, skill levels determined placement more in some categories than in others. The kinds of skills shown by literacy rates were clearly most important among the salaried employees. Literacy was considerably less important among owners; in this group accumulation of capital, business experience, and contacts, factors which may or may not have signified literacy, particularly among the self-employed, were presumably more important in placement in the labor force. Among wage laborers, jobs in retailing and in the lodgings and restaurant business required a greater level of skills, at least as measured by literacy, than did most factory jobs.

Such a structural division of the labor force based on the terms of employment—though it does reveal the change in the number of owners, salaried employees, and wage laborers as well as their gender, age, marital status, and literacy—is not altogether satisfactory. It groups, very unsatisfactorily, more than one-quarter of the labor force into personal

6. PM 1902, I, 2, i, 12–17.

TABLE 6   TERMS OF EMPLOYMENT AND LITERACY, 1902

Terms of Employment	Males			Females			Totals		
	Total	Literate	Percent Literate	Total	Literate	Percent Literate	Total	Literate	Percent Literate
Employers	24,799	20,739	83.6	8,269	5,534	66.9	33,068	26,273	79.5
Employers of own family	3,556	2,427	68.3	1,384	734	53.0	4,940	3,161	64.0
Self-employed	22,186	14,804	66.7	12,327	6,182	50.2	34,513	20,986	60.8
All owners	50,541	37,970	75.1	21,980	12,450	56.6	72,521	50,420	69.5
Factory clerks	7,153	7,097	99.2	323	297	92.0	7,476	7,394	98.9
Clerks, other manufacturing	3,014	2,933	97.3	319	307	96.2	3,333	3,240	97.2
Clerks, transport	10,427	10,342	99.2	1,354	1,350	99.7	11,781	11,692	99.2
Clerks, lodgings, restaurants	2,979	2,809	94.3	210	177	84.3	3,189	2,986	93.6
Clerks, retail	29,662	29,228	98.5	1,990	1,933	97.1	31,652	31,161	98.4
All clerical employees	53,235	52,409	98.4	4,196	4,064	96.9	57,431	56,473	98.3
Factory workers	78,056	54,585	69.9	29,725	5,740	19.3	107,181	60,325	56.0
Workers, other manufacturing	82,550	55,230	66.9	24,551	8,914	36.3	107,101	64,144	59.9
Workers, transport	37,227	22,296	59.9	452	55	12.2	37,679	22,351	59.3
Workers, lodgings, restaurant	29,711	21,778	73.3	1,936	407	21.0	31,647	22,185	70.1

TABLE 6 (*continued*)

Terms of Employment	Males			Females			Totals		
	Total	Literate	Percent Literate	Total	Literate	Percent Literate	Total	Literate	Percent Literate
Workers, retail	19,688	15,737	79.9	1,154	413	35.8	20,842	16,150	77.5
All workers	247,232	169,626	68.6	57,818	15,529	26.9	305,050	185,155	60.7
Domestics	7,965	5,842	73.3	70,763	19,120	27.0	78,728	24,962	31.7
Day laborers	6,212	3,222	51.9	2,706	312	11.5	8,918	3,534	39.6
Unemployed	11,755	9,120	77.6	6,362	1,894	29.8	18,081	11,014	60.8
Total labor force	506,216	386,505	76.4	249,010	107,853	43.3	755,226	494,358	65.5
Total population over age 5	570,838	428,752	75.1	437,401	216,645	49.5	978,239	649,397	66.0

Source: *PM 1902,* I, 2, i, 6–7.

and professional service, a category that includes both salaried employees and wage laborers as well as jobs ranging from physician to domestic servant. It does not present actual jobs held and conceals large differences within categories. The category "factory and plant worker," for example, covers a wide range of jobs and factory workplaces. But according to a contemporary worker:

The world of the factory is completely different from that of the plant. It has its own conditions and numerous peculiarities. The work and the payments of a factory worker are radically different from the work and wages of a skilled plant worker (*zavodskii masterovoi*). Therefore these two large groups of workers should at no time be compared. Even if they do have some common features, the difference in their working conditions is tremendous.[7]

Using the 1902 and 1912 censuses, it is possible to locate, albeit laboriously, actual occupational categories, such as teacher, tailor, turner, and so on. These occupational categories, as well as the numbers employed in them in 1902 and 1912, are presented in Appendix A. The structure of the labor force may be understood better by noting the relative increase or decrease in the city's occupations. To do this, I have selected eighteen large and representative occupations; as is shown in table 7, these eighteen occupations constituted almost one-third of the entire labor force in 1912. Four of them—cabdrivers and draymen, nursemaids, chambermaids, and cooks—experienced an absolute decline, particularly significant in years of rapid population growth. All four were semiskilled or menial jobs that reflected the decline in domestic service and the modernization of municipal transport. Another group of four—shoemakers, building superintendents, cabinetmakers, and weavers—showed only moderate increases, which did not keep pace with the average for the entire labor force. Like the previous group, this group consisted of manual jobs, including two skilled crafts. The remaining occupations displayed greater than average increases, and two—peddlers and bookkeepers—actually more than doubled in number. With the exception of the waiters, all manual jobs in this group were skilled and included trades such as printing and metalworking where organizational activity has been noted in several studies of labor politics.[8]

7. Timofeev, "Zavodskie budni," 31. As Thomas Owen pointed out to me, D. Mendeleev makes a more technical distinction between factory and plant in his article "Zavody," *Entsiklopedicheskii slovar'*, 12:100–4.
8. See Bonnell, *Roots of Rebellion*, chaps. 3, 5, 7, passim; Engelstein, "Moscow and the 1905 Revolution: A Study in Class Conflict and Political Organization," Ph.D. dissertation (Stanford University), 406–7; Koenker, *Moscow Workers*, 70–71 and chap. 4, passim.

TABLE 7   MOST COMMON OCCUPATIONS, 1902
AND 1912

Occupation, trade or craft	Number employed		Percent Increase or Decrease,
	1902	*1912*	*1902–12*
Sales clerks	20,776	33,885	63.1
Tailors[b]	20,880	33,569	60.8
Cooks, Kitchen help	36,029	32,381	−10.1
Building superintendents (*dvorniki*)[a]	20,859	25,167	20.7
Weavers[b]	22,007	21,976	− 0.1
Office clerks	14,140	22,185	56.9
Cab drivers, draymen (*izvozchiki*)	24,638	19,716	−20.0
Mechanics, fitters (*slesari*)[b]	10,935	18,524	69.4
Teachers	8,992	16,269	80.9
Metal smiths[c]	6,888	13,262	92.5
Shoemakers[b]	10,557	12,936	22.5
Chambermaids	13,569	12,331	− 8.7
Governesses, nursemaids	10,407	10,709	5.1
Printers	5,493	10,141	84.6
Cabinet makers[b]	9,020	10,127	12.3
Waiters, Waitresses	5,455	10,040	84.1
Bookkeepers, cashiers	4,237	9,572	125.9
Peddlers (*raznoschiki*)[b]	4,182	9,194	119.8

Source: *PM 1902*, I, 2, i, 46–115; I, 3, iii, 170–215; *SEMMG*, 68–73.
[a] Includes guards, doormen
[b] Includes both "self-employed" and "worker." In 1912, however, figures for self-employed weavers, mechanics, shoemakers, and cabinetmakers not available, making percentage increase slightly smaller than it would be otherwise.
[c] Working nonprecious metals, such as tinsmiths, wiremakers.
[d] Includes lithographers, typesetters, and other printers.

Although identifying the city's occupational groups is a step beyond using the rather broad categories based on terms of employment in examining the labor force, it does not provide a new structure to replace the old. A new order can be imposed by regrouping the labor force into nonmanual and manual or white-collar and blue-collar workers and, within these categories, ranking the various jobs and trades listed in Appendix A. Such a ranking will provide a different tool for analyzing changes in the structure of the Russian labor force, will facilitate a more detailed probe of job hierarchies, and finally will permit speculation on the complex and important issue of occupational mobility in terms more familiar to contemporary scholars.

WHITE-COLLAR, BLUE-COLLAR MOSCOW

At the outset, a few definitions, categories, and procedures must be clarified. This is all the more important given that, first, the concepts "white-collar" and "blue-collar" were not used as such by the Russian census compilers, and second, no standardized occupational classification exists for nineteenth-century Russia. It might not be too difficult to find the "white-collar" and "blue-collar" positions in the censuses as presently compiled, but the real difficulty comes when the historian tries to compare, for example, the censal category "wage laborer" with the category "blue-collar" or tries to make subdivisions such as "low white-collar" or "semiskilled blue-collar." Concerning the former case, it will be remembered that in 1902 40 percent of the entire self-supporting population were classified by the census as "wage laborers." Does this mean that 40 percent could be classified by the census as "blue-collar," and if so, what proportions might have held skilled, semiskilled, or unskilled jobs?

The lack of a standardized occupational classification poses an equally serious problem. Given the unavailability of the manuscript schedules and the ambiguity of many of the census aggregates, as well as the absence of socioeconomic indicators such as consistent income data, creating an occupational hierarchy has more than its share of pitfalls. Moreover, as a recent study of American occupational statistics argues, the bias of the compiler is built into the choice of a hierarchy and the placement of occupations in that hierarchy. Status is frequently substituted for skill, particularly in the difficult "judgment calls" on the borders between manual and nonmanual or between skilled and semiskilled, in placement of new or ascendant skills and old or declining skills, and in determination of the degree of skill dilution.[9] Finally, a classification created specially for Moscow in

9. Margo Anderson Conk, *The United States Census and the New Jersey Occupational Structure, 1870–1940* (Ann Arbor, Mich., 1978), and "Occupational Classification in the United States Census," *Journal of Interdisciplinary History*, 9, no. 1 (Summer 1978), 111–30. (I am grateful to David Montgomery for calling Conk's book to my

1900 could be too specific and make comparison with the labor force of other cities impossible.

A borrowed classification system is likewise not without problems. It might have job categories inappropriate for late-nineteenth-century Moscow. Given that most occupational (as opposed to sectoral) classification systems are products of the twentieth century, they might include too many "modern" occupations or attach different values to older occupations. Such values suggest biases concerning status, and a borrowed occupational classification might bring the bias of a different country, class, culture, and century to Moscow. Finally, even if similar jobs could be classified together, any notion of a hierarchy of jobs could be totally different from one society to another.

Until more information becomes available to make it possible to create an occupational classification for Moscow, or until an "outside" classification becomes universally recognized, a compromise seems the best solution. Accordingly, I have chosen the classification schedule of the American census statistician Alba Edwards, used extensively by Stephan Thernstrom in *The Other Bostonians*, with several modifications to account for the specific features of the Moscow labor market when ranking a particular occupation or trade.[10]

Justification on the basis of convenience for comparison is insufficient unless I can demonstrate that such a classification schedule, devised for the American economy of the 1930s, is appropriate for the Russian economy of the turn of the century. Thernstrom himself has supplied part of that justification by arguing that the classification schedule is applicable to late-nineteenth-century Boston and, by implication, other large American cities, on the grounds that by 1880 the urban labor force had already taken on an essentially industrial and modern character.[11] Of course, by 1880 the United States was well on

---

attention and to Robert Johnson and Diane Koenker for sharing their thoughts on occupational structure and mobility.) For a similar argument, see James Henretta, "The Study of Social Mobility: Ideological Assumptions and Conceptual Bias," *Labor History*, no. 2 (Spring 1977): 165–78. For two inquiries into historical social mobility in the European context, see William H. Sewell, Jr., "Social Mobility in a Nineteenth-Century European City: Some Findings and Implications," *Journal of Interdisciplinary History*, 7, no. 2 (Autumn 1976): 217–33; and David Crew, "Definitions of Modernity: Social Mobility in a German Town, 1880–1901," *Journal of Social History*, 7, no. 1 (Fall 1973): 51–74.

10. Stephan Thernstrom, *The Other Bostonians: Poverty and Progress in the American Metropolis, 1880–1970* (Cambridge, Mass., 1973), 289–92. In *Outcast London*, Gareth Stedman Jones uses a schedule which is fundamentally similar to that used by Thernstrom (pp. 355–56).

11. Thernstrom, *The Other Bostonians*, 289–92.

the road to industrialization while Russia was still at the tollgate. Boston's economy may have been essentially industrial and modern, but can the same be said for Moscow's? It must be noted that it is unclear what a purely "modern" occupational structure would be. Large and seemingly "modern" cities everywhere retain many traditional occupations (or traditional functions even if the job titles change). Naturally, technological change creates new jobs and destroys old jobs, but that does not provide insurmountable obstacles in ranking occupations. A quick comparison of the American occupational categories with those used in the 1902 Moscow census showed that virtually every job category in the latter had its place among the former. The mix, of course, was frequently quite different, but the most important thing is that the equivalent jobs were there. Moscow's economy was sufficiently industrial and "modern" to make comparisons with the labor forces of more advanced countries meaningful.

Although any American notion of an occupational hierarchy or of status associated with a particular job could have been inapplicable to nineteenth-century Russia, Moscow's census compilers themselves tended to put jobs in a loose hierarchy based in part, it appears, on status. The category "self-employed proprietors" follows "employers of wage labor" in all censuses. The more skilled metalworkers tended to be grouped ahead of textile mill hands. The unemployed, domestic servants, and casual laborers were invariably at the end of the occupational listings. Such a hierarchical arrangement of occupational categories, however imprecise, conforms reasonably well to the more modern-sounding classifications, such as "semiprofessional," "sales-clerical," "skilled worker," and so on. It would appear that even though the census compilers did not compile *precisely* in terms of such categories, they were already beginning to *think* in such terms in their arrangement of the data. Although these divisions are based on value judgments concerning status, they were made by professionals, and it is unlikely that such value judgments were drastically different from one nineteenth-century metropolis to another.

Naturally, the census compilers were educated officials doing nonmanual labor, and their notions of status or occupational hierarchy may have been radically different from those of the muzhiks themselves. Although the potential bias here must be recognized, there is evidence, as will be shown below, that workers themselves absorbed and transmitted such notions of status and hierarchy and thereby may have been just as judgmental as the census compilers.

The structure of the labor force according to the categories of white-collar and blue-collar jobs is summarized in table 8. A few of the difficult judgment calls in placing occupations in this hierarchy should be noted at the outset. One of the most difficult concerned the single proprietors and the self-employed artisans (*khoziaeva-odinochki*). Despite the manual labor frequently performed and the income levels that were often below those of skilled workers, Thernstrom placed them in the category "low white-collar" rather than in "skilled blue-collar." In brief, Thernstrom argues, holders of low white-collar jobs generally had more education, were younger, had greater regularity of income, were less often unemployed, and had generally more favorable working conditions. Perhaps even more important, they had more opportunities for career advancement, had greater ability to pass on advantages to the next generation, and had higher status than skilled blue-collar workers had. Thernstrom also observed in passing that the skilled artisan had almost died out in the Boston economy by 1880.[12] Finally, it must be noted that Moscow's census compilers placed the self-employed in the general category "owners" or "proprietors," a fact that must be at least reckoned with. However, did the group exhibit the same characteristics as its American counterpart?

To begin with, the self-employed artisan had not died out in Moscow by 1900. Admittedly, in the most skilled metal trades it was an endangered species. However, in 1902 the self-employed artisan constituted almost 20 percent of the shoemakers and over 40 percent of the tailors.[13] Other socioeconomic characteristics, such as the low proportion of Moscow-born and the relatively high proportion of illiterates, suggest that the group more closely resembled skilled blue-collar workers than nearby low white-collar workers. Contemporary accounts of the sweated trades certainly do not indicate that the self-employed artisan enjoyed more favorable working conditions than did the skilled workers. Income data are lacking for this group, but there is no reason to believe that income was more regular or that the self-employed were less frequently unemployed. In fact, artisans were prominent in countless studies of slum housing and welfare, suggesting that the economic position of this group was very precarious.[14]

12. Ibid., 296–301.
13. *PM 1902*, I, 2, i, 46–115; 3, iii, 170–215.
14. Raevskii, "K voprosu," 86, 108; Kurnin, *O nekotorykh usloviiakh*, 18–19. For additional sources, see note 76 below. For a journalistic description of working conditions, see Giliarovskii, *Moskva i Moskvichi*, 23–45, 72–81.

TABLE 8 WHITE-COLLAR, BLUE-COLLAR MOSCOW, 1902

Occupational Ranking	Men		Women		Total Labor force	Percent Men
	Number	Percent	Number	Percent		
High white-collar						
Professionals	8,929	1.8	5,903	2.4	14,632	61.0
Major proprietors, managers, officials	15,948	3.2	7,802	3.2	23,750	67.1
All high white-collar	24,877	5.0	13,705	5.6	38,382	64.8
Low white-collar						
Sales-clerical	43,598	8.8	4,231	1.7	47,829	91.2
Semiprofessionals	8,576	1.7	7,769	3.2	16,345	52.5
Petty proprietors, managers, officials	47,332	9.5	15,520	6.4	62,852	75.3
All low white-collar	99,506	20.0	27,520	11.3	127,026	78.3
Unclassified white-collar	14,107	2.8	20,647	8.5	34,754	40.6
Total white-collar	138,290	27.8	61,872	25.4	200,162	69.1
Blue-collar						
Skilled	112,881	22.7	21,360	8.8	133,821	84.4
Semiskilled and service	142,237	28.6	85,318	35.2	227,585	62.3
Unskilled and menial service	71,663	14.4	45,174	18.6	116,837	61.3
Unclassified blue-collar	24,034	4.8	25,136	10.3	49,170	48.9
Total blue-collar	350,815	70.5	176,988	72.9	527,413	66.5
Total white- and blue-collar	489,105	98.3	238,860	98.3	727,575	67.2
Unclassified	8,449	1.7	4,156	1.7	12,605	67.0
Total labor force	497,554	100.0	243,016	100.0	740,570	67.2

Source: *PM 1902*, I, 2, i, 46–115; I, 3, iii, 170–215.

Whether the condition of ownership or the possession of capital, however small the amount, offset the insecurity of income is impossible to judge.

My solution to the problem has been to place the self-employed in manufacturing, construction, or transport (including self-employed artisans) in the category skilled blue-collar workers under the assumption that in terms of skills, culture, and ways of life there was not a significant difference between a wage-earning cabinetmaker and a self-employed cabinetmaker: both were essentially manual laborers. Similarly, I have placed those self-employed in retailing and services with other small businessmen and proprietors, that is, with others performing nonmanual labor, in the category low white-collar.

To take another example, the distinctions between skilled, semi-skilled, and unskilled blue-collar workers are not always easy to make, and another difficult "judgment call" is the case of many of the city's factory workers, especially textile workers. Other socioeconomic factors may assist in the placement of various factory jobs. The average annual wage of operatives at the cotton mills was only half that of certain skilled trades, such as machinists, gold- and silversmiths and cabinetmakers.[15] Both literacy and Moscow birth were much higher among workers in the more skilled printing and metal trades than among textile workers. Urban occupations with a low proportion of women, such as the metal, machine-tool, and printing trades, tended to be the most skilled and therefore the highest blue-collar rungs of the ladder; jobs of the lowest skill and status, such as domestic service, had a high proportion of women, and others, such as jobs in the textile industry and the clothing trades, occupied the middle rungs.[16] Finally, recent Western research into factory life and detailed examinations of certain trades, such as metalworking and printing, suggest that factory labor per se may not have been the most important criterion in stratification; rather, skill, apprenticeship training, urban expe-

15. In 1900 the maximum wage paid to men at Tsindel' and Prokhorov was 1 ruble per day for approximately 275 working days during the year. The average annual wage in Moscow was 264 rubles, 400–600 rubles for a skilled machinist, and 420 rubles for gold- and silversmiths. At the other end of the scale, the minimum wage at Prokhorov and Tsindel' for females was 77 rubles. Wage data can be found in *Rabochie Rossii*, 123; "Report for the Year 1908 on the Trade and Agriculture of the Consular District of St. Petersburg," no. 4323 (1909), 20; Pazhitnov, *Polozhenie rabochego klassa*, 74; Schulze-Gävernitz, *Krupnoe proizvodstvo*, 83; Shestakov, "Materialy dlia kharakteristiki fabrichnykh rabochikh v Moskve," 165; Kut'ev, "Dokumental'nye materialy," 14; Kir'ianov, *Zhiznennyi uroven'* 103–4, 122, 124; Engelstein, "Moscow in the 1905 Revolution," 176.

16. Kadomtsev, *Sostav*, 64; *PM 1902*, I, 2, table 6.

rience, and self-esteem set the skilled workers distinctly apart from most textile operatives.[17] In the ranking system used here, I have placed more emphasis on craft and skill than on place of work. Consequently, most of the workers in the metal trades emerge as skilled blue-collar, as do the tailors, while most textile operatives appear in the category "semiskilled blue-collar."

Though such job distinctions may seem at times arbitrary, they were no less real to contemporaries. We have seen that the skilled metalworker Semen Kanatchikov denigrated the village ways of some of his fellow workers. Patternmakers such as himself didn't tuck their trousers into their boots, but they did tuck their shirts into their trousers, had a sense of personal worth, were family men and city dwellers, and had savings for a rainy day.[18] Another skilled metalworker, P. Timofeev, observed the sharp distinctions between the foremen, skilled workers, semiskilled operatives, and menial laborers at the metal plants. In addition to their considerable power over the workers on the shop floor, the foremen (*mastera*) could always be distinguished by the fact that they carried their rulers in their upper jacket pocket, whereas the workers carried their rulers in their lower jacket pocket or in their trousers pocket. If a worker carried his ruler openly, his buddies would laugh at him.[19] Among the workers themselves, there was a big difference between the skilled workers (*masterovye*) and the regular workers (*rabochie*) in wages and ways of life. The latter, in turn, had more status than the common or unskilled laborers (*chernorabochie*), employed in gangs by the metal shops where they were jokingly referred to as the servants (*pridvornye*) by the skilled workers.[20] According to Timofeev, these menials possessed neither literacy nor skills nor imagination: only brawn.

Dragging iron bars, loading and unloading freight cars, carrying more than three tons of cast iron, lifting unbelievably heavy loads, digging and filling holes—those are some of the jobs of the common laborers.[21]

According to this hierarchy of manual and nonmanual jobs, a strikingly high proportion of Moscow's self-supporting population held blue-collar jobs—not the 40 percent classified as "wage laborer" by the census, but over 70 percent. Several blue-collar jobs not included in the

17. For example, see Bonnell, *Roots of Rebellion*, 43–69.
18. Kanatchikov, *Iz istorii*, 17–18.
19. Timofeev, "Zavodskie budni," 38.
20. Ibid., 20–21. See also Bonnell, *Roots of Rebellion*, 47–48.
21. Timofeev, "Zavodskie budni," 35.

census category "wage laborers" account for the difference: family members working for the head of the household in manufacturing, apprentices, day laborers, the unemployed (whom I assume were, or had been, in the main, blue-collar workers), domestic servants, soldiers, policemen, firemen, those living on relief, and a wide range of manual and menial service jobs performed for public and private institutions. As is readily apparent, although one-fifth of the city's self-supporting males were skilled blue-collar workers—an impressive figure by itself—more than two-fifths of the self-supporting males and two-thirds of all blue-collar workers were semiskilled or menials. Placement in this manual/nonmanual job hierarchy can be studied further by examining the available supportive data from the 1902 census on gender, age, and birthplace. Then, using the 1902 and 1912 censuses, structural changes may be observed and compared with those structural changes noted earlier using terms of employment as the criteria.

Although women were represented at all occupational levels, they were slightly better placed in high white-collar positions. This occurred primarily because women dominated among teachers and rentiers; many of the latter presumably were widows who had inherited property. If these two groups were removed from the high white-collar positions, women, having barely penetrated other professions or positions of major ownership, would have been very poorly represented. The placement of women in low white-collar and in blue-collar positions followed a distinct pattern: women fared markedly worse at the upper levels within each division. Only one of ten sales-clerical jobs and one of seven skilled blue-collar jobs were held by a woman. Moreover, given the preponderance of elderly female self-employed and small proprietors, many owed their positions not to expanding opportunities for women per se in these areas but to acquiring small businesses in widowhood. Among the sales-clerical jobs, women were well represented only among the cashiers; among the more prestigious and rapidly expanding jobs, such as sales clerks, bookkeepers, accountants, and office clerks, women fared badly. Likewise, women had made inroads into only a few of the skilled blue-collar occupations, such as tailors, dressmakers, hatters, glovemakers, and confectioners. Of forty-six skilled crafts listed, twenty had four or fewer women.[22]

Women were better represented on the lower rungs within each division: in semiskilled jobs in the textile and clothing industry and of

22. *PM 1902*, I, 2, i, 46–115; 3, iii, 170–215.

course in domestic service. In 1902 almost 40 percent of the semi-skilled and menial jobs were held by women. In addition, almost three-quarters of those on relief in institutions were women.[23] Although the phenomenon of structural shifts from 1902 to 1912 will be taken up below, it is worth noting here that the proportion of women in the unskilled and menial jobs, that is at the bottom of the job hierarchy, actually increased, whereas the proportion in the category of semiskilled immediately above decreased. Other notable increases in female employment occurred in high white-collar positions and in small proprietary and managerial jobs.

Women happened to fare better in several occupations which had a disproportionate number of persons over the age of forty—rentiers, self-employed, small proprietors, and domestics. In addition to gender, age was an important factor determining placement on the occupational ladder. Using the 1902 census, it is possible to isolate occupations filled primarily by the young or by the elderly.[24] By comparing those younger than twenty-five with those older than forty, it is also possible to locate persons who were at their first jobs and those who were at their last. (See Appendix C.)

Understandably, high white-collar jobs had an older labor force. For example, only 13.6 percent of the entire male labor force was aged 40–49, whereas 30.5 percent of the manufacturers and 29.2 percent of the managers fell into this age group. By contrast, only 3 percent fell into the age group 20–24. Because of the need to build up capital, experience, and business connections, the small proprietors and the self-employed were older than average. Interestingly, a similar pattern prevailed among several semiskilled blue-collar workers, such as cooks and weavers, 23 percent of whom were aged 40–49, as well as among menial workers, such as day laborers, menials of institutions, and building superintendents.

Other occupations had a distinctly youthful labor force. Among the low white-collar jobs, office clerks stand out, with their largest number, both absolutely and proportionately, in the 20–24 age group. The proportions of office clerks found in the 25–29 age group declined slightly and then dropped to only 8 percent in the 40–49 age group. Similar patterns prevailed among many skilled craftsmen such as silversmiths, machinists, turners, painters, typesetters, and shoemakers; and among stocking knitters, bakers, waiters, and other restaurant

23. Ibid.
24. *PM 1902*, I, 2, i, 46–115.

workers in the semiskilled trades. All occupations exhibited a greater than normal relative decline after age 30; for example, there were 500 fewer waiters aged 20–24 than aged 15–19.

Several of the occupations mentioned above—painters, bakers, stocking knitters, waiters, and other restaurant workers—had disproportionately large numbers of immigrants and consisted almost exclusively of outsiders in the younger age groups. Immigration played an important role in determining placement on the labor force, both within occupational groups as a whole and within certain age groups. A comparison of the 1902 occupational distribution according to terms of employment of the Moscow-born with that of the newcomers is an appropriate starting point.

Remember that 12.2 percent of the active male population was Moscow-born. Among the city's occupational groups, this proportion was by no means uniform. The group of white-collar employees and several of the professional groups had the greatest proportion born in Moscow, while most groups of blue-collar workers had the lowest proportion of Moscow-born. Businessmen, proprietors, and the self-employed were close to the average. Table 9 shows the numbers of male and female immigrants on the Moscow job market in selected occupations. Moscow-born women were relatively more prominent than Moscow-born men in most occupational categories. The greatest single source of female employment was domestic service, and one out of every three women who migrated to the city ended up in this job. Accordingly, the best way to avoid this job was to have been born in the city. More than one-third of the city's female employers, more than one-quarter of its self-employed, and almost one-half of its employees were born in Moscow. As might be expected, the city's managerial, professional, and proprietary jobs tended to have relatively more need of male Muscovites, who presumably had the greater opportunity to acquire the necessary experience, training, capital, or connections.[25] Nevertheless, it is still striking that more than 80 percent of the city's employers, more than 90 percent of its self-employed, and even 85 percent of those in health care were newcomers. No single occupational category contained more than 50 percent male Muscovites. By the same token, certain middle- and high-level occupations, it seems, were by no means closed to immigrants. Thus, the city birth gave certain but by no means exclusive advantages.

25. PM 1902, I, 2, i, 8–11. For further commentary on managerial, professional, and proprietary positions, see GPD 1902, VI, 35.

TABLE 9 LABOR FORCE AND BIRTHPLACE

Occupational Group	Men 1902			Women 1902			Men 1912			Women 1912		
	Total	Moscow-born Total	Percent	Total	Moscow-born Total	Percent	Total	Moscow-born Total	Percent	Total	Moscow-born Total	Percent
All occupations	506,216	61,356	12.2	249,010	45,688	18.3	684,981	86,773	12.7	366,282	68,002	18.6
Selected occupations												
Employers	24,799	4,876	19.7	8,269	3,040	36.6	32,600	6,064	18.6	11,623	4,002	34.4
Self-employed	22,186	2,173	9.8	12,327	3,347	27.2	33,622	3,617	10.8	25,489	6,198	24.3
Employees, retail	29,662	6,869	23.2	1,990	963	48.4	—	—	—	—	—	—
All employees	53,235	12,729	23.9	4,196	1,944	46.3	81,541	19,305	23.7	10,834	5,535	51.1
Factory workers	78,056	5,422	6.9	29,725	2,510	8.4	115,189	10,226	8.9	49,995	5,429	10.8
All workers	247,232	14,991	6.1	57,818	7,753	13.4	318,566	22,236	7.0	84,756	12,877	15.2
Government officials	4,031	1,144	28.4	471	208	44.2	—	—	—	—	—	—
Selected professions												
Legal	2,117	627	29.6	152	84	55.3	—	—	—	—	—	—
Health care	5,827	963	16.5	4,756	957	20.5	—	—	—	—	—	—
Science, literature, arts	5,286	1,475	27.9	1,475	250	16.9	—	—	—	—	—	—
Domestic servants	7,965	256	3.2	70,763	3,625	5.1	6,761	181	2.7	92,313	4,157	4.5
Day laborers	6,212	695	11.2	2,706	343	12.7	8,811	1,139	12.9	3,586	507	14.1
Unemployed	11,755	2,229	19.0	6,362	799	12.6	19,720	3,952	20.0	9,692	1,463	15.1

Source: *Pm 1902*, 1, 2, i, 8–11; *SEMMG*, 68–73.

The degree to which broader categories conceal large differences among occupations is shown by the percentages of Moscow-born males. Holders of higher managerial, proprietary, and professional jobs were more likely to have been born in Moscow than the average, although the lower white-collar category of office clerks actually had the highest proportion of natives. Blue-collar workers were less likely to have been born in Moscow, although 39 percent of the typesetters on the upper rungs and 33 percent of those on poor relief on the lower rungs were Moscow-born. On the other hand, a tiny 1 percent of the city's carpenters, cotton and wool weavers, bakers, cabdrivers, draymen, and deliverymen were born in Moscow.[26]

Did immigrants gravitate to certain jobs immediately upon arrival in the city? Using census data on the occupation and length of residence in the city of immigrants and comparing the group resident in the city less than one year with all immigrants, it is possible to locate common jobs that gave the immigrant an "entry" into the metropolitan labor force.[27] We find that those just entering the city were not likely to take upper-level jobs: only 2.1 percent of this group were listed as employers, compared with 4.5 percent of all immigrants. We might expect that wage laborers would be overrepresented among the new arrivals; in fact, factory workers and other industrial laborers were underrepresented: approximately 24 percent of the men who had just arrived in the city went to blue-collar jobs in manufacturing, compared with almost 33 percent of all immigrant men. This suggests that industrial workers, too, were relatively less likely to find such jobs immediately upon arrival. A leading Soviet labor historian has stated:

The road of yesterday's peasant to industry was not always direct—from wooden plough to factory workbench—but passed through several traditional stages; work in small-scale industry, in the construction trades, in the carrying trades, in domestic service, and so forth.[28]

This was also true of blue-collar positions in retailing. The three blue-collar groups that did appear to provide more entry-level jobs were the transport trades, the housing and restaurant business, and apprenticeship. Surprisingly, casual labor did not provide a disproportionate

26. *PM 1902*, I, 2, i, 46–115.
27. Ibid., 8–11.
28. Ivanov, "Preemstvennost'," 73.

share of entry-level jobs for men. For newly arrived women, domestic service was the largest source of employment.[29]

Moscow birth gave advantages to those entering the labor force in many occupations, including upper managerial, proprietary, and professional jobs. There were 1,231 male manufacturers, for instance, of whom 428, or 34.8 percent, were Moscow-born. Yet 51 percent in the age bracket 25–29 but only 35 percent in the age bracket 40–49 were Moscow-born. The change was even more striking among directors and managers, of whom the proportion of Moscow-born varied from 25 percent (the groups as a whole) to 74 percent at ages 25–29, to 20 percent at ages 40–49.[30] Moscow birth was advantageous among several occupations with a youthful labor force on the upper rungs of their divisions—office clerks among low white-collar jobs and turners, typesetters, and lithographers among the skilled blue-collar jobs. On the other hand, male newcomers in several semiskilled blue-collar trades stood as good a chance, if not better, as Muscovites to enter the labor force.

The lower white-collar groups—office clerks, salespeople, small proprietors, and the self-employed—exhibited in part the same pattern as did the upper white-collar groups with greater proportions of natives at the younger ages. The difference between the proportions of Moscow-born in younger and older age groups, however, was not nearly so noticeable as that in the high white-collar jobs and barely existed for the self-employed. Interestingly, for the blue-collar workers the pattern was reversed. With a few exceptions, the proportion of Moscow-born was higher in the age group 30–39 than in the age group 20–24. If this pattern had prevailed only among skilled workers, then the explanation might be simple: natives were at an advantage when it came to the skilled trades and were able to enter them quickly after apprenticeship. But the pattern prevailed not only among skilled workers but among semiskilled and unskilled as well. Clearly, for outsiders the blue-collar occupations were more easily entered.

Were the immigrants all cut from the same cloth or did birthplace play a role in job placement? A close inspection of the 1902 census shows that male immigrants from more industrial regions or from

29. *PM 1902*, I, 2, i, 8–11. It has been observed that there is much recruitment to casual jobs from second- and third-generation urban residents who enter the urban labor market at its lowest level. See Edwin Eames and Judith Granich Goode, *Urban Poverty in a Cross-cultural Context* (New York, 1973), 144.

30. *PM 1902*, I, 2, i, 46–115.

areas of widespread seasonal migratory labor were better represented on the upper rungs of the occupational ladder. According to investigators of the Moscow zemstvo, a disproportionate share of skilled laborers, such as engravers and typesetters, came from Moscow province.[31] Likewise, as Appendix B shows, a disproportionate share of Moscow's blue-collar workers came from Tula, Riazan', Kaluga, and Smolensk, regions with less developed industry and less of a tradition of seasonal migratory labor. Of 1,213 peasants surveyed at the Tsindel' mill, more than 50 percent came from Riazan' and an additional 25 percent from Tula.[32] Similarly, within Moscow province itself, the industrial county of Bogorodsk sent a disproportionately large share of employers, self-employed, and factory white-collar employees and a small share of blue-collar workers.

Why would peasants from Tver', Vladimir, and Iaroslavl' fare better than their brethren from Tula, Riazan', and Smolensk on the Moscow labor market? In contemporary accounts, one now and then runs across the image of the brighter, quicker, shrewder Iaroslavl' peasant and the duller and slower brand from Kaluga, Tula, and Riazan' ("from the steppe"), but this begs the question.[33]

It is quite likely that a longer tradition of seasonal migratory labor in the industrial regions around Moscow gave Vladimir and Iaroslavl' peasants better connections in the city. Perhaps even more important, peasants from Vladimir, Tver', and Iaroslavl' were more literate than their counterparts from Riazan', Tula, Kaluga, and Smolensk, which had below average literacy rates for European Russia. The peasant from an industrial region seeking an industrial job would have had less need to come to Moscow; thus, relatively more Vladimir and Bogorodsk immigrants were apt to have been white-collar workers.[34] Similarly, blue-collar workers in Vladimir or Bogorodsk may have transferred to white-collar jobs upon arrival in Moscow.

Whatever the differences between Iaroslavl' and Riazan' peasants in job placement, the fact remained that in the labor force as a whole

31. Peskov, *Sanitarnoe issledovanie*, 113; Svavitskii and Sher, *Ocherk*, 8.

32. Shestakov, *Rabochie*, 20, 35; *PM 1902*, I, 2, iii, 26–33; I, 2, i, 40–45; Peskov, *Sanitarnoe issledovanie*, 138–39. See also E. Bergman, "Poslednie perepisi," 127; Antonova, *Vliianie*, 188–90; and A. Kurbatov, "Zapiski starogo povara," *Nash sovremennik*, 1 (1967): 99.

33. Dement'ev, *Fabrika*, 11–13, 22, 31–32; Shestakov, *Rabochie*, 35.

34. Kirillov, "K voprosu," 270. Kirillov found that of 120,000 registered migratory laborers employed in nonagricultural jobs in Iaroslavl' province in 1893, only 8,500 (6.5 percent) were employed in factory jobs. See also my "Patterns of Peasant Migration" and the studies of Anderson and Guroff and Starr cited in chapter 4, n. 95.

there was virtually no decrease in the proportions of immigrants. The incessant flow of newcomers caused great concern among Muscovites. Particularly distressing was the fact that the proportion of immigrants actually increased on two of the lowest rungs of the occupational ladder—casual labor and domestic service. Although the proportions of immigrants in any occupational group did not rise or fall dramatically from 1902 to 1912, the rate of growth of the major occupational divisions displayed considerable variation. Such varying rates of growth reflect important structural changes in the labor force, the final aspect of white-collar and blue-collar Moscow to be inspected.

We have seen that in the decade 1902–1912, the labor force increased by 41.1 percent. However, as table 10 shows, the blue-collar division increased by only 35.4 percent, whereas the white-collar division increased by 56.8 percent. High white-collar workers increased by 72.1 percent, and professionals exhibited the greatest increase (86 percent) of all groups. In the low white-collar division, sales-clerical jobs grew three to four times as fast as did semiprofessional and lower proprietary, managerial, and government jobs. A similar unevenness prevailed in the blue-collar division, in which increases for skilled jobs were above average, near average for unskilled jobs, and considerably below average for semiskilled jobs.[35]

As a result of such varying growth rates, on the eve of World War I a larger proportion of Moscow's labor force was employed in all high white-collar divisions, in sales-clerical jobs, and in skilled blue-collar jobs. A smaller proportion of the labor force found blue-collar jobs, and particularly semiskilled jobs, as well as semiprofessional and lower proprietary and managerial jobs. Owing to the modernization and diversification of the economy, nonmanual occupations in general, and professional, technical, managerial, and clerical positions in particular, grew the fastest. Likewise, there was a greater need for skilled manual jobs, particularly in the metal and machine-tool industries. On the very bottom rungs of the ladder, unskilled and menial service jobs expanded in approximately the same proportion as that for all jobs.

35. *PM 1882*, II, pt. 2, 101–340; *PM 1902*, I, 2, i, 116–59; *SEMMG*, 68–73. It will be remembered that I chose to place the self-employed artisans in the category skilled blue-collar rather than in the category lower proprietary white-collar. This has the statistical effect of depressing the figures in the latter category. Likewise, the inclusion of all textile operatives, jobs exhibiting slow growth rates, in the category semiskilled rather than skilled blue-collar has the effect of depressing the figures in the former category.

TABLE 10 WHITE-COLLAR, BLUE-COLLAR MOSCOW: STRUCTURAL CHANGE, 1902–1912

Occupational Ranking	Men 1912			Women 1912			Labor force 1912			
	Number	Percent male labor force	Percent Increase 1902–12	Number	Percent female labor force	Percent Increase 1902–12	Number	Percent total labor force	Percent men	Percent Increase 1902–12
High White-collar										
Professionals	14,744	2.1	65.1	12,474	3.4	111.3	27,218	2.6	54.2	86.0
Major proprietors, managers, officials	23,113	3.4	44.9	15,730	4.3	101.6	38,843	3.7	59.5	63.5
Total high white-collar	37,857	5.5	55.2	28,204	7.7	105.8	66,061	6.3	57.3	72.1
Low White-collar										
Sales-clerical	75,237	11.0	72.6	10,160	2.8	140.1	85,397	8.1	88.1	78.5
Semiprofessionals	9,127	1.3	6.4	10,612	2.9	36.6	19,739	1.9	46.2	20.8
Petty proprietors, managers, officials	61,735	9.0	30.4	24,275	6.6	56.4	86,010	8.2	71.8	36.8
Total low white-collar	146,099	21.3	46.8	45,047	12.3	63.7	191,146	18.2	76.4	50.5
Unclassified white-collar	23,609	3.4	67.4	33,013	9.0	59.9	56,622	5.4	41.7	62.9
Total white-collar	207,565	30.2	50.1	106,264	29.0	71.7	313,829	29.9	66.1	56.8

Blue-collar

Skilled	159,212	23.3	41.0	42,275	11.6	97.9	201,487	19.2	79.0	50.6
Semiskilled, service	175,206	25.6	23.2	97,513	26.7	14.3	272,719	26.0	64.2	19.8
Unskilled, menial service	87,436	12.8	22.0	75,651	20.7	67.5	163,087	15.5	53.6	39.6
Unclassified blue-collar	41,276	6.0	71.7	35,676	9.8	41.9	76,952	7.3	53.6	56.5
Total blue-collar	463,130	67.7	32.0	251,115	68.8	41.9	714,245	68.0	64.8	35.4
Total white- and blue-collar	670,695	97.9	36.2	357,379	97.8	49.4	1,028,074	97.9	65.2	40.5
Unclassified	13,873	2.0	64.2	7,831	2.1	88.4	21,704	2.1	63.9	72.2
Total labor force	684,568	100.0	37.6	365,210	100.0	50.3	1,049,778	100.0	65.2	41.7

Source: *SEMMG*, 68–73; *PM 1902*, I, 2, i, 46–115; I, 3, iii, 170–215.

While the growth of the labor force demonstrates an expansion of job opportunities at all levels, the structural shifts reveal greater relative expansion in many nonmanual jobs. To what degree did these structural changes reflect individual or generational changes? That is to say, were the relative increases in certain occupations the result of individuals moving from one occupational level to another? If, for example, the labor force in 1912 had more plumbers and fewer water carriers than in previous years, does this mean that water carriers, or the sons of water carriers, became plumbers? Or did the "extra" plumbers enter the labor force from the outside, while the city's water carriers remained immobile? Although it is impossible to determine directly and systematically individual occupational changes, this should not prevent a preliminary investigation of the problem of occupational mobility.[36]

OCCUPATIONAL MOBILITY

The metalworker P. Timofeev claimed that during his ten years among workers, only rarely did he meet a worker who did not dream about changing his job:

They cherished the hope of sooner or later, having saved up even just a little money, leaving the plant and being free from all the bosses and whistles. Some dreamed about a little house in the city, some about the village, and others about some kind of business.[37]

Other contemporary studies and accounts leave an impression of a certain degree of job turnover, beyond what might be expected on account of age or technological and structural changes alone. Many observers, Russian and foreign alike, considered the Russian laborer an "industrial nomad," so often did he allegedly switch jobs.[38] In his memoirs, Semen Kanatchikov noted that in the 1890s workers were always in demand; although he lost his first Moscow job at the Bromley Works in 1897, he "immediately" found a new one at the Mytishch Railway Works. One year later he moved to Petersburg.[39] At the Tsindel' mill almost one-fifth of 693 workers surveyed in 1910 had been there less than one year and another one-fourth from one to

36. It is impossible to sample individual occupational changes, because manuscript censuses and tax rolls are not available and city directories do not include the laboring population in their listings.
37. Timofeev, "Ocherki," 72.
38. I. I. Ianzhul, *Iz vospominanii*, 4–5, 160; Ia. T. Mikhailovskii, "Zarabotnaia plata," 274–75.
39. Kanatchikov, *Iz istorii*, 55.

three years.[40] Oliunina found that about one-half of her tailors had
changed jobs during the year before the survey.[41] Surprisingly, one-
fourth of Moscow's printers, a profession one would have thought to
be less "nomadic," had been at their current factory less than one
year. According to Svavitskii and Sher, this turnover was especially
noticeable among the typesetters and bookbinders, two skilled trades
whose labor was less mechanized.[42]

Job turnover, while suggesting a fluid labor force and the opportunity for moving from one job to another, or lateral mobility, does not
necessarily indicate occupational changes from one level to another.
Such vertical occupational mobility was represented by Ivan Slonov,
an upwardly mobile Moscow businessman who wrote in his laconic
memoirs in 1914, "I was able to change from a poor man into a
businessman and Moscow property-owner, and from a Kolomna
townsman into a hereditary honored citizen."[43] Slonov had a right to
end his memoirs on an upbeat and smug note. He had come to Moscow in adolescence in the late 1860s and had begun work as an errand
boy amid the "Asiatic caravan" of shops and stalls known as the
Trading Rows. Apprenticed later to a shoemaker, the enterprising
Slonov bought out the business upon his master's death in 1872. He
then later changed his trade to a dealer in gold, silver, and bronze.
After fifteen more years, which included trips to England, France,
Italy, and Germany to master the trade, this self-made man was made
an honored citizen.

Such striking upward mobility warmed the hearts of the preachers
of hard work and respectability all over Victorian Europe and America—and Russia was no exception. One does not have to believe in
the typicalness of such rapid mobility as Slonov's to recognize the
possibility of climbing from "rags to responsibility" if not "rags to
riches." Alongside the myriad familiar examples of poverty, cases of
modest upward mobility oblige historians to examine such opportunities. Even though it is impossible to chart individual careers, it is
possible to make inferences concerning individual occupational
changes from data on the length of residence of the city's immigrants. In this way, it will be possible to examine the jobs immigrants were most likely to have held upon arrival and speculate on

40. Quoted in Antonova, *Vliianie*, 190.
41. Oliunina, *Portnovskii promysel*, 177–78.
42. Svavitskii and Sher, *Ocherk*, 12.
43. Slonov, *Iz zhizni*, 227.

their likelihood of changing occupations the longer they remained in the city.

Unfortunately, such an arrangement of the data is far from ideal. Occupations are categorized according to the terms of employment, not according to occupational groups. The very concept of "length of residence" was never defined precisely by the census compilers, a regrettable omission given the transient sojourns and multiple entries into the city of many of its peasants. Those immigrants resident in the city for more than eleven years included persons who could have spent nearly a lifetime in Moscow. Perhaps even more important, each group of immigrants included only those who stayed in Moscow; but many immigrants left after only a short sojourn in the city. This parameter of occupational mobility will be treated separately below. Despite the obstacles, we have several distinct groups of immigrants who lived varying numbers of years in the city, as is shown in table 11.

If immigrants had remained at the same occupational levels at which they entered the labor force, little change should be noted in the occupational dispersion of the short-term and long-term immigrants. If many immigrants had entered the city in the upper occupational groups—that is, if nonlocal manufacturers, businessmen, upper officials, or professionals had moved to Moscow—an almost insurmountable barrier would have existed for those on middle and lower rungs of the occupational ladder in the city. In fact, more of the long-term residents were able to find higher jobs on the occupational ladder. This phenomenon was particularly marked for employers, female self-employed, and male clerks. Likewise, proportionately more of this group than of the new arrivals had found blue-collar jobs in manufacturing. On the other hand, this group showed less representation in blue-collar jobs in the transport trades, in retailing, and in the restaurant and housing business. Age, of course, was a factor here, and the census does not permit us to correlate occupation, age group, and length of residence. Presumably, those resident in the city at least eleven years were older than those resident in the city less than one year; that the former group should have had more persons in proprietary and managerial positions was certainly due in part to this fact. However, the former group also had more persons in manufacturing positions where one would not expect age to play as important a role. This fact, plus the marked difference between the two groups in the proportions of upper white-collar jobs held, suggests that age was not the only factor.

TABLE 11 MIGRATION, PERSISTENCE OF RESIDENCE, AND OCCUPATION, 1902

Immigrants, by years resident in Moscow

Occupation	Total	%	Moscow-born Total	%	All immigrants Total	%	Less than 1 Total	%	More than 11 Total	%
					Men					
All labor force	506,216	100	61,356	100	444,860	100	62,257	100	165,590	100
Selected occupations										
Employers	24,799	4.9	4,876	7.9	19,923	4.5	1,332	2.1	15,369	9.3
Self-employed	22,186	4.4	2,173	0.4	20,013	4.5	2,049	3.3	11,292	6.8
Clerks, factory	7,153	1.4	2,130	3.5	5,023	1.1	484	0.8	2,508	1.5
Clerks, other manufacturing	3,014	0.6	696	1.1	2,318	0.5	253	0.4	948	0.6
Clerks, transport	10,427	2.1	2,675	4.3	7,752	1.7	939	1.5	2,963	1.8
Clerks, housing and restaurant	2,979	0.6	359	0.6	2,620	0.6	198	0.3	1,408	0.9
Clerks, retail	29,662	5.9	6,869	11.2	22,793	5.1	1,670	2.7	10,557	6.4
Workers, factory	78,056	15.4	5,422	8.8	72,634	16.3	7,670	12.3	29,487	17.8
Workers, other manufacturing	81,936	16.2	5,749	9.3	76,187	17.1	7,591	12.1	29,569	17.9
Workers, transport	37,227	1.4	2,000	3.2	35,227	7.9	6,607	10.6	10,264	6.2
Workers, housing and restaurant	29,711	5.9	769	1.2	28,942	6.5	4,826	7.8	8,783	5.3
Workers, retailing	19,688	3.9	1,051	1.7	18,637	4.1	2,464	4.0	6,114	3.7
Domestic servants	7,965	1.6	256	0.4	7,709	1.7	974	1.6	2,907	1.8
Day laborers	6,212	1.2	695	1.1	5,517	1.2	929	1.5	2,438	1.5
Unemployed	11,755	2.3	2,229	3.6	9,526	2.1	1,504	2.4	4,719	2.8

TABLE 11 (continued)

					Immigrants, by years resident in Moscow					
			Moscow-born		All immigrants		Less than 1		More than 11	
Occupation	Total	%	Total	%	Total	%	Total	%	Total	%
					Women					
All labor force	249,010	100	45,688	100	203,322	100	27,902	100	81,839	100
Selected occupations										
Employers	8,269	3.3	3,040	6.7	5,229	2.6	230	0.8	4,183	5.1
Self-employed	12,327	5.0	3,347	7.3	8,980	4.4	299	1.1	6,296	7.7
Clerks, retail	1,990	0.8	963	2.1	1,027	0.5	137	0.5	436	0.5
All clerical employees	4,196	1.7	1,944	4.3	2,252	1.1	232	0.8	943	1.2
Factory workers	29,725	11.9	2,510	5.5	27,215	13.4	3,061	11.0	7,566	9.2
All workers	57,818	23.2	7,753	17.0	50,065	24.6	4,725	16.9	18,203	22.2
Domestics	70,763	28.4	3,625	7.9	67,188	33.0	12,200	43.7	21,088	25.8
Day laborers	2,706	1.1	343	0.8	2,363	1.2	107	0.4	1,538	1.9
Unemployed	6,326	2.5	799	1.7	5,563	2.7	599	2.1	2,526	3.1

Source: *PM 1902*, I, 2, i, table 2. Calculations are my own.

The long-term residents could have had the same proportions in all occupations when they first arrived in the city, in 1891 or earlier. If this had been true, then there would have been no mobility at all. Having no census for 1892, nor for any of the intervening years, it is impossible to assess the occupational distribution at time of arrival for any of these groups. Using the 1882 census, however, we can discern whether there was any similarity in the pattern of occupational distribution and, by extension, the likelihood that entry-level occupations were held the duration of residence in Moscow. The pattern of occupational distribution in 1882 is strikingly similar to that of 1902. Less than 2 percent of the new arrivals were owners, whereas more than 10 percent of males resident eleven or more years held this position. White-collar employees and blue-collar workers in manufacturing were more prominent among the longtime residents; blue-collar workers in the transport trades, the restaurant and housing business, and in retailing were more prominent among the fresh arrivals to the city.[44]

Such similarity suggests that, barring exceptional years, the pattern did not change significantly at the end of the nineteenth century. Those taking low-level first jobs were not locked into working years on the low rungs of the occupational ladder and had some chance to experience upward mobility. (The chances to experience downward mobility will be examined in the next section.) Places on the lower rungs were easily filled by waves of new arrivals. To the enterprising newcomer who stayed in the city long enough to make the proper connections, acquire the necessary skills and experience, or amass some capital, doors were open.

As they were everywhere else, doors were open wider for some than for others. Doors were open wider for natives as a group than for newcomers, but doors may also have been open wider for those in certain age groups or occupational groups, whether native or newcomer. Again, in the absence of direct data, indirect and inconclusive evidence must serve. The 1902 census did give a detailed listing correlating occupation with gender, age, and birthplace. (Unfortunately, length of residence in the city is unavailable here.) I shall assume that occupational groups with a disproportionate share of young persons would be occupations from which one would have had a greater likelihood to move to different occupational destinations; by the same

44. *PM 1882*, II, 37–42.

token, occupational groups with greater than average proportions of middle-aged persons would be occupations one might hold at the peak of one's working years and earning power.

Certain occupational groups, some of which have already been noted, had an especially youthful labor force. The category of office clerks stands out, with the largest number, both absolutely and proportionately, found in the 20–24 age group. The proportions of office clerks found in the 25–29 age group declined slightly then dropped after age 30. Similar patterns prevailed among silversmiths, turners, painters, typesetters, and lithographers among the skilled trades; and stocking knitters, bakers, waiters, and other restaurant workers among the semi-skilled trades. In all of these groups, there was a marked decline in the numbers after age 30, a decline which cannot be explained by the general decline in the proportions of age groups over 30 in the labor force or by the physical demands of the job alone. The five hundred waiters, who represent the decline in absolute numbers between the ages 15–19 and 20–24, moved on to other jobs, perhaps minor proprietary or white-collar in the restaurant and tavern business. Similarly, painters very likely moved up in the construction business.

An examination of the age structure of occupational groups may give some additional information on the small proprietary and self-employed positions. The decrease in the number of the self-employed, especially in manufacturing, between 1882 and 1902 suggests that competition was keen for this group, particularly in years, such as 1902, of a sluggish economy. This group may have been prone to downward mobility, as former single proprietors were forced to take lower manual jobs. On the other hand, more and more of the self-employed, far from experiencing downward mobility, could have been expanding their operations and hiring laborers and thereby shifting into the census category "employer." Close inspection of the age data suggests that the latter was not the case. The small proprietors and self-employed had one of the highest proportions of persons in the 30–39 and 40–49 age groups and, correspondingly, one of the lowest in the entry-level ages. Since a relatively small portion of the self-employed were at the entry-level ages, self-employment was not a springboard for subsequent jobs, such as higher proprietary and managerial jobs. Rather, in Moscow as in many other cities, small business ownership or self-employment was usually a final step in a work career which began at another job.

Small business ownership or self-employment have been in many societies a final step which began in a manual job, and as such they have provided the greatest opportunity for mobility from manual to nonmanual careers.[45] Although such mobility was no doubt possible in a city of one million, the precariousness of self-employment, as well as the slow rate of growth of semiprofessional and lower managerial jobs, suggests that the barriers between manual and nonmanual jobs were formidable. There were two possible ways to cross the barrier, so to speak: crossing the barrier between generations and crossing the barrier before (or while) arriving in the city.

It is regrettable that one very important parameter of mobility—intergenerational mobility—cannot be subjected to even the crude speculations I have offered for intragenerational mobility. Occupation of father is nowhere revealed in the census, and the evidence presented in a few studies of specific factories or trades is at best fragmentary. We know, for example, from Peskov's study of Moscow mills in 1880 that the fathers of more than two-fifths of the textile workers surveyed were also factory workers; among weavers, the proportion exceeded two-thirds. We also know that a surprisingly large proportion of male workers had long factory records: more than two-thirds had been factory workers at least six years, and more than two-fifths had been factory workers at least fifteen years. Twenty years later the city census showed that certain categories of textile workers—weavers, for instance—showed a disproportionate share in the older age brackets.[46] This suggests occupational stagnation or dead-end jobs rather than mobility. Twenty years after Peskov's study, Shestakov correlated the age of first factory job with occupation of father and demonstrated that those workers whose fathers were also factory workers were much more likely to enter the factory at an early age.[47]

These figures, fragmentary as they are, indicate a degree of stability of factory employment. As V. Sher, then, and Reginald Zelnik, more recently, have argued, this stability was particularly noteworthy in

45. Studies have shown that the greatest amount of occupational shifting has occurred on either side of the manual/nonmanual barrier and that permanent crossings of the barrier are rare. Although American cities have shown somewhat greater mobility than have European, the barrier has been high even in the "land of opportunity." See Thernstrom, *The Other Bostonians*, 232–33; Wilbert E. Moore, "Changes in Occupational Structures," in Neil Smelser and Seymour Martin Lipset, eds., *Social Structure and Mobility in Economic Development* (Chicago, 1966), 203; Seymour Martin Lipset and Reinhard Bendix, *Social Mobility in Industrial Society* (Berkeley, 1959), 170–77.

46. Peskov, *Sanitarnoe issledovanie*, 122, 134; PM 1902, I, 2, i, 46–115.

47. Shestakov, *Rabochie*, 24.

years of economic contraction.[48] Many factory workers, especially in
the more skilled trades, apparently passed on their jobs, or at least
some kind of factory job, to their sons. Nevertheless, the data are also
significant for what they do not reveal. We do not know the entry-
level occupation of the "fathers" in question and therefore cannot
ascertain their own career mobility. Nor do we know the final occupation of the "sons." One statistic I have yet to see is the proportion of
factory fathers who begat tradesmen, clerks, or artisans rather than
factory sons. The image of generation after generation of factory
workers following their fathers' footsteps to loom and lathe would
have been altered drastically if the "fathers" in either Peskov's or
Shestakov's study had started their careers outside the factory gates
and if the "sons" had left the factory grounds at the first opportunity,
particularly in years of economic expansion. How many of them made
it to white-collar occupations and how many of *their* sons started their
careers at Tsindel', we do not know. However, it seems clear that one
reason such a high and remarkably constant proportion of Moscow's
factory workers were born elsewhere is that an insufficient number of
Moscow-born factory sons were staying at the factory.

Immigration itself could have been another way to get around the
formidable barriers to occupational mobility. Contemporary accounts
repeatedly depict Moscow as the land of opportunity, and the large
number of peasant businessmen is one final testimony to the opportunities for occupational advancement that the city provided. The industrial and commercial expansion of Moscow greatly expanded the opportunities for peasant business ownership: given the small size of
most provincial and county towns, nowhere else within hundreds of
miles were there so many opportunities for entrepreneurial ability and
self-employment.[49] A large proportion of the city's employers and a
large majority of its self-employed were first- or second-generation
peasants. Although the data on the ownership of industrial and com-

48. V. Sher, "Fabrichno-zavodskoi rabochii Moskovskoi gubernii," *Vestnik Evropy*,
49, no. 4 (April 1914): 320–21; Reginald Zelnik, "Russian Workers and the Revolutionary Movement," *Journal of Social History* (Winter 1972–73), 214–36. The expansion of
the industrial economy is one explanation for the odd phenomenon that whereas in the
mid-1880s Dement'ev recorded 55 percent of the workers of Moscow province having
factory fathers (*Fabrika*, 46), thirty years later another statistician of the Moscow
zemstvo found only 44 percent of the workers having factory fathers. (I. M. Koz'minykh-Lanin, *Ukhod na polevye raboty fabrichno-zavodskikh rabochikh Moskovskoi gubernii* [Moscow, 1912], 8.) I would add that in years of *general* economic expansion,
opportunities outside the factory may have lured away more factory sons.
49. *Sbornik svedenii po Rossii za 1884–85* (St. Petersburg, 1886), 2–9; *Obshchii
svod*, 1: pt. 2, 6–7; Kurkin, *Statistika*, 22–23; Rashin, *Naselenie*, 101.

mercial enterprises published by the municipal statistical committee cover only the 1880s, they are indicative of significant presence of peasant businessmen in the city's manufacturing, wholesale, and retail economy. Approximately one-third of all commercial and industrial establishments were owned by peasants. Moreover, this proportion increased steadily during the 1880s despite the industrial slump of the economy as a whole. These data, however, give but part of the picture, as only establishments hiring two or more persons were included. According to the 1882 census, which included the self-employed, 34,098 out of 69,923 proprietors were peasants.[50]

These small peasant producers, retailers, builders, and carters were ubiquitous and appear more frequently in the observations of contemporaries than in the advertising section of the city directory or in official listings of manufacturing and retailing establishments. Most likely, the data we have are conservative estimates, to say the least. In all branches of production except textiles, peasants were the most numerous businessmen: in 1882, peasant ownership approached 54 percent of wood-processing establishments, 58.3 percent in the food industry, and 70 percent in the construction industry. In the various branches of retailing and services, peasant ownership reached 68 percent of the business of peddling, street vending, and hawking, and 88 percent of the carrying trades.[51] A special study of the carrying trades in the mid-1890s confirmed that peasants had virtually taken over the business: of 2,595 establishments, 2,255, or 86.9 percent, were owned by peasants.[52]

The preponderance of peasant ownership does not mean, of course, that peasants controlled the industrial or commercial wealth of the city. The most important industry, textiles, was in the hands of the merchants; the value of output was greater (albeit not markedly) in merchant-owned businesses; peasant-owned enterprises employed fewer wage and salaried personnel; and in all likelihood the proportion of peasant-owned businesses decreased somewhat at the turn of the century.[53] Nevertheless, the tenacity or, perhaps more accurately, the vitality of the peasant entrepreneur in the metropolis suggests that small-scale organization was well suited to the vagaries of the Moscow market and the industrial cycle, to the demand for made-to-order and

50. *PM 1882*, II, 303–16; *TPZ*, 15, 34–38, 65–66.
51. *PM 1882*, II, 303–16; *TPZ*, 16–18.
52. *Nekotorye svedeniia o lomovom izvoze v Moskve* (Moscow, 1896), 14.
53. *TPZ*, 36–40, 49–52.

luxury items, and to the demand of a vast internal market of peasants in and around the city. Paradoxically, at a time when the proportion of the total population born in Moscow was increasing slightly, the proportion of Moscow-born employers, presumably one of the most stable elements of the population, actually decreased slightly from 1882 to 1902. The remarkable consistency in the proportion of immigrant employers is testimony to the continued opportunities in the city as well as to the possibilities for upward occupational mobility.

In 1905 P. Timofeev wrote that he had rarely met a worker who had not dreamed about changing his job. He added, though, that "these dreams, of course, rarely materialize, and a large majority [of workers] spend their entire lives in the shop, retaining the same name—worker."[54] Although he did not address this issue specifically, Timofeev indicated that few workers rose to be foremen. A skilled worker applying for a job might have to demonstrate his skills, Timofeev continued, "if the foreman himself had been a worker"—as if that was the exception rather than the rule.[55] The author did suggest ways to please the foreman (including marrying his daughter) and thereby climb up, but occupational advancement was not considered.[56]

Although I have inferred on the basis of structural change and aggregate data that Moscow's laborers could experience upward or lateral occupational mobility, the evidence of occupational stability (immobility) and downward mobility is too pervasive to ignore. Evidence concerning housing conditions, skid-row neighborhoods, and agencies of poor relief, as well as the increasingly shrill rhetoric of the authorities and reformers, will be examined in subsequent chapters. Here we will examine evidence concerning occupational and spatial turnover, casual labor, and unemployment.

IMMOBILITY, DOWNWARD MOBILITY, AND CASUAL LABOR

The indirect evidence for upward occupational mobility for some of the city's new arrivals concerns only those who stayed in Moscow. From 1882 to 1902 almost 100,000 left Moscow every year.[57] This was far larger than the number who experienced upward occupational mo-

---

54. Timofeev, "Ocherki," 72.
55. Timofeev, "Zavodskie budni," 39.
56. Timofeev, "Ocherki," 73.
57. PM 1882, II, pt. 2, 31–34; PM 1902, I, 2, i, 8–11. See also Johnson, *Peasant and Proletarian*, 43–44.

bility within the city. A part of this contingent, to be sure, were seasonal laborers who never had any intention of staying, older peasants returning to their home villages, and peasants who had "made it" in the city. The latter, as contemporaries observed, enriched their cottages with store-bought furniture, table lamps, mirrors, and samovars.[58] Even if such peasants may be regarded as upwardly mobile, it is highly unlikely that the majority left the city with table lamps and samovars. Those who left probably had worse occupational prospects than those who stayed, and in many cases departure signified failure. Moves that did not improve job prospects or marketable skills, or that were the result of poor job prospects and few marketable skills, brought about an aimless drifting at the lower end of the occupational scale, a source of great concern among reformers.

Even among those immigrants who did not experience this aimless drifting but who settled down in the city, occupational stability was a common experience. For example, although immigrants who had resided in Moscow more than ten years were better represented on the upper rungs of the occupational ladder than were newly arrived immigrants, immigrants who had resided in the city for intermediate periods of time displayed stability rather than upward mobility. This was particularly noticeable among employers; immigrant employers resident in the city one to five years were actually less likely to hold employer positions than were new arrivals.[59]

Occupational immobility and downward mobility and the aimless drifting at the bottom of the occupational ladder contributed to the growth of a casual labor force. Like Paris and London, Moscow during the second half of the nineteenth century had a chronic glut of unskilled laborers, employed intermittently or casually. In every trade, the nucleus of permanently (or more or less permanently) employed was surrounded by a casual fringe which worked on the waterfront, in the transport, construction, carting, and hauling trades, in the wholesale markets, and as hawkers, messengers, vendors, draymen, and laborers in low-grade and unhealthy factory jobs. Although reformers at the end of the nineteenth century decried the loss of craft skills, a large, economically marginal reserve population in every sector of the

58. Zhbankov, *Bab'ia storona*, 66–69; Kirillov, "K voprosu," 291; V. P. Semenov, *Moskovskaia promyshlennaia oblast'*, 104.

59. *PM 1902*, I, 2, i, 8–11. On the other hand, Thernstrom speculates that in the large cities the opportunities may have been even greater than in small towns for the advancement of low manual workers; accordingly many stayed in the metropolises. (*The Other Bostonians*, 247–48.)

economy from manufacturing to domestic service was vital to the metropolis at this stage of development and economic organization.

Casual employment is marginal, peripheral, unstable, and redundant. It comes about when sporadic demand leading to intermittent employment coincides with an oversupply of potential laborers. It also comes when modern organizational methods have incompletely penetrated certain sectors—construction, transport, retailing, and services, for example—of a dynamic, expanding economy. Many casual trades, being residual occupations in a modernizing economy, pay low wages per unit of energy or time: dock work, ditchdigging, manual bricklaying, ice-cutting, refuse removal, scavenging, ragpicking, domestic service, message delivery, street vending, and door-to-door peddling are examples of such occupations.[60] Because of the imperfectly differentiated economies of the largest cities, the rapidly expanding employment opportunities for common labor in trade, transport, services, and construction in central districts, and the inadequate system of public transport, hiring took place at outdoor marketplaces, the most important of which were in the city center, which added greatly to their prominence and notoriety.

Even worse than the low level of income is the insecurity of income and the erratic nature of demand. The construction trades, for example, were erratic both in their seasonality and in their sensitivity to the business cycle. Some common labor in the construction trades actually paid very well. A brick carrier who could carry a goatskin bag (*koza*) of thirty to thirty-five bricks on his back could earn at least 1 ruble 25 kopeks per day, a wage which, had it been regular and year-round, would have meant an annual income of over 350 rubles, more than that of many skilled workers. Of course, such a wage was not regular, and many day laborers worked only half the week "in season" and came upon hard times in the "off season." According to one observer, in the winter the same brick carriers were driven to clear snow, collect garbage, or beg. The lack of jobs coupled with the influx of several thousand laborers from the villages made the spring and fall bad seasons; during the former, "many day laborers gather nettles, sorrel, the buds of birch and pine trees, worms, and so forth, to keep from starving."[61] Also very seasonal were the clothing trades, as a

60. A. Gorovtsev [Gor-ev], "K kharakteristike ekonomicheskikh i bytovykh uslovii zhizni bezrabotnykh," *Mir Bozhii*, no. 10 (October 1899): 38. See also Eames and Goode, *Urban Poverty*, 118, 125, 257.

61. Gor-ev, "K kharakteristike," 37–38.

1914 study noted; periods of intense work alternated with periods of unemployment:

In the busy season one notices constant overtime work and a mad rush, so that the tailor doesn't even have enough time for meals and sleep. But in the slack season there is often nothing to eat. Starving workers at this time roam from workshop to workshop looking for jobs.[62]

Such erratic employment made it impossible to keep anything resembling a budget, and was, according to Oliunina, responsible for the endemic alcoholism among tailors and prostitution among seamstresses.[63] A "budget" was arguably even more of a problem for common laborers than for tailors. The former group was far less "settled," took jobs all over the city, and was forced to eat at the nearest soup kitchen or tavern. As a result, according to municipal investigations, common laborers spent half their wages on breakfast and dinner and the rest on supper, drink, and lodging. Any day without work was disastrous.[64]

Employment in occupations where the demand was not clearly seasonal (such as cigarette making, candy wrapping, flower vending, itinerant repairing, and ragpicking) could be even more erratic. The writer N. A. Leikin describes common women laborers looking for work at an outdoor labor market. One woman complains, "This is already the fourth day I've come here and haven't earned a penny. . . . One day I'll work and then four days there'll be nothing."[65] Such sporadic employment was compounded by the erratic and random way that such laborers learned about jobs. In Leikin's novel *Working*, the women laborers "hear" that before the Easter holidays is a good time to get such jobs as charwomen and learn about the other jobs by rumor, word of mouth, and chance encounters. Arina and Akulina, the two major characters, go off to get a job at a junkyard because of a chance encounter with a woman who once worked there.[66] Hiring itself was frequently erratic: at the factory gates or the workshop door, in taverns and tearooms, at city squares such as Haymarket in St. Petersburg and Khitrov in Moscow, at construction sites, the docks or the railroad freight yards, or on streets such as Arbat and Tverskaia, for domestic servants.[67]

62. Oliunina, *Portnovskii promysel*, 7.
63. Ibid., 324.
64. Gor-ev, "K kharakteristike," 38.
65. Leikin, *Na zarabotkakh*, 130.
66. Ibid., 90, 127.
67. D. Gomberg, "K voprosu ob uchrezhdenii Gorodskoi posrednicheskoi kontory," *IMGD*, 30, no. 17 (September, 1906): 14–15.

Jobs in the junkyards, in refuse collecting, in ragpicking and scavenging provide examples of menial labor in the metropolis. In 1902 Moscow had only 152 registered ragpickers (64 of whom were women), 1,092 street cleaners, and 811 garbage collectors, but such menial occupations, and ragpicking and scavenging in particular, relied on the surplus of unskilled laborers who came to the junkyards when there was no other work.[68] Usually old women, fit for no other jobs, worked full time in the junkyards. Leikin describes a junkyard in Petersburg, and one can assume that the junkyards beyond the Sushchevo or Rogozh' wards did not differ appreciably:

Sheds and tottering, decrepit wooden canopies were scattered about a huge yard. Under the canopies one could see all kinds of junk—overturned carts, old crates, old wheels, axles, carriage shafts, the chassis of city coaches broken in two, even an omnibus without wheels and lying on its side. Junk was piled up between the canopies, the junk almost reaching the roof. On looking at these piles more closely, one could see iron hoops, rusty nails, bones, broken glass, cork, spools, tin cans and jars.[69]

Groups of women and young boys, usually hired straight from the villages, collected the junk, in return for food, shelter, and clothing. They went from yard to yard with bags and three-pronged hooks collecting refuse. The ragpickers and scavengers occasionally had specialized tasks:

Some would buy up rags, bones, bottles, jars, and so forth, and then resell it all. Others would only search for refuse on the streets, in yards, in garbage cans, and in the trash piles. All are brought back for inspection by the junkyard's owner.[70]

This was not the end of the working day, however: after scavenging all day in the city's dumps, the ragpickers at home had to sort out and clean the rags and separate the flax from cotton and the broken glass from unbroken bottles. Sorting the bones was tolerable, but the stench and filth made sorting the rags almost unbearable. Damp rags were hung out in the courtyard and even in the living quarters to dry. What was fit to be washed was washed and stored until the next Sunday, when rags were taken to the mills, bones to the glue factory and rendering plants, and old clothes to the flea markets. The ragpickers lived alongside the junk in sheds that were excellent carriers of disease,

68. PM 1902, I, 2, i, table 6; Leikin, Na zarabotkakh, 158.
69. Leikin, Na zarabotkakh, 152–53.
70. G. Gertsenshtein, "Gde i kak iutitsia peterburgskaia bednota?" Severnyi vestnik, no. 3 (1898): 141.

one reason why municipal ordinances forbade junkyards within the city limits.[71]

Certain menial occupations stood out in the eyes of contemporaries because of the ubiquitousness of persons engaged in them or because of certain character traits or style of dress associated with certain jobs in the popular mind. One such occupational group was the *dvornik*, a job which combined the functions of concierge, janitor, and building superintendent, obliged, according to municipal ordinances, to clean the streets and sidewalks (including snow and ice removal in winter) and to help the police keep public order and apprehend suspicious characters.[72]

The superintendent is such a distinctive type that, even if he is without his broom, you will recognize him immediately in his apron, his greasy cap, his peasant shoes (*koty*) on his bare feet, leaning on the gatepost of his master's house. . . . His facial expression is usually dull and angry, and his entire figure expresses laziness and apathy, no doubt a consequence of a disagreeable job that forces him either to root around constantly in the garbage or manure, or spend the whole night unlocking the gate for residents. No doubt for these reasons he is usually sulky and unsociable.[73]

Superintendents were prominent not only because they were colorful: 17,214 of them in 1902 sulked in the streets and courtyards of Moscow, making them an occupation exceeded in number only by sales clerks, soldiers, domestic servants, cooks, weavers, and tailors.[74]

Casual labor figured prominently in the writings of reformers. Again and again "parasitic elements," "vagrancy and idleness," or the inability to prove one's means of livelihood appear on the pages of journals at the end of the nineteenth century. It was easily assumed that those who had sporadic employment were lazy and that the metropolis attracted such persons. Despite the increasingly shrill rhetoric from the authorities and reformers, no one tackled the arduous task of estimating the number of casual laborers. The hard core, so to speak, of the casual labor force were those appearing in the census as "unemployed," "unskilled," "day laborers," and "on relief." Around this core was the remainder of the category of unskilled laborers and menial service workers, numbering 116,837 in 1902 and 163,087 in 1912, approximately 15 percent of the labor force. This category in-

71. Ibid., 141–42; Leikin, *Na zarabotkakh*, 160.
72. Moskovskaia gorodskaia duma, *Sbornik obiazatel'nykh dlia zhitelei goroda Moskvy postanovlenii* (Moscow, 1914), 50.
73. Golitsynskii, *Ulichnye tipy*, 36–37.
74. PM 1902, I, 2, i, table 6.

cluded such precarious occupations as washerwoman, janitor, coachman, building superintendent, chambermaid, and other menials of private or public institutions. In addition, many semiskilled laborers were
prone to casual employment as the market temporarily needed, for
example, fewer draymen, weavers, cigarette-makers, seamstresses,
waiters, and cooks. By 1912 the category of "semiskilled" constituted
one-quarter of the labor force. Finally, other categories, such as artisans, petty tradesmen and landlords, and those supported by relatives,
were also prone to casual employment.[75]

Several municipal reports of mendicancy, housing conditions, slum
life, and the City Workhouse suggest not only which occupations were
prominent among the casual labor force but also which occupations
were prone to downward mobility. The majority of flophouse residents and wards of the Workhouse were currently engaged in begging,
unskilled day labor, domestic service, or menial jobs such as washerwoman. Nevertheless, survey after survey showed that from 25 to 40
percent of this population were currently employed as artisans. Artisans also figured prominently whenever the investigators were told
previous occupation or training. In the files of the Workhouse one
employee wrote that though few listed a current artisanal occupation,
most declared that by training they were skilled craftsmen.[76] One
survey of occupational groups among 15,000 wards of the Workhouse
in 1900 showed that approximately one-quarter were artisans (including a surprising 1,455 in the metal trades), as well as nearly 1,000 in
sales-clerical positions. Twelve years later the Vocational Center had
40,000 applicants, more than 45 percent of whom called themselves
artisans. By contrast, usually no more than 20 percent of the population surveyed were factory workers.[77] For example, the largest number
of laborers applying for aid from the Municipal Guardianship of the
Poor in 1895 were artisans (38 percent), while only 7 percent of the
applicants were factory workers.[78] Thus, although most artisanal occu-

75. *PM 1902*, I, 2, i, 46–115; I, 2, iii, 170–215; *SEMMG*, 68–73.
76. TsGAM, f. 184, op. 2, d. 852, l. 60.
77. Moskovskoe gorodskoe obshchestvennoe upravlenie, *Moskovskii gorodskoi
dom trudoliubiia i Rabotnyi dom v ego proshlom i nastoiashchem*, compiled by S.
Sharov (Moscow, 1913), 25–26, 72; Raevskii, "K voprosu," 86, 108; S. Sharov, "Kharakteristika klientov Moskovskogo Doma trudoliubiia," *IMGD*, 38, no. 3 (March
1914): 10; M. Pozner, "Nochlezhnye doma i nochlezhniki v Moskve," *IMGD*, 15, no. 6
(1891): 34–38; Kurnin, *O nekotorykh usloviiakh*, 18–19; K. V. Karaffa-Korbut,
"Nochlezhnye doma v bol'shikh russkikh gorodakh," *Gorodskoe delo*, no. 10 (May 15,
1912): 642; S. V. Kurnin, "Bezrabotnye na Khitrovom rynke v Moskve," *Russkoe
bogatstvo*, no. 2 (February 1898): 169.
78. Gor-ev, "K kharakteristike," 118.

pations have been ranked here as skilled blue-collar, this does not necessarily mean that their employment prospects were secure. Indeed, this precariousness of his job is an additional justification for not placing the self-employed artisan in the low white-collar category.

The census counted a curiously small number of unemployed—only 18,117 in 1902 and 29,412 in 1912. Such figures, like those for "day laborer" and "unskilled," must be treated with great caution; given that the census taker was asking for occupation rather than current job status, it is likely that the figures for the number unemployed are seriously underestimated. There were relatively more natives among the 11,755 officially unemployed males than among the labor force as a whole. This was particularly noticeable among all categories of wage laborers, where the proportion of Moscow-born was more than double the proportion of Moscow-born in the entire labor force. Moreover, temporary unemployment was a more common phenomenon than long-term unemployment, if the former is defined as unemployed less than one month and the latter as unemployed more than six months. Using these criteria, almost one-quarter had been unemployed less than one month, while 15 percent had been unemployed more than six months.[79]

Given these basic parameters, two questions may be posed. Were outsiders more prone to long-term unemployment than natives? And did Moscow residence help keep immigrants from being jobless, or at least from being jobless a long time? The first question may be quickly answered in the negative. Moscow-born laborers were approximately twice as likely to have been unemployed for one year or more; and whereas 25 percent of the immigrants were temporarily unemployed, only 15 percent of the Moscow-born fell into this category. Surprisingly, the natives hardest hit were in categories of white-collar labor, and in particular clerical workers in the housing and restaurant business.[80] It would seem that these jobs were the insecure white-collar jobs whose holders were prone to downward occupational mobility. It is fair to assume that in addition to those clerical workers who lost their jobs, others fell to blue-collar jobs.

The second question is more difficult to answer. It would seem that an immigrant who stayed in the city for two years lessened the chances of being unemployed for a long time. A three-year or longer stay, however, seemed to increase those chances, although not to the level

79. *PM 1902*, I, 2, i, 189–205; *SEMMG*, 68–73.
80. *PM 1902*, I, 2, i, 198–205.

of the outsider who had just arrived. At the same time, the outsider who had stayed three or more years was slightly less likely to have been temporarily unemployed.

The Moscow-born fared poorly among the ranks of the unemployed for several reasons. Recent arrivals had a greater chance of not being reported, thus skewing the proportions in favor of the more permanent residents. Minors, women, and the elderly may have been thrown out of work more easily, and there were more native-born among these groups. However, it is not likely that this alone could account for the greater proportion of unemployed native wage laborers, especially in such trades as transport which had miniscule proportions of minors, women, and the elderly. Finally, Moscow-born laborers who lost their jobs may have had no choice but to remain in Moscow to look for other jobs, thus increasing their chance of appearing in the unemployment statistics. Immigrants who lost their jobs were more inclined to engage in unskilled or casual labor (categories with small representation of Muscovites), move elsewhere, or return home. There is statistical as well as fictional evidence that the village continued to remain a safety valve for the unemployed peasant.[81]

❖   ❖   ❖

Upon arrival, the city's immigrants entered a complex labor force consisting of virtually all crafts and occupations known in late imperial Russia. Because of the preponderance of immigrants who could bring dependents to Moscow only with great difficulty, as well as the demand of a booming metropolitan economy, the labor force constituted approximately 70 percent of the entire population, a higher proportion than that of any other major Russian or European city at the time. Although the city censuses present a very full picture of the labor force, using categories based on branch of the economy or terms of employment, I have gone one step beyond such an arrangement in an effort to examine the parameters of placement on the labor force, structural changes, and individual occupational changes. I have grouped the population into white-collar and blue-collar workers and have ranked occupations in a hierarchy ranging from high white-collar (largely professionals) to unskilled menial jobs.

More than two-thirds of the labor force were blue-collar, and of the

81. See, for example, Semenov, *Dvadtsat' piat' let*, 170–71, and Chekhov, "Peasants." See also Bulgakov, *Peredvizhenie*, 6; and Kurkin, *Statistika*, 502–3.

blue-collar labor force, two-thirds were semiskilled or menial workers. The lower blue-collar jobs attracted proportionately more immigrants and women than did skilled blue-collar or most white-collar jobs. Although many women were found in certain high white-collar occupations, such as teachers, they had barely penetrated other professions or positions of major ownership and fared markedly worse than men in skilled blue-collar and sales-clerical jobs, two occupational categories offering rapidly expanding opportunities at the beginning of the twentieth century. At the bottom rungs of the occupational ladder, the proportion of women holding unskilled jobs, such as domestic service, actually increased. Although natives had an advantage over immigrants in managerial, professional, and proprietary jobs (and particularly in sales-clerical jobs), the higher rungs on the occupational ladder were by no means closed to newcomers. Blue-collar jobs in transport, the housing and restaurant business, and domestic service were the easiest entries into the labor market for the newcomer. Not only the fact of being an immigrant but also actual birthplace influenced placement on the labor force. Immigrants from regions with some manufacturing and a long tradition of seasonal migratory labor were much more likely than immigrants from more agricultural regions to enter white-collar jobs. Finally, literacy and skill level, as might be expected, influenced placement on the labor force. Those jobs where women, immigrants in general, and immigrants from agricultural regions in particular had a markedly poor showing—professional, upper managerial, and proprietary, to be sure, but also sales-clerical and skilled blue-collar—were jobs requiring a much higher degree of literacy and skills than the occupational categories immediately below.

Significantly, professional, upper managerial, and proprietary, sales-clerical and skilled blue-collar jobs presented the most rapidly expanding opportunities in a labor force whose structure was shifting gradually. An increasingly modern economy had in particular greater need for professionals, technicians, and sales-clerical personnel. The rate of increase in the number of white-collar workers in proprietary and employer positions was neither as high nor as constant. In poor economic years, such as those just preceding the 1902 census, their number barely increased, but in good years, such as those preceding the 1912 census, the rate of increase of employers, and even of the self-employed, outpaced that of wage laborers. Given the sectoral changes in the economy discussed in chapter 3, trade and commerce provided the best opportunity for businessmen in the years 1902–1912. Not only was there an overall gradual structural shift as white-collar jobs made gains at the expense of blue-collar jobs, there were shifts within these two large divisions. Thus, for example, the category sales-clerical made marked gains over semiprofessional and lower managerial and professional white-collar jobs, and skilled blue-collar jobs made gains over semiskilled blue-collar jobs.

While direct evidence of individual career patterns is lacking, such structural shifts, as well as indirect evidence that those immigrants who stayed long periods of time in the city improved their job prospects and entrepreneurial skills, suggest that lateral and upward mobility were attainable in the metropolis. Long-term immigrants were more likely than new arrivals to find higher jobs, and those taking low-level first jobs were not locked in but had chances for upward mobility. The nonmanual–manual barrier, while crossable, presented formidable obstacles. No doubt there were some nonmanual sons of manual fathers, but the data on intergenerational mobility provide even weaker grounds for speculation than do the data on intragenerational mobility. The actual process of immigration itself provided the best opportunity to cross the nonmanual–manual barrier, and the myriad of peasant businessmen demonstrate that in part Moscow lived up to its image as a place of opportunity.

Unfortunately, for many Moscow was a place of thwarted opportunity, and much more noticeable to the authorities, as will be shown in Part Three, were occupational stagnation and downward mobility. While frequent change of jobs may have produced upward occupational mobility in some cases, it was more often a sign of aimless drifting at the lower rungs of the occupational ladder. Nearly 100,000 persons left Moscow every year, and though many had had no intention of staying, the job prospects of those who left were worse than of those who stayed. An expanding yet erratic and poorly organized metropolitan economy demanded that those with poor job prospects and little or no skill continue to come to the city. A supply of casual laborers was essential to the rapid growth of the city: common laborers could be hired by the job, and a myriad of street vendors, hawkers, and draymen were essential, given the incomplete penetration of modern methods of retailing and distribution. In addition, the Moscow market attracted more skilled craftsmen than could find employment at any one time, making artisans prone to downward mobility, as study after study of the city's skid row or of welfare cases showed. Artisans as well as casual laborers faced an erratic market, erratic hiring practices, and frequent periods of unemployment.

A booming but volatile and dualistic metropolitan economy generated a booming but volatile and dualistic labor force. More brains were needed than ever before; at the same time more brawn was needed to build, move, haul, and clean. Occupational stratification was becoming more and more complex; one contemporary noted that "the world of the factory is completely different from that of the plant," and the difference in skill levels and working conditions for the skilled metalworker and the menials ("servants") was increasing. Never had opportunities been greater for the skilled and enterprising; given that the position of the unskilled laborer is more precarious in a skilled, urban society than in an agrarian society, never had the consequences of missing those opportunities been more disastrous. These consequences were vividly illustrated by the city's increasingly overcrowded housing market and by the households of the city's muzhiks, the subject of the next chapter.

CHAPTER SIX

Housing and Households

For Moscow's laboring population, second only to a pressing need to find employment was the need to find shelter. The two to three million immigrants beckoned by the job opportunities of a booming metropolitan economy between 1880 and 1900 put considerable pressure on the city's housing stock and had a marked impact on the city's household and family structure. For centuries Moscow's transient immigrants, with little stake in the city and a strong stake in the village, had been used to finding makeshift urban accommodations while maintaining their real home elsewhere. Although an increasing number of skilled workers were settling and making Moscow their permanent home, the expanding and volatile economy demanded that more and more immigrants come. Consequently, the majority of the labor force still had to find makeshift urban accommodations as the conditions of their employment permitted.

By the end of the nineteenth century housing had become a major issue for the authorities and reformers. Many contemporary studies used housing as a criterion by which to differentiate among blue-collar workers. Schulze-Gävernitz, for example, to a great degree based his stage theory of the Europeanization of Russian workers on the type of housing. The hardships the muzhiks faced in the city were frequently epitomized by their housing conditions. The breakdown of traditional morals and family virtues that reformers feared in the teeming metropolis was epitomized by the composition of households and the nature of the family life among the muzhiks. Moreover, the deleterious housing conditions and alleged family breakdown were not confined to a few isolated neighborhoods or distant working-class suburbs: the muzhik was everywhere in the city. Accordingly, the purpose of this chapter will be to analyze the city's housing market and the housing conditions of the laboring population as well as to examine the composition and spatial distribution of the city's households. An analysis of these parameters of the daily lives of the laboring population in this chapter will provide a link to the subsequent analysis of the perceptions of these parameters and of the policies implemented on the part of the municipal authorities and reformers.

THE HOUSING MARKET

At first glance it would not appear that Moscow's housing market would have been severely strained by the influx of immigrant laborers. Before the emancipation of the serfs, Russian cities were no more thickly settled than those of medieval Europe, and foreign travelers without exception noticed the vast tracts of unused land and the sprawling one-story wooden buildings. The official *Military-Statistical Review of the Russian Empire* in 1853 noted that half of Moscow's territory consisted of gardens, orchards, ponds, and rivers.[1] Fifty years later, according to a survey of the Ministry of Internal Affairs, only two-thirds of Moscow's total area was built up.[2] The density of population per unit of land was lower than in western Europe largely because the use of wood for building material prevented construction of tall, compact housing. In 1853 only 5,785 out of approximately 18,000 buildings were made of stone. More complete information from the 1882 and 1912 censuses allows us to make a comparison of two thirty-year intervals. Despite the building boom at the end of the century, wood continued to be the primary construction material in the metropolitan area: the proportion of wooden buildings actually increased because of the nearly exclusive use of wood in the city's rapidly growing suburbs. That the proportion of wooden buildings within the city limits declined only gradually from 1882 to 1912 reflects the continued reliance on the cheaper building material and more rapid construction to house a rapidly growing population even in the heart of the city.[3]

1. *Voenno-statisticheskoe obozrenie Rossiiskoi imperii za 1853*, cited in *Istoriia Moskvy*, 4:58–59.
2. *TsGIA*, f. 1290, op. 5, d. 195, ll. 1–15.
3. *PM 1882*, I, 48–60; *SEM za 1913–14*, 30, 34–37, 46–47. The 1853 figure is quoted in *Istoriia Moskvy*, 4:58–59.

The continued use of wood for construction immediately suggests a predominance of one- and two-story buildings. So great was this predominance in 1882 that less than 5 percent of the city's residential buildings had more than two floors above ground. Thirty years later this proportion had increased almost threefold, and the 1915 guidebook breathlessly observed that four- and five-story buildings were growing "like mushrooms and radically altering the physiognomy of the city."[4] The fact remains, however, that seven out of every eight residential buildings were only one- or two-story on the eve of World War I.[5] The continued predominance of wooden residential buildings suggests that the housing stock was not improving greatly at the beginning of the twentieth century. At the same time, the many one- and two-story residences suggest that Moscow did not have the problems of high-rise tenement housing that beset Western metropolises. Construction materials and building height, however, are only the two most visible features of the city's housing stock. In order to get a more complete picture of Moscow's housing situation, several other factors must be considered.

The key to understanding Moscow's housing problems lies in the number of apartments per building and the number of residents per apartment. Although the density of population per unit of land was relatively low, the density per housing unit was high. According to the 1912 census, 39,051 residential buildings contained 164,022 housing units. With 8.5 persons per housing unit, Moscow was twice as densely settled as European capitals, where 3.9 Berliners, 4.2 Viennese, and 4.5 Londoners occupied each housing unit in those metropolises.[6] Given that there had been 8.9 persons per housing unit in 1882, this congestion had gone virtually unchanged during the previous three decades, despite a 43 percent increase in the number of occupied housing units during the decade 1902–1912 alone. With nearly as many residents per housing unit, the suburbs, so sprawling and village-like in outward appearance, were just as densely inhabited as the city proper.[7] For example, in 1882 the average number of persons per apartment was highest in Lefort and Sepukhov, two outlying wards. These two wards also had the highest proportion of per-

4. *Moskva: Putevoditel'* (Moscow, 1915), 117.
5. *SEM za 1913–14*, 48.
6. *GPD 1912*, 16–17.
7. *PM 1882*, I, pt. 2, 1–4; *GPD 1912*, 30, 34–37.

sons living in apartments containing twenty or more residents and the second and third highest ratio of residents per room.[8]

These averages, like all others, conceal a great amount of variation in the size of housing units and number of rooms, and comparisons over time are not always possible. A reasonably accurate barometer of housing congestion were the basement apartments, almost synonymous with the "housing question" and the subject of a special 1885 study. Approximately 10 percent of Moscow's apartments were found in basements; this proportion remained virtually unchanged for thirty years despite the greater proportion of apartments located above the second floor. Perhaps more alarming, the proportion of the population occupying basement apartments had jumped 50 percent by 1912; in absolute terms 119,585, or one out of every eight apartment-renters, lived in a basement. Basement living quarters frequently doubled as workshops and sweatshops, thus combining two of the worst features of the housing market: basement residence and the combination of working and living quarters. In 1895, for example, 64 of 334 bakeries were located underground.[9] Basement apartments were rather evenly scattered throughout the city. The inner Sretenka ward had the largest proportion of the population living in basement apartments in 1882; other wards with more than 10 percent of the population living in basements were Tver', Prechistenka, Presnia, and Meshchane.[10]

Another barometer of housing conditions was the presence of modern conveniences. Both the 1882 and 1912 censuses noted the number of living units with indoor plumbing and with flush toilets. Unlike the constant proportion of basement apartments, which suggests an unimproving housing market, there were improvements in the more purely technological area of modern conveniences. In 1882, 15,496 living units, or 22 percent of those for which figures were available, had either indoor plumbing or flush toilets or both. Thirty years later this proportion had grown two and one-half times. More than 800,000 persons, or almost 60 percent of the city's population, lived in housing units with at least one of the two modern conveniences. Even more impressive, by 1912 more than 90 percent of the housing units in

8. *PM 1882*, I, pt. 2, 86–88, 116–19, 137–38.
9. *PM 1882*, I, pt. 2, 61; *SEM*, 66–67; Moskovskaia gorodskaia uprava, *Moskovskie khlebopekarni v 1895 g.* (Moscow, 1896), 17.
10. *PM 1882*, I, pt. 2, 62.

many of the central wards (including an astonishing 98.4 percent in Tver's second precinct) had either indoor plumbing or flush toilets.[11]

However, in both 1882 and 1912 the central wards were notably better serviced than were the outlying wards. In 1882 the proportion of housing units in the central Tver' ward with indoor plumbing was ten times greater than that of Rogozh' on the southeast side.[12] Given the technologies, as well as the politics, involved in this form of housing improvement, it is only to be expected that central districts would have a piped water supply sooner than outer districts.[13] The gap remained wide thirty years later. By 1912, when more than 98 percent of the housing units of one central precinct had either plumbing or toilets, only 18 percent of the housing units in the second precinct of the southern Serpukhov ward had either convenience.[14]

Throughout this discussion I have used the term "housing units" or "living quarters" rather than "homes" or "apartments." The reason is that the rapid growth of the metropolitan economy, the massive influx of immigrants, and the shortage of housing space on the private-apartment market created a housing market with a variety of self-contained, subdivided, communal, and institutional housing units, for which the term "apartment" is misleading. Table 12 shows the variety of living units available in the city. In 1912 one-quarter of the population lived in hotels and boarding houses, communal (artel') apartments, special quarters for building superintendents and doormen, school and factory dormitories, shelters, almshouses, hospitals, prisons, jails, barracks, monasteries, and housing for laborers in the home of the employer.

Despite the ambiguities in the arrangement of the data and the overlapping of individual units, certain broad categories of housing can be discerned: institutional, "company," commercial, communal, and "private." Institutional units were those provided for the wards of private, municipal, or state institutions. The institutions singled out by the census compilers were monasteries and convents, schools, prisons and jails, barracks for soldiers, policemen, and firemen, hospitals, almshouses, and shelters. As might be expected, institutional housing had the largest number of persons per unit; in 1897 the average institutional unit housed 43.2 persons.[15] Although the number housed in

11. *PM 1882*, I, pt. 3, 37; *SEM*, 38–39, 62.
12. *PM 1882*, I, pt. 3, 37.
13. Bater, "Some Dimensions of Urbanization," 46–63.
14. *SEM*, 38–39.
15. *PVP*, 24a, pt. 1, 4–7.

such facilities increased from 56,789 in 1882 and 63,354 in 1897 to 92,095 in 1912, the proportion of the population so housed actually declined from 7.6 percent to 6.6 percent.[16] Large numbers of institutionally housed residents were found in the Serpukhov, Rogozh', Lefort, Meshchane, Sushchevo, and Khamovniki wards. Among these institutional units, almshouses, shelters, and all forms of welfare housing will be discussed in subsequent chapters.

Similar to institutional housing was "company" housing, that is, housing provided to employees by their employers. One of the forms of "company housing" were noninstitutional units provided to civil servants, officers, and municipal employees and variously termed *kvartiry po sluzhbe* or *sluzhebnye kvartiry* in the censuses. Other employer housing included those provided to employers of commercial enterprises such as taverns and the public baths and those provided to domestic servants, superintendents, and guards by their masters. The latter often lived in notoriously undesirable accommodations, "crowded, low, slanting quarters under the second-floor landing where you can stand upright only at the entrance." The largest numbers of this kind of company housing were located in the central business district.[17] I have chosen to treat "company" housing separately because certain small-scale varieties would be difficult to place in the category "institutional" and because this form of housing was particularly important to blue-collar workers.

The stereotypical form of company housing was that provided to workers by the manufacturers and usually taking one of three basic forms: lodging in the living quarters of the employer himself, sleeping at the workplace, and housing in specially constructed dormitories at the larger factories. The first two forms were not new in late-nineteenth-century Moscow. An employer, whether a textile middleman or an artisan, lodging a few laborers, apprentices, or journeymen was a commonplace in Europe, too, in the early stages of industrialization; the custom remained prevalent in the sweated trades in the metropolises well into the early twentieth century. Sleeping at the workplace was also an old tradition in both rural and urban Russia. A study of the Moscow textile industry in the late 1870s revealed that most weavers slept at the workplace; of fifty workshops for handloom weavers, only two had separate sleeping quarters:

16. *PM 1882*, I, pt. 2, 1–4; *PVP*, 24a, pt. 1, 4–7; *SEM*, 52–59.
17. Gertsenshtein, "Gde i kak iutitsia?" 125–26; *PM 1882*, I, pt. 3, 40–45, 50–55.

TABLE 12:   STRUCTURE OF MOSCOW'S HOUSING MARKET

Type of living unit	1882 Units		1882 Residents		1912 Units		1912 Residents	
	Number	Percent	Number	Percent	Number	Percent	Number	Percent
Institutional	2,417	2.5	56,789	7.6	2,015	1.3	92,095	6.6
Dormitories[a]	705		12,724		164		13,009	
Shelters, almshouses	561		13,611		528		21,999	
Hospitals, maternity wards	308		7,012		385		14,704	
Prisons, jails	67		3,939		65		6,281	
Barracks	877		16,561		272		21,561	
Quarters for police, firemen[b]	—		—		537		10,961	
Monasteries, convents[c]	399		2,942		64		3,578	
Company (provided by employer)	14,887	15.4	161,286	21.4	32,317	20.1	207,205	14.8
Quarters for office workers	9,839		58,912		12,736		58,501	
Workers' dormitories	424		22,142		1,129		50,138	
Other quarters for workers[d]	4,430		80,232		8,088		66,553	
All worker housing	4,854		102,374		9,217		116,691	
Quarters for domestics, superintendents	—		—		10,364		32,013	
Independent communal housing	951	1.0	17,548	2.3	530	0.3	20,207	1.4
Artel apartments	—		—		304		9,260	
Other communal units	—		—		226		10,947	

Source: PM 1882, I, pt. 2, 1–4; SEM, 4:52–59.

Commercial housing[e]	1,457	1.5	45,988	6.1	305	—	17,963	—
Hotels and inns	629		20,240		—		—	
Boarding houses	332		13,845		—		—	
Lodging houses	234		9,664		—		—	
Other	262		2,239		—		—	
Ordinary, private housing	57,525	59.5	469,880	62.5	124,031	77.0	1,047,501	74.9
Occupied only by owner and family	—		—		7,791		57,580	
Occupied only by tenants, families, servants	—		—		48,977		298,790	
Apartments with subletting of rooms	—		—		46,198		407,831	
Apartments with subletting of parts of rooms, beds	—		—		21,065		283,300	
Other private living units	—		—		1,791	1.1	13,702	1.0
Units exclusively for industrial, commercial use	13,759	14.2	—		—		—	
Vacant units	5,763	6.0	—		—		—	
All Housing Units	96,759	100.0	751,491	100.0	160,989	100.0	1,398,672	100.0

[a] Affiliated with educational institutions.

[b] Most likely counted under "barracks" in 1882.

[c] Includes all ecclesiastical units in 1882.

[d] Includes housing for both factory and artisanal workers. However, a footnote in the census states that only half of the city's laborers were included. Excluded were, among others, workers living in the same housing unit as their employers, factory workers not housed by the factory, and day laborers. Living quarters for superintendents, domestics, and some outworkers may have been included in the category "ordinary apartments."

[e] Figures very incomplete in 1912 census.

The top of the loom usually serves as a bed, where sometimes an entire family can be found on the corded boards. Sacks stuffed with hay or straw act as bedding, but that is rare; more often the workers sleep on their own clothes or on some dirty, torn shreds, sometimes on felt strips or mats.[18]

The lack of sleeping quarters for the handloom weavers was not considered too unusual, since

handloom weavers, being primarily country folks and not having completely lost the habits and attitudes acquired in the villages, perhaps see in the loom something familiar, reminiscent of their own home and their own possessions, especially, if they and their family sleep on them.[19]

Widespread factory housing was both more recent and more common in Russia than in the West. It grew out of a need to house homeless migrant laborers from far-off provinces, a lack of cheap, private accommodations in factory villages and a shortage of such in the big cities, the tradition of serf factory labor, the need to house the workers away from the workbench when the factory became mechanized and went on shifts, and finally the need to attract cheap woman and child labor. A zemstvo survey of factory villages in Moscow province revealed that in the 1880s more than 50 percent of the factory workers were housed in factory housing, 25 percent lived at home, and only 18 percent rented housing on the private market.[20]

The barrack-style housing at the larger factories consisted of three- or four-story units with several large sleeping rooms connected by a long corridor. Some dormitories had separate apartments, or family rooms, often with kitchen facilities. In both communal and family rooms, men and women, singles and couples, minors and adults, and unrelated persons and families were all mixed together. The beds were bare-plank beds and bunks, and the workers themselves had to provide their own bedding, usually their own clothing. Having surveyed both types of housing in 1880, Peskov judged the dormitory-type rooms to be better constructed, ventilated, and heated than family apartments. Despite the fact that the latter were always full (with boarders squeezed into corners) and poorly ventilated because of their proximity to the kitchens, workers and their families preferred these rooms. General sleeping quarters offered less privacy, and the same plank beds were used by two or more different workers as the factory shifts changed.[21]

18. Peskov, *Sanitarnoe issledovanie*, 205.
19. Ibid., 208.
20. Dement'ev, *Fabrika*, 39–42. See also, Pazhitnov, *Polozhenie*, 98–103.
21. Peskov, *Sanitarnoe issledovanie*, 192; Pazhitnov, *Polozhenie*, 108. For additional descriptions of dormitory-style factory housing, see S. T. Semenov, "Briukhany," in *V rodnoi derevne*, 369; and "Iz zhizni Makarki," 437, 444.

Peskov did not see later models of progressive worker housing—the barracks run by the Tsindel' and Prokhorov calico-print factories. Prokhorov, for example, on the eve of World War I provided four different types of housing units, including thirteen barracks, two separate units with apartments, and buildings rented by the company from private landlords. Seven barracks provided sleeping quarters for 2,800 single men and women. The sleeping rooms had from 50 to 150 iron beds (the latest in bed technology and surpassing the wooden plank beds) complete with mattress, stool, and cupboard. Over 700 working couples without children were housed in three-story stone barracks; 51 large rooms were designed to accommodate four families in each. Over 300 workers with children were housed in small family units with one family to a room; two kitchens on each floor served 12 rooms. Finally, a set of private apartments contained 253 separate rooms for single workers and couples without children. A total of 4,252 workers, approximately 90 percent of the labor force, received free housing from the factory.[22] No doubt jubilee company publications overstated their case: the best factory housing was still overcrowded and unsanitary. Yet, since the barracks were free, the management had little incentive to make an extra ruble by squeezing in more workers.[23] Despite the disadvantages, worker demands for free factory housing often created waiting lists. The housing was only the beginning of the paternalistic services provided by the company, which included a consumer's cooperative, hospital maternity ward, technical school for employees and workers, kindergarten, library, Bible readings, orchestra, and chorus.[24] One would need only to add the catering services, group vacations, and Party activists and one would recognize contemporary Soviet "company paternalism."

The factory owners' motivations for building worker housing is an issue better left to a study of labor and management.[25] It should be pointed out that the Russian worker was mistrusted, and his movements were watched all the easier if he lived at the workplace. Two hundred years ago contemporaries observed that the worker could not go out alone, he had to be in groups; he was obliged to attend church

22. *Materialy k istorii Prokhorovskoi trekhgornoi manufaktury*, 397; Sviatlovskii, *Zhilishchnyi vopros*, 4:257.
23. Francis Palmer observed that to get around regulations concerning overcrowding, factory owners would count two children under fourteen or four children under ten as "one" person. (*Russian Life*, 272–73.)
24. In addition to the Prokhorov company histories, see *Dvadtsatipiatiletie Tovarishchestva sittsenabivnoi manufaktury Emil' Tsindel' v Moskve*, 24.
25. See Sviatlovskii, *Zhilishchnyi vopros*, 4:129–77, 244–89.

services and sing fitting (*blagopristoinye*) Russian songs at work.[26] The need for surveillance and control of peasants continued after the emancipation when operatives were no longer bound to the landlord or the state. Naturally, provision of the best housing was (and still is) used as a reward to certain workers. Factory owners generally provided housing for only the most skilled workers. Once the worker was in company housing, management had great leverage over its tenants. One student of the housing question remarked of the company housing: "Workers value them so much, that the threat of being deprived of an apartment is everywhere the most effective disciplinary measure in the hands of the factory management."[27]

What is perhaps more important for my purposes than the motivations behind such company housing are the proportions of city residents (and of workers) so housed and the changes over time. In 1882, 161,286 persons, or 21.4 percent of the city's population, lived in company housing. By 1912 this figure had increased to 207,205. However, the *proportion* of the population so housed decreased to 14.8 percent. Particularly noteworthy was the drop in the proportion of factory workers housed by the factory. In 1882, 57,385, or 90 percent, of the workers and their families were housed by the factory owners.[28] Thirty years later 50,138 workers and their families were housed in workers' dormitories; this constituted only 29.9 percent of the city's factory workers and their families.[29] This decline seems almost too precipitous and could be in part the result of imprecise categories. However, even if we take the total number of the city's laborers and their families, the proportion housed by their employers declined from 42 percent in 1882 to 24 percent in 1912.[30] Although still important, it would appear that company housing was losing its prominence, especially among blue-collar workers.

The category "commercial" housing included hotels, inns (*postoialye dvory*), boarding (or rooming) houses (*meblirovannye komnaty*),

---

26. Gol'denberg, *Planirovka*, 112; *Istoriia Moskvy*, 2:263.
27. Sviatlovskii, *Zhilishchnyi vopros*, 4:216.
28. *PM 1882*, I, pt. 2, 1–4, 37.
29. *SEM*, 52–59, 68–74.
30. Altogether the number of laborers of all kinds housed by their employers increased from 81,257 in 1882 to 148,704 in 1912, although the proportion—slightly less than 11 pecent—remained virtually unchanged. The 1882 figures are in all probability incomplete, since living quarters for superintendents, domestics, and outworkers were apparently included in the large category "ordinary" apartments. *PM 1882*, I, pt. 2, 1–4; II, pt. 2, 393–94; *SEM*, 4:52–59; *SEMMG*, 68–74; *Promyshlennye i torgovye zavedeniia*, 4:42–43.

lodging houses (*nochlezhnye doma*), and other similar establishments which provided shelter for a profit. Although in absolute terms, the number of persons so housed was never great, such living arrangements, as succeeding chapters will show, loomed larger than they actually were in the eyes of municipal officials and reformers. In 1882 an estimated 17,696 persons lived at one of the city's 573 inns. Found primarily on the scruffy outskirts of the city, such as in the Sushchevo and Rogozh' wards, the inns, as well as taverns, and all-night teahouses (*nochnye chainye*), provided shelter for a motley clientele of transient cabdrivers, shopkeepers, workers between shifts, casual laborers, prostitutes, and thieves. They were also a natural stopping place for newly arrived peasants, seeking employment but without family, friends, or fellow villagers to turn to, such as Ivan Andreev in Semenov's story, "Two Brothers."[31] Reformers decried the overcrowding, the illicit sale of vodka, and the prostitution and crime. But as the economist A. P. Chuprov pointed out, "the large accumulation of working people without families . . . find themselves refuge in the inns and drinking parlors."[32]

In addition to the 17,696 inhabitants of inns, teahouses, and taverns, the 1882 census recorded 23,509 inhabitants of boarding and lodging houses, that is, houses (excluding hotels, considered separately by the census compilers) where one could obtain lodging for a night, a week, or a month, and concentrated in the inner wards. The distinction between the Bowery-type lodging houses and the boarding (or rooming) houses with furnished rooms usually lay in the nature of the patrons, the prices charged, and the method of payment. In a rooming house, for example, lodgers paid the landlady (as most of the proprietors were women, often widows) by the week or the month, while lodgers in transient lodging houses paid by the night. Because of the relatively fewer private homes in Russian cities, because of the inability of the mass of urban blue-collar (and even many lower white-collar) workers to afford private rooms in a boarding house, and because so many immigrants sought room and board with fellow villagers in subdivided apartments, the boarding house was never as prominent a part of the

---

31. S. T. Semenov, "Dva brata," *V rodnoi derevne*, 38–39. For a description of the inns, see V. D'iakonov et al., "O postoialykh dvorakh," *Otchet o deiatel'nosti Moskovskoi gorodskoi upravy za 1885* (Moscow, 1887), 165–78.
32. Chuprov, *Kharakteristika Moskvy*, 39. See also Slonov, *Iz zhizni*, 165; Vasilich, "Ulitsy i liudi," 10; *Ushedshaia Moskva*, 147–48; and *Moskovskii listok*, no. 16 (January 19, 1913): 2.

urban fabric in Russia as it was in the West, particularly in the United States.[33]

The same could be said for the lodging houses, although one might not know it from the notoriety they received. In the 1860s Moscow had an estimated 50 private lodging houses. The 1882 census counted 234 lodging houses and 9,664 lodgers, and later surveys estimated more than 10,000 lodgers.[34] Such estimates were subject to considerable error. The estimates of the surveys and the census, taken in the winter, were subject to seasonal fluctuation: the spring influx of workers into the city, for example, added approximately 1,500 to 2,000 to those already in lodging houses. In addition, the proprietors concealed overcrowding so as not to incur fines (apparently rarely levied) by the police or by the sanitation inspection. As we shall see later, police reports themselves noted the large numbers of peasants without proper papers who most likely never registered at the lodging houses. One municipal report estimated that the actual number of lodgers may have been twice the number given by the proprietors.[35] In 1882, 60 percent of the city's lodgers lived in the Miasniki ward; Rogozh' and Khamovniki were the only other wards to have 10 percent of the total number of lodgers.[36]

Although conditions varied among lodging houses, certain descriptions are typical. Upon entering a flophouse, one investigator working for the local Guardianship Council wondered how the municipal government tolerated such houses in the city's center:

These people live in impossible conditions: filth, stench, suffocating heat. One can't stay standing for half an hour in these apartments. They lie down together barely a few feet apart, there is no division between the sexes, and adults sleep with children. The air is saturated with the most dreadfully foul language.[37]

The horror stories abounded. Half of the dwellers owned no warm clothing; two-thirds either did not have a hot meal every day or ate

    33. *PM 1882*, I, pt. 2, 1–4; D. D. Duvakin, "Nochlezhnye doma," in *Otchet o deiatel'nosti Moskovskoi gorodskoi upravy za 1885*, 74; Moskovskaia gorodskaia uprava, "Neskol'ko dannykh o moskovskikh koechno-kamarochnykh kvartirakh," *IMGD*, 1 (1899): 110. Moscow had one lodging house for every 1,328. With one lodging house per 1,045 population, New York was the closest of American cities, most of which had twice as many lodging houses per capita as did Moscow. (Albert B. Wolfe, *The Lodging House Question in Boston* [Boston, 1906], 38.)
    34. Duvakin, "Nochlezhnye doma," 75–76.
    35. Moskovskaia gorodskaia uprava, *Ischislenie naseleniia g. Moskvy v fevrale 1907 g.*, pt. 1 (Moscow, 1907): 9.
    36. *PM 1882*, I, pt. 3, 50–55. See also Duvakin, "Nochlezhnye doma," 75–76.
    37. Alaverdian, *Zhilishchnyi vopros*, 46.

food of dubious quality. ("Ah, there wasn't nothing to eat but I drank three glasses of vodka!") Most of the living quarters consisted of one room with plaster walls and wooden floors. Meals were eaten on bunks; lodgers placed bread and potatoes on the foul bedding. An all-purpose tub served as sink, washtub, and garbage disposal. The boarders claimed that it was so noisy and uncomfortable that only drunks could sleep at night (all the more incentive to get drunk?). Lodgers slept wherever possible, often on the floor; a regulation did prohibit putting drunk lodgers on the plank beds.[38] The toilet facilities consisted of outhouses (*otkhozhie mesta*), occasionally of brick, with primitive stools, cold and covered with urine and excrement. Needless to say, the smell permeated the apartments. Many units, of course, had no toilet facilities except the courtyard or a ruined basement.[39]

Every late-nineteenth-century investigation observed that the lodging houses exceeded the numbers of lodgers allowed by structural, police, or sanitary norms. The system of subletting whereby the lessee of individual apartments within the lodging houses sublet space to lodgers for a few kopeks led to widespread partitioning, further reducing the amount of space and air per person. Although most rooms had a little window opening, the cold weather and 24-hour occupancy prevented the vents from being opened and the rooms aired out. Writing in *Russkaia mysl'*, Vladimir Ovtsyn described the gloomy atmosphere and unbelievable stench of the notorious Rzhanovskaia "fortress" near Smolensk Square.[40] The novelist Tolstoi, a census taker in 1882, summed up the population pressure:

All apartments were full, and all cots were occupied, and not by one person but often by two. . . . All the women were drunk and slept like corpses with men. Many women slept on narrow cots with totally strange men. . . . One apartment, and then another, and then three, ten, twenty, with no end. And everywhere the same stench, heat and congestion, the same mixing of the sexes, the same men and women in a drunken stupor, and the same fear, submissiveness and guilt on all faces.[41]

38. Duvakin, "Nochlezhnye doma," 71.
39. Ibid., 11–12, 71; Pozner, "Nochlezhnye doma i nochlezhniki," 49; Kurnin, *O nekotorykh usloviiakh*, 4–6.
40. Vladimir Ovtsyn, "K istorii i statistike gorodskogo proletariata," 71.
41. Tolstoi, "Tak chto zhe nam delat'?" 49. More material on the overcrowding and other features of such lodging houses is contained in TsGAM, f. 46, op. 14, d. 1212, l. 36; Alaverdian, *Zhilishchnyi vopros*, 57; Pozner, "Nochlezhnye doma i nochlezhniki," 10; and Imperatorskoe russkoe tekhnicheskoe obshchestvo, *Doklad komissii po ozdorovleniiu Khitrova rynka* (Moscow, 1903), 8.

Of course, there were lodging houses and lodging houses, and strange as it may seem, not all reports were so negative. In Leikin's novel *Working*, the two heroines, Arina and Akulina, and a group of women casual laborers head for a lodging house after an unsuccessful afternoon at the labor market. Admittedly, the action is set in Petersburg, but there is no reason to believe that similar circumstances could not have prevailed in Moscow. Run by the Society of Lodging Houses, the particular establishment where Arina and Akulina ended up offered for five kopeks a plank bunk bed, a hot supper consisting of a bowl of cabbage soup and kasha or a piece of bread, and a mug of tea with a lump of sugar for breakfast. The impression made on the laboring poor was not as universally gloomy as that made on the intellectuals. Akulina was almost ecstatic:

Akulina looked around her and was moved by the lodging house's conveniences. . . . "You know, if you hadn't brought us here we never would have known what good lodgings you could get for a nickel. . . . This place is really good. Soup in the evening, everyone has a place to sleep, and then you get tea in the morning. This is simply paradise!"[42]

Closely related to the inns, boarding houses, and lodging houses, as well as to some of the institutional and company housing, were various private communal living quarters. The most distinctive type of communal living units were those of the informal associations of migrant workers known as artels. Semen Kanatchikov recalled that when he first came to Moscow, he and fifteen other young factory workers rented an apartment together as an artel. To get and prepare food, they hired a woman; this way, they could come home for lunch from the factory, obviously nearby. For Sunday entertainment the whole group occasionally went to the Tret'iakov or Rumiantsev museums or, whenever possible, ran to watch fires.[43]

Watching fires was free entertainment, and most artel workers, with families back home in the village, lived frugally, even by Russian standards. Up to one-third of their wages was sent home. Watching fires also provided a diversion from the crowded living conditions, as described by a fellow worker:

Once I had the opportunity to visit a common laborer. He lived in a communal (*artel'naia*) apartment along with seventeen others. The apartment consisted of a large, smokey room with two windows. At one time the walls had

---

42. Leikin, *Na zarabotkakh*, 145.
43. Kanatchikov, *Iz istorii*, 10, 14. See also L. Fedorovich, *Zhilye pomeshcheniia rabochikh* (St. Petersburg, 1881), 33.

been papered over, but the wallpaper had since pealed away exposing boarded walls. Cockroaches swarmed along the walls. . . . Wooden bunks, no doubt a haven for bedbugs, circled the room. A long table perched on blocks, and two long benches stood in the middle of the room. A small kerosene lamp hung on the wall between the windows, and below it hung a woodcut depicting the royal family. A blackened icon hung in the corner. Next door was a kitchen which also doubled as the entryway. The cook slept in the corner. There, you have an entire apartment for eighteen people.[44]

Unfortunately, it is virtually impossible to determine how many lived in artel or other communal apartments, and despite its obvious importance in Russian social life, no special study was undertaken of communal housing as such. In 1882, 120,536 persons, or 19.3 percent of the city's population, lived communally outside communal institutional units (*zhivushchie obshchezhitiiami vne obshchezhitel'nykh zavedenii*).[45] This number had grown to 193,260, or 18.6 percent of the population of 1897. More noteworthy, the number of women living communally almost doubled from 23,078 in 1882 to 43,784 in 1897.[46] In 1897 approximately 9 percent of Moscow's households fell into the category of communal or, more precisely, households of artels, and laborers and servants living away from their employers or the head of the household (*khoziaistva lits, ne sviazannykh rodstvom: arteli, otdel'no ot khoziaev zhivushchie rabochie i prisluga*).[47] This 9 percent compared with 1 percent in Warsaw, 2 percent in Odessa and Tula, 5 percent in Iaroslavl' and 6 percent in Petersburg. Even more striking is the fact that fully 25 percent of the entire male population (and 10 percent of the female) lived in such artel-based households. Serpukhov with 26 percent and Iaroslavl' with 20 percent of the males were the only towns close to Moscow; Warsaw and Odessa had only 2 percent and 7 percent, respectively, of their male population living in households of unrelated persons. Even Petersburg had but 15 percent.[48]

In both the 1882 and the 1912 census (as table 12 shows) ordinary private apartments constituted a clear majority of the total number of

---

44. Timofeev, "Ocherki," 21–22. For more on worker communal living, see Zelnik, "Russian Bebels," 259–60.
45. *PM 1882*, I, pt. 3, 156–59.
46. *PVP*, 24a, pt. 1, 4–7.
47. The comparable figures cannot be found in the 1912 census, although two categories—artel apartment and "other common living units"—registered 20,207 persons, or 1.4 percent of the total populations. Such a precipitous decline from 19.3 percent and 18.6 percent to 1.4 percent is unlikely, and those living communally in 1912 were most likely grouped with subletted apartments. *SEM*, 52–59.
48. *PVP*, 24:6–9; 24a, pt. 1, 4–7; 37, pt. 1, 4–7; 44:6–9; 47:4–5; 50:6–9; 51:4–5.

housing units and housed a majority of the total population. The latter census isolated apartments occupied only by owners, by tenants and their families and servants, and apartments with subletting of rooms or parts of rooms. Assuming that the categories were comparable in the two censuses, the proportion of the population housed in the private-apartment market increased slightly. Fortunately, there exist several studies of particular types of private housing, so that one does not have to rely on the censuses.[49] Not only do specialized studies have the advantage of depicting a more limited universe of living quarters, but by directing particular attention to the city's worst housing, the studies allow us to examine more carefully the housing of the laboring population exclusively.

The private-apartment market did not escape the problems of over-crowding, endemic in the communal, institutional, and company housing units. In 1882 the average private apartment had three to four rooms and almost nine residents, that is, from two to three residents per room. The smaller the apartment, the greater the density; six persons lived in the average one-room apartment.[50] The situation had improved little by 1897 and 1912, when the average number of residents of private households still exceeded eight. In comparison with a random sample of cities of the empire, Moscow had a markedly large average household size: Warsaw, Odessa, Iaroslavl', and Volokolamsk all had average household sizes ranging from five to six residents; only Tula (6.3), Serpukhov (6.1), and Petersburg (7.9) exceeded six persons per household.

It might be mentioned in this context that the compilers of a survey of the city's printers observed that workers had difficulty in responding to the question about family size and included not only the conjugal family or economic unit (*khoziaistvennyi soiuz*) but all relatives regardless of their residence. It might be supposed that the census figures for household size might be inflated and include family mem-

49. Based on private and municipal investigations, the studies are "Neskol'ko dannykh o moskovskikh koechno-kamarochnykh kvartirakh"; I. Verner, "Zhilishcha bedneishego naseleniia Moskvy," *IMGD*, 26, no. 19 (1902): 1–27; "Doklad Komissii po zhilishchnomu voprosu," *Doklady Moskovskoi gorodskoi upravy*, no. 184 (1905); and N. M. Kishkin, "Zhilishchnyi vopros v Moskve i blizhaishie zadachi v razreshenii ego Gorodskoi dumoi," *Gorodskoe delo*, no. 5 (1913): 291–300, and no. 6 (1913) 351–60. In addition, see the many studies of lodgings at the Khitrov slum cited in note 110, chapter 7.

50. *PM 1882*, I, pt. 3, 86–88, 116–19, 137–38. In principle, landlords could have their license to rent living space revoked for overcrowding, though this doesn't appear to have happened too often. See "Stolichnye prikazy Moskovskogo Ober-Politseimastera po politsii," no. 130 (11), quoted in *IMGD*, 25, no. 6 (June 1901), 30.

bers living elsewhere. In fact, the average family size of village-born workers was 6.7 persons and that of city-born workers was 3.8 persons. Although only 3 percent of the latter had family size greater than 9, 22 percent of the former had such large families. This clearly reflects the greater ability of immigrants to keep excess family members elsewhere.[51]

What brought about these crowded conditions was the bane of the housing of Moscow's laboring population: the subdivision of living space. In 1912, 691,131 persons, or half of the entire population and two-thirds of the population on the private-apartment market, resided in living units where the owner or tenant rented out part of his own living space. Forty percent of this population lived in apartments where parts of rooms (and even beds) themselves were subdivided. This type of housing was the subject in 1899 of one of the most thorough housing investigations, which surveyed 16,478 such apartments and provided data for 15,922, housing 180,919 persons.[52]

When the owner of the building or even the tenant of an apartment decided to defray expenses, he rented a "cot" (koika), or "corner"; a room became a "cot" apartment where several unrelated tenants and their families and even boarders all lived on cots with nothing separating them; and a majority of such apartments consisted of one room. Often the rooms were curtained off into separate quarters or small chambers called kamorki: hence the name "cot-chamber" apartment (koechno-kamorochnaia kvartira).[53] The most salient differences between such apartments and "ordinary" private apartments were the former's subdivision of rooms and a propensity for overcrowding, the poor sanitation standards, and the lack of privacy and the mixing of ages, sexes, and families. In addition, the sublessor had the peculiar double function of lessor and lessee; rents collected by greater subdivisions often became a major source of income. One-quarter of the apartments were located in basements (where the average was twelve persons per apartment), 70 percent on first or second floors (where the average was eight persons per apartment), and 6 percent in attics. On the outskirts, where over 80 percent of the apartments were found, such units often occupied an entire house, usually a one- or two-story wooden structure. In the center, the apartments were spread among stone houses and usually occupied only a part of the building—a

51. Svavitskii and Sher, Ocherk, 4, 16–17.
52. "Neskol'ko dannykh," 95.
53. Ibid., 101; Verner, "Zhilishcha," 3.

basement, an attic, a wing.[54] Although 17 percent of the city population lived in cot-chamber apartments, the proportions varied from
ward to ward. In general the inner wards had fewer cot-chamber
apartments, though one precinct in Miasniki and both Sretenka precincts exceeded the average. The second Presnia precinct with 36.7
percent, the second Rogozh' precinct with 31.5 percent, and the third
Meshchane precinct with 30.6 percent had the largest proportions of
their populations living in cot-chamber apartments.[55]

Increased speculative buying of real estate and housing put pressure
on the housing market, and apartment values and rents soared at the
end of the nineteenth century. The pressure on the housing market can
be ascertained by figures showing the number of vacant housing units:
whereas in 1882 approximately 7 percent of the city's living units
were unoccupied, thirty years later only 2 percent were unoccupied.[56]
According to one contemporary study, land prices in the city rose
more than 50 percent from 1897 to 1912. Obviously, both the housing pressure and the value of land were reflected in the apartment
rents, which rose almost 100 percent from 1882 to 1912.[57] Among
cot-chamber apartments, the average price for a chamber was estimated to be almost 6 rubles per month: for a single bed, almost 2
rubles per month; and for a double bed, almost 3 rubles per month.
The more crowded the apartment, the higher the price for the space
available. Prices increased relatively more for cheaper, more crowded
apartments because the demand for them was greater. Rent had only a
slight correlation with living space or comfort, and the average cost of
space in the basement and attic (where presumably those worst off
lived) was about the same as in the first and second floor, although the
per capita cost was higher.[58]

Exactly who profited from all this is unclear. One municipal statistician calculated that the proprietors, whose households comprised
approximately one-third of the apartments' inhabitants, lost 135,000
rubles a month. Subtracting the rent which the proprietor did *not* have
to pay to himself, the statistician arrived at a net monthly loss of only

---

54. "Neskol'ko dannykh," 96–97; Verner, "Zhilishcha," 4–5; Pazhitnov, *Polozhenie*, 115.
55. "Neskol'ko dannykh," 105.
56. *PM 1882*, I, pt. 2, 1–4; *SEM*, 34–37.
57. Alaverdian, *Zhilishchnyi vopros*, 29–31.
58. A. Gibshman, "Neskol'ko dannykh o kvartirnykh usloviiakh sluzhashchikh v
Moskve," *IMGD*, 35, no. 1 (January 1911): 16–18; Sviatlovskii, *Zhilishchnyi vopros*,
4:19; Verner, "Zhilishcha," 21–22.

35,000 rubles, or roughly half a ruble per person in the proprietor's family. Since the proprietors were also poor, it was difficult to lower rents or improve living conditions. Yet, elsewhere the city's report of 1899 claimed that subleasing was a major source of income for many proprietors. Not all cot-chamber apartments were as unprofitable as the above figures indicate. If the apartment had less than five cubic feet of living space per person, or if the number of dwellers in the apartment exceeded ten, then rent exceeded the cost of the apartment. The incentive for squeezing in more and more boarders, sharing cots, and making further subdivisions was obvious.[59] The pressure for increased subdivisions is shown by comparing the 1899 investigation with the 1912 census. In the latter year a total of 20,555 apartments consisting of 73,406 rooms had rented partitioned chambers and cots. Altogether 29,942 rooms, 11,340 partitioned chambers, 46,612 corners and cots, and 5,343 spaces on bunk beds were rented. While the number of subdivided units increased by 28 percent in a little more than a decade, the number of residents increased by 57 percent.[60]

Over half of the tenants were judged to be living in excessively cold apartments; almost 90 percent were said to be living in excessively damp apartments. According to one investigator, the survey teams often took marginal notations, such as "the building is old and dirty," "the building hasn't been repaired and is decrepit," "the building is completely unfit for inhabitation."[61] The chambers were usually located near windows; although the proprietors insisted otherwise, the partitions, made of thin boards stuffed with newspaper, made ideal breeding grounds for cockroaches. The entryway usually led from a courtyard through a common and cold corridor. If heated, the corridor was also often used as living quarters. The courtyards themselves were often little better than open cesspools.[62] Conditions were especially difficult for the approximately 36,000 who rented no more than a cot. Total strangers often shared double cots and even single cots: one slept at night, the other during the day.

The resident who rents a cot gets three bare boards laid on bricks, logs, or leather. He gets no mattress or straw sack, and more often than not he doesn't have one himself; instead he usually sleeps on the shirt off his own back. For

59. Verner, "Zhilishcha," 22–23. See also S. T. Semenov, "Vnizu," V rodnoi derevne, 564.
60. SEM, 58–59; "Neskol'ko dannykh," 107; Verner, "Zhilishcha," 17.
61. Verner, "Zhilishcha," 5.
62. Ibid., 8. See also K. T. Tupitsyn, "O podval'nykh zhilykh pomeshcheniiakh v Moskve," IMGD, 9, no. 1 (January 1885): 187–89.

this reason, during the day the cots present a disgusting picture of old boards and undetermined rumpled bedding.[63]

Even worse were the almost one thousand who paid rent but took a different place every day—on top of the stove, on a vacant cot or the vacant half of a double cot, or on the floor.[64] Remember that nearly one-quarter of Moscow's cot-chamber apartments were in basements housing almost 60,000 persons. Tolstoi happened into one such while participating in the 1882 census:

The apartment was laid out thus: a stove stood in the middle of a room measuring 180 square inches. Four partitions, constituting four chambers, emanate from the stove like a star. The first chamber contained four cots and had two persons—an old man and a woman. Another chamber followed right away with a young proprietor, a good-looking pale *meshchanin* dressed in a gray, cloth sleeveless coat. On the left from the first corner was the third chamber with one man sleeping, probably drunk, another man, and a woman in a pink blouse, open in front and tied behind. The fourth chamber behind the partition was the proprietor's chamber.[65]

Small wonder that then, as now, "company" housing was considered a prize for skilled and deserving workers.

So far the discussion has concerned the different types of housing units that at least provided shelter, however unsatisfactory it may have been. Like other metropolises, then and now, Moscow had a laboring and a nonlaboring population with no residence, which floated from inns or all-night tea houses to lodging houses to open freight cars or the riverbank during the summer. One municipal study estimated that at the beginning of the twentieth century Moscow had 15,000 homeless,[66] but we will most likely never know how many had no shelter: the task of estimating the numbers of the homeless was no less formidable to the municipal authorities than it is to the historian today. The compilers of the 1907 census noted with due gravity that a partial census of lodgings undertaken by the municipal statistical bureau and the sanitary physicians had included, among other havens, the

haystacks on the riverbank which serve as a place of lodging for the homeless in [the neighborhood of] Danilovka. . . . Data on the numbers of persons living in boats and on rafts on the Moscow River were gathered indirectly by two sanitary physicians and two census takers and can thus be considered only approximate. Even less exact are the data on the numbers of persons spending

63. Verner, "Zhilishcha," 8.
64. Ibid., 13.
65. Tolstoi, "Tak chto zhe nam delat'?" 39.
66. *Sovremennoe khoziaistvo*, 107–8.

the night in empty frieght cars in the railroad yards, in lumber yards, and in manure heaps.

It should be pointed out that the census was taken in February when the average Moscow temperature is 14° F (−10° C).[67]

FAMILY AND HOUSEHOLD

The preceding discussion of Moscow's housing has focused on the housing units—their number, size, construction, type—as the necessary background for an analysis of the residents themselves, particularly of their position in the housing unit, their relationship, if any, to other residents, and the nature of the household or family formed. Here the focus of the discussion is on the private, rather than the institutional, company or commercial housing, although related persons and even an entire family could live in nonprivate housing. Three types of sources will provide the basis for the following analysis. First, the 1882 and the 1897 censuses provided data on the numbers and types of residents of the city's various forms of households; the 1897 census has the added advantage of permitting comparisons with households in other cities of the empire. Second, the investigations of the lodging houses and of various types of apartments, such as the "cot-chamber" apartments mentioned above, provide additional data on marital status, occupation, and estate of the residents. Finally, memoir literature and fiction will occasionally amplify certain of the quantitative observations. All these sources, particularly the censuses and the municipal investigations, suffer from an inconsistency in the categories used such that comparison over time is virtually impossible.

The 1882 census provides the most detailed differentiation of the members of households (*khoziaistva*). When the census compilers entered Moscow apartments on the night of January 24, they were looking for the following kinds of residents: the heads of the households and their children and grandchildren, relatives and their children, laborers earning their keep (*promyshlennye sluzhashchie*), domestic servants and their children, tutors and their pupils, boarders (*nakhleb-niki*), other members of the household, and lodgers (*zhil'tsy iz vtorykh ruk, nochlezhniki*). (See table 13.) The census compilers did not define these categories, and the distinction is not always clear. A household was defined as an economic and spatial unit, usually though not al-

67. *Ischislenie*, pt. 1:9. For a discussion of Moscow's climate, see V. P. Semenov, *Moskovskaia promyshlennaia oblast'*, 33–43.

TABLE 13   MOSCOW'S POPULATION BY POSITION IN
HOUSEHOLD, 1882

Position in household[a]	Males	Females	Total	Percent
Heads of household	52,443	55,794	108,237	21.5
Children of head	50,371	50,623	100,994	20.0
Grandchildren of head	1,017	1,092	2,109	0.4
Relatives of head	10,860	24,100	34,960	6.9
Relatives' children	1,476	1,788	3,264	0.6
Laborers (*promyshlennye sluzhashchie*)	63,216	15,418	78,634	15.6
Domestic servants	17,488	49,025	66,513	13.2
Children of domestic servants	1,111	1,398	2,509	0.5
Tutors	203	1,652	1,255	6.2
Boarders (*nakhlebniki*)	3,067	1,707	4,774	0.9
Students	560	775	1,335	0.3
Other members	2,850	6,519	9,369	1.9
Lodgers (*zhil'tsy iz vtorykh ruk*)	24,549	24,459	49,008	9.7
Lodgers' children	6,389	6,649	13,038	2.6
Night lodgers (*nochlezhniki*)	14,234	13,683	27,917	5.5
Totals	249,834	254,032	503,916	100.0

Source: *PM 1882*, I, 156–57.

[a]Includes only private households. Excluded are institutional, company, communal, and commercial housing units.

ways of blood relatives, living together and having a common budget. It seems that a common budget was a particularly important criterion in categorizing residents of the various housing units. Laborers earning their keep were apprentices, journeymen, and outworkers in the employ of the head of the household. Boarders, a very small group, were those whose rent included meals and who were therefore considered part of the core household but who were not working for the head of the household. Lodgers rented space but received no board and were not considered members of the core household. It is possible that many lodgers were fellow villagers of the proprietor or tenant. Many of S. T. Semenov's stories illustrate peasants arriving in the city and looking for a fellow villager to put them up for the night or help them find a job. Ivan Andreev in "Two Brothers" goes back and forth between fellow villagers and inns while looking for a job. In "The Superintendent" Gerasim stays with both relatives and fellow villagers upon arrival in Moscow, while the latter try to get him a job as a superintendent.[68] Despite the importance of the phenomenon of *zem-liachestvo*, it is impossible to determine how many entering peasants may have found temporary lodgings this way. Unfortunately, the 1897 census used different and broader categories. Heads of households, children, grandchildren, and relatives are all grouped together as "family members." Laborers, domestic servants, and the various types of boarders and lodgers are hidden together in the category "outsiders" (*postoronnye*) or as "residents" in households headed by single persons or in households of unrelated persons.

One thing is clear from both censuses: as table 14 shows, little more than one-third of the city's inhabitants lived together with members of their own family. Moreover, this proportion did not rise appreciably during the fifteen years between censuses. Between 1897 and 1910 there was likewise little change: a hospital survey found that only one-third of the patients rented accommodation as a family member. If one looks at the male population alone, only slightly more than one-quarter lived with other members of their own family. No other Russian city had fewer than 50 percent of its men and 70 percent of its women living with members of their own family. Even if one considers only private households of related persons, as the 1897 census was able to do, only slightly more than half of the residents were actual family members. This fact necessitates a modification of the statement made earlier concerning the large size of Moscow housing units and households. Although the average private household of related persons contained 8.2 residents in 1897, that average household contained only slightly more than 4 persons of the same family. In 1882 only slightly more than 1 out of every 4 family members was actually the head of the household. Only 1 resident in 7 was a head of a household; according to a survey of hospital patients, only 1 in 6 was a head of a household thirty years later.[69]

Family size frequently varied according to job and urban experience, as a study of Moscow's printers revealed. Although the average

68. S. T. Semenov, "Dva brata," 38; "Dvornik," *V rodnoi derevne*, 91–92; "Iz zhizni Makarki," 441; and "Katiusha," *U propasti i drugie rasskazy* (Moscow, 1904), 84.

69. Moskovskaia gorodskaia uprava, *Perepis' bol'nykh, prizrevaemykh v lecheb-nykh, rodovspomogatel'nykh i blagotvoritel'nykh uchrezhdeniiakh Moskovskogo gor-odskogo obshchestvennogo upravleniia 11-go dekabria 1910 g.* Compiled by V. P. Uspenskii, 2 vols. (Moscow, 1912), 1:19, 21; 2:32.

TABLE 14 HOUSEHOLD SIZE AND COMPOSITION, 1897

	Private Households of Related Persons						Households of Unrelated Persons			
			Percent Residents						Percent City's Residents	
			Family members		Strangers					
Location	Number households	Average size	Men	Women	Men	Women	Number households	Average size	Men	Women
Moscow	87,607	8.2	29.6	43.9	32.9	33.9	9,097	21.2	25.3	9.8
Selected Wards										
Prechistenka	4,168	7.8	37.8	42.1	33.5	39.5	279	17.0	17.5	5.2
Presnia	6,763	7.9	34.8	40.5	37.6	38.0	407	19.1	16.9	4.6
Meshchane	9,610	7.8	33.2	46.4	34.6	31.8	685	20.6	18.9	7.2
Lefort	5,478	8.0	26.2	42.0	25.8	28.8	841	24.2	34.1	18.7
Rogozh'	7,382	7.9	31.8	50.7	30.7	32.0	808	19.4	27.1	6.8
Selected Cities										
Petersburg	127,734	7.6	34.8	48.2	35.1	35.7	10,483	12.3	15.0	4.4
Warsaw	104,487	5.8	65.4	72.2	17.2	22.4	1,196	7.8	1.9	0.8
Odessa	62,412	5.6	60.3	75.9	15.4	17.1	1,299	13.3	7.0	1.1
Iaroslavl'	11,580	5.3	54.6	73.3	16.3	15.1	653	13.0	19.9	2.6
Tula	16,955	6.3	60.8	79.5	20.0	13.2	339	16.9	8.2	1.1
Volokolamsk	472	5.5	58.1	78.2	12.8	12.8			14.4	0.8
Serpukhov	4,281	6.1	53.0	71.3	9.6	11.0			26.1	11.1
Volokolamsk County	13,950	5.3	90.3	92.5	6.5	9.5			2.1	0.5
Serpukhov County	14,671	5.1	81.0	91.1	8.4	5.0			8.8	1.2

Source: *PVP*, 24, pt. 1, 4–7; 37:4–7; 51:4–5; 50:6–9; 44:6–9; 24:6–9.

family was 5.2 persons, that of immigrant workers was 6–7 persons and that of native workers was 3–5 persons. Though only 3 percent of the latter group had families of more than 9, 22 percent of the immigrant workers had such large families. The unskilled workers had larger families than the skilled; at 4.3, the lowest family size was found among the typesetters.[70]

Between one-half and two-thirds of the population lived apart from members of their own family in 1882 and 1897, and all the available data indicate that this did not change drastically by 1912. That is to say, approximately five hundred thousand in 1882 and almost seven hundred thousand in 1897 were laborers earning their keep, servants, boarders, lodgers, or residents of households of nonrelated members. Indeed, more than half of Moscow's private households of related persons contained laborers or servants. Only two-fifths of Petersburg's, one-third of Warsaw's, and one-quarter of Odessa's households had laborers or servants. Similarly, no city in the empire except Petersburg approached the proportions of lodgers (or "outsiders") reached in Moscow.[71] The phenomenon of households containing nonfamily members such as laborers and boarders was not confined to distinct parts of the city. Because of the many small shops and workshops, the central districts of Gorod, Tver', and Miasniki had the highest proportion (nearly one-third) of households with hired laborers. Nearly two-fifths of the households of Presnia, Meshchane, Lefort, and Rogozh' had boarders. Surprisingly, more than one-quarter of the households of outlying lower-class districts, such as Rogozh', Serpukhov, Presnia, and Lefort, had servants.[72]

If Moscow exceeded other Russian cities in the prominence of nonfamily members, one could imagine how Moscow might have compared with other European cities. The compilers of the 1882 census frequently compared Moscow with Berlin; such a comparison is particularly revealing in the area of households.[73] While less than one-third of all Muscovites resided as members of a nuclear family, more than three-quarters of all Berliners were either heads of households or spouses and children. All family members (including lateral relatives) composed 82.7 percent of Berlin's population, more than twice the proportion of Moscow's. Far fewer Berliners resided in households as

70. Svavitskii and Sher, *Ocherk*, 16–17.
71. *PVP*, 24, pt. 1, 4–7; 37, pt. 1, 4–7; 47:4–5; 51:4–5.
72. Ibid.
73. *PM 1882*, I, pt. 2, 75–76.

laborers, or domestic servants; in the proportion of lodgers, Berlin slightly exceeded Moscow. A negligible proportion of Berliners, according to the 1880 census, lived communally.

If one looks at the proportions of households which included various members, the differences between Moscow and Berlin stand out even more. Twice as many Muscovite households contained lateral relatives, indicating in the eyes of the compilers the "great tenacity of patriarchal life in the Moscow family."[74] Laborers rarely lived with their employers in Berlin, where only 4.8 percent of households contained such laborers. This phenomenon was much more common in Moscow, where 22.8 percent of private households contained laborers earning their keep. Households with lodgers and domestic servants were more frequent occurrences in Moscow than in Berlin.

The terms "head of the household," "laborer," "boarder," and "lodger" suggest more stratification in the household than there may actually have been, particularly in the so-called cot-chamber apartments. If occupation is used as a criterion, there was often little difference between proprietors, tenants, and subtenants. The most typical kinds of landlords of low-cost housing were small investors, usually artisans and shopkeepers, who had saved a little money and whose income as landlords depended on the excessive subdivision described above. Although sketchy, the survey data also refer to factory workers, laborers in the transport and construction trades, and even unskilled and casual laborers as being landlords or sublessors of housing space. Lodgers of cot-chamber apartments ran the occupational gamut from artisans and shopkeepers to unskilled and casual laborers and domestic servants. Understandably, artel apartments tended to have more artisans and workers in the construction and transport trades. Even a large majority of printers, judged to have better accommodations than the city's textile workers, were unable to rent an entire apartment; most either rented a room or a cot.[75] Some of the worst accommodations—lodging houses, "cots," and such nooks and crannies as kamorka pod lestnitsei, ugol v kukhne, and kamorka pri kukhne—housed not only domestics and day laborers but also artisans. According to a survey of hospital patients, certain low-grade occupations, such as domestic servants, candywrappers and cigarette-wrappers, held almost exclusively by women,

74. E. T[arnovskii], "K voprosu o brodiazhestve," Iuridicheskii vestnik, no. 12 (December 1886): 766.
75. Svavitskii and Sher, Ocherk, 34–35.

went hand in hand with residence in kitchens, under stairways, and in the entryways.[76]

Given the large proportion of the population not living in households as family members, as well as the excess of men, it might be expected that a large portion of the city's population would not be married. The large proportion of lodgers, boarders, and laborers, as well as the large number of communal households, would not seem to be favorable for married persons. In fact, more than half the persons over age fifteen were married, and the proportion of married men (although not of women) was higher in Moscow than in Petersburg, Odessa, and all European capitals.[77] Indeed, if one looks at the marital status of the male population, Moscow most closely resembled, not Petersburg, Odessa, or Berlin, but the town population of Riazan' province. Clearly, village marriage customs and the fact that unlike urban laborers, Moscow's peasants did not have to delay marriage age were reflected in the high proportion of married persons in the city.[78] Yet, despite the increase of peasants in the city from 1882 to 1902, the proportion of married persons over age fifteen remained virtually constant. This apparent lack of change concealed a slight decrease in the proportion of married men and a slight increase in the proportion of married women.[79]

The most plausible explanation for this increase is simply that more married women were moving into the city. The compilers of the preliminary results of the 1912 census observed that men brought women (presumably married) into the city more often than in the past, and the consensus of most studies of Moscow's workers is that there was a gradual increase in the proportion of workers who had their wives and children in Moscow. On the other hand, an increased city marriage rate, coupled with the more stable, if not somewhat declining, rate for the province as a whole, also suggests that more single women migrated into the city and married men there rather than in the villages.[80] Women, after all, were beginning to break the fetters which had tied them to the village longer than men, and a greatly expanding city offered more jobs, from spinner to charwoman, than ever before.

76. Verner, "Zhilishcha," 17–19; *Perepis' bol'nykh,* 2:30–32, 64, 74, 105. See also Giliarovskii, *Moskva i Moskvichi,* 76, 342.

77. *GPD 1902,* IV:5.

78. See also Johnson, "Family Relations," 265–72.

79. *PM 1882,* II, pt. 2, 10–14; *PM 1902,* I, 1, i, 9–10.

80. *SEM,* no. 3 (Moscow, 1911): 25; Kurkin and Chertov, *Estestvennoe dvizhenie,* 23.

The increase in the number of women in the city's households brought with it an increase in the number of children. The number of children under age five per 1,000 total population increased from 56 in 1871 to 77 thirty years later.[81] In view of the fact that there were more than twice as many children, the percentage increase certainly could not be called spectacular. It must be kept in mind that the total population almost doubled during this period, thus almost keeping up with the increase in the number of children under age five. Another, and perhaps more sensitive, indicator of the increase in the number of children is the change in the child–woman ratio, that is, in the ratio of children under age five to women of childbearing age, ages fifteen to forty-five. The number of children per 1,000 women increased from 247.4 in 1871 to 256.0 in 1882 to 306.6 in 1902.[82] Did the statistical increase in the proportion of children to women of childbearing age mean that these women were actually having more children?

In fact, sharp increase in child–woman ratios among the laboring groups, led by the peasants, concealed a decline in this ratio among the city's privileged groups.[83] It is possible that the proverbially fecund peasant women were just as productive in the city as in the villages. However, since the city's birthrate decreased slightly from 34.9 per 1,000 in 1868 to 33.5 per 1,000 in 1912, and since peasant laborers made up the majority of the population, it is unlikely that birthrates among the peasants in the city could have been increasing significantly.[84] The experience of Western cities in the process of industrialization and urbanization indicates that the average number of children born per woman tends to decrease over time, and there is no reason to think this might not have been happening in Moscow at the beginning of the twentieth century.[85] Moreover, better reporting of births and more extensive hospital and maternity ward facilities also tended to keep birthrates from declining as much as they might have.

If increased fertility was not a factor, we still have to account for

---

81. *Statisticheskie svedeniia o zhiteliakh*, 8–9; *PM 1882*, II, pt. 2, 4–11; *PM 1902*, I, 1, i, 12–13.
82. *Statisticheskie svedeniia*, 8–9; *PM 1882*, II, pt. 2, 21–25; *PM 1902*, I, 1, i, 4. The child-woman ratio measures the proportion of the population present at the time of the census which is under the age of five. It is neither a birthrate nor a fertility rate, for children born during the period January 1877–January 1882 may have died, left the city in infancy, or entered the city in infancy. The proportion of the population under age five, then, is a net result of the attrition rate of children in their first few years of life.
83. *PM 1882*, II, pt. 2, 4–11; *PM 1902*, I, 1, i, 12–13.
84. *SEM*, no. 3, 25; Kurkin and Chertov, *Estestvennoe dvizhenie*, 25.
85. E. A. Wrigley, *Population and History* (New York, 1969), 180–202.

the increasing number of children. First, the city experienced a decline in infant mortality from an average of 360 per 1,000 in the period 1868–1872 to 270 per 1,000 in the period 1908–1912;[86] a large survival rate of even fewer babies could have yielded a larger population under age five. Second, the proportion of married women increased slightly. Accordingly, more women of childbearing age who were actually married could have explained the increase in the number of children. Finally, more children under age five could have been entering the city with their parents, or with their mother, than had been the custom in earlier times. More important, the increased child–woman ratio suggests that more women were staying in the city and that fewer children under age five may have been sent back to be raised in the villages.

The increased marriage and child–woman ratios still do not account for the discrepancy between the great bulge in the number of women of childbearing age and the small number of children, particularly among the peasants. The preponderance of adult immigrants kept the child–woman ratio low among peasants. Although more women were most likely marrying and having and raising children in the city, most young peasant women who migrated to the city continued to return to the villages to bear or rear children. In the novel *Working*, unskilled women laborers are constantly talking about their little children back in the village.[87] More important is the fact that many of these children were raised in the villages and came to Moscow (if at all) only as they approached apprenticeship, or at least working, ages.

A perfect example of a city-born but village-bred child is provided by Semenov's story "At the Brink" ("U propasti"). Dar'ia Pavlova comes to Moscow as a young girl and gets a job as a servant. She starts keeping company with a laborer (*artel'shchik kakoi-to*) working in the store on the first floor of the building where she lived. Dar'ia becomes pregnant, and the laborer runs off with another girl. On the advice of close friends, she gives the infant to someone in the village. Thus little Polia was nursed and raised in the village (and supported by a monthly 3 rubles from her mother) for fifteen years. The wet nurse, Kidinova, brings Polia to Moscow to help her mother, not yet forty but weary after almost twenty years of hard work and wanting to "save a little money, rent a corner and rest a bit, at least live

86. *SEM*, no. 3, 25; Kurkin and Chertov, *Estestvennoe dvizhenie*, 23, 25.
87. Leikin, *Na zarabotkakh*, 103.

without any bother for half a year."[88] The story shows that although
single peasants met and conceived in Moscow, if they did not always
marry there, they often sent their progeny back to be raised in the
village. This pattern of course was particularly characteristic of illegitimate children of servant girls, but there is reason to suspect that it was
not an isolated phenomenon.[89]

The influence of immigration on household patterns in the city may
be seen also by comparing the peasants with other estate groups.
Raising children in the villages was an option not open to the *meshchane* and guild artisans, groups close to the peasants in status and
occupation. Indeed, both these "urban" groups had the highest child–
woman ratios in 1882 and 1902 as well as the highest rate of
increase.[90] This is all the more noteworthy because the age structure of
the *meshchane* and guild artisans was considerably older than that of
the peasants.[91] It is difficult to believe that a decline in infant mortality, an increase in the married population, or an increase in fertility
could have produced such a sharp increase in the proportion of children. More *meshchane* and guild artisans married to each other would
have accounted for more city babies; this would suggest that peasants
married to each other still raised children in the village. The hereditary
gentry, on the other hand, were the only major social group (besides
foreigners) with a child–woman ratio lower than that among peasants. This low ratio was due in part to an older age structure, a small
proportion of married persons, and a higher marriage age.[92] At the
same time, one would expect that infant mortality would have been
lower than among the peasantry, enabling more babies to survive and
thus producing a larger child–woman ratio. In fact, it is more likely
that the lower proportion of gentry infants registered by the census
takers was due to a higher proportion of infants leaving Moscow to be
raised in the countryside. This low proportion is further confirmed by

88. S. T. Semenov, "U propasti," 8. For a similar phenomenon, see his story "Katiusha," 82.
89. Schulze-Gävernitz, *Volkswirtschaftliche Studien aus Russland* (Leipzig, 1899),
129–71; S. N. Prokopovich, "Krest'ianstvo i poreformennaia fabrika," in A. K. Dzhivelegov et al., *Velikaia Reforma* (Moscow, 1911), 6:273–74. Anthropologists have also
observed that city peasants often have their children raised in the village. See Aidan
Southall, "Urban Migration and the Residence of Children in Kampala," in William
Mangin, ed., *Peasants in Cities: Readings in the Anthropology of Urbanization* (Boston,
1970), 152, 156.
90. *PM 1882*, II, pt. 2, 4–11; *PM 1902*, I, 1, i, 12–13. The calculations are my
own.
91. See note 90 above.
92. Ibid.; *PVP*, 24a, pt. 2, 58–59.

the fact that within the gentry estate itself, the child–woman ratio was lower among the more immigrant hereditary gentry than it was among the personal gentry.[93] This similarity in child–woman ratios suggests that because of immigration patterns, the top and bottom of Russian society may have had some child-rearing patterns which appear statistically similar through the prism of the census, even if they were motivated by different reasons.

The nature of the household units, as well as the configuration of the city's gender and age structure, suggests certain peculiarities of family and residence ties. That nearly 20 percent of the population lived in communal households suggests that associations of laborers, such as the artel that formed or disbanded according to the needs of the casual labor market, still fulfilled important social functions. The artel was, in part, a collective response to the urban housing shortage, a shortage in particular of private, single-family units. In turn, of course, the very existence of this old labor association, the surrogate "family" of ten to fifteen male laborers, and the cheap way by which they could be housed provided a disincentive for more rapid construction of the tenement-style single-family units, more prevalent in the West. Moreover, by entering the Moscow housing market collectively, or at least collectively through the representation of the artel boss (*starosta*), the communal households shielded individual members and preserved collective values and village ways among their members and thereby among a significant proportion of Moscow's population. At the same time, the opportunity to live communally, or at least the opportunity to avoid entering Moscow's housing market on one's own, no doubt enabled more immigrants to come to the big city for temporary sojourns than might otherwise have done so.

These temporary sojourns and the temporary housing arrangements they fostered suggested a tenuousness of family ties *within* the city itself. The small proportion of the population living together as a family is the most striking illustration. Without question, this small proportion is related to the gender ratios; yet, gender ratios alone cannot account for the small proportion of the population living as a family. While the proportions of women married and living as a family were virtually identical (44 percent) in 1897, 57 percent of the males were married and only 30 percent were living as a family. In fact, in 1897 only 7 percent of Moscow's laborers lived with their *entire* family in the city.

93. *PM 1882*, II, pt. 2, 4–11; *PM 1902*, I, 1, i, 12–13; *PVP*, 24a, pt. 2, 58–59.

The remainder either were single or had all or parts of their large family back in the village. The male population in particular had tenuous family ties, because even as late as 1897 married men in the city had wives living elsewhere, chiefly back home in the village. Since the 30 percent of the males living as a family unit presumably included children and others not married, the percentage of *married* men living as a family unit was even smaller, most likely less than half of the city's total married male population.[94] Similarly, a fairly large proportion of the residents of households of single persons, of unrelated persons, and institutional households were married with spouses living elsewhere. As a result, the legal concept of "married" did not necessarily mean living with one's spouse. "Moscow's immigrant population," wrote the compilers of the 1902 census, "has for years been working alone in Moscow, without family members, who are left behind in the villages. Often its marital status is more accurately stated: left wife in village, lives in Moscow."[95] Reformers, as Part Three will discuss in more detail, regarded workers' lives as family-less. A discussion of garden settlements for workers stated that "measures to improve the life of the working-man are tied most closely to the opportunity for a family life, and a necessary prerequisite for the latter is some kind of comfortable and inexpensive home (*ochag*)."[96]

Popular fiction and memoirs of the time are filled with accounts of peasants living in Moscow while their spouses lived elsewhere, not an encouraging way of life from the point of view of reformers. The hero of Podiachev's *Mytarstvo* winds up in the Workhouse while his wife is back in Zvenigorod.[97] In Semenov's "The Fat Cats" ("Briukhany") written in 1904, which describes a small dyeing factory on Moscow's north side, three workers had wives back in the village. One worker from Tula had seen his wife only once in many years. As the story shows, however, the tenuousness of family ties cannot be attributed solely to village residence of workers' dependents: two workers had family in Moscow but did not live with them. The wife of one worked at another factory, and either accommodations or distance permitted only occasional visits; another had a wife and daughter who lived "somewhere on Nemetskii Street and begged for a living."[98] Transi-

94. *GPD 1902*, IV:3.
95. Ibid., 53.
96. "Rabochii poselok pod Moskvoi," *IMGD*, 9 (May 1906): 4.
97. Podiachev, "Mytarstvo," 168.
98. S. T. Semenov, "Briukhany," *V rodnoi derevne*, 373–75. Other characters created by Semenov find themselves in similar situations. See, in the same anthology, "Aleshka," 429; "Turki," 210; "Soldatka," 72.

tory and consensal unions were common means of coping with long separation. According to Giliarovskii's description of the night-lodging houses of the slum:

> The proprietor was never alone; he always lives with his wife although never with his legal wife. The proprietors left their legal wives in the villages and brought in cohabitants, usually Khitrovka natives and often without passports.[99]

The German expert on Russia's textile industry, Schulze-Gävernitz, noted the same phenomenon among immigrant mill hands:

> Now he may leave his wife and child back on his allotment, but in the city or at the factory he marries again, not legally by a priest; all his interests are concentrated in the second marriage.[100]

The conversation between Akulina and a flirtatious young laborer she meets in Leikin's *Working* is revealing:

> "You're getting pretty forward with a young girl! What are you a bachelor, or a widower?"
> "We're all bachelors here in Peter."
> "But you still have a wife back in the village, don't you?"
> "For sure. I've got a farm and a house in the village. You can't have a farm without a woman. So I've got a wife and children. I won't hide it."[101]

The tone of Akulina's first question suggests some doubt that the young man is a bachelor or a widower. His first answer suggests that in a big city immigrant laborers were de facto bachelors. Later in the novel Akulina, working with a group of women along the river outside Petersburg, starts "living together" ("shacks up" in the most literal sense) with another common laborer. His flirtatious and flippant attitude, though, finally drives this independent young woman away.

Not surprisingly, illegitimacy was a fact of life among the laboring population and a source of great concern among reformers. According to data compiled by zemstvo statistician P. I. Kurkin, for the ten-year period 1888–1897, 56,631 out of 250,256 births in Moscow were illegitimate. Even allowing for the immigration of pregnant peasant

---

99. Giliarovskii, *Moskva i Moskvichi,* 42. See also Pozner, "Nochlezhnye doma i nochlezhniki," 27–30.
100. Schulze-Gävernitz, *Krupnoe proizvodstvo,* 139. One study of St. Petersburg estimated that 18 percent of the couples living together were not married. (M. and O., "Tsifry," 92.)
101. Leikin, *Na zarabotkakh,* 52.

women, at 22.6 percent, the illegitimacy rate in the city compared badly with a rate of 2.4 percent in Moscow province.[102]

To establish an independent household in Moscow was much harder than in European capitals:

If the presence of a relatively greater number of laborers in the household is explained partly by custom and partly by our predominantly unsettled population, then the large number of lodgers (*zhil'tsy iz vtorykh ruk*) . . . shows even better the difficulty in "living in one's own house."[103]

On the basis of data on municipal workers, the compilers of the 1882 census concluded that peasant migrants looking for work faced an interruption of at least several years in their family life. The housing shortage, the high cost of living, and the uncertainties of the labor market were clear deterrents to urban family life. The skilled Petersburg metal-fitter P. Timofeev, who described the communal apartment for eighteen cited above, wondered why men who had not seen their wives for five years did not have them move to the city. "Just how could they even move here?" an artel worker responded. "Here today, but God knows where we'll be tomorrow! You have a job today, but tomorrow you get thrown out onto the street—with a family, no less! So we all live by ourselves."[104] It is unlikely that laborers themselves regarded this situation as unfavorably as did the statisticians who studied them, and in any case, the economic necessity, as well as the source of peasant savings to be had from village residence of family members, gave the peasant little choice. Such considerations suggest that the peasant laborers were only very gradually, if at all, severing their ties with the village and becoming more "settled" in urban households.[105]

Tenuous family ties provided an atmosphere less favorable for the upbringing of children. In 1882, 36 percent of all households were headed by a single person; 23 percent were headed by a single woman. This meant that 19 percent of all children were brought up in house-

102. Kurkin, *Statistika*, 150–51, 166, 535. See also Tsentral'nyi statisticheskii komitet, *Statistiki Rossiiskoi imperii*, 18: *Dvizhenie naseleniia v Evropeiskoi Rossii za 1886–1890* (St. Petersburg, 1890), 2–8; Tsentral'nyi statisticheskii komitet, *Sbornik svedenii Rossiiskoi imperii za 1890* (St. Petersburg, 1890), 6–9; V. Krasuskii, *Kratkii istoricheskii ocherk Imperatorskogo Moskovskogo vospitatel'nogo doma* (Moscow, 1878), 233. For a discussion of the problem of illegitimacy elsewhere, see Bater, *St. Petersburg*, 201–2; Chevalier, *Laboring Classes*, 18, 21, 311; and Eames and Goode, *Urban Poverty*, 172–73, 196.
103. *PM 1882*, I, pt. 2, 115.
104. Timofeev, "Ocherki," 22; and "Zavodskie budni," 42.
105. For another view, see Ivanov, "Preemstvennost'," 98–120.

holds headed by a single woman. The economic necessity, especially for single, divorced, or widowed women, to take in lodgers meant that 25 percent of Moscow's children were brought up in households that contained hired laborers, and 43 percent in households that contained lodgers.[106] The files of the city Workhouse give many examples of what today would be called "broken homes" and delinquent (*bezprizornye*) youths.[107] Even more than the transitory and consensual unions, the number of children brought up by single parents or in households with lodgers caught the eye of reformers, who again and again decried this "unhealthy" mingling of young children with strangers.

The large number of people living as lodgers and boarders, as domestics in the homes of their masters, and as laborers in the homes of their employers suggests that the mingling of social and occupational groups, and the widespread practice of subdivision and subleasing in large households, were common social phenomena touching most social groups. The data also suggest that a certain degree of mingling of social groups took place within neighborhoods as well as within large households. Although the inner wards were certainly more fashionable and generally speaking had a higher proportion of Muscovites over muzhiks than did the outer wards, it is impossible to isolate completely rich and poor districts. The above discussion of the housing market and of households has already indicated that in terms of density, proportions of basement and cot-chamber apartments, and proportions of nonfamily residents of households, there was not a sharp variation from ward to ward. At this point it is appropriate to consider additional factors—estate group, birthplace and length of residence, marital status and occupation—to determine the distinctiveness of households in different parts of the city.

RESIDENTIAL SEGREGATION

We may start with the highest group on the social scale, the titled gentry. Almost 16 percent of all titled gentry lived in the Arbat ward in 1871, and 40 percent lived in the three wards of Arbat, Prechistenka, and Tver'—the closest thing Moscow had to London's wealthy West End. At the same time, the titled gentry constituted 15.8 percent of Arbat's total population and 11.8 percent of Prechistenka's. Since

106. *PM 1882*, II, pt. 1, 77, 93–96, 119.
107. Sharov, "Kharakteristika," 1–47.

this group constituted an average of 4 percent of the population in
each of Moscow's wards, it is clear that with three to four times the
city average, the "gentry nests" were a statistical as well as a literary
reality.[108]

That was true in 1871. By 1902, little more than 10 percent of this
estate lived in Arbat, and 33 percent lived in Arbat, Prechistenka, and
Tver'. Similarly, the proportion of Arbat's total population which was
titled gentry declined from 15.8 percent to 12.8 percent. In 1902 a
greater share of this group was registered in outer districts, such as
Lefort, Rogozh', Presnia, and Meshchane, and the southwestern ward
of Khamovniki just beyond Arbat; the Sushchevo ward of artisans and
small proprietors, for example, had almost as large a proportion of
Moscow's gentry as Arbat and Prechistenka had.[109] The overall trend
points to a dispersion of this group throughout the city, with no one
outer ward becoming a fashionable suburban neighborhood. The hard
times facing the gentry made it impossible for some to maintain mansions in the gentry nests and forced them to acquire less-expensive
property on the outskirts of town; the impression of contemporaries
that merchants were moving into traditional gentry neighborhoods was
confirmed, as both Arbat and Prechistenka had an increasing proportion of all merchants in 1902.[110] At the same time, continued migration
of gentry into the city may have forced the more recent arrivals to seek
residence in parts of town other than in the old "gentry nests."

A glance at the censuses quickly shows the even distribution of
townsmen and peasants throughout the city. The proportion of the
city's townsmen living in the Sushchevo, Rogozh', and Meshchane
wards increased considerably from 1871 to 1902; but this reflects the
fact that these wards became the three most populous rather than any
notable concentration of townsmen. With 22.3 percent of its population consisting of townsmen, the south-side Iakimanka ward had the
largest proportion in the city; yet this was a relatively small ward, and
the 6.1 percent of the city's townsmen living there does not indicate a
large concentration. One could argue that townsmen were leaving the
nicer central wards: for example, 29.3 percent of Arbat's population
in 1871 but only 18.5 percent in 1902 consisted of townsmen; Prechistenka and Tver' experienced similar, if less precipitous, declines.[111]

---

108. *Statisticheskie svedeniia*, 70–71.
109. *PM 1882*, III, 20–25; *PVP*, 24a, pt. 1, 46–48; *PM 1902*, I, 1, iii, 137–39.
110. See notes 108 and 109 above.
111. *Statisticheskie svedeniia*, 70–71; *PM 1882*, II, pt. 2, 20–25; *PM 1902*, I, 1, iii,
137–39.

Any decrease in the proportion of townsmen living in the central districts was offset by the continued, and increasing, peasant presence. Thanks to the scattering of occupational groups such as artisans, retailers, proprietors and laborers in drinking and eating establishments, and domestics, several central wards had near-average proportions of peasants, and one, Gorod, had the second largest percentage of peasants in 1902. On the other hand, no great concentration was observed in Miasniki 3, the precinct containing the city's skid row. Domestic servants, as well as craftsmen, attracted by the need for small-scale producers and retailers of articles of consumption, and even casual laborers meant that more than half of the population of the gentry neighborhoods of Prechistenka and Arbat was peasant. Furthermore, the proportion of the population consisting of peasants in these central wards was increasing at a pace with the increase for the city as a whole. As might be expected, the outer precincts did have the highest proportions of peasants: Lefort 2 had the largest (81 percent), and both Khamovniki precincts, Sushchevo 2, Meshchane 2, Basman 2, Lefort 1, Rogozh' 2 and 3, Piatnitsa 2, and Serpukhov 2 all had peasant concentrations of 70–76 percent.[112]

The available evidence suggests that neither were the major estate groups in the city segregated nor was there a distinct trend toward segregation at the end of the nineteenth century. Moscow's traditional settlement patterns described in chapter 2 provide a partial explanation. A sharp spatial segregation of different social groups never had existed in Moscow, and even the elite had been concentrated not in one but in several dispersed areas. Superimposed on the traditional settlement patterns were the rapid growth of the outer districts and the slow growth of the central districts, which appear statistically as a movement of the population from the center. This counteracted any tendency for social groups to concentrate in a few sharply defined districts. The lack of peasant concentration in the outer, sleazy districts or in selected pockets in the central districts can be explained most simply by the fact that there were too many to be absorbed by these districts alone. Furthermore, inasmuch as peasants worked in all parts of the city, they were forced to live in all parts of the city.

Of course, the term "peasant" covers many different varieties, and although this estate group was found everywhere, better-off peasants, Moscow-born peasants, or peasant businessmen and their families

112. See note 111 above.

may have concentrated in the central wards, leaving the poorest peasants in the outer wards. If this were so, the censuses might show greater precinct deviation from the averages when other factors—proportion of immigrants, length of residence, literacy, and occupation—are taken into account. Specifically, even though no pronounced (or increasing) concentration of the privileged estate groups was found in the central wards, one might expect to find in the better parts of town a noticeably lower proportion of immigrants, greater residential persistence, higher literacy, and more persons holding white-collar jobs.

All indicators point to uniformity rather than diversity of households across the city. As chapter 4 has already demonstrated, immigrants were evenly distributed throughout the city, and there was no single neighborhood with a large concentration of households of new arrivals. Nor does the uniformity of literacy rates suggest a sharp spatial differentiation of muzhik and Muscovite. As table 15 shows, in 1902 three-quarters of the men and one-half of the women were literate. Yet, in no precinct were fewer than 66 percent or more than 87 percent of the men literate. The central Tver', Gorod, Miasniki, Arbat, and Prechistenka wards had the highest literacy rates, although several outer precincts also had higher than average rates.

A comparison of occupation and residence is more complicated. First, both terms of employment and actual occupational categories can be correlated with residence. Second, patterns are more difficult to identify with the scores of occupational categories than with literacy or birthplace. In certain occupational categories a clear clustering can be observed. For example, factory workers were concentrated near the mills of Khamovniki, Presnia, Lefort, Basman, Piatnitsa, and Serpukhov. More noteworthy was the rather even spatial distribution of many other occupational groups, including employers, workers in nonfactory manufacturing establishments, apprentices, tailors, managers, office clerks, cabinetmakers, bakers, washerwomen, carpenters, and even domestic servants.[113]

With working hours up to eleven and twelve hours in the factories and longer in the small-scale establishments not subject to factory legislation, many laborers were obliged to live near their place of work because of the absence of convenient, rapid, and low-cost public transport.[114] In 1900 a ride from the center to the workers' district of

113. *PM 1902*, I, 2, iii, 164–215.
114. This was also the conclusion of one of the censuses of commerce and manufactures. See *Promyshlennye i torgovye zavedeniia*, 4.

TABLE 15   LITERACY AND PRECINCT, 1902

Precinct		Men[a]	Literate	Percent Literate	Women[a]	Literate	Percent Literate
Gorod		12,398	10,140	81.8	4,823	2,340	48.5
Tver'	1	7,910	6,889	87.1	7,610	4,749	62.4
Tver'	2	15,460	13,343	86.3	12,130	7,491	61.8
Tver'	3	9,249	7,768	84.0	7,553	4,362	57.8
Miasniki	1	10,448	9,168	87.7	7,734	4,787	61.9
Miasniki	2	7,492	6,244	83.3	5,667	3,312	58.4
Miasniki	3	10,812	7,622	70.5	8,419	3,794	45.1
Prechistenka	1	9,743	8,070	82.8	10,783	6,301	58.4
Prechistenka	2	9,154	7,527	82.2	9,939	5,991	60.3
Arbat	1	8,165	6,859	84.0	10,054	6,439	64.0
Arbat	2	9,876	8,378	84.8	10,572	6,336	59.9
Sretenka	1	10,886	8,430	77.4	9,832	4,693	47.7
Sretenka	2	13,460	10,942	81.3	11,432	5,893	51.5
Iauza	1	6,752	5,628	83.4	6,891	4,226	61.3
Iauza	2	9,936	7,689	77.4	7,134	4,174	58.5
Khamovniki	1	16,882	11,610	68.8	14,363	6,340	44.1
Khamovniki	2	18,733	13,020	69.5	12,554	5,912	47.1
Presnia	1	13,256	9,332	70.4	12,429	5,125	41.2
Presnia	2	11,510	9,072	78.8	10,557	5,545	52.5
Presnia	3	14,355	10,622	74.0	11,933	5,539	46.4
Sushchevo	1	21,511	16,973	78.9	18,498	9,467	51.2
Sushchevo	2	18,706	12,701	67.9	10,165	4,648	45.7
Sushchevo	3	21,682	16,303	75.2	17,729	9,107	51.4
Meshchane	1	16,299	12,566	77.1	11,219	5,681	50.6
Meshchane	2	10,366	7,931	76.5	7,080	3,463	48.9
Meshchane	3	23,080	17,106	74.1	18,555	8,793	47.4
Meshchane	4	13,684	9,719	71.0	10,779	4,582	42.5
Basman	1	12,930	10,281	79.5	10,222	5,658	55.4
Basman	2	10,922	7,956	72.8	8,261	3,822	46.3
Lefort	1	22,505	16,039	71.3	15,546	6,571	42.3
Lefort	2	9,982	6,612	66.2	8,174	2,599	31.8
Lefort	3	11,624	8,762	75.4	6,301	2,793	44.3
Rogozh'	1	11,704	8,720	74.5	9,177	4,366	47.6
Rogozh'	2	25,033	17,426	69.6	18,011	7,699	42.7
Rogozh'	3	25,794	17,462	67.7	13,362	5,436	40.7
Iakimanka	1	12,735	9,476	74.4	9,995	4,899	49.0

TABLE 15 (continued)

Precinct		Men[a]	Literate	Percent Literate	Women[a]	Literate	Percent Literate
Iakimanka	2	15,698	11,790	75.1	12,438	6,451	51.9
Piatnitsa	1	15,945	12,144	76.2	10,868	5,578	51.3
Piatnitsa	2	21,812	15,472	70.9	14,267	5,816	40.8
Serpukhov	1	5,315	3,700	69.6	4,133	1,516	36.7
Serpukhov	2	17,034	11,260	66.1	10,212	4,351	42.6
Totals		570,838	428,752	75.1	437,401	216,645	49.5

Source: PM 1902, I, 1, iii, 114–19.
[a]Age five and older.

Preobrazhenskoe cost 15 kopeks; a monthly round-trip would have cost at least 7 rubles, almost one-third the monthly wage of a printer or approximately equal to the monthly rent of a room.[115] It was not until 1906 that a garden suburb for workers to be serviced by commuter trains was proposed.[116] Because of poor housing, municipal services, and unhealthy conditions, one might think that those who could have afforded it would have lived in the better residential areas, and that this would have led to a greater degree of residential segregation. That this was not the case or that this trend was operating only very gradually is explained partly by the arduous journey to work. The public transit system which served the city's laborers also served all but the most wealthy, who could afford their own carriages and coachmen. Accordingly, most middle-level managerial and professional groups could not afford to live far from their place of work.[117]

The apparent mixture of social groups even in the so-called fashionable central districts concealed a segregation within buildings as peasant laborers, tradesmen, and domestics resided in cellars and attics. Apartment rents were highest for first- and second-floor apartments; basement and attic apartments were the cheapest and attracted

115. GPD 1902, II:10. For contemporary wage and rent correlations, see Svavitskii and Sher, Ocherk, 35; for more recent correlations, see Kir'ianov, Zhiznennyi uroven', 96–101, 259–62. For the total number of streetcar rides, see SEM, no. 3: 116–18.
116. "Rabochii poselok," 1.
117. L. A. Kirillov, "Moskovskie domovladel'tsy v 1892 godu," Sbornik statei po voprosam, otniosiashchimsia k zhizni russkikh i inostrannykh gorodov, 12 vols. (Moscow, 1895–1901), 6:10–11, 13, 16.

those with less ability to pay.[118] A budget study of Moscow workers observed the construction of new buildings with a large number of apartments for rent beginning in the 1870s, a decade after the first wave of post-emancipation immigrants. These new buildings, it was observed, sprung up in all districts and even on the same streets as and between large mansions. Social differentiation occurred by floor not by house. The first floor housed the professional, administrative, and official elite; lower ranks of the same professions lived above, and higher still lived the lowest-level officials, artisans, and students.[119] The historian Kizevetter did not remember many new buildings but did observe residential integration:

Entire streets and especially side streets were nothing but lines of one-story houses and the largest of the two-storied mansions—genuine aristocratic manors—which were interrupted by wooden shacks (*khibarki*) and grubby little shops (*lavchenki*).[120]

Popular fiction also gives a hint of the vertical segregation of social groups and of the location of stores or small workshops on the ground floor of fashionable apartment buildings. Dar'ia Pavlova, the maid in Semenov's "At the Brink," describes how she met the father of her daughter Polia: "Very simple. I was in our master's maids quarters, and he was in the store below."[121] It would appear that Moscow had retained a preindustrial horizontal if not vertical mixture of social groups and occupations.

It has been observed that social groups became more residentially segregated in European and American cities during the course of the nineteenth century. The Anglo-American pattern saw the wealthy and the status-conscious, upwardly mobile middle classes begin to desert the central city, particularly where public transport facilitated the opening of distant suburbs and made possible the continued link with the central business district.[122] The continental pattern differed in that, although migration of the wealthy to distant suburbs was rarer, en-

118. *GPD 1902*, II:58–59; *SEM*, no. 2:214–15. See also, Bater, *St. Petersburg*, 405–7.

119. E. O. Kabo, *Ocherki rabochego byta: Opyt monograficheskogo issledovaniia rabochego byta* (Moscow, 1928), 157–58. See also Pinkney, *Napoleon III*, 8–9.

120. A. A. Kizevetter, *Na rubezhe dvukh stoletii: Vospominaniia, 1881–1914* (Prague, 1929), 14.

121. S. T. Semenov, "U propasti," 9. See also A. Levitov, "Moskovskie komnaty snebel'iu," in Voronov and Levitov, *Moskovskie nory*, 191–320.

122. The literature on the beginning of the movement to the suburbs, especially in American cities, is voluminous. For example, see Sam Bass Warner, *Streetcar Suburbs: The Process of Growth in Boston, 1870–1900* (Cambridge, Mass., 1962); David Ward, *Cities and Immigrants: A Geography of Change in Nineteenth-Century America* (New York, 1971); Thernstrom, *The Other Bostonians*.

claves of the wealthy in the central districts and working-class suburbs promoted residential segregation.[123] One student of the problem has described London:

> In the course of the nineteenth century, the social distance between rich and poor expressed itself in an even sharper geographical segregation of the city. Merchants and employers no longer lived above their places of work. . . . Vast tracts of working-class housing were left to themselves, virtually bereft of any contact with authority except in the form of the policeman or bailiff. The poor districts became an immense terra incognita periodically mapped out by intrepid missionaries and explorers who catered to an insatiable middle class demand for travellers' tales.[124]

In the 1860s, London's central business district was experiencing a decrease in the residential population and an increase in the daytime population: "An extensive no man's land of offices, government buildings, railway yards, warehouses and wharves insulated upper-class from working-class London."[125]

Although I have emphasized the relative lack of spatial segregation in Moscow, I do not mean to imply that there were no barriers between social groups. We should not assume from the previous examination of vertical segregation and horizontal integration that there was any social intercourse between Prechistenka's peasant laborers and the Golitsyns, no matter how proximate their residences. Although easing somewhat in the last decades of the old regime, Russia's legal, social, and cultural barriers prevented the upper social groups from relating to those below them as neighbors except in the most narrowly spatial sense. Legally, the empire's estate system segregated the city's peasants as effectively as any slum residence could have. Socially and culturally, the system of status, privilege, and deference made it certain that all inhabitants of the city knew their place even if they were spatially integrated.

In fact, it could be argued that Moscow's horizontal integration was possible precisely *because* the sharp legal and cultural segregation made neighborhood segregation superfluous. A nobleman did not need to demonstrate his superiority by his choice of neighborhood: his superiority was granted by law, rank, privilege, and deference. By the same token, spatial integration, the peasant-dominated labor force, and the gradual penetration of relationships based on occupational,

---

123. Pinkney, *Napoleon III*, 165.
124. Jones, *Outcast London*, 13–14.
125. Ibid., 166.

rather than juridical, groupings made the archaic estate system all the more necessary to those who benefited from it the most.

❖   ❖   ❖

The immigrant laborer entered a housing market far more complex than that of the surrounding villages, mill towns, or provincial capitals. This complexity reflected not only the size of the city but also the diversity of the immigrant population itself and the wide range of employment opportunities. Given the immigrants' transience and frequent job changes, it was likely that at one time or another most of the newcomers lived in many different types of housing units. This complexity of the housing market reflected a complexity of leasing and subleasing arrangements and accordingly of landlord-tenant-lodger relationships. Similarly, although the contrast in the metropolis between the mansions of Arbat and Prechistenka and the hovels of the factory suburbs or the flophouses of skid row were as striking as that in the mill town between factory barracks or shanties on the waterfront and the mansions of the factory owners on the hills above, the interstices of the housing market in the metropolis were far more numerous than in the mill towns.

A myriad of reports on the housing question as well as data extracted from the censuses point to an overall deterioration in housing conditions: the growth in housing stock could not keep pace with population growth; rents increased sharply at the end of the century, causing increased subdivision and overcrowding; families found it difficult to live together; and a growing number of sleazy flophouses catered to a homeless casual labor force. Central neighborhoods such as those around Sukharev tower, Smolensk market, and the infamous Khitrov market became eyesores that received mounting publicity.

Yet, it would be an oversimplification to say that there were no improvements at all in housing. Despite the tenuousness of family ties, the continued importance of communal living arrangements, and the continued subdivision and overcrowding of units, there is reason to believe that more Moscow residents were becoming independent in their housing arrangements and that an element of choice was increasingly entering the determination of housing. The decline in the number of persons dependent upon institutions or their employers for their housing, and the increase in the number renting housing from private landlords, showed that a segment of the laboring population was becoming free from at least one form of social control of the employer. Such independence may have been worth the price of the overly subdivided private apartments that were arguably worse than the best company housing. A striking factory worker living outside the company gates may have had less fear of losing the roof over his head as well as his wages or job than his brothers living in factory dormitories. Despite the great subdivision of private housing space, a recent Soviet study has documented that more of the better-paid laborers and their families were able to rent an entire room for themselves rather than merely a cot, a "corner," or a "chamber." Writing about worker housing in the suburbs of Petersburg as early as 1895, one public health doctor observed that married workers tried to make their apartments more comfortable with pictures, mirrors, soft furniture, and good beds and blankets.[126] A 1912 article in *Pravda,* surely no source of excessively rosy views of the living conditions of workers, observed that Petersburg workers earning 60 rubles per month (at the time the average wage at both the Putilov and Nevskii plants exceeded 600 rubles per year) who could rent a room for 15 rubles might have "bookshelves with books and portraits of writers on the walls and a clean tablecloth and a lamp with a lampshade on the table."[127] The proportion of the factory workers' budget allotted for food decreased, per capita meat consumption increased, and more and more workers ate with their families at taverns and cafeterias.

Such improvements in housing and households that were within the reach of the better-off laborers went largely unnoticed by the authorities and reformers, increasingly preoccupied by the widespread deleterious conditions. To the extent that improvements were observed, they made the deleterious conditions even more unacceptable to reformers. What did the municipal administration do to alleviate the worst aspects of the urban environment? How successful were policies of the local government in altering the urban environment and in transforming the habits of the city's immigrant laborers? Let us now see how Muscovite confronted muzhik in the second half of the nineteenth century—the perceptions of social problems in the eyes of Muscovites and the evolution of policy responses in the broad area of welfare.

126. Kir'ianov, *Zhiznennyi uroven',* 257. See also my review in *Kritika.*
127. Ibid., 258.

1. THE KREMLIN WALL AND THE TOWER OF THE SACRED GATE.

"If ever a city expressed the character and peculiarities of its inhabitants, that city is Moscow,
the 'heart of Russia' in which the Russian 'wide
nature' (*shirokaia dusha*) is abundantly obvious.
The character, life and tendencies of the people
are seen in much greater purity here than in St.
Petersburg and are much less influenced by
Western Europe, though even Moscow is rapidly
becoming modernized of late years"

(Karl Baedeker, *Russia with Teheran,*
Port Arthur, and Peking, 277).

2. FLEA MARKET ON NEW SQUARE AT THE END OF THE
NINETEENTH CENTURY.

"Every day from morning till night a most colorful and dirty crowd pushes and shoves. . . . The
very essence of the flea market [literally "shoving market" (*tolkuchii rynok*)] lies in this dirty,
unshaven, tattered, hideous crowd moving back
and forth"

(Golitsynskii, *Ulichnye tipy*, 43–45).

3. OLD MAN AT THE FLEA MARKET, EARLY TWENTIETH CENTURY.

"The second-hand goods are generally so well used up that they may be placed on dirty cobblestones without receiving further injury"

(John Bell Bouton,
Roundabout to Moscow, 303).

4. FRUIT JUICE VENDOR, BEGINNING OF THE
TWENTIETH CENTURY.

"They carry food in large baskets all over
the city and yell not only during the day
but also at night"

(Slonov, *Iz zhizni torgovoi
Moskvy*, 53).

5. SELLING CLOTH IN MOSCOW, EARLY TWENTIETH CENTURY.

"Moscow is fast becoming a great centre of
manufacturing and a commercial and business
city with a railroad system affording the means
for the reception of material and the distribution
of products"

(Curtis Guild, *Britons and
Muscovites*, 176).

6. STREET RETAILING, EARLY TWENTIETH CENTURY.
NOTICE THE BAST SHOES CALLED LAPTI,
A MARK OF RURAL ORIGIN.

"Moscow clothes a significant proportion of the
Russian population"

(Oliunina, *Portnovskii promysel v Moskve i v derevniakh Moskovskoi i Riazanskoi gubernii*, 20–21).

7. OPEN-AIR MARKET, EARLY TWENTIETH CENTURY.

"Any poor man who can't spend more than a ruble for a jacket or half a ruble for a pair of pants, or who needs an old cap for a few kopeks, can go to the flea market and immediately find everything"

(Golitsynskii, *Ulichnye tipy*, 43–45).

8. SELLING OLD SHOES AT SUKHAREV MARKET, LATE NINE-
TEENTH CENTURY.

Shoemakers also remade shoes from scraps of
leather collected at the city's marketplaces and
junkyards. The product was colloquially known
as "shoddy" (*lipovaia*) shoes for their flimsiness.

"It is among the multitude who spread dilapidated treasures on the ground that the most
amusing incidents are to be noted by the inquisitive stranger"

(John Bell Bouton, *Roundabout to Moscow*, 303).

PART THREE

Muzhik Faces Muscovite

CHAPTER SEVEN

Welfare: Relief and Repression

By the end of the nineteenth century, Moscow, despite the persistence of its "overgrown village" image, had all the ingredients of a bustling metropolis. Foremost among the factors shaping the character of the city and the process of urbanization were Moscow's muzhiks. By 1900 they numbered three-quarters of a million, entered the city at an annual rate of 100,000–150,000, and left at an annual rate of almost 100,000, were distributed among virtually all white- and blue-collar jobs, and resided in all quarters of the city. Like bustling metropolises everywhere, Moscow was the center of unprecedented economic expansion and employment opportunities which acted as a magnet for a large hinterland. But at the same time, also like bustling metropolises everywhere, Moscow was a center of urban blight and destitution. Massive immigration, a booming yet unorganized and erratic labor market, housing congestion and shortages, and the seeming tenuousness of family and household ties were common strains accompanying rapid urban growth, which alarmed the authorities toward the end of the nineteenth century.

The notoriety of urban pathologies increased largely because the pathologies themselves worsened and because the perceptions of the nature of these pathologies changed. But the attention the Muscovite paid to the muzhik and to the strains of urbanization increased also because different groups of Muscovites faced different muzhiks. In the mid-nineteenth century, Muscovites—largely officials of imperial agencies and institutions, the police, and writers of a populist bent—observed the colorful characters of the streets, particularly the city's beggars, vagrants, runaways, and drifters. Indeed, as the tip of the iceberg, these elements of the subordinate classes contributed much to the prevailing image throughout the nineteenth century of Moscow as an "overgrown village," in the eyes of foreign visitors and natives alike. The attention given the laboring population as a whole, the submerged iceberg, was sporadic. Only toward the end of the century did Muscovite—now joined by municipal officials and professionals—recognize the deleterious effects of congested and unsanitary housing, irregular employment, and slum living, not just on the city's more colorful inhabitants but on its entire laboring population.

Although the imperial government, "estate" and ecclesiastical associations, and an increasing number of private organizations tried in various ways to cure urban pathologies, city governments were increasingly looked to for solutions to the most serious urban problems. By the end of the century, urban problems appeared more urgent, and the resulting policies became more systematic in organization, broader in scope, and more self-consciously reformist in expression. Yet, despite greater municipal activism, the city faced formidable difficulties. While some of these difficulties stemmed from fiscal and policy limitations of the city governments themselves, to an even greater degree they stemmed from economic and social forces beyond the control of the municipalities, as well as from the social and cultural disparity between the common people, who were allegedly responsible for urban problems, and the educated elite, who tried to solve them. The purpose of this and the following chapter is to trace the changing attitudes of the authorities and philanthropists toward the problems of the muzhik in the city, the formulation of concrete solutions to these problems in the areas of poor relief and housing, and the evolution of an ethos of individual and social reform.

BEGGARS AND VAGRANTS

Although the number of Moscow's beggars, tramps, and vagrants struck both Russian and foreign observers, such extreme examples of indigence and homelessness were present everywhere in nineteenth-century European and American cities, especially in the metropolises. London reportedly was constantly inundated with "plagues of beggars." The prefect of the Paris police observed in 1831: "On every hand destitution rears its ugly head. The number of beggars is growing daily. Were we to arrest the lot, the jails could not hold them. . . .

There are also far more vagrants around."[1] The *Journal des Débats* complained:

Beggars are displaying themselves in Paris and adjacent communes in every hideous and distressing guise. They pursue passers-by in the streets, besiege the doors of churches, creep into houses, hold shopkeepers to ransom and everywhere present a shocking contrast of abject poverty in the midst of wealth and plenty, of idleness and vagrancy amid the most thriving industry and the most polished civilization.[2]

Another Parisian put the latter thought into different words: "Indigence in the great cities has a far more disturbing mien than poverty in the country; it inspires disgust and horror, for it assails all the senses at once."[3] Even the land of opportunity harbored tramps and paupers who appeared to be descending on the large cities. According to one Bostonian, foreign paupers merely add to

our native poor, who remove to Boston from the country for the purpose of getting aid from the charitable institutions of the city. They find help more readily than at home, where they are better known. . . . Every tramp knew . . . that there was free soup in every station house in Boston. . . . He goes to Boston with the feeling . . . that he shall not starve to death when he gets there.[4]

Certain themes frequently cited in the literature of European and American cities were repeated again and again in Moscow. Like European metropolises, Moscow had always been, and had always been *perceived* as, a mecca for beggars and vagrants. In the seventeenth century there were complaints about the horrible state of "begging children who roam about the streets in throngs. They learn nothing except thievery." As if to ensure their visibility in the seventeenth and eighteenth centuries, beggars and vagrants concentrated in Red Square and at the Stone Bridge, in the heart of Moscow.[5] A report of the Moscow Alms Committee for 1847, indicating that two-thirds of its 3,592 wards were from outside the city, concluded that Moscow was still a mecca for the indigent.[6] Indeed, the popular impression was that

1. Quoted in Chevalier, *Laboring Classes*, 268.
2. Ibid.
3. Ibid., 360.
4. Quoted in Nathan Irvin Huggins, *Protestants against Poverty* (Westport, Conn., 1970), 71.
5. M. I. Pyliaev, *Staraia Moskva* (St. Petersburg, 1891), 418–19. See also S. Bakhrushin, *Maloletnie nishchie i brodiagi v Moskve* (Moscow, 1913), 2; Geinike, *Po Moskve*, 259; *Istoriia Moskvy*, 2:192, 328.
6. *Otchet Moskovskogo komiteta o prosiashchikh milostyniu za 1847* (Moscow, 1848), 7.

beggars congregated almost exclusively in the big cities, whose concentration of wealth, marketplaces, and opulent churches offered a more profitable place for begging. According to two students of the problem, the many employment opportunities of cities attracted not only the "sincere" indigent looking for work but also "professional beggars who figure they can trick unsuspecting individuals more easily in the cities and more safely lead a life of idleness and drink."[7] In addition, by the end of the nineteenth century, it was also widely believed that the mere presence of many charitable societies and welfare institutions attracted paupers to large cities.[8]

The theme of disgust, horror, and offense at the mere sight of beggars and vagrants could also be found in Russia. Like the Frenchman quoted above, August A. Levenstim regarded beggars as an unseemly sight:

Pilgrims stand at the church entrance, defining a narrow pathway along which people can barely pass. It's hard to imagine a more revolting sight. After a heavenly service, people come out into a dirty crowd of ragged creatures who deliberately shove their rags and open wounds into the faces of passers-by.[9]

Particularly offensive was the cynical use of children and even infants, also a common practice in Europe, to elicit more sympathy from the potential almsgiver:

Children at Khitrov market were in great demand: from infancy they were rented out, almost auctioned to beggars. Sometimes a dirty old woman, often still infected with some awful disease, takes an unfortunate child, stuffs a dirty rag and a piece of bread in its mouth to suck on, and drags him out onto the cold streets. Cold and dirty all day, the child rests in her arms, poisoned with the rag, and moaning from the cold, from hunger, and from constant stomach pains; this arouses the sympathy of passers-by for the "poor unfortunate orphan." There have been times when the child dies in the beggar's arms in the morning, but not wanting to lose a day, the beggar woman keeps going until night for alms.[10]

7. P. I. Georgievskii, *Prizrenie bednykh i blagotvoritel'nost'* (St. Petersburg, 1894), 43; Levenstim, *Professional'noe nishchenstvo*, 23. See also M. Poludenskii, "Mnenie o istreblenii v Moskve nishchikh," *Chteniia Obshchestva istorii i drevnostei rossiiskikh*, Vol. 2 pt. 5 (1861): 181; I. V. Andreev, "Filantropy i nishchie," *Delo*, no. 7 (1868): 17.

8. Linev, *Prichiny russkogo nishchenstva*, 39; S"ezd po obshchestvennomu prizreniiu, sozvannyi Ministerstvom vnutrennikh del, *Trudy* (Petrograd, 1914), 459–62.

9. Levenstim, *Professional'noe nishchenstvo*, 50.

10. Giliarovskii, *Moskva i Moskvichi*, 36, 41–42. For similar descriptions, see Tolstoi, "Tak chto zhe nam delat'?" 17, 28; Vasilich, "Ulitsy i liudi," 6; Obshchestvo pooshchreniia trudoliubiia v Moskve, *Letopis' pervogo dvadtsatipiatiletiia* (Moscow, 1888), 94.

Despite the disgust that beggars and vagrants aroused among some well-heeled Muscovites, to others such street people remained a picturesque phenomenon, curiosities, relics of the "patriarchal Muscovite" past, representatives of an unkempt rural Russia still untouched by civilization, and as such attractive to writers and artists of a populist bent. The composer Modest Mussorgsky described his first trip to Moscow in 1859:

> I ascended the "Ivan the Great" tower from the top of which I had a wonderful view. Roving through the streets I remembered the dictum "All Muscovites bear a distinctive hallmark." This is certainly true of the common people. Nowhere else in the world could beggars and rogues of the same kind be found. They have a strange demeanor, a nimbleness of motion that struck me particularly. In short I feel as if I had been carried into a new world, the world of yore—an unclean one, but one which nevertheless impresses me most favorably. You know I was a cosmopolitan; now I feel reborn and quite close to all that is Russian.[11]

It may be no mere coincidence that several popular studies of this aspect of Russian life were published in the 1860s and 1870s, among which were *Wandering Pilgrims,* a four-volume compendium of poems, folk songs, legends, and ballads compiled by Slavicist Peter Bessonov; *Street Folk,* a collection of illustrated sketches of Moscow's street people; Ivan Pryzhov's *Beggars in Holy Russia;* and the ethnographer Sergei Maksimov's *Wandering Begging Russia.*[12]

Pryzhov claimed, though without supporting evidence, that in the early 1860s Moscow had 40,000 beggars, as well as an undetermined number of prophets, holy fools, and women possessed by the devil. The central marketplace, the Trading Rows, was

> jammed with beggars who, from early morning to late in the evenings bustle all over, giving neither passage nor place to customers and tradesmen, like locusts who fly in every day from all corners of the capital and cling to everything they meet.[13]

Among the more colorful of the prophets and holy fools Pryzhov described in the magazine *Entertainment* in 1865 were Feodosii and Evdokiia. The former, a peasant from Dmitrov who discovered that

---

11. M. D. Calvocoressi, *Modest Mussorgsky: His Life and Works* (Fair Lawn, N.J., 1956), 32–33.
12. P. A. Bessonov, ed., *Kaleki perekhozhie: Sbornik stikhov i issledovanii,* 4 vols. (Moscow, 1861–1864); Golitsynskii, *Ulichnye tipy;* I. G. Pryzhov, *Nishchie na sviatoi Rusi: Materialy dlia istorii obshchestvennogo i narodnogo byta v Rossii* (Moscow, 1862; reprint Kazan', 1913); Pryzhov, *Ocherki, stat'i, pis'ma* (Moscow, 1934); S. V. Maksimov, *Brodiachaia Rus' Khrista-radi* (St. Petersburg, 1877).
13. Pryzhov, *Ocherki,* 155–56.

being a holy fool was profitable, wandered barefoot wearing iron chains and uttering his prophecies in Khamovniki, which had recently become a "haven for all kinds of charlatans."[14] Evdokiia, from Tambov, could always be found in the Rogozh' district, near either Taganka Square or the Pokrov gates,

in vacant lots, strewn with refuse, where all kinds of holy fools and charlatans gather. She'll stop any passerby and ask: "Dear brother" or "Dear sister, you can be blessed for a kopek." If she gets the kopek she'll bless the donor, but if not, she'll send them to hell, and you know how they're afraid of these things in Zamoskvorech'e. . . . When someone invites her in, she sits down on the floor and starts telling tales of apparitions and visions she has seen, after which she'll ask for some vodka.[15]

The popular impression, of course, was that beggars, prophets, and holy fools shared an attraction to vodka. Pryzhov, whose best-known work was a history of Russian taverns, estimated that approximately three-fourths of the almost 4 million rubles collected each year on the streets of Moscow was spent on alcohol.[16]

Perhaps even more colorful than the tales of Pryzhov were the *Street Folk* of A. Golitsynskii published in 1860. If one wanted to know the Russian people, Golitsynskii began his sketches, one should study their street life:

At home our common man is a guest, frequently a very formal guest, and you'll hardly get a word out of him. He appears at home mainly to grab a bite to eat, rest and, if you please, die. His entire personal and public life is expressed on the street: here he works, drinks, passes time, quarrels, trades, cheats.[17]

With an eye for detail rivaling his more celebrated contemporary, Henry Mayhew, Golitsynskii described the subculture of Moscow's street folk and of its beggars in particular. Beggars formed their own corporate estate, much like the gentry and the merchants, with their own "aristocrats," their own scoundrels and honest people, their own "offices" (*dokhodnoe mesto*) and "English Clubs." There were even "bankers who keep their money not of course with the Board of Trustees but in their boots or in the soles of their sandals." Just as laborers frequently found work through a subcontractor (*podriad-*

14. Ibid., 55.
15. Ibid., 54.
16. Ibid., 163–64. His history of taverns is *Istoriia kabakov v Rossii v sviazi s istoriei russkogo naroda* (St. Petersburg, 1870). See also Levenstim, *Professional'noe nishchenstvo*, 46–47.
17. Golitsynskii, *Ulichnye tipy*, 3.

chik), so too many village beggars relied on a "subcontractor" or agent (*otkupshchik*) who, for a cut, found reliable and safe places to beg. The inhabitants of entire villages not far from Moscow allegedly lived by begging.[18] As if to confirm notions of beggars being professionals, one confided,

I have been in Moscow many times and know all the benefactors like the palms of my hand. I can show you places where our brothers will never get turned down. Besides, I know two merchants and a princess who would always give every penny they had. And to boot, I know how to approach them and what to say. Of course, I can explain everything to you, but only if you'll add a farthing.[19]

Such agents were joined by beggar-chiropractors operating in the public baths, "Sevastopols" (discharged soldiers who claimed they were wounded at Sevastopol), "drummers" who begged by knocking on windows, "writers" who wrote letters to philanthropists, and many more.[20]

According to Golitsynskii, the aristocrat of the women beggars was the "cape-woman" (*salopnitsa*), so named for her "short, silky, well-worn, faded cape."[21] Almost always the widow of a lower civil servant "who had worked forty years for five rubles a month and died of pauperism, alcoholism and hemorrhoids," the cape-woman

has a strikingly supple character. The cape-woman is created precisely for the proletariat: at the same time she can be a matchmaker, gossip, and make cosmetics; she is a devotee, a mourner, a sponger, a fortune-teller, a thief—everything you could want.[22]

In characteristically tongue-in-cheek style, Golitsynskii bids farewell to the cape-woman thus:

In conclusion you can always see her coming out of the beer hall. But, God forbid, she didn't have a drop there; she only begged for a kopek for the poor and that's why on leaving, she piously crosses herself and praises the Lord. The fact that her nose is a reddish-purple, well, that's because, no doubt, she's been crying from morning till evening, and the bitter tears have discolored her nose.[23]

18. Ibid., 8; Linev, *Prichiny russkogo nishchenstva*, 193; A. I. Svirskii, *Pogibshie liudi*, 3 vols. (St. Petersburg, 1898), 3: *Mir nishchikh i propoits*, 20–25.

19. Svirskii, *Pogibshie liudi*, 3:19.

20. Golitsynskii, *Ulichnye tipy*, 12; Ia. Kharlamov, *Khristovym imenem: Ocherki zhizni peterburgskikh nishchikh* (St. Petersburg, 1898), 159; Levenstim, *Professional'noe nishchenstvo*, 47–49, 66; E. D. Maksimov, *Proiskhozhdenie nishchenstva*, 68–69.

21. Golitsynskii, *Ulichnye tipy*, 8–9.

22. Ibid. For more on widows of civil servants on relief, see Poludenskii, "Mnenie," 181.

23. Golitsynskii, 9–10.

One message Golitsynskii conveyed to his readers, a message that was repeated frequently in later, more scholarly, studies of pauperism as well, was that beggars were not always what they appeared to be. In particular, they were not helpless or suffering but frequently were skilled operators who preferred begging to any other trade. They were on the streets to hoodwink the unsuspecting Muscovite:

Don't think that the one sitting with closed eyes at the street corner has wrists attached to his shoulder blades or that he crawls over the sidewalk all day like a lizard because of an amputated leg. At the proper time, this blind man will recover his eyesight and the mutilated arm will straighten. And that acrobat who was crawling around, he'll chug a bottle of vodka after his day's work and do a *trepak* [a Russian folk dance] so fast that no instrument could ever accompany him.[24]

Perhaps this was the "nimbleness of motion" that struck Mussorgsky!

Citizens of the street, such as the holy fools, the cape-woman, the "crippled" beggar who danced the trepak after hours, may have been exceptional; street life itself was not. Although locust-like beggars were certainly annoying when they swarmed in the central business district and even disgusting when they shoved open wounds into the faces of well-heeled Muscovites after church, they still represented picturesque extremes of the ordinary life of the streets, of the "proletariat," in Golitsynskii's usage of the word. To the Slavicist, linguist, or ethnographer like Bessonov and Maksimov, they were valuable objects of study, if not actual possessors of some inner virtue, as quintessential representatives of the Russian people. Although such observers recognized the moral and social problems of begging, vagrancy, and pauperism, particularly when connected with alcoholism and crime, the street people did not present serious cases of need. In the bucolic words of one observer,

The Russian pauper is not a landless proletarian like his Western counterpart. No matter how poor, almost all have their own hut where, even if it is way off in the sticks, they can very easily spend the rest of their lives. . . . Consequently the most important thing is to provide the have-nots with food, but this is not too difficult a matter.[25]

The street people, even the deviant street people, remained curiosities, certainly not hard-core welfare cases.

24. Ibid., 3.
25. A. Kudriavtsev, *Nishchenstvo, kak predmet popecheniia tserkvi, obshchestva i gosudarstva* (Odessa, 1885), 83.

ALMSGIVING, REPRESSION, AND RELIEF

Colorful curiosities, yes, but beggars and vagrants could not be ignored. By the mid-nineteenth century three common remedies for the problems of begging and vagrancy had evolved: almsgiving, expulsion or incarceration, and relief administered either in institutions or by a charitable society or agency. The first was by far the most widespread, the second attempted to repress the problem by removing it from the city's streets, and the third attempted to relieve the problem by providing appropriate aid. All three, of course, had their equivalents in Europe at the time, and despite changing perceptions of the problem of the laboring poor and increasing criticism of such "primitive" relief, they remained widespread in Russia at the close of the nineteenth century.

"Muscovites are indeed solicitous toward beggars; they give them what they can, clothe and feed them, and even take them into their homes."[26] Foreigners commonly observed that Muscovites were generous in giving alms, and the alleged godliness of the seeker of alms "for the sake of Christ" (*Khrista radi*) or "in Christ's name" (*Khristovym imenem*) in Russian culture is well known. Pryzhov estimated, although it is unclear on what basis, that the average beggar in Moscow collected 25 kopeks per day; the 40,000 beggars he estimated to be in the city on any given day would collect 3,600,000 rubles in one year, or 6 rubles per year from every man, woman, and child in the city.[27] Although such figures are highly speculative, Muscovites were perceived as being generous, perhaps even overly generous, and one detects in both Pryzhov and, especially, Golitsynskii a chiding tone: that beggar, that pilgrim or wandering soothsayer, that cripple or holy fool, they are saying, may be, not what they appear, but frauds, out to hoodwink bighearted, pious, or superstitious Muscovites.

There were, of course, those Muscovites who were less interested in living examples of the folkways of the Russian nation than were Golitsynskii or Pryzhov and for whom "locust-like" beggars in the Trading Rows or fraudulent holy fools on the church or cemetery grounds were a nuisance, a moral offense, and a threat to public order. Expulsion from the city of beggars or vagrants whose birthplace or place of residence was known, and also criminal punishment, were the major

26. Pyliaev, *Staraia Moskva*, 418.
27. Pryzhov, *Ocherki*, 163–64. This estimate is based on an 1871 population of 601,969.

repressive means of dealing with the problem of vagrancy and mendicancy. According to the Code of Laws issued in 1857, a person begging because of laziness or habitual idleness could be sent to jail for
one to three weeks for a first offense and up to three months for a
second. Those who accompanied their begging with impertinence and
rudeness, abusive and profane language, or with fraud in the form of a
faked wound or injury or of someone else's child carried to enlist
greater sympathy were liable to a jail sentence of three to six months.[28]
Such laws obviously tried to make a distinction between the "professional" or "fraudulent" beggar and the honest pilgrim or cripple.

More serious an offense in Russia, as elsewhere, was vagrancy.
"The beggar is the dregs of society," a Muscovite could have read in
the 1860s, "with no feeling of personal worth, but at least he has a
place to live and a family." The vagrant is "animal-like"; he has the
"force of a wild beast." "Whereas the beggar is passive and inert, the
vagrant is active and energetic."[29] According to the Criminal Code,
someone who could not remember his next of kin or who refused to
indicate his occupation or means of support and permanent residence
or who gave false information was a vagrant and could be imprisoned
for up to four years.[30] But it is clear that the vagrant was judged in
part for his alleged lack of family and for his unruly, rebellious nature.

The laws on the books were one thing; practice, however, was
another. It appears that very few were actually sentenced for mendicancy or vagrancy. At a time when Moscow allegedly had 30,000–
40,000 beggars, fewer than 3,000 were rounded up annually by the
police.[31] If beggars were indeed as plentiful as locusts, or if they made
it difficult to make one's way out of church, and if they were as
cunning and fraudulent as many observers believed, it is odd that so
few were apprehended or convicted. Of those apprehended by the
police, by no means all were actually sentenced; the more common
form of repression for those who disclosed an out-of-town residence
was expulsion and return home by police convoy (*po etapam*).[32] From

28. *Svod zakonov Rossiiskoi imperii* (St. Petersburg, 1857), 15: *Ulozhenie o na-
kazaniiakh ugolovnykh i ispravitel'nykh*, articles 1274, 1275; *Entsiklopedicheskii slovar'*, 41:209–10; A. Likhachev, "Nakazanie i pomoshch' nishchim," *Trudovaia pomoshch'*, 2, no. 1 (January 1899): 11–12.

29. N. Radiukin, "Brodiagi i nishchie," *Delo*, no. 6 (1867): 98.

30. *Svod zakonov* (1885 ed., reprint St. Petersburg, 1912–1914), 15, articles 950–
954.

31. M. N. Kurbanovskii, *Nishchenstvo i blagotvoritel'nost'* (St. Petersburg, 1860),
54.

32. See the discussion of illegal residents of the city's lodging houses below.

the sketchy data available, it would seem that even this form of repression was not widely used. In fact, when existing measures of combatting mendicancy and vagrancy came under increasing fire at the end of the century, it was frequently argued that far fewer were convicted of mendicancy or vagrancy in Russia than in western European countries with smaller populations and more narrowly conceived vagrancy laws. One student of the problem pointed out that while an average of 1,323 beggars were sentenced during the period 1891–1895 in the entire Russian empire, from 1892 to 1896 in France 14,638 were sentenced annually for mendicancy and 18,000 for vagrancy, and in Austria 28,000 were sentenced annually for begging alone.[33]

ORGANIZED CHARITY

Organized poor relief was the third method of dealing with the problems of mendicancy and vagrancy and of indigence in general. Such relief consisted of aid to the needy from charitable societies and agencies and of institutionalization of certain categories of indigence. These of course are very basic forms of poor relief, and the combination of institutional and noninstitutional welfare was present in Moscow throughout the nineteenth century. Many relief institutions and agencies were extremely small in their operations, had a very limited clientele, or had limited objectives.[34] Somewhat broader in its scope of activities was, for example, the Sheremetev Wayfarer's Home. Founded in 1803, the Wayfarer's Home offered material handouts to the poor (particularly on holidays) and allowances for poor brides, and ran an almshouse and hospital from a building on Moscow's near north side, whose classical facade was one of the city's architectural landmarks.[35] The most common form of aid in all of these charitable societies was the almshouse (*bogadel'nia*). Almshouses provided total maintenance for those who were too old, infirm, or ill to work, such as Polikarpych, an aging building superintendent in Semenov's "Dvornik." In addition, many of the larger parish churches maintained an almshouse, often on

33. E. Tarnovskii, "K voprosu o brodiazhestve," 18; Likhachev, "Nakazanie i pomoshch'," 13.

34. *SSS 1889*, viii–xii, 4–6; *SSS 1901*, passim; *Letopis'*, 88, 180, 199; *Sbornik ocherkov*, 1–7, 16–18; P. M. Kapustin, "Moskovskii ispravitel'nyi priiut," *Vestnik Evropy*, 5, no. 8 (August 1871): 608; "Priiut dlia neimushchikh pristanishcha lits, vykhodiashchikh iz Staro-Ekaterininskoi bol'nitsy dlia chernorabochikh," *Russkaia mysl'*, 3, no. 2 (February 1882): 106.

35. *SSS 1901*, 247; *Strannopriimnyi dom gr. Sheremeteva v Moskve, 1810–1910* (Moscow, 1910), 1–2, 12, 486–88.

the church grounds. According to one survey of the city council, in the 1880s almost 15,000 persons were on relief at 107 almshouses.[36]

At mid-century Moscow's larger welfare agencies and institutions all had imperial sponsorship or were run directly or indirectly by the central government. Such were the Imperial Philanthropic Society, the Institutions of Empress Maria, and the Offices of Public Welfare. Founded in 1802, the first supervised a Guardianship of the Poor which managed several orphanages, almshouses, vocational schools, and clinics and also paid money allowances to the poor.[37] Two other agencies of the Imperial Philanthropic Society were the Society to Encourage Industriousness and the Fraternal Apartment Agency for the Needy.[38] A similar variety of welfare agencies and institutions was run by the Office of the Institutions of the Empress Maria, after 1828 the Fourth Section of His Majesty's Own Imperial Chancery, one of the oldest welfare offices in continuous operation in Moscow. Subordinate to the Institutions of the Empress Maria were the Moscow Charity Society founded in 1837, whose major purpose was to provide vocational training to poor girls; the Moscow Council of Children's Shelters founded in 1842; and the Ladies Guardianship of the Poor founded in 1844, which gave money allowances to the poor and ran several shelters, including the Mary Magdalene shelter for former prostitutes.[39]

THE IMPERIAL FOUNDLING HOME

What put the Institutions of the Empress Maria on the welfare map, though, was neither the Mary Magdalene shelter nor any of the other shelters or agencies, but Moscow's largest, best known, and most controversial welfare institution: the Imperial Foundling Home. Standing on the banks of the Moscow River not far downstream from the Kremlin, the Foundling Home sheltered thousands of foundlings per year and gave showplace tours to foreign travelers in one of the city's most prominent edifices.

Foundling homes had become widespread in seventeenth- and eigh-

36. *SSS 1889*, xxi–xxii; S. T. Semenov, "Dvornik," 94; "Bogadel'ni," *Entsiklopedicheskii slovar'*, 4:141–43.

37. Imperatorskoe Chelovekoliubivoe obshchestvo, *Istoricheskii ocherk Soveta Imperatorskogo Chelovekoliubivogo obshchestva i podvedomstvennykh emu blagotvoritel'nykh uchrezhdenii* (St. Petersburg, 1898), 15 ff; *SSS 1889*, xiv–xv; *SSS 1901*, 45–46.

38. *Letopis'*, 209; *SSS 1901*, 60–61.

39. *SSS 1889*, xiii–xiv, 13–15; *SSS 1901*, 18–19, 24–25, 31–32, 36–37.

teenth-century Europe, particularly in France, when mercantilist policies tried to increase national wealth by, among other things, increasing
population. Child abandonment and infanticide, allegedly in epidemic
proportions and clearly objectionable on moral grounds, also deprived
the state of too many potentially productive citizens. Louis XIV was
alleged to have said that "the lives of foundlings must be preserved,
since they can be useful to the state in the future," and Napoleon
regarded male foundlings as potential soldiers for the nation.[40]

Russia's first foundling institution was an asylum for illegitimate
children created in 1706 at the Kholmo-Uspenskii monastery near Novgorod. Peter I created hospitals on church grounds which also took
infants secretly. The first actual foundling home opened in 1764 (only
twenty-three years after that in London) when Catherine II founded the
Imperial Foundling Home in Moscow. Both the institution and its
wards (*pitomtsy*) acquired certain privileges: the home was tax exempt,
and it could buy and sell villages, houses, and land, run workshops and
factories, and run lotteries and keep one-quarter of the proceeds. The
wards themselves and all their descendants enrolled in the *meshchanstvo* and could never become enserfed.[41] Clearly, these privileges
were designed to persuade poor peasant women to leave their infants at
the Foundling Home rather than to abandon or kill them, although
estimates of the numbers of infanticides or babies abandoned "on the
doorsteps, in gardens, in railway carriages" do not appear in the
literature.[42] After an 1828 law prohibited the building of more provincial foundling homes, the Moscow home became the only institution to
provide services for the central region.

From its inception, the Foundling Home was intended to admit not
only illegitimate infants but also the legitimate offspring of destitute
parents and orphans up to age thirteen. According to one traveler:

The managers of the hospital informed us that a large proportion of the
children brought to the hospital were of legitimate birth, their parents being of
the laboring classes and at service at such low wages that they could give
neither the time nor the means to bring up their children and being assured of

40. "Vospitatel'nye doma," *Entsiklopedicheskii slovar'*, 7:274–80. I am grateful to
Katherine Lynch for pointing out the many similarities between the Russian and French
institutions.
41. Ibid., 276.
42. A. I-ov, "Vospitatel'nye doma v Rossii," *Vestnik Evropy*, 25, no. 6 (June
1890): 490–98; N. N. Ginzburg, "Prizrenie podkidyshei v Rossii," *Trudovaia pomoshch'*, 7, no. 4 (April 1904): 500–13; B. P. Brukhanskii, "Ocherk istoricheskogo
razvitiia i sovremennogo sostoianiia Imperatorskikh Vospitatel'nykh Domov," S"ezd po
obshchestvennomu prizreniiu, *Trudy*, 154–59.

better care than they could give, resigned them here, with the hope of claiming
them before they reached the age of ten years.[43]

The Home accepted infants from the municipal and provincial authorities, maternity wards, and midwives if the mother had died or if a
physician certified that the mother was incapable of breast-feeding the
infant. Upon the reception of the infant, no questions were asked
except the infant's name, age, and whether it had already been
baptized.[44] Other infants were taken in secretly, as poignantly described by John Bell Bouton, an American traveler in the 1880s:

Many a baby, over whom the Moskwa [sic] would otherwise close its dark
and swift waters, is saved to become a good soldier for the Tsar or a modest
and prettily dressed housemaid, simply because the newborn could be put by
its mother within the folds of the foundling asylum and none be the wiser. She
has only, in the darkness of night, to place the child in a sort of cradle
attached to a door outside the building and pull the bell. This gives a signal
and starts some machinery. The door revolves on its hinges, landing the little
stranger on the inside. At the same time a nurse responds to a summons and
takes charge of the baby. . . . If she wants to keep her painful secret forever to
herself, she may be sure that her child will be well-fed, neatly clothed, taught
to read and write, cared for in health and morals, and trained in the religion of
the Greek church till he or she is old enough to be apprenticed, or adopted out
by some respectable citizen and put in the way of honest living.[45]

The revolving cradle—the tour—and the secret admission of infants
clearly beckoned destitute mothers of legitimate as well as illegitimate
children. The "success" of the Foundling Home in its admissions policy can be seen in the increasing number of foundlings taken in
annually.[46] The Home's administration appeared to be pleased with a
large number of foundlings. One English traveler saw the nurses
standing around waiting for arrivals. The superintendent remarked
that "only five" had arrived on that day, which was "but few indeed"
and "it was getting late" so that "today would be a bad day." Since
there were usually about thirty-five nurses in the room, one could
assume that approximately that number of foundlings came in on an
average day. The traveler suggested that after the emancipation, the

43. Guild, Britons and Muscovites, 174–75.
44. A. I-ov, "Vospitatel'nye doma," 490–98; Ginzburg, "Prizrenie," 502–9; Krasuskii, Kratkii istoricheskii ocherk, 40–52.
45. Bouton, Roundabout to Moscow, 262–63. See also Charles A. Stoddard,
Across Russia (New York, 1891), 176.
46. A. I-ov, "Vospitatel'nye doma," 518–19; Krasuskii, Kratkii istoricheskii ocherk,
50.

people were becoming more moral and marrying more, at which the superintendent laughed.

It was clear that this engaging person looked at the credit of the establishment first and that this consisted in numbers. Her pride was in hosts, as a preacher would feel pride in a crowded congregation, or a general in added legions. Any check upon the maintenance of the lady's legions in the shape of matrimony or morality she would hold to be an invasion of the domain. The superintendent was a true official.[47]

Once the infant was admitted, it was weighed, measured, examined, washed, and dressed before being given to a wet nurse. Bouton described the nurses' room and the nurses themselves in the 1880s:

It was a long apartment, spotless as to wooden floor and whitewashed ceiling. Along one side was a row of strong, wooden cradles; on the other side were the nurses' beds with frames of iron. . . . There were ten or twelve nurses present, each one rocking a cradle or holding a child to her breast. Ruddier and more robust women I never saw. They were mostly under thirty. The contour of their faces was more oval than the type of head seen in Petersburg and Moscow and they were handsomer in other respects. . . . Inquiring, I learned that the best nurses came from the provinces south of Moscow, and that most of these were of that select class. . . . Near the end of the line stood a nurse, who had no baby in her arms. The cradle just behind her was empty. Death had removed its little tenant.[48]

What brought a peasant woman from Riazan' to Moscow's Foundling Home to be a wet nurse? Allegedly, they were often the mothers of children just deposited, but it is impossible to estimate the accuracy of this belief. According to the regulations, a mother who wanted to nurse the infant she was submitting had to be admitted and given payment. Others left their own children at home and came to the Foundling Home for better wages, much as a construction worker might look for better employment in the city. Indeed, wet nursing was one village trade which could be said to have been thriving, as "married women, having lost their own offspring by death, came into the hospital for a few months to earn money by suckling little outcasts."[49]

---

47. Lowth, *Around the Kremlin*, 117–20.
48. Bouton, *Roundabout to Moscow*, 269–71. Most of the other travelers made similar comments on the wet nurses—they were stupid-looking, had "abundant facilities," often nursed two infants at once, and were stout, strong, healthy, clean, robust, or "fine specimens of a peasantry," as Lowth put it (p. 113). Note the reference to the iron bed frame, an advancement over wooden plank beds.
49. John Foster Fraser, *Russia of Today* (London, 1915), 209–10. See also Guild, *Britons and Muscovites*, 174.

Although there is no way to estimate the social origins of the mothers or the infants themselves deposited "in the darkness of night," the women employed by the Home as wet nurses and unskilled laborers were almost exclusively young peasant women. The Foundling Home was a bigger source of female employment than any factory, and the nature of employment was perfectly suited to the transient peasant labor force: no skills were required, and there was almost a constant demand for wet nurses.

The travelers who visited the Foundling Home received rosy tours and were duly impressed. Bouton was guided from the nurses' ward through the laundry, the hospital, the kitchen, and the cafeteria. Sitting at the tables were

boys and girls, simply and neatly dressed in uniform style. They all rose as we entered and held up their spoons in salute. . . . It was plain that the older children, as well as the babies themselves, were the objects of a provident care which would shame many parents. Not otherwise can I explain the bright eyes, contented faces and chubby bodies I saw in that refectory. Many of the children were strikingly good looking.[50]

Another traveler summarized the overall impression of many foreign visitors:

It is impossible to go through the Foundling Hospital without being struck with the admirable order and completeness of detail, brilliant cleanliness and attention to health which reign throughout all departments of this magnificent establishment. There is nothing superior to it in any country in all its substantial richness of material employed and in the intelligent knowledge displayed in carrying out the object in view.[51]

The medical care was highly rated; nurses trained in childhood diseases were in attendance, and a special department equipped with an incubator was devoted to premature births.

The original intention was for the Foundling Home not only to nurse infants but to raise its wards to become the sober urban citizenry the empire lacked. However, inadequate facilities, a greater number of infants than expected, and a shortage of wet nurses caused an almost 100 percent death rate in the first few years of the Home's existence. To reduce the death rate as well as to accommodate the large number of babies, the fosterage system, recently discussed by David Ransel, was created, whereby after an average of three weeks at the Foundling Home, infants were sent to villages to be nursed in

50. Bouton, *Roundabout to Moscow*, 272–73.
51. Lowth, *Around the Kremlin*, 106–7.

peasant homes.[52] Nursing and raising those infants who survived the first few weeks of life became a cottage industry with which the city provided village families. Several contemporary studies, the writer Semenov, and Ransel have described the system by which infants were "put out" through enterprising intermediaries. One traveler encountered a train from Petersburg to Moscow filled with peasant women carrying infants from the Petersburg Foundling Home to be put out in the villages.[53] Given the tight peasant budget, the extra 3 rubles a month, the average monthly allowance in the second half of the nineteenth century, no doubt more than offset the marginal cost of an extra mouth to feed and provided the peasant family with badly needed cash. In addition, a mother who nursed her baby in the Foundling Home itself and then wanted to take it back to the village was entitled to receive a daily allowance in the village for two years. Such payments could almost be regarded as a form of "outdoor" poor relief to peasant families. Moreover, male foundlings could count as part of the peasant family for recruiting purposes.[54] Every two weeks an inspector (*ob"ezdnoi*) from the Foundling Home made the rounds of the wards in the villages to see whether they knew their prayers and to check the literacy of those in school. In Semenov's "Someone Else's Child" ("Chuzhoe dite") poor Dashka was dressed up as much as a Potemkin villager, and not without reason. If the inspector found something wrong, he could refuse to sign the card which enabled the foster family to get paid, levy a fine, or give the child to another foster family.[55]

What became of the foundlings—or those that survived (a problem to be raised later)? No doubt, many remained in the villages in which they were raised. One common career pattern was state service: the boys made "good soldiers for the tsar," and the girls became uni-

52. Krasuskii, *Kratkii istoricheskii ocherk*, 146–53; Ginzburg, "Prizrenie," 506–7; *Materialy dlia istorii Imperatorskogo Moskovskogo vospitatel'nogo doma*, 2 vols. (Moscow, 1914), 1:95–131. See also David L. Ransel, "Abandonment and Fosterage of Unwanted Children: The Women of the Foundling System," in Ransel, ed. *The Family*, 189–217.

53. Isabel F. Hapgood, *Russian Rambles* (Boston, 1895), 319; S. T. Semenov, "Chuzhoe dite," *V rodnoi derevne*, 148–64; "Moskovskii vospitatel'nyi dom," *IMGD*, 30, no. 5 (March 1906): 218–21; Moskovskaia gorodskaia uprava, *Smertnost' naseleniia g. Moskvy, 1872–1889* (Moscow, 1891), 49; Ginzburg, "Prizrenie," 605–21; Ransel, "Abandonment," 201–17.

54. S. T. Semenov, "Chuzhoe dite," 148–64; Ginzburg, "Prizrenie," 605–21; A. I. Lebedev, "Ocherk deiatel'nosti Moskovskogo vospitatel'nogo doma (1764–1896 gg.)" *IMGD* (July–August 1898), 34–47.

55. S. T. Semenov, "Chuzhoe dite," 152–53, 159–60.

formed servants of government institutions for educating upper-class
girls. Female orphans of indigent servants of the royal family were
given a free education at the Home's Nicholas Institute, and then they
served six years as teachers or governesses in the provinces. Older girls
frequently came back to work in the Foundling Home as attendants,
choir members, seamstresses, or even, as one foreigner found, as superintendents, who were

> of a higher class, being of those who were brought to the institutions as
> orphans, daughters of deceased officers and employees of the Government and
> who, having returned to the hospital as their home, find a congenial occupa-
> tion in these large nurseries. . . . The superintendents were all, I observed,
> cheerful people with pleasing countenances and many of them wore unmistak-
> able signs of good birth in face and manner.

Those especially talented were taught dancing and some even entered
the imperial ballet.[56]

Such were the objectives, procedures, and scope of Moscow's largest welfare institution in mid-century. The Home was subject to much
criticism, and one senses that the rosy tours of foreigners—and apparently this was the only institution or agency that gave tours to foreigners—were designed in part to forestall criticism. The complaints
surrounding the infant mortality rates, the abuses of the fosterage
system, and most of all the open admissions policy reached a cre-
scendo in the 1880s and 1890s, and we will return to these problems
in the next chapter. For the moment, it should be clear that because of
its objectives and scope, as well as its size, the Foundling Home far
surpassed Moscow's other institutions. Its original goal, formulated in
the liberal and "humane" era of Catherine the Great, was to raise a
solid urban citizenry, a third *chin,* or third estate, whose existence
seemed to be a sign of economic and social advancement in the West
at the time. In practice this goal was abandoned soon after the Home
opened, and the "success" stories trotted out to foreign tourists or
noted in laconic institutional reports suggest that government service
(just the *opposite* of the ethos of the third estate) was the customary
attainment of the foundlings who made it to adulthood. However, the
mere presence of such articulated goals distinguished the Foundling
Home from most other welfare agencies or institutions and charitable

---

56. Lowth, *Around the Kremlin,* 113–14. See also Lebedev, "Ocherk," 47–57;
Fraser, *Russia,* 210–12; Stoddard, *Across Russia,* 179. Some foundlings eventually
discovered their parents. See A. N. Ostrovskii, "Bez viny vinovatye," in *Polnoe sobranie
sochinenii,* 16 vols. (Moscow, 1949–1953), 9:217–18.

societies, which, at least at mid-century, were chiefly concerned with immediate relief or maintenance. The Home served not only the city but the entire Central Industrial and Agricultural regions. The elaborate system of collecting, nursing, distributing, and providing foster care for "little outcasts" became a thriving cottage industry and reflected the close relationship between the old capital and the surrounding villages in the second half of the nineteenth century.

THE WORKHOUSE

In the broad scope of its operations, the Foundling Home resembled the other major edifice of welfare, the Moscow Workhouse. The second largest institution of poor relief in Moscow and in the entire Central Industrial Region, the Workhouse and its affiliated agencies purported to combine the functions of total (and frequently punitive) maintenance and, with the addition of a Vocational Center at the end of the nineteenth century, job training and job placement. Unlike many smaller, private institutions but like the Imperial Foundling Home, it was the subject of conscious social policy especially after it came under municipal management in the 1890s.

The origin of the workhouse can be traced back to the Poor Laws of Elizabethan England. The institution was conceived as a method of punishing vagrancy and mendicity at a time when village pauperism was beginning to be regarded as a social problem and lack of work as a moral offense. For a long time, however, the administration of such punitive poor relief in England was very unsystematic, control over the workhouse was allegedly lax, and most relief in the parish was "open," that is, not provided in institutions. In the early nineteenth century, the Speenhamland system, and what we might call today the "open relief rip-off" or the alleged abuses of "welfare chiselers" who were supported at home at the taxpayers' expense, came under fire. With the amendment of the English Poor Laws in 1834, the workhouse system—with total, and usually punitive, maintenance replacing "open relief" and a centralized board of guardians replacing local parish control—became more repressive. With an increasing number of vagrants produced by the industrial revolution, and with the popular assumption that vagrants had an aversion to labor and were potential if not actual criminals, the workhouse became widespread in England and later on the continent and in the United States. The overriding principle was that if "relief were given only to the able-bodied poor in a well regulated workhouse under conditions inferior to those of the humblest laborer outside," then the allegedly clever pauper would be forced to turn from mendicancy to labor and learn the virtues of thrift and self-help.[57]

In England poor relief in general and the workhouse in particular were barometers which reflected broad changes in the social and cultural climate. The origin of the workhouse in the seventeenth century reflected a harsh attitude toward idleness and vagrancy. A more tolerant, or at least a more indifferent, eighteenth century was more generous and less punitive in its poor relief, to the great dismay of Malthus. The more judgmental Victorian era reinstated the stern, prison-like workhouse, the workhouse of Dickens. Finally, an explosion of charitable organizations, a renewed emphasis on open relief, and a resulting de-emphasis on the workhouse characterized the turn of the twentieth century.

Before the reign of Catherine the Great, Russia's aged and infirm had been supported in parish almshouses, and able-bodied vagrants had been frequently conscripted to factories, mines, or the military. The edict which created the institutions of provincial government in 1775 also created Offices of Public Welfare (Prikazy obshchestven-nogo prizreniia) and proposed creating workhouses to punish the lazy and enable the needy to support themselves. The lazy were of particular concern, and the edict hinted at the efforts of character reformation that were to become prominent a century later:

In order to remove the opportunities for wanton idleness among loafers, accustomed to roaming about (*prazdno shatat'sia*) shamelessly begging for alms, a workhouse should be established under the jurisdiction of the local police.[58]

Built in Moscow in 1782, Russia's first workhouse reflected the policy of the Offices of Public Welfare of providing primarily "indoor" or "closed" relief, that is the care of the needy in institutions, usually in

57. Robert H. Bremer, *American Philanthropy* (Chicago, 1960), 61–62; Kathleen Woodroofe, *From Charity to Social Work in England and the United States* (London, 1962), 17–18; "Poor Laws" and "Vagrancy" in *Encyclopedia of the Social Sciences* (New York, 1934), 12:231, and 15:205–6, respectively. See also Arthur Redford, *Labour Migration in England, 1800–1850*, 3d ed. (Manchester, 1976), 20–34, 81–131; David Matza, "The Disreputable Poor," in Smelser and Lipset, eds., *Social Structure and Mobility*, 329–31; Jones, *Outcast London*, 254–55; and Eames and Goode, *Urban Poverty*, 69–82.

58. *PSZ*, 1st ser., 20, no. 14394 (1775), especially articles 386–390; I. Tarasov, "Moskovskii Gorodskoi Rabotnyi Dom," *Russkoe obozrenie*, 43, no. 1 (January 1896): 337–38. See also *Sbornik ocherkov*, 2–3; M. B. Vasilevskaia, "Novaia organizatsiia gorodskoi blagotvoritel'nosti v Moskve," *IMGD*, 19, no. 4 (April 1895), 4; and E. Maksimov, "Prikazy obshchestvennogo prizreniia" *Trudovaia pomoshch'*, 4, no. 6 (June 1901), 54.

almshouses or orphanages. The Offices were not charged with the task of studying the needy, let alone administering "outdoor" or "open" relief. Thus, in marked contrast to the humane goals of the Foundling Home, although the rhetoric of Catherine's legislation contained the seeds for later liberalization, the punitive attitude of the eighteenth-century state toward paupers and vagrants was akin to that of the seventeenth-century English state.

In 1836 the Workhouse was transferred to the Committees to Investigate and Aid Beggars (Komitety po razboru i prizreniiu prosia-shchikh milostyniu), which replaced the Offices of Public Welfare. Under the authority of the Ministry of Internal Affairs, the Moscow Workhouse not only continued its punitive function of detaining vagrants and beggars sent by the local police, but began the charitable function of providing a haven and work for those who voluntarily sought a refuge. This was connected with the idea of soliciting volunteers, or creating "guardians of the poor," examining individual cases of need, and administering noninstitutional relief. At this time vocational centers (*doma trudoliubiia*, or literally, "homes of industriousness") sprang up in many Russian cities, including Moscow, in an effort to teach trades to the poor as well as to help artisans and domestics find jobs. Although they were not very active until the end of the nineteenth century, the vocational centers were intended to fulfill more preventive and charitable than correctional and punitive functions.[59] Thus, at the same time that the new poor laws were ushering in a more repressive era in England, it appeared that Russia's welfare institutions were being liberalized. Nevertheless, the changes in the management of the Workhouse itself in 1836 were more reflective of the charitable ideals of the Alexandrian era and of the bureaucratic reorganizations of the early Nicholaevan era than they were of any fundamental change in the nature of the institution. In spite of the high hopes that it could become primarily a haven and place of work for the needy of Moscow's streets, the Workhouse remained for all practical purposes a place of detention.[60]

59. *PSZ*, 2d ser., 13, pt. 2, no. 11514 (1838); G. G. Shvittau, *Trudovaia pomoshch' v Rossii*, 2 vols. (Petrograd, 1915), 2:195.

60. Tarasov, "Rabotnyi dom," 338–40; *Sbornik ocherkov*, 4; D. P. Beloshapkin, "Moskovskii Rabotnyi dom," *Trudovaia pomoshch'*, 6, no. 3 (March 1903): 325–26. Additional material on the changes in urban institutions during the Nicholaevan era can be found in Zelnik, *Labor and Society*, 8–68; Walter Pintner, *Russian Economic Policy under Nicholas I* (Ithaca, N.Y., 1967), 91–102; P. G. Ryndziunskii, *Gorodskoe grazh-*

Both Workhouse and Foundling Home were established with high hopes of stamping out idleness and of creating a new urban citizenry; but both became service institutions of the imperial government to detain and process the city's outcasts. Both Foundling Home and Workhouse were responses to the needs of a specific clientele—unwanted children and beggars—whose exceptional plight gave them attention out of proportion to their numbers. The less spectacular cases of need, as well as the problem of poverty in general, were not addressed by these institutions or by most organized charity in Moscow. However, with the expansion of the metropolitan economy and mounting peasant immigration during the last third of the nineteenth century, the more mundane instances of need increasingly overshadowed the more spectacular cases of child abandonment and mendicity. At the same time, with the creation of organs of municipal self-government, the needs of the city's laboring population more broadly conceived—not just its beggars and vagrants—gradually received more and more attention. Although the various types of need and accordingly the perceptions of them among the authorities were frequently related, two issues stood out most in the public eye: congested and unsanitary housing, and the development of a skid row where the urban pathologies of disease, death, deprivation, depravity, and demoralization were vividly concentrated.

CHANGING NEEDS AND PERCEPTIONS, 1860–1890

THE HOUSING QUESTION

Moscow's laborers found a housing market consisting primarily of private, extensively subdivided, cramped tenements scattered throughout the city. In addition, company housing provided by the larger manufacturers and various forms of institutional or charitable housing accounted for a noticeable portion of housing units. Conspicuously absent among the various types of housing available to the city's laborers were the boarding and lodging houses that in the West frequently served newcomers, transients, and single persons. Not only

---

danstvo doreformennoi Rossii (Moscow, 1958), 209–52; B. N. Kazantsev, Rabochie Moskvy i Moskovskoi gubernii v seredine XIX veka (Moscow, 1976), 53–108; and W. Bruce Lincoln, "N. A. Miliutin and the St. Petersburg Municipal Act of 1846: A Study in Reform under Nicholas I," Slavic Review, 30, no. 1 (March 1974): 55–68.

did Western cities have more private boarding and lodging houses, but municipal governments in London, Glasgow, Manchester, and Berlin were increasingly building or acquiring housing for the needy. In Moscow, as in most Russian cities, such housing was provided either by private initiative or by the provincial administration with philanthropic societies covering the cost of upkeep. In 1848, for example, a Petersburg joint-stock company called the Society for the Betterment of Living Quarters for the Laboring and Needy Population of Petersburg began providing housing for the poor.[61] Before the 1860s, neither the shortage of housing for laborers nor the lack of municipal involvement in housing received much attention. However, the intensity of need and the perceptions of it were to change quickly.

In 1863 the Moscow police chief, Nikolai I. Ogarev, like a latter-day traffic reporter hovering in his helicopter above a metropolitan area during morning rush hour, noted the influx of laborers into the city and in a memorandum to the governor-general, V. A. Dolgorukov, suggested the construction of municipal lodging houses for immigrant laborers.[62] Ogarev attributed this influx of laborers to the convergence of several railroad lines in Moscow and to the emancipation of the serfs. He was of the opinion that although most immigrants had no factory or trade skills, they nevertheless constituted an important part of the city's summertime labor force: a pool of casual, day laborers employed in construction and in the railroad yards. Without Moscow residence permits these illegal residents were driven to a few private lodging houses for shelter, where they easily concealed their identity from the authorities. These lodging houses allegedly subjected the honest laborer to physical deprivation, cold, and filth, and exposed him to thieves, vagrants, drunks, deserters, prostitutes, and hardened criminals.

As presented by the police chief, the housing problem was really a police problem: the presence of the "honest" laborer in the midst of the dens and rookeries of Moscow made it more difficult for the police to do its job of combatting crime.

The police is taking all possible measures to wipe out crime, pauperism, vagrancy and idleness in the city. Nighttime searches are often undertaken in such apartments. Residents of other towns who have no passports are expelled by the hundreds . . . several hundred beggars a month are handed over to the

---

61. Pozner, "Nochlezhnye doma," 2–3; Sviatlovskii, *Zhilishchnyi vopros*, 4:124; Kishkin, "Zhilishchnyi vopros," 8.
62. Moskovskaia gorodskaia duma, Komissiia po delam o pol'zakh i nuzhdakh obshchestvennykh, "Doklad ob ustroistve i soderzhanii kvartir dlia nochlezhnikov," *Doklady Moskovskoi gorodskoi upravy* (June 20, 1866), 1.

Alms Committee; Moscow *meshchane* and guild artisans, caught for not having passports or for various crimes, are dispatched to their associations. But all
of this hardly puts a dent in the level of vagrancy and idleness in the city. It
grows and grows, and those expelled from Moscow reappear within a few
months to resume their criminal trades. Among those rounded up by the
police are those who have been expelled from the city or handed over to their
own associations ten or more times.[63]

The night lodgers rounded up by the police "reveal that they are
casual laborers, have no permanent residence and sleep wherever they
can," but they "cannot be detained if they have their papers in order."
Investigations of suspicious people would "bog down the police in
useless work."[64]

If the municipality would provide lodging houses, according to
Ogarev, those unafraid of registering their whereabouts with the police would have a decent place to go, and the existing rookeries could
be eradicated:

Then, failure to present one's papers, vagrancy at night, a lack of proper proof
for one's nightly whereabouts or means of livelihood will all take on a different meaning. Such people can then be assumed to be malevolent and can be
expelled from the city if they are from other towns, or, if they are local
meshchane and guild artisans, they can be sent for investigation by their own
association.

The police "would have more opportunity to investigate those who gain
their livelihood by nefarious means."[65] Overcrowded housing per se
was not yet the issue. The police were overburdened, or at least anticipated being overburdened, with exclusively *administrative* tasks and
prevented from locating and isolating criminals. Given the stories about
the good life and abundance in Moscow which were allegedly spread in
the villages, Ogarev argued, the city attracted those elements more
prone to sloth and idleness. He feared that, with easier access and more
job possibilities for a greater number of people in the city, the criminal
and parasitic elements not only would multiply and infect the "honest
laborer," but could easily achieve anonymity and escape detection in a
labyrinth of inns, lodging houses, and rookeries. The police solution to
the undesirable cohabitation of the "honest laborer" with the criminal
element and ne'er-do-wells was to "quarantine" the latter.[66]

63. Ibid., 2–3.
64. Ibid. For a description of police raids in lodging houses and all-night tea houses,
see Leonid Andreev, "Neskol'ko eskizov iz moskovskoi zhizni," *Polnoe sobranie sochinenii* (St. Petersburg, 1913), 6:221.
65. "Doklad ob ustroistve i soderzhanii kvartir," 4.
66. Ibid., 5–6.

SKID ROW

The rapid and alarming development of a skid row was the most vivid example of need during the second half of the nineteenth century. While Moscow, like metropolises such as Paris and London, offered the greatest number and variety of employment opportunities and the most elegant neighborhoods for hundreds of miles around, it also had the most serious problems of unemployment, casual employment, and urban blight. Many of the city's casual laborers and unskilled workers, complemented by an undetermined but sizeable contingent of vagrants, beggars, paupers, runaways, drifters, malcontents, and criminals for whom the opportunities for work, relief or a refuge in the metropolis acted like a magnet, gravitated to various forms of slums or skid rows, frequently near the heart of the metropolis. Public health officials, statisticians, and reformers in every metropolis from Chicago to Moscow publicized the problems brought about by crowded housing, poor sanitation, and unemployment and warned that the failure of efforts to clean up the slums would have serious consequences for the health and social stability of the city.

One such skid row, arguably the empire's most notorious, was Moscow's Khitrov market. It inspired the novelist, and occasional census taker, Tolstoi to write *What Is to be Done?* in 1882; it provided colorful and poignant subject matter for the sketches of writers such as Aleksandr Levitov and Vladimir Giliarovskii; and it provided the background for the actors of Stanislavsky's production of Maxim Gorky's *The Lower Depths*.[67] Not only was Khitrov market notorious and colorful, as the symbol of urban blight and destitution it received mounting attention from the authorities and reformers. At the same time, at the slum were congregated both skilled and unskilled laborers, transient and permanent residents, and legal and illegal business activity; these dualities of development, coupled with the slum's power of attraction, made the community notably resistant to reform. The complexities of the slum and the evolution of policies designed to renovate it provide an instructive case study of the difficulties facing Russia's largest cities in the late imperial period.

Khitrov market had not always been a slum. In 1823 Major-General N. Z. Khitrovo purchased a vacant lot just east of the crooked con-

67. Tolstoi, "Tak chto zhe nam delat'?"; M. Gor'kii, *Na dne*, 3d ed.(St. Petersburg, 1903); A. I. Levitov, *Sochineniia*, 2 vols. (Moscow, 1884), and *Zhizn' moskovskikh zakoulkov: Ocherki i rasskazy* (Moscow, 1875); Giliarovskii, *Moskva i moskvichi*, and *Trushchobnye liudi* (Moscow, 1957).

gested streets of the neighborhood known as the Zariad'e and just north
and west of the Foundling Home and the confluence of the Moscow
and Iauza rivers. Khitrovo intended to build an enclosed meat and
produce market, but he died in 1826, and only an open-air winter meat
market materialized. With the rapid growth in the city's population
beginning in the 1860s, the same decade that saw police interest in the
housing shortage, Khitrov Square became a labor market, its most important function throughout the remainder of the nineteenth century, as
will be shown below.[68] Photographs taken at the turn of the twentieth
century show crowds milling around and under a latticed iron canopy,
called the *balagan,* rather resembling ornate railroad stations of the
period and providing rudimentary protection from the elements. Surrounding the square were two-story private lodging houses, apartment
buildings, sleazy taverns, and narrow side streets dimly lit by kerosene
lamps, giving the neighborhood an added element of mystery and in-
trigue for the respectable visitor, especially on a foggy evening. According to the journalist Vladimir Giliarovskii, Khitrov market was

a big square in the center of the capital, near the Iauza River, surrounded by
peeling stone houses. It lies in a low place into which lead several side streets,
like streams into a swamp. It's always bursting, especially toward evening.
When it's a little foggy or just after a rain, standing at the top of one of the
side streets, you can barely make out the figures below you descending into a
crawling, putrid pit.[69]

We can learn more about the crowds milling around the canopy by
turning to contemporary investigations. According to the 1902 city
census, 21,676 persons resided in the third precinct of the Miasniki
ward, the precinct containing Khitrov Square.[70] The manuscript census being unavailable, it is impossible to determine the numbers living
in the confines of the slum. The municipal authorities did try to count
the numbers residing in the slum's lodging houses: 8,768 were counted
in 1885, 9,486 in 1899, and 6,496 in 1907.[71] As the previous chapter
indicated, the actual number of lodgers may have been twice the number given by the proprietors. An additional 2,000 to 3,000 lived in the

68. P. V. Sytin, *Iz istorii moskovskikh ulits,* 275–76. The city's population increased from an estimated 364,148 in 1864 to 601,969 by the time of the first census of
1871. (*GPD 1912,* 6).
69. Giliarovskii, *Moskva i moskvichi,* 23.
70. In 1882 the population was 18,270. By 1912 the population was 22,914. From
1902 to 1912 the population grew by 5.7 percent, a slow rate of increase comparable to
that of Moscow's other central districts. See *PM 1882,* II, pt. 2, 50–62; *PM 1902,* I, 1,
iii, 4; *GPD 1912,* 8.
71. Karaffa-Korbut, "Nochlezhnye doma," 637.

dozens of apartment units in the neighborhood. When one totals the lodgers, the apartment dwellers, and those who came to Khitrov market seeking employment, food, or entertainment but who resided elsewhere, it is clear that at least 20,000–25,000 persons frequented the slum in the daytime or after dark.

Though outwardly Khitrov market did not appear to be as densely populated as tenement districts of New York or London, it was more congested. In 1902, in Miasniki's third ward the average apartment had 14.3 residents; the average at this time for the entire city was 8.7 residents, approximately double that for Berlin, Vienna, and London. The number of apartments actually decreased by 6.3 percent from 1902 to 1912.[72] An 1899 investigation estimated that twice the number permitted by existing structural, police, or sanitary norms actually inhabited the private lodging houses. By 1910 the situation was worse. According to one police investigation, accommodations intended for 2,828 persons housed approximately 7,000.[73]

The concentration of both skilled and unskilled laborers illustrates the economic duality of Khitrov market. All over Russia at this time, especially in the northern industrial centers or the market towns of the south, which attracted large numbers of migratory workers, seasonal and casual jobs such as those described in chapter 5 were filled by hiring at outdoor labor markets.[74] The most important outdoor hiring markets of large cities, such as Moscow's Khitrov and Petersburg's Haymarket, were located in the center, adding greatly to their prominence and notoriety. As early as 1863, Moscow's chief of police noted the increasing number of casual laborers from miles around who converged on the city in the summer months. Fifty years later a study of the city council noted:

Every year a large number of migrant laborers from different provinces head for Khitrov market in search of work: carpenters, painters and navvies all pass through Khitrov market during the summer months. Usually there are up to 2,500 of these migrant laborers.[75]

Desperate laborers, frequently grouped in artels of ten to fifteen persons, would gather under the canopy as early as 4:00 A.M. and wait

72. GPD 1912, 16–20, 29.

73. TsGAM, f. 46, op. 14, d. 1212, l. 36; Doklad komissii po ozdorovleniiu Khitrova rynka, 8; Alaverdian, Zhilishchnyi vopros, 49, 52, 57.

74. See also Timothy Mixter, "Of Grandfather-Beaters and Fat-Heeled Pacifists: Perceptions of Agriculture Labor and Hiring Market Disturbances in Saratov, 1872–1905," Russian History, 7, pts. 1–2 (1980): 139–68.

75. TsGAM, f. 179, op. 21, d. 2009, l. 49.

for a contractor (*podriadchik*) to come and offer a job.[76] Employed
sporadically in the transport and construction trades, in the wholesale
markets, and as waiters, bakers, hawkers, messengers, draymen, vendors, and laborers in low-grade and unhealthy factory jobs, many
ended up staying in the city during the winter when there was less
demand for unskilled labor. The presence of the hiring market explains the occupational categories predominant among the slum's residents: "day laborers," "unskilled laborers," domestic servants, washerwomen, as well as "no occupation" and "unemployed." More of
the city's day laborers and unemployed came from Miasniki's third
precinct than from any other part of the city.[77]

Along with the menial laborers who worked in distant freight yards
were skilled workers and tradesmen who provided the slum population with essential goods and services and whose importance illustrates the economic complexity of the neighborhood. According to an
1891 survey of residents of the slum's lodging houses, 41 percent gave
artisan as their current occupation.[78] Most common were the shoemakers, tailors, and cap-makers. Working in part for the local population, they easily set up improvised (and illegal) workshops in the lodging houses. Setting up workshops was greatly facilitated by the fact
that the proprietors of the Khitrov lodging houses did not evict lodgers
during the day, as was customary at many other lodging houses.[79]
Shoemakers, for instance, "made" shoes by softening, stretching, sewing, tanning, and cleaning scraps of leather collected at Khitrov market and at the city's junkyards. The product, colloquially known as
"shoddy" (*lipovaia*) shoes for their flimsiness, was sold to local residents. Similar "shoddy" clothes were sewn by local tailors from rags.[80]
The tailors would frequently double as "exchangers" (*smenshchiki*)
and would buy old clothes from passersby in the city's open-air markets. They would wash the old items at the public baths, mend them,
and then return them to the market for resale. Women, too, dominated a variety of trades. Local "florists" made flowers from paper
and dried plants. Cigarette-makers and candy-wrappers sold their

76. Gor-ev, "K kharakteristike," 38–39.
77. *PM 1902*, I, 2, i, 164–65. Almost one-quarter of the city's male day laborers
lived in this ward. Almost 30 percent of the male population of Miasniki 3 were either
day laborers or unemployed, compared with 4.3 percent of the male population in the
city as a whole.
78. Pozner, "Nochlezhnye doma," 38.
79. Sytin, *Iz istorii moskovskikh ulits*, 277.
80. Gor-ev, "K kharakteristike," 42, 120.

wares at Khitrov and at other large market squares. Stale bread, om-
elettes made from rotten eggs, moldy cheese, rotten sausage, and rotten
berries were peddled on the street as well as in the lodging houses.[81]

Proprietors of lodging houses and of eating and drinking establishments also provided essential services to all other workers. The lodging houses catered not only to laborers working in the surrounding
neighborhood but also to casual laborers who worked far away. According to a report of the city council:

> Up to 250 day laborers go off to work every day at 4:30 A.M. to the Nicholas
> and Archangel railways. After work, willing or not, they drag (*volei-nevolei
> tianutsia*) back to Khitrov market: there are no lodging houses near their jobs
> and they won't get turned down at Khitrov. Thus the absence of lodging
> houses near those places where the greatest concentration of day laborers
> work—the railroad stations, freight yards, and lumber yards—is one of the
> reasons for the accumulation of workers at the Khitrov houses.[82]

Similarly attractive were the slum's thirty-five eating and drinking
establishments, which ranged from taverns to hot-water stands, the
latter being essential because many lodgers ate in their rooms.[83]

Such a symbiotic occupational duality whereby artisans, tradesmen,
and proprietors provided goods and services and casual laborers provided customers accounts in part for a demographic duality. Khitrov
market was a center both for transients passing through and into Moscow and for a more or less permanent population. According to one
investigation, among the lodgers 73 percent were peasants and 90 percent of all estates were immigrants.[84] It was commonly acknowledged,
however, that the number of lodgers "resident" in the lodging houses
was subject to seasonal fluctuations; most estimates were calculated in
the winter, not the season of maximum occupancy. The spring influx of
laborers added approximately 1,500 to 2,000, and many more casual
laborers slept outside during the summer months. Almost one-third of
the male lodgers of two lodging houses for which data are available had
lived in those lodging houses less than one year. At the same time, more
than 50 percent of the residents of two lodging houses had lived in the

---

81. Ibid., 42–44. Skilled workers could also be found at the slum: printers, typesetters, and mechanics worked nearby, and members of the Khitrov "intelligentsia" copied
plays and sometimes lectures by hand.
82. TsGAM, f. 179, op. 21, d. 2009, l. 49.
83. Gor-ev, "K kharakteristike," 122–23; Duvakin, "Nochlezhnye doma," 72.
84. Kurnin, O nekotorykh usloviiakh, 16.

houses more than ten years.[85] More than any other set of figures, these proportions clearly illustrate the importance of Khitrov Square as both a magnet for transients and a skid row for the city's destitute from which removal was very difficult.

Writing about the city's tavern trade, the economist Chuprov noted the "large accumulation of working people without families." Indeed, additional data on age and marital status indicate that the residents of the lodging houses were far less likely to be married and have dependents than were inhabitants of the city as a whole; 58 percent of all Moscow men but only 48 percent of male lodgers were married.[86] In part this was due to the age structure of the lodging houses' residents; while 43 percent of Moscow's population were over thirty in 1882, 64 percent of the lodging houses' residents were over thirty.[87] Yet, even among those aged twenty to thirty, a lower than average proportion of the residents of the lodging houses were married, and a higher than average proportion were widows.[88] Because of the larger proportion of the elderly and of widows, women were more likely than men to have been residents of the lodging houses for ten years or more.[89]

As has already been suggested, casual laborers and skilled artisans, tradesmen and proprietors existed symbiotically. This occurred not only in legal business activity but also in illegal pursuits, and the coexistence of a thriving aboveground world of manufacturing and retailing and an equally thriving underground world was a third duality in the development of Khitrov Square. The symbiotic nature of many of the relationships between the aboveground and the underground worlds made policies of reform that much more difficult to implement.

The authorities assumed that as a center of disease, deprivation, depravity, and demoralization, the slum threatened the physical and

---

85. Ibid. Unfortunately, the author does not indicate whether the concept "ten years" meant uninterrupted residence in the lodging houses, regular but seasonal residence, or merely occasional residence beginning ten years previous. The same could be said for a census of women at one lodging house in 1913, which showed that 87 percent of the total woman-nights spent over a three-week period were repeated occupancies and that 60 percent of the women had been resident ten years or more. ("Delo ob ozdorovlenii Khitrova rynka," TsGAM, f. 179, op. 21, d. 1715, l. 60.)

86. PM 1882, II, pt. 2, 10–14; PM 1902, I, 1, i, 9–10; Pozner, "Nochlezhnye doma," 27–30.

87. PM 1882, II, pt. 2, 1–2; PM 1902, I, 1, i, 4; Pozner, "Nochlezhnye doma," 27–30.

88. Pozner, "Nochlezhnye doma," 27–30.

89. TsGAM, f. 179, op. 21, d. 2009, l. 49; Kurnin, O nekotorykh usloviiakh zhizni, 16, 27.

moral well-being of the rest of the city, a common perception among municipal authorities in Europe and America during the nineteenth century. As one Parisian perceived the slums of central Paris in 1840:

If you venture into those accursed districts in which they live, wherever you go you will see men and women branded with the marks of vice and destitution and half-naked children rotting in filth and stifling in airless, lightless dens. Here in the very home of civilization, you will encounter thousands of men reduced by sheer besottedness to a life of savagery; here you will perceive destitution in a guise so horrible that it will fill you with disgust rather than pity.[90]

Descriptions of the Moscow slum abound with lurid tales of the underworld of thieves, gamblers, and card sharks, "professional" beggars (called *strelki*), vagrants, runaways, prostitutes (called "princesses"), and pimps (called "cats") that hung out at the lodging houses and taverns of Khritrov market. The slum was also a mecca for children and minors running away from parents, orphanages, master artisans, and workshops. The opportunities for child abuse were expectedly great and ranged from young girls entering the life of prostitution to infants "helping" beggars attract sympathy. Runaways of another type were reflected in the popular names attached to the taverns at the local lodging houses: "Convoy," "Siberia," "Hard Labor." The ease of procuring a false passport, or "eyes," and of finding the contacts necessary to escape the detection by the police was legendary.[91] A lively and profitable trade in stolen goods and liquor flourished in the lodging houses and in the back rooms of taverns. Just as Moscow today has its contingent of black marketeers, so prerevolutionary Moscow had its contingent of dealers (*baryshniki*) who engaged in the marketing of a great variety of goods—new, used, and stolen. The richer *baryshniki* dealt in stolen goods and operated from inside the taverns and lodging houses directly with the thieves themselves, and it was not without reason that the proprietors took special care to guard the rooms of thieves from the police.[92]

Though not always illegal, shady business practices took place in the food and drink trade, much to the consternation of public health

90. Chevalier, *Laboring Classes*, 360. See also Zelnik, *Labor and Society*, 240–82; and the selections by Anthony Wohl, George Rosen, Richard Schoenwald, Eric Trudgill, and Gertrude Himmelfarb in H. J. Dyos and Michael Wolff, eds., *The Victorian City*, vol. 2 (London, 1973).

91. Moskovskoe gorodskoe obshchestvennoe upravlenie, *Otchet gorodskogo popechitel'stva o bednykh Khitrova rynka*, 4 (Moscow, 1907): 1; Giliarovskii, *Moskva i moskvichi*, 24.

92. Gor-ev, "K kharakteristike," 44–49, 119–20, 122–23.

officials. One of the canteens (*kharchevni*) in the area was notorious for a cheap soup that consisted of "scraps of meat and bones, thrown out at the pubs and restaurants. . . . [They] chop [it] up into a pulp, warm it up, add pepper and bay leaves—and the soup is ready."[93] A similar practice was common in the wine cellars. Liquor bought by the bottle would be taken over to a corner where an "opener" (*ottykalo*) sat with a corkscrew and mug. The "openers," usually winos themselves, also collected leftover vodka from bottles, mugs, and dishes; when up to one-half of a bottle of leftovers (*slivki*) had been accumulated, the "opener" turned it in to the proprietor. Then, the next lone patron without a buddy or two to split a bottle, called an "80-proofer" (*sorokovka*), might find leftover liquor poured into his drink. Such leftover liquor also found its way quickly to the lodging houses via the sublessors (*s"emshchiki*) who, to supplement their income from renting extra space in an apartment or room, engaged in a lively illicit vodka trade.[94]

In many reports one finds the theme of the honest, unsuspecting laborers from the countryside, who end up at Khitrov market because of bad luck or loss of work, or who "have no will power," and who come in contact with "the depraved residents of the lodging houses and are subject to their demoralizing influence."[95] The unsuspecting passerby or resident in the lodging houses could easily become a victim of the underworld and be drawn into criminal activities:

Thieves, sharpers, and pickpockets pursue their dark deeds. By hook or by crook they pounce on, disrobe and steal from any sleeping boarder, especially from the new arrival, his passport, clothes and tools—they will even take away the means of getting a job from an honest laborer—and then they skip the premises. The unclothed lodger has no recourse but to beg or steal. Absolute depravity reigns in this environment. In spite of the regulations, men and women sleep together in all apartments. Any form of family life is impossible. Cohabitation is shocking and prostitution is rampant.[96]

The saying "once you've eaten Khitrov soup, you'll never leave" expressed the impression that this influence was irreversible. Indeed, municipal investigators and police alike were convinced that those picked up at Khitrov market for misdemeanors, vagrancy, or begging,

---

93. Podiachev, "Mytarstvo," 23–24.
94. Gor-ev, "K kharakteristike," 127.
95. Gor-ev, "K kharakteristike," 118, 122, 126; "Doklad ob ustroistve i soderzhanii kvartir," 3–4. See also Jones, *Outcast London,* 218–19, for similar sentiments in London.
96. Sviatlovskii, *Zhilishchnyi vopros,* 4:233. See also Chevalier, *Laboring Classes,* 142.

even if expelled from the city to their place of official residence, would soon be back. The resulting "demoralization" was particularly alarming because it allegedly spread both shiftlessness and a loathing for work (*otvrashchenie k trudu*) and alcoholism, assumed rampant where there was "a tavern on every corner and liquor sold right in the lodging houses" and where "everyone drinks, from old men and women to children."[97]

Such was the evolution of the Khitrov slum. In and around Khitrov market congregated casual laborers as well as tradesmen and skilled artisans, transients as well as longtime city residents, persons engaging in normal business activity, as well as the thieves, pimps, and prostitutes of the city's underworld. The shortage of lodging houses for transients and casual laborers and the development of the eyesore of Khitrov Square in the heart of the city were two aspects of urbanization which in the second half of the nineteenth century made the authorities aware of the more general, mundane, and less picturesque social problems and of the magnitude of need in the old capital. To be sure, there were other related and equally urgent problems—education, crime, sanitation and public health, transportation, waste removal, water supply, and the like—but the previous discussion should suffice to illustrate the increasingly pressing needs of the laboring population. The greater the amount of attention received by these issues, particularly the issue of the slum, the more the authorities viewed the life of the common people as one of disease, deprivation, depravity, and demoralization. What remedies, then, were proposed to solve these problems, particularly those of the slum?

POLICE, CITY COUNCIL, AND THE SLUM

One of the earliest proposals for attacking these problems came, as we have seen, from the Moscow chief of police. Disturbed by the influx of homeless common laborers into the city, Ogarev recommended that the municipality build its own lodging houses, primarily as a means of aiding the police in preventing and detecting crime. Municipal lodging houses that could be policed more easily would be a shelter for the "honest laborer," and the existing rookeries could be eradicated. Although Ogarev's recommendations touched primarily the problem of the shortage of low-cost housing for the casual labor

97. Gor-ev, "K kharakteristike," 51, 126, 129.

force, the memorandum to the governor-general clearly raised many related issues, such as slum renovation, public health, and crime.

The governor-general approved the police recommendations and sent the memorandum to the mayor who, in turn, passed the memorandum on to a committee of the city council called the Commission for Matters of the Commonweal (Komissiia po delam o pol'zakh i nuzhdakh obshchestvennykh).[98] A subcommittee of five appointed to study the proposal concluded two years later that while the desire of the police to improve the living conditions of the city's "honest laborers" and to eradicate the undesirable housing was commendable, such facilities would not solve the problems of crime and vagrancy. In a clear rebuttal to the police, the committee charged that "what is important here is vigilance on the part of the police to prevent crime or nip it in the bud."

The difficulties which the police now face in investigating and expelling from the city vagrants without passports stem from various factors, and therefore it would be futile to expect the opening of new lodging houses and the closing of the existing facilities to lead immediately (as the former police chief argues) to the eradication of idleness, vagrancy, pauperism, depravity, theft, and other crimes in the city.[99]

The Commission for Matters of the Commonweal did recognize that a clear welfare need existed and that it was "obviously impossible to expect either discrimination in accepting boarders or surveillance of their conduct from private persons engaged in the operation of lodging houses." Although Ogarev had recommended that the city take over the existing lodging houses, the commissiia proposed that the city council set up a few experimental lodging houses; if such facilities were cheap, clean, safe, and sanitary and had a superintendent with quasi-police functions, then the trustworthy elements would allegedly be attracted to them. The commission differed from the police also in that it proposed closer municipal (rather than provincial) control over the operation of the facilities ("without any interference from the city police"), noting rather sarcastically that such facilities would come under the surveillance of the city police anyway. Whereas the police proposal recommended the expulsion of out-of-town residents, the committee's proposal stated that these facilities should admit out-of-town residents and Moscow *meshchane* and guild artisans whose

98. "Doklad ob ustroistve i soderzhanii kvartir," 4–5.
99. Ibid.

papers were in order.[100] Thus, although the city council had initially disclaimed any responsibility for Moscow's immigrants, in the end it realized that such facilities inevitably had to cope, albeit on an experimental basis, with the massive influx of peasant immigrants. The city council finally decided to appropriate 5,000 rubles annually for the acquisition, establishment, and upkeep of four lodging houses.[101]

While the city organs were taking their time on the issue of providing low-cost or free municipal housing, charitable societies began to respond to the newly perceived need. As early as 1861 the Fraternal Apartment Agency for the Needy was founded under the auspices of the Imperial Philanthropic Society to provide free or low-cost apartments to women, particularly widows with children.[102] In 1875 the Liapin Brothers and the Society to Encourage Industriousness (another agency of the Imperial Philanthropic Society) requested municipal aid for joint construction of one lodging house. The city council, not yet convinced of its responsibility to provide housing for the city's immigrant laborers, filed the request. The Liapin Brothers themselves opened a free lodging house in 1879, and five years later the Society to Encourage Industriousness opened a similar facility.[103] The Liapin Brothers' Lodging House became the only free lodging house in the entire Khitrov slum. The Belov Lodging House, run by the Society to Encourage Industriousness and located at Smolensk Square near a seedy riverfront neighborhood, was a more commerical operation costing 5 kopeks a night. Nevertheless, its free morning and evening tea and its strict rules and regulations distinguished it from the basic kind of private lodging house. An estimated 304,486 persons were given shelter during the first three years after the house opened.[104]

The threat posed by Khitrov's private lodging houses to public health finally convinced the city council in 1879 that it had to provide low-cost municipal housing, if for no other reason than to make the city healthier and to prevent epidemics. It was generally acknowledged

---

100. Ibid.

101. Kishkin and Alaverdian incorrectly argued that the city council rejected the requests of the chief of police and the governor-general. The city council committee certainly rejected the reasoning behind the proposals of the provincial authorities and did not provide free housing (the fee for lodgings was meant to be the average of the prevailing fees, yet enough to cover the annual costs of rent, heat, lighting, repairs, and the superintendent's salary), but it did at least approve construction in 1869. See Kishkin, "Zhilishchnyi vopros," 294–95; Alaverdian, *Zhilishchnyi vopros*, 47–48.

102. *SSS 1901*, 60–61.

103. Pozner, "Nochlezhnye doma," 9–10.

104. *Letopis'*, 266–68 and Appendix, 22–24, 53.

that Khitrov market was the breeding ground for contagious diseases that spread throughout the city, though in all fairness to Khitrov Square, the rest of the city was not markedly healthier.[105] Disease at Khitrov market was more dangerous than at, say, a factory on the city's outskirts because at the lodging houses there resided artisans, peddlers, cabdrivers, draymen, small shopkeepers, domestics, clerks, and prostitutes, who were in constant contact with the general public and who, particularly if they were illegal residents, avoided sanitation officials and hospitals for fear of being turned over to the police.[106] Fearing that crowded private lodging houses, commonly acknowledged to be more negligent about public hygiene, would be potential breeding grounds for epidemics, such as the outbreak of the plague in Astrakhan', the city council proposed the first free municipal housing in 1879.[107] Opened in late 1879, the Morozov Municipal Lodging House was designed to accommodate 510 lodgers. However, located approximately one mile from Khitrov Square, the Morozov Lodging House did not mark an immediate improvement in the slum's housing problem.[108]

Because of its reputation as a skid row of disease-ridden beggars, vagrants, tramps, and unemployed, and because of the central location of this symbol of urban degeneration, Khitrov market received mounting publicity from the police, public health officials, and welfare reformers in the 1880s and 1890s, much as did districts of central Paris in the 1830s and 1840s.[109] However, as frequently happens in Russian history, it was not until this publicity was accompanied by institutional expression and official investigations that the problems of the city's transients and of the slum itself were addressed. A sanitary inspection and a census of the lodging houses were undertaken in 1884 and 1889, respectively; a broader investigation of the city's tenements was undertaken in 1898. In 1897 the Moscow Division of the Imperial Technical Society established a Commission for Renovating

---

105. Kurnin, *O nekotorykh usloviiakh*, 6–7; "Spravka Moskovskoi gorodskoi upravy o meropriiatiiakh po preduprezhdeniiu epidemii kholery i po bor'be s neiu," *IMGD*, no. 6 (1910): 2; Kishkin, "Zhilishchnyi vopros," 292; Alaverdian, *Zhilishchnyi vopros*, 48; "Delo po meditsinskomu otchetu Moskovskoi gubernii," TsGIA, f. 1297, op. 289, d. 160, l. 60.

106. Sviatlovskii, *Zhilishchnyi vopros*, 4:127. See also Chevalier, *Laboring Classes*, 345, 461; *Doklad Komissii po ozdorovleniiu Khitrova rynka*, 3.

107. Pozner, "Nochlezhnye doma," 11–12.

108. Ibid., 12–15.

109. On the central location of the slums of Paris, see Chevalier, *Laboring Classes*, 369.

Khitrov Market, and in 1902 the Municipal Guardianship of the Poor, itself created in 1894, established a special district Guardianship for Khitrov Market. The creation of these bodies was accompanied in rapid succession by two detailed investigations in 1898 by the Commission for Renovating Khitrov Market and in 1899 by the city council itself.[110] Several proposals for municipal housing went hand in hand with proposals for measures to improve public health. Thus during the 1880s a Commission of Sanitary Physicians employed by the city council undertook many ad hoc measures to combat epidemics: sanitary stations scattered throughout the city gave free medical aid, baths, and vaccinations; disinfection brigades inspected marketplaces and eating establishments, tenements, cemeteries, and water supplies; and temporary canteens served free meals and boiled water.[111] By the mid-1880s, the Society to Encourage Industriousness alone ran ten public cafeterias serving free or low-cost hot meals.[112]

The most far-reaching proposals to meet the housing shortage and the skid row of Khitrov Square came at a time when slum renovation was beginning to receive widespread publicity. To hardly anyone's surprise, the 1898 report of the Imperial Russian Technical Society described the neighborhood as a den of iniquity, a refuge for convicts, and a breeding ground for disease. On March 28, 1899, a special committee under the supervision of the municipal

110. The relevant investigations and commentaries on them are Duvakin, "Nochlezhnye doma"; Pozner, "Nochlezhnye doma i nochlezhniki; A. G. Petrovskii, *Khitrov rynok, ego sanitarnoe i obshchestvennoe znachenie* (Moscow, 1898), and "Khitrov rynok i ego obitateli," *Vestnik Evropy*, 29, no. 6 (June 1894): 579–93; Kurnin, *O nekotorykh usloviiakh zhizni naseleniia Khitrova rynka*, and "Bezrabotnye na Khitrovom rynke v Moskve," *Russkoe bogatstvo*, no. 2 (February 1898): 165–79; Gor-ev, "K kharakteristike ekonomicheskikh i bytovykh uslovii zhizni bezrabotnykh"; Imperatorskoe russkoe tekhnicheskoe obshchestvo, *Ozdorovlenie Khitrova rynka* (Moscow, 1899), and *Doklad komissii po ozdorovleniiu Khitrova rynka* (Moscow, 1903); "Neskol'ko dannykh o moskovskikh koechno-kamarochnykh kvartirakh"; Verner, "Zhilishcha bedneishego naseleniia Moskvy"; "Doklad Komissii po zhilishchnomu voprosu," no. 184 (1905), and "Doklad Komissii po ozdorovleniiu Khitrova rynka," no. 110 (1910), no. 171 (1911) in *Doklady Moskovskoi gorodskoi upravy; Otchet gorodskogo popechitel'stva o bednykh Khitrova rynka*; "Delo ob ozdorovlenii Khitrova rynka," TsGAM, f. 179, op. 21, d. 1715; Karaffa-Korbut, "Nochlezhnye doma v bol'shikh russkikh gorodakh"; and Kishkin, "Zhilishchnyi vopros v Moskve."
111. "Novye vrachebno-sanitarnye meropriiatiia moskovskogo gorodskogo obshchestvennogo upravleniia," *Sbornik statei*, 5 (1897): 180–95; *Sbornik ocherkov*, 23; Kut'ev, "Dokumental'nye materialy," 5; TsGIA, f. 1297, op. 291, d. 64, l. 337; *Sovremennoe khoziaistvo*, 148–52; *Istoriia Moskvy*, 5:727. Smallpox vaccinations were actually introduced by the zemstvo before the municipal authorities. The frequency of disease lowered after regular vaccinations, but even in 1900 an estimated 47 percent of the children were still not vaccinated. (TsGIA, f. 1297, op. 289, d. 160, l. 29.)
112. *Letopis'*, 78, 221, 249, Appendix, 22–24.

statistical board and composed of members of the executive board, the Committee on Matters of the Commonweal, and the City Guardianship of the Poor of Khitrov Market conducted an investigation of the neighborhood's lodging houses and, regarding immediate slum renovation as urgent, recommended the following: (1) complete municipalization of the slum's private lodging houses; (2) construction of lodging houses for 10,000 in other parts of the city to supplement those at Khitrov; (3) strict regulation and supervision of existing facilities until new ones opened; and (4) creation of a special employment agency closely connected with the lodging houses.[113]

The response of the city council to more than three decades of proposals was hardly vigorous. It took fifteen years after the initial proposal of the police before the municipal authorities approved the conversion of a building into a city lodging house. Responding to the more far-reaching proposals of 1899, the city council did authorize construction of six new lodging houses.[114] The first, named the Ermakov House, opened in 1909, almost a mile from Khitrov Square. Not only was it electrically lighted to enable newly arrived laborers to locate it, but it actually advertised at railroad stations within a radius of sixty miles from Moscow and sent out announcements to township authorities, measures the city council a few decades earlier would have regarded as ill-advisedly attracting too many migrant laborers. Considered a model of its time, the six-story building had thirty sleeping rooms accommodating fifty persons each (although ideally accommodating forty), with one iron cot per boarder; in addition, the unit had a kitchen, four cafeterias, a bath, a laundry, and a clinic. While admitting that the floors and beds were in unsatisfactory condition, the modest words of the house's first published accounts described the

bright, high-ceilinged chambers which meet the minimum requirements of hygiene, neatness and quiet, and separate beds for each lodger [which] sharply

113. *Doklad komissii po ozdorovleniiu Khitrova rynka*, 3; Moskovskaia gorodskaia duma, *Stenograficheskii otchet o sobranii* (February 4, 1903), 63; Alaverdian, *Zhilishchnyi vopros*, 49; Kishkin, "Zhilishchnyi vopros," 297–98.

114. The authorization can be found in "Doklad Komissii po zhilishchnomu voprosu," Appendix 3, and in "Doklad Komissii sanitarnykh vrachei po voprosu o vybore mestnostei v g. Moskve dlia postroiki nochlezhnykh domov," TsGAM, f. 179, op. 21, d. 2009, ll. 34–59. The appropriation can be found in "Zakliuchenie Finansovogo komiteta po dokladu Komissii po zhilishchnomu voprosu" (February 16, 1906), TsGAM, f. 179, op. 21, d. 2009, ll. 60–64.

distinguish the Ermakov house from other similar institutions and attract a mass of lodgers in spite of its relatively high price (6 kopeks).[115]

The response to the other recommendations of 1899 was less than adequate and reveals the limited degree of success the municipality enjoyed in solving the problems of urban poverty and blight. No action was taken on the first recommendation, to municipalize the slum's privately owned lodging houses, or on the third, to regulate and supervise more strictly the existing flophouses until new facilities were built. Enforcing the existing housing and sanitation codes or putting stricter ones on the books, measures frequently proposed to the city council, were not without difficulty. Most investigators pointed out that although fining proprietors or closing a flophouse for violations of municipal ordinances might set a good example, many owners would not be able to meet expenses if the number of lodgers permitted were reduced. Higher rents or the closing of buildings would evict dwellers who might not be able to find alternative housing, especially given the slowness with which the city council or private builders were providing acceptable low-cost housing. On the eve of World War I, the journal *Gorodskoe delo* observed that although the police had the power to limit overcrowding, the city still had not passed any strict sanitary ordinances, since to do so would close most apartments and lodging houses inhabited by the poor, and throw the lodgers out onto the streets.[116]

Similarly, the authorities were divided among those who wanted to raze the whole slum, those who wanted to build bigger and better lodging houses in the Khitrov market area, and those who wanted to build new units in other neighborhoods. According to the third approach, alternative lodging houses scattered around the city would disperse the diseased and depraved population, relieve some of the housing pressure at Khitrov market, and thereby indirectly help to renovate the slum. Accordingly, the six new lodging houses authorized in 1899 were to be built in neighborhoods removed from Khitrov Square.[117] However, this solution meant lengthy consideration of

115. Moskovskoe gorodskoe obshchestvennoe upravlenie, *Otchet o deiatel'nosti gorodskogo nochlezhnogo doma im F. Ia. Ermakova za 1909* (Moscow, 1912), 4. See also Alaverdian, *Zhilishchnyi vopros*, 53–54; Karaffa-Korbut, "Nochlezhnye doma," 640–41.

116. Duvakin, "Nochlezhnye doma," 76–77; *Gorodskoe delo*, no. 2 (1912): 127.

117. TsGAM, f. 179, op. 21, d. 2009, ll. 34–59. Most sites were near railroad stations (such as Kalanchevskaia Square, location of the three most crowded passenger stations) or freight and lumber yards (such as the Kursk and Nizhnii Novgorod freight

location as well as housing construction, and approval was not always forthcoming. For example, fearing the consequences of the
proximity of two groups of dangerous elements, as well as the passage of prison officials or convoys past such housing units, the City
Prefect (Gradonachal'nik) and the Prison Administration objected to
building low-cost housing in the Rogozh' district near the provincial
prison.[118]

In 1899 the city council did approve a resolution to establish an
employment office to "organize correctly the mediation (*posredni-
chestvo*) between the demand and the supply of labor." The main
office opened in 1906, and one year later the first annex opened at
Khitrov market. Statistics gathered by the city council after the first
two years of the office's operation, however, show that the total
number of applicants was four to seven times the number of jobs
filled.[119] Although the data are incomplete, one suspects that the
itinerant laborers who most needed employment to break out of the
vicious circle of disease, depravity, and demoralization received the
least help.

Led by the Imperial Philanthropic Society, municipal and private
charity had begun to meet the challenge posed by the housing shortage
and by the slum. By 1889 there were eleven free lodging houses and
eighteen low-cost apartment buildings; by 1901 there were forty-seven
free or low-cost soup kitchens or tearooms.[120] Modest improvements
at Khitrov market were indeed made at the turn of the century: the
number of its lodgers may have declined somewhat at the beginning of
the twentieth century, and improvements in housing and employment
may have contributed to the greater than average increase in the proportion of married men living in Miasniki's third precinct. Improvements in public health were evidenced, and the third precinct of Miasniki was not as lethal as it had been. In 1901 a city councilman, S. V.
Puchkov, who claimed to have spent his childhood not far from Khitrov market, asserted that there had been a tremendous improvement

---

stations in the Rogozh' ward) where day laborers, carpenters, masons, and bricklayers
were in demand, and where the existing lodging houses, inns, taverns, or even the
lumber yards and empty freight cars themselves provided inadequate or nonexistent
shelter.

118. Kishkin, "Zhilishchnyi vopros," 298–99; *Sovremennoe khoziaistvo*, 177–79.

119. M. Dukhovskoi, *Soobrazhenie po voprosu ob ustroistve Moskovskim gorod-
skim upravleniem posrednicheskoi kontory dlia ukazaniia raboty v g. Moskve* (Moscow,
1895), 200–1; *Otchet Moskovskoi gorodskoi upravy za 1908* (Moscow, 1909), 229–30.

120. *SSS 1889*, xiv–xxiii; *SSS 1902*, v.

in the previous twenty years.[121] However, the efforts of municipal and private charity fell short, and not until 1911 did the city council authorize construction of low-cost apartment units (as distinguished from lodging houses). A cholera epidemic in 1909 once again exposed the housing deficiencies, and another Commission to Renovate Khitrov Market concluded that another lodging house for 3,000 should be built.[122]

❖   ❖   ❖

The evils of substandard housing or slum residence certainly did not touch all of the city's laboring population. For decades prior to the mid-nineteenth century, Muscovites were largely aware of the more picturesque or exceptional cases of deprivation—the street life of the city's beggars and vagrants or the abandonment of infants. Until the 1860s, neither the economic opportunities of the city nor the level of immigration put excessive strain on the housing stock, created a large casual labor force, or spawned a slum. The few modest charitable societies coupled with the larger imperial institutions such as the Foundling Home and the Workhouse seemed to be able to handle the worst cases of need. These worst and most visible cases of need were concentrated at opposite ends of the age spectrum: infancy and old age. It was generally assumed that the majority of the adult population, having few dependents anyway, could fend for itself. Moreover, before the era of the Great Reforms the social problems that did persist received little attention from an almost nonexistent public.

However, during the second half of the nineteenth century, the strains of urbanization became more severe and touched more and more of the city's muzhiks, particularly more and more of the adult laborers. As a result, the problems of the laboring population began to change from the exceptional to the common, calling for broader measures than rounding up a few vagrants or providing a home for abandoned infants. It was only natural, therefore, that more general prob-

121. *Stenograficheskie otchety o sobraniiakh Moskovskoi gorodskoi dumy za mai, iun', avgust, 1901 g.* (Moscow, 1901), 276–77. The proportion of married men in Miasniki 3 increased from 35.3 percent in 1882 to 45.6 percent in 1902. The significance of this fact, however, is qualified by the corresponding proportions of married women, which were 30.3 percent in 1882 and still only 31.2 percent in 1902. The additional married men apparently were not living with their wives at Khitrov market. (*PM 1882*, II, pt. 2, 2–3; *PM 1902*, I, 1, iii, 112.)

122. TsGAM, f. 179, op. 21, d. 1715, ll. 61–62; Kishkin, "Zhilishchnyi vopros," 298–99; *Sovremennoe khoziaistvo*, 177–79.

lems, such as congested and unsanitary housing, casual labor, and slum residence, should receive attention. Simultaneously, the municipality itself, quite reluctantly, began to face the problems of urban blight. In this connection, the observations and recommendations of the chief of police in 1863 marked an important step in the evolution of attitudes toward the muzhik and toward public assistance. First, Ogarev astutely observed that the influx of casual peasant laborers was becoming a serious social problem. To be sure, Moscow had its own contingent of poor laborers, artisans, and lower officials, and the wretched state of the *meshchane* in urban Russia is legendary. Yet the sheer magnitude (and the rapid increase) of the immigrant needy meant that the issue of public assistance had changed dramatically and required immediate attention. Second, although the chief of police acknowledged the participation of private individuals and societies in charity, he argued that the municipality must take the responsibility and initiative in public assistance. Clearly, the needs of masses of the jobless and homeless in Moscow could not be met by the limited and unsystematic nature of private charity or by the specialized aid of imperial institutions such as the Workhouse and Foundling Home. In this perception of the problem, the chief of police anticipated more thorough public assistance programs at the end of the century.

Yet, Ogarev's perceptions also looked backward to more patriarchal, ordered times, and no innovations in municipal welfare were made in the 1860s and 1870s. Ogarev suggested no measures to reform the individual (let alone society): the honest laborer was simply to be separated from the alleged idlers and criminals. Public housing would merely supplement basic police work. Moreover, the chief of police viewed Moscow's peasant multitudes as legal residents elsewhere. Peasant vagrants could simply be expelled from the city: neither they nor their problems were the concern of the municipality. These solutions were, therefore, primarily administrative rather than reformist. Likewise, the city council only reluctantly began to provide municipal lodgings, and then primarily because of the threat to public health.

However, further evaluation of the city's attempts to meet the needs of its laboring population must wait: perceptions of these "needs" and accordingly of the city's "success" changed. Beginning in the 1890s relief and repression came to be viewed more and more as a means too administrative and simplified to deal with the needy muzhik. True welfare, it was to be argued, must aim at reform—of the individual, of society—and with a vision of rationalization and regeneration Muscovite faced muzhik at the beginning of the twentieth century. This effort to transform the muzhik into a responsible citizen of the urban and industrial system contains the evolution of the ideas of individual and social reform, the subject of the next chapter.

9. VIEW ALONG THE IAUZA RIVER TAKEN FROM THE
ANDRONIKOV MONASTERY IN 1889. IN THE
BACKGROUND IS A TANNERY.

"Under bushy willows meanders the dirty Iauza, dyed
all colors of the rainbow by industrial discharge.
Along its banks are factories surrounded by vast
tracks of wasteland and truck gardens"

(Geinike, *Po Moskve*, 290).

10. WORKERS' CAFETERIA AT A BREWERY, 1896.

"The creation of an intelligent, sober, literate, honest workingman is a goal dear to every Russian who wants to see our industry and productivity flourish"

(*Letopis' pervogo dvadtsatipiatiletiia Moskovskogo Obshchestva pooshchreniia trudoliubiia*, 276–77).

11. YOUNG LABORERS ON MOSCOW'S SOUTH SIDE. AGAIN, NOTICE THE BAST SHOES.

"Every year a large number of migrant laborers from different provinces head for [the city] looking for work: carpenters, painters, and navvies all pass through . . . during the summer months"

(TsGAM, f. 179, op. 21, d. 2009, l. 49).

12. CAB STAND, EARLY TWENTIETH CENTURY.

"Upon leaving the railway station, you will see a long row of carriages. To hire a driver, you must go up to him, since they are not permitted to drive up to the platform"

(*Nastol'no-spravochnaia adresnaia kniga* [1878], 14).

"For the unfamiliar traveler, hiring a driver is no easy matter. Since there are no fares, drivers usually try to charge twice as much as it ought to cost"

(*Putevoditel' po Moskve* [1890], 152).

"Moscow has a multitude of unpoetical and noisy horse cars that tear along the streets at a furious gallop with a perpetual and generally inopportune tinkling of bells"

(Theodore Child, ed., *The Tsar and His People*, 250).

13. BLIND BEGGARS, TURN OF THE CENTURY.

"Muscovites are indeed solicitous toward beggars; they give them what they can, clothe and
feed them, and even take them into their homes"

(Pyliaev, *Staraia Moskva*, 418).

"Our welfare system, or rather, the absence of any
system, affects the poor as rain affects mushrooms—it multiplies them"

(K. I. Odynets, *Dom trudoliubiia*, 2:28–29).

"Work assistance is designed . . . to wipe out
once and for all the current practice of irrational
aid and to replace it with more expedient forms
of charity and public assistance."

(G. G. Shvittau, *Trudovaia pomoshch'*, 2:10).

14. KHITROV MARKET, NOW GORKY SQUARE, EARLY
TWENTIETH CENTURY.

"A big square in the center of the capital, near
the Iauza river, surrounded by peeling stone
houses. It lies in a low place into which lead several side streets, like streams into a swamp. It's
always bursting especially toward evening. When
it's a little foggy or just after a rain, standing at
the top of one of the side streets, you can barely
make out the figures below you descending into
a crawling, putrid pit"

(V. Giliarovskii, *Moskva i moskvichi*, 23).

15. UNEMPLOYED AT KHITROV MARKET, LATE NINETEENTH
CENTURY. NOTICE THE CANOPY (*BALAGAN*)
IN THE BACKGROUND.

"But in the slack season there is often nothing to
eat. At this time starving workers roam from
workshop to workshop looking for jobs"

(Oliunina, *Portnovskii promysel*, 7).

CHAPTER EIGHT

Welfare: Reform and Regeneration

The great metropolises across Europe and America during the nineteenth century, including Moscow, were centers of unprecedented employment opportunities as well as concentrations of those for whom "the special condition of employment, extreme mobility of demand and perpetual changes in manufacturing processes . . . leave by the wayside."[1] This casual labor force was complemented by an undetermined but sizeable contingent of vagrants, beggars, paupers, runaways, drifters, and criminals for whom the metropolises acted like a magnet, and also by a growing number of laborers who at one time or another during their working years in the city needed some form of assistance. The alleged intemperance, indolence, and improvidence of these groups not only threatened the health and social stability of the city but also deviated more and more from the values of sobriety, industriousness, and frugality preached by social reformers. Accordingly, municipal authorities and professionals attempted to instill in the allegedly indifferent and hostile lower classes the values of discipline, self-reliance, providence, and respectability. Systematic reform of character and ways of life began to supplement and even replace older, limited, and more punitive methods of treating indigence.[2]

As they were in Europe and America, Russian urban welfare insti-

---

1. Chevalier, *Laboring Classes*, 169.
2. See Christopher Lasch, *Haven in a Heartless World: The Family Besieged* (New York, 1977). See also Huggins, *Protestants against Poverty*; Bremer, *American Philanthropy*; Woodroofe, *From Charity to Social Work*; and Roy Lubove, *The Professional Altruist: The Emergence of Social Work as a Career, 1880–1930* (Cambridge, Mass., 1965).

tutions, especially in Moscow and St. Petersburg, were on the cutting edge of social reform efforts at the beginning of the twentieth century. Moreover, welfare agencies and institutions, neglected by historians of Russian institutions and urban administration,[3] had an added dimension in urban and industrial life: their efforts to create a reformed, responsible, and self-reliant poor reflected a vision of a reformed, responsible, and self-reliant Russia—a hardworking, purposeful, modern society and a provident citizenry. The city council and the police, as well as the public health officials, sanitary physicians, charity workers, statisticians, scholars, and penologists who made up the urban Third Element, were well aware that their success or failure in this endeavor had important consequences for the health and stability of the urban community.

Despite the existence of all the charitable agencies discussed in the previous chapter, despite the size of the Foundling Home and the Workhouse, despite the many proposals submitted to the city council for housing construction and slum clearance, at the end of the nineteenth century poor relief in Moscow found many critics who feared that the city's charity would be overrun by needy muzhiks. Several problem areas emerge from the specialized literature of the period: the lack of knowledge about the laboring population or about poverty; the inability of existing charity to get at the root causes of need— individual, economic, or institutional; the lack of local control and alleged remoteness of the larger institutions; the lack of systematic organized relief as well as a lack of moral and financial support; and the potentially demoralizing effect of indiscriminate aid and welfare abuse. Out of this criticism came investigations into the nature and causes of poverty, major changes in the city's poor relief, and a liberal reformist idea based on rationalization of services, character regeneration, and integration of Moscow's laborers into urban-industrial society and its dominant values. The criticisms and innovations at the turn

---

3. The few published studies of urban administration or of Moscow at the end of the nineteenth century have neglected welfare reform and institutions of poor relief. See the articles by Walter Hanchett and Michael Hamm in Hamm, ed., *The City in Russian History;* Robert Thurston, "Police and People in Moscow, 1906–1914," *Russian Review*, 39, no. 3 (July 1980): 320–38; and Bater, "Some Dimensions of Urbanization." One of the few studies of urban institutions that discusses welfare and welfare reform is Walter Hanchett, "Moscow in the Late Nineteenth Century: A Study in Municipal Self-Government," Ph.D. dissertation (University of Chicago, 1964), especially pp. 341–69. The most complete study of Russia's charitable institutions is Adele Lindenmeyr, "Public Poor Relief and Private Charity in Late Imperial Russia," Ph.D. dissertation (Princeton University, 1980).

of the century, as well as the ingredients of an idea of reform which will be discussed in the concluding chapter, can be seen better by analyzing the crackdown at the Foundling Home, the municipalization and devolution of certain services, the idea of work assistance and the reformed Workhouse, and the new District Guardianships of the Poor.

"THE ALL-RUSSIAN ALMSHOUSE"

To begin with, it was apparent to any thoughtful Muscovite that the needy were everywhere, that existing agencies and institutions were being seemingly overrun by muzhiks, and that, in the words of a commission of the city council, Moscow faced the prospect of becoming the "all-Russian almshouse."[4] Yet, no one really knew how many of the city's muzhiks were truly needy, either constantly or intermittently. Nor was there any consensus concerning what constituted need or indigence, pauperism, and poverty. One of the agencies that was in the business of knowing such things, the Office of the Institutions of the Empress Maria, undertook two mammoth surveys of charity in the Russian empire. Relying on data from the 1897 census, the surveys estimated that more than 400,000 persons and their dependents engaged in begging. At the same time, more than 100,000 were on relief in welfare institutions; of these almost three-quarters were in cities, representing 48 of every 10,000 urban inhabitants.[5] Applying this ratio to Moscow, a city of approximately 1 million, 4,800 would have been receiving institutional relief. As the compilers of the survey admitted, these estimates, particularly those of the number of beggars, were probably too low, owing to the difficulty in making such estimates and to the understandable reluctance of most beggars to reveal an illegal occupation to the census takers. A municipal survey of the city's welfare system in 1889 counted 73,633 persons receiving institutional relief and an additional 353,933 receiving noninstitutional relief; the latter figure did not include those receiving free lodgings or meals.[6] However, these figures include a whopping 386,108 receiving medical care. If this

4. Moskovskaia gorodskaia uprava, "Doklad Komissii o pol'zakh i nuzhdakh ob-shchestvennykh po voprosu o peredache dela prizreniia nishchikh v Moskve v vedenie Gorodskogo obshchestvennogo upravleniia," no. 117 (October 14, 1891), in *IMGD*, no. 11 (1891): 2.

5. *Blagotvoritel'nost' v Rossii*, 1:v, x–xi.

6. *SSS 1889*, iii, v, xix.

number and the numbers of children and students are deducted from the total, only 18,668 adults were receiving systematic assistance.[7]

Other estimates may be obtained by examining the city censuses. In 1902, for instance, 18,263 were recorded in the category "on relief" (*prizrevaemye*).[8] This corresponds reasonably well to the figure of adults on relief in 1889. However, such a figure represents the number on relief frozen at one point in time. The actual pool of needy contributing to the censal category "on relief" may have been much larger. In occupational terms, all or most of the city's 18,117 unemployed, for example, contributed to this pool, as did most of its 116,837 menial blue-collar workers. One might even argue that in very broad terms *all* the city's blue-collar workers (more than 500,000) or even its blue-collar and low white-collar workers combined (more than 625,000) were *potential* if not actual cases of need.[9] Moreover, these occupational categories represented only the active population; dependents, frequently more prone to need, were not included. However, estimating the total number of needy on the basis of occupational categories is not entirely satisfactory. Above the unemployed and notoriously precarious occupations such as common laborer, ragpicker, and domestic servants, the further up the occupational ladder we climb, the more difficult it becomes to label all the laborers holding a particular job as consistently contributing to the pool of the needy. This would be especially true if the jobs in question were reasonably steady and if the laborers holding them were in entry-level stages of their careers.

Mindful of the discussion of housing and households in chapter 6, one might want to define the needy in terms of their living arrangements. Although the data come from various years, more than 350,000 persons, including an estimated 15,000 homeless and 180,919 in the cot-chamber tenements, lived in transient, subdivided, crowded, unsanitary housing. From another perspective, more than 100,000 lived in basement apartments, approximately 500,000 had neither indoor plumbing nor flush toilets, and from a half to two-thirds of a million did not live with their family. Since lack of wherewithal presumably made it impossible for various numbers of people to pay for better accommodations or to support dependents, one might suppose that one or a combination of the above categories was evidence of need. How-

7. Ibid., xxv. The compilers of the municipal survey acknowledged the difficulties in separating those on welfare from those receiving medical aid.
8. *PM 1902*, I, 2, i, 46–115.
9. See Appendix A, "Occupations in White-collar, Blue-collar Moscow."

ever, trying to locate cases of need on the basis of housing yields a wide range of numbers, and the method may not offer much improvement over that employed above using various occupational categories. The best that can be said is that both methods yield figures that create a range so wide as to encompass all contemporary estimates.

A French statistician of the 1830s devised a method, used by Chevalier in his pioneering study but unknown, as far as I can tell, to nineteenth-century Muscovites, for estimating the extent of poverty in Paris.[10] Assuming that one would have avoided at all costs the nineteenth-century hospital, an object of fear on the part of the people, deaths recorded in hospitals would represent cases of poverty. Although this method would include deaths from causes that struck the population randomly—accidents, for example, or even instances of epidemics that by no means struck only the poor—it might be worthwhile to apply it to Moscow.

For the years 1897–1906 there were annually 7,485 deaths at the city's nine municipal hospitals. This number constituted approximately one-quarter of all annual deaths. I shall add the average annual number of deaths at the Foundling Home (4,148 for the period 1892–1906), under the assumption that these deaths represented rather severe cases of need. Thus, during the period there were 11,633 deaths that may be assumed to have represented deaths of the needy population.[11] During the same period, Moscow's death rate was approximately 27 per 1,000 population, that is, 1 death for every 36 inhabitants. In some of the city's poorer outlying districts, however, the number of deaths per inhabitant was much higher—1 death for every 30 in Serpukhov's second precinct, 1 for every 23 in Meshchane's fourth precinct. Assuming that among the poor there was 1 death per 30, or a death rate of 33.3 per 1,000, the pool of needy supplying the city with 11,633 deaths per year numbered 349,339.[12]

Thus, extrapolating from the number of deaths in municipal hospitals and in the Foundling Home, it is possible to estimate that Moscow's needy numbered nearly 350,000. As can be seen, this figure happens to approximate the 357,660 living in inns, lodging houses, and cot-chamber tenements or living communally or having no home. It also happens to approximate the 365,371 semiskilled, menial, or unemployed workers. Finally, it approximates the 353,933 the city

10. Chevalier, *Laboring Classes*, 352.
11. *SEM za 1906–7* (Moscow, 1908), 52–53, 70–71.
12. See chapter 1, note 41, and figure 2.

estimated to be receiving some form of noninstitutional relief. Moreover, the figure derived from deaths in hospitals falls roughly halfway
between figures for all blue-collar and low white-collar workers and
those living away from their families, on the one hand, and figures for
the homeless and the unemployed, on the other. The point here,
though, is not to arrive at a precise figure for the city's poor (an
impossible task given the subjective nature of the concepts "poor,"
"needy," "indigent"), nor to derive a foolproof method for doing so,
but to give some rough idea of the magnitude of need in the city. As
criticism of welfare in Moscow mounted toward the end of the nineteenth century, there was a fear that needy muzhiks would inundate
city services unless the latter were rational, properly organized, effi-
cient, and able to reach the root causes of poverty, and had procedures
commensurate with the goal of regeneration and reform. One institution whose procedures were increasingly seen as not commensurate
with these goals was the Foundling Home.

THE FOUNDLING HOME: CRITICISM
AND CRACKDOWN

The Imperial Foundling Home during the last quarter of the nineteenth century was busy shepherding foreign visitors around one of
the largest buildings in the city; alone among Moscow's welfare institutions, it was also preparing an exhibit of its operations for the 1896
Exposition of Industry and the Arts at Nizhnii Novgorod.[13] And well
it might have been engaged in such public relations, for its procedures
received much criticism at the end of the century. To begin with, the
foster care system led to child abuse. Although they were a source of
income for peasant foster families, foundlings were often treated
worse than the peasant's own children. Child abuse of the *shpitonki*,
the village slang for the wards of the Foundling Home, is illustrated in
Semenov's "Someone's Else's Child" ("Chuzhoe dite"). Dashka had
been sent to a village family which had just lost its own child. However, the family had one other child who survived infancy, and Dashka
became a virtual slave for taking care of the foster family's own, and
more favored, child. Dashka breaks the last straw when she tells the
inspector (*ob"ezdnoi*) that she was being mistreated, thus incurring a

---

13. Vserossiiskaia promyshlennaia i khudozhestvennaia vystavka, *Podrobnyi ukazatel' po otdelam Vserossiiskoi promyshlennoi i khudozhestvennoi vystavki 1896 g. v
Nizhnem-Novgorode* (Moscow, 1896), 1.

fine on her foster mother. She later contracts a fever, is neglected, and dies at the age of eleven.[14] Even setting such open forms of abuse aside, the sudden transfer of infants from the hothouse Foundling Home to unhygienic village huts, the unsupervised transfer of children from one family to another, and the rather casual and pecuniary attitude of peasant families to the foster children—all contributed to a death rate of foster children in Moscow province of nearly 400 per 1,000 at the turn of the century.[15]

Abuse and mortality among foster children affected, after all, children who had *survived* the first weeks of infancy in the Foundling Home. An alarming number of infants did not survive, and this was a second cause for criticism of the system. In another of Semenov's stories, "On the Brink," Daria Pavlova decides not to send her illegitimate daughter to the Foundling Home ("where you'd never find her again") but gives her to an acquaintance in the village. She thanks her fate she did the right thing:

Thank God I didn't secretly give you up to the Foundling Home then. There you either would have died long ago or they would have sent you far away and I never would have found you.[16]

A character in Kharlamov's sketches of paupers in St. Petersburg echoes the same sentiment when someone suggests she take her baby to the Foundling Home so that she can find work: "To the Founlin'! Hey, you try it. You'll torture yourself—have a baby and then desert it like a puppy at the Founlin'."[17] The common people, it seems, did not have to read annual reports of the Home or mortality tables to understand that it was a deathtrap, perhaps hardly better than abandonment itself. Those who did like to read annual reports or mortality statistics, however, would have noticed an increase in the number of deaths from an annual average of 3,684 from 1878 to 1883 to 5,635 from 1884 to 1889.[18] The proportion of all infant deaths in Moscow from 1880 to 1889 attributed to deaths in the Foundling Home aver-

14. S. T. Semenov, "Chuzhoe dite," 148–64.

15. "Moskovskii vospitatel'nyi dom," 218–21; *Smertnost' naseleniia g. Moskvy,* 49; Ransel, "Abandonment and Fosterage," 201–17.

16. S. T. Semenov, "U propasti," in *U propasti i drugie rasskazy,* 2d ed. (Moscow, 1904), 10, 22.

17. Kharlamov, *Kristovym imenem,* 135–36. "Founlin' " is an approximation of the colloquial "shpitatel'nyi," used instead of "vospitatel'nyi."

18. *Smertnost' naseleniia,* 16–18; Ginzburg, "Prizrenie podkidyshei," 606. In all fairness to the institution, 93 percent of the foundlings were received in the first two weeks of life, the most vulnerable period of an infant's first year under any circumstances.

aged 45.2 percent and was as high as 56.4 percent in 1888.[19] So great was the impact of the Foundling Home on the city's overall infant mortality and death rates (almost one-fifth of the city's deaths in the 1880s) that most compilations of municipal population statistics had to specify whether figures from the Foundling Home were included.

Child abuse in the foster system and high mortality rates in the Foundling Home itself demonstrated that while the Home may have been a humane way of taking abandoned or unwanted infants, it had not succeeded in bringing many of them into childhood, let alone adulthood. Such "medical" failures were joined by the "moral" failures in the eyes of critics. This kind of criticism centered on the mounting number of infants deposited in the Home and particularly on the "open admissions" policy. The number of infants deposited increased steadily in the 1880s, from 13,860 in 1880 to a high of 17,114 in 1888, and by the end of the decade approximately one-third of the city's annual births enrolled in the Foundling Home.[20] The connection between the Foundling Home and illegitimacy in a city where between one-quarter and one-third of the annual births were illegitimate was inescapable.[21] Even worse, according to critics, the liberal admissions policy and the *tour* mechanism with its secret deposit not only virtually beckoned admission of illegitimate infants but encouraged mothers of legitimate babies to deposit unwanted children. One foreign visitor claimed that because many parents of the "laboring classes" brought legitimate babies to the Home "with the hope of claiming them" later, "notwithstanding its excellent management, the institution may perhaps in many respects be considered a questionable charity."[22]

Regulations permitted not only the admission of legitimate children but also the admission of their mothers if they wanted to nurse their own children or if there was a shortage of wet nurses. Thus, critics maintained, working-class mothers were being paid by the state to nurse their own children—hardly a sign of propriety and responsibility, on the part of either state or citizens. In theory, such "official" admission of mothers and babies, whether the babies were legitimate or not, forced the mother to experience "shame" for her conduct. More disturbing, however, was the abuse of the system by mothers

19. *Smertnost' naseleniia*, 20–22, 46.
20. "Ocherk deiatel'nosti Moskovskogo vospitatel'nogo doma," *IMGD*, 22, no. 1 (July–August 1898): 6; *Smertnost' naseleniia*, 21, 41, 47.
21. Maksimov, *Proiskhozhdenie nishchenstva*, 92.
22. Guild, *Britons and Muscovites*, 174–75.

who secretly left their babies at the door and then returned as wet nurses and tried to get their own babies back, and also money for their support. In the words of one foreign traveler:

Unfortunately, this famous refuge has corrupted all the villages around Moscow. Peasant girls who have forgotten to get married send their babies to the institution and then offer themselves in person as wet nurses. Having tatooed their offspring, each mother contrives to find arrangement with the nurse to whom it has been assigned. As babies are much alike, the authorities cannot detect these interchanges and do not attempt to do so. In due time, the mother returns to her village with her own baby whose board will be paid by the State at a rate of eight shillings a month, and possibly the next year and the year after she will begin the same game over again.[23]

Finally, Moscow was in danger of becoming a center for unwanted children. Since 1828 a ban had existed on establishing foundling homes in the provinces.[24] As a result, most illegitimate or unwanted children from nearby provinces were sent to Moscow. In Tula "the provincial zemstvo runs an orphanage, but the children are not kept long and are sent to Moscow"; "there was a Foundling Home in Belev, but it was considered more expedient to send babies to Moscow and so it was closed in 1888"; in Iaroslavl', the county seat of Rybinsk "has a Foundling Home but the extras are sent to Moscow."[25] Excessive centralization of the foundling home system was the final criticism of the institution toward the end of the nineteenth century.

The liberal admissions policy, the mounting number of applicants, often from remote rural areas, alleged abuses, and the inability of the system to inculcate the subordinate classes with the values of responsibility and self-discipline gave the Foundling Home a bad press for promoting "immorality and fraud." In the 1890s a crackdown on admissions finally came. Regulations of 1890 and 1894 tried to decrease the number admitted by restricting the secret depositing of infants and insisting on more documentation for each infant submitted. Such documentation included birth and baptismal certificates, identification of the person submitting the infant, and verification of the mother's death, if this was given as the reason for submission. Secret admission was still possible, though made more difficult: the *tour* was dismantled, and in the absence of the mother a parish priest,

23. A. J. C. Hare, *Studies in Russia* (London, n.d.), 282. For a similar description, see Leikin, *Na zarabotkakh*, 208.

24. *PSZ*, 2d ser., 4 (1828), no. 2125.

25. M. A. Oshanin, "O prizrenii pokinutykh detei," S"ezd po obshchestvennomu prizreniiu, *Trudy*, 2:12–13, 110, 139.

a representative of a charitable society or the police had to bring in the infant. All of this was aimed at preventing the "fraud" of mothers trying to submit their own children secretly and at "curbing the access to the Foundling Home for those children who, by virtue of their social position or material condition, have no right, such as legitimate children, who were constantly submitted earlier as illegitimate."[26] Finally, as a step toward decentralizing the system, in 1898 the ban on establishing foundling homes in the provinces was lifted.[27]

Although a causal connection cannot be established conclusively, it would seem that the changes in the rules contributed to a reduction in the number of admissions. From 16,466 in 1890, the number of admissions dropped to 10,724 in two years and then dipped under the 10,000 mark for several years in the late 1890s. Although the number of admissions rose slightly in the first decade of the twentieth century, exceeding 11,000 for the years 1904–1906, in most years the figure hovered at close to 10,000. The infant mortality rate also dropped from highs of 43.1 percent and 44.8 percent of admissions (1888–1889) to 24.2 percent in 1892; however, it rose again and averaged between 30 and 40 percent after the late 1890s.[28] The crackdown was also accompanied by a search for alternatives—such as labor colonies—both to the foster care system and to orphanages in general.[29] Whether the crackdown on admissions or the prospect of children's labor colonies had any effects on the values and habits of the muzhiks is problematical. Judgment on this issue is best suspended, for the reform at the Foundling Home took place in the context of other reforms in Moscow in the 1890s—reforms which were prompted by similar issues: decentralization, eligibility for relief, responsibility for dispensing aid, and moral regeneration.

MUNICIPALIZATION

Frequent criticisms of poor relief in Moscow and throughout Russia were the lack of agreement concerning the responsibility for dispensing aid, the confusing jurisdiction of the many government agencies and private societies in the provision of relief, and the ill-

---

26. Ginzburg, "Prizrenie podkidyshei," 84–85; S"ezd po obshchestvennomu prizreniiu, *Trudy*, 2:169; *SSS 1901*, 4–5.
27. *PSZ*, 3d ser., 18 (1898), no. 15131.
28. "Ocherk deiatel'nosti," 6; K. I. Anufriev, "Osnovy obiazatel'nogo prizreniia bednykh," S"ezd po obshchestvennomu prizreniiu, *Trudy*, 2:206.
29. S"ezd po obshchestvennomu prizreniiu, *Trudy*, 2:78, 83.

defined eligibility for welfare. Closely related, and particularly important as far as Moscow was concerned, was the lack of municipal
control over the administration of assistance within the city. Major
agencies and institutions such as the Foundling Home and the Workhouse, as well as the police itself, were outside the jurisdiction of the
municipality. Ultimate supervision of welfare agencies and institutions
rested with the Ministry of Internal Affairs, whose approval was
needed for the establishment of any charitable society. Several vaguely
worded articles of the 1870 City Statute stated that charitable institutions and hospitals were under the jurisdiction of the municipality, but
the senate subsequently interpreted this as meaning the city had the
right to establish charitable institutions and hospitals but not the
obligation.[30]

By the late 1880s, however, the Ministry of Internal Affairs began
to consider the reorganization of the empire's welfare system. Although in the literature this period is frequently labeled the time of
"counterreform," paradoxically the late 1880s and early 1890s mark
the beginning of a period of devolution (or municipalization) of welfare in general and of many of the organizations the Ministry of
Internal Affairs supervised, in particular.[31] In 1887 the State Council
gave the ministry the go-ahead to consider discontinuing its Moscow
Welfare Office and approved the transfer to the municipality of several charitable organizations, almshouses, and hospitals.[32] In 1888 a
commission of the city council chaired by I. N. Mamontov investi-
gated the municipal management of all the city's private, public, and
state welfare institutions.[33] The following year the Ministry of Internal

30. *Svod zakonov Rossiiskoi imperii* (St. Petersburg, 1876), 2, part 1; "Doklad
Komissii o pol'zakh i nuzhdakh obshchestvennykh," 7.
31. Most histories of Russian institutions do not mention the changing administration of welfare in the context of the counterreforms. See for example Eroshkin, *Ocherki*,
304–5, and P. A. Zaionchkovskii, *Rossiiskoe samoderzhavie v kontse XIX stoletiia*
(Moscow, 1970), 411–28.
32. Transferred to municipal management were the Ekaterina and Demidov almshouses, the Akhlebaev Wayfarers' Home, the Gorikhvostov and Preobrazhenskii hospitals, the Bakhrushin Home for the Blind, the Abrikosova Maternity Home and Gyneco-
logical Clinic, the Lepekhin Maternity Home, and the Rukavishnikov Correctional and
Vocational Shelter for Juvenile Delinquents. See *PSZ*, 3d ser., 7 (1887), no. 4554;
Sbornik ocherkov, 1–7, 16–18; Moskovskoe gorodskoe obshchestvennoe upravlenie,
Otchet po rodil'nomu domu im. A. A. Abrikosovoi (Moscow, 1909), 61, and *Otchet po
gorodskomu rodil'nomu domu im. S. V. Lepekhina* (Moscow, 1909), 35–37, and
Otchet o deiatel'nosti gorodskogo sirotskogo priiuta im. br. P., A., i V. Bakhrushinykh
(Moscow, 1909), 5–12. The buildings and the grounds of this former home for the
blind are now those of Mir Publishers, my employers for a year in Moscow.
33. "Doklad Komissii o pol'zakh i nuzhdakh obshchestvennykh," 27, 35, 39–40;
Moskovskoe gorodskoe obshchestvennoe upravlenie, *Vremennoe polozhenie o gorodskikh uchastkovykh popechitel'stvakh o bednykh v Moskve* (Moscow, 1894), 1–7.

Affairs proposed that the city either continue to fund the existing Committee to Investigate and Aid Beggars or take over this committee's operations altogether.[34] The Commission for Matters of the Commonweal under the chairmanship of Vladimir Ger'e, as well as the Mamontov Commission, recommended that the city take over the functions of this committee, and indeed the City Statute of 1892 abolished the committee in Moscow (although not in Petersburg, where the enthusiasm for municipalization was less forthcoming) and transferred its functions to the city.[35]

Devolution and municipalization were part of a larger reexamination of welfare in the empire, best associated with the Grot Commission, created in November 1892 to examine the poor laws to draw up new legislation.[36] The Grot Commission, named after its chairman, State Secretary K. K. Grot, soon found out that the existing laws did not specify who should get relief; when, from what agency, and in what form relief should be administered; what means should be used to finance aid; and whether limited private initiative or more extensive governmental obligation should determine the form of assistance.[37] The Grot Commission, which met until 1897, solved none of these problems, and none of its proposals were enacted.[38]

Neither the many commissions, nor municipalization, nor the 1892 City Statute solved another issue, absolutely crucial as far as poor relief in Moscow was concerned. Like the city population as a whole, the needy were dominated by those born elsewhere. In the 1880s and 1890s approximately 40 percent of the infants brought to the Foundling Home, for example, were born elsewhere; considering that most of the babies were brought in during the first weeks of life, this is a remarkable proportion.[39] Figures of lodgers at the flophouses and at countless other institutions reveal the preponderance of immigrants; the police and municipal authorities repeatedly complained of the numbers apprehended with no passports.[40] Even changes in the passport laws in 1894, including a provision that persons exiled for mendicancy not be reissued a pass-

34. "Doklad Komissii o pol'zakh i nuzhdakh obshchestvennykh," 1.
35. *PSZ*, 3d. ser., 12 (1892), no. 8708.
36. *Materialy k voprosu ob obshchestvennom prizrenii* (Odessa, 1895), 4.
37. Ibid., 17, 60–65.
38. Anufriev, "Osnovy," 212; Adele Lindenmeyr, "Public Poor Relief and Private Charity," 24–25.
39. I-ov, "Vospitatel'nye doma," 525.
40. *Otchet o deiatel'nosti Moskovskoi gorodskoi upravy za 1902*, 217.

port for two years, seemed to have little effect on curbing the entry of the needy into Moscow.[41]

For welfare reformers the problem posed by the police in 1863 and debated by the city council in the 1870s and 1880s continued to stare Muscovites in the face: should the city assume responsibility for immigrants? Before the 1890s it was not too difficult for the city council to deny responsibility for aiding the city's immigrants: it denied ongoing responsibility for aiding the city's needy, period. With the municipalization of certain services and the prospect of even greater involvement in the 1890s, the issue resurfaced. The issue was discussed not only by the local Mamontov and Ger'e commissions but by the Grot Commission and, demonstrating that none of these bodies solved it, as late as 1914 by the Conference on Welfare organized by the Ministry of Internal Affairs. It was pointed out at this conference that, although by 1914 most European countries believed that relief must be provided at the place of domicile of the applicant, that is, "provided by the community where the economic activities of a given individual are directed at the moment of need," Russian law still regarded birthplace as determining the locality for dispensing aid.[42] Although the issue was never resolved in principle, different interpretations had important practical applications in the rules and regulations of Moscow's newest welfare organizations, the District Guardianships of the Poor. However, before turning to a discussion of this organization, one more consequence of municipalization must be introduced: the reformed Workhouse.

THE REFORMED WORKHOUSE

The Committee to Investigate and Aid Beggars, which passed into municipal hands in 1892, had maintained the Workhouse. By the 1880s weeds were growing in the cracks of this venerable institution: in 1889 only 136 were admitted.[43] However, reformers anticipated that it would play a critical role in a coming vigorous campaign to rid the city's streets of the indigent, in new efforts at job training and placement, in new programs of "work assistance," and in a policy of

41. PSZ, 3d ser., 14 (1894), no. 10709.
42. N. V. Nesmeianov, "Material'nye zatrudneniia krupnykh gorodov v dele prizreniia bednykh i mery k ikh ustraneniiu," S"ezd po obshchestvennomu prizreniiu, Trudy, 2:440–41; V. I. Ger'e, "Zapiska, predstavlennaia v Vysochaishe uchrezhdennuiu Komissiiu dlia peresmotra deistvuiushchikh zakonov o prizrenii bednykh," Materialy, 63, 71.
43. SSS 1889, 22.

systematic character regeneration through an institutional regimen, "love of work," and moral awakening.

All these goals were to be unified in a system of social and even individual reform. The Mamontov Commission had argued that the city could direct social policy away from the indiscriminate expulsion or incarceration of individual beggars or vagrants and toward a more rational and coordinated program of relief. Those physically unable to work were to be sent to a municipal almshouse affiliated with the Workhouse; special facilities were to exist for the chronically ill and children. Only the beggars and vagrants apprehended by the police would continue to be sent to the Workhouse itself, which would retain its punitive character. Those referred by a charitable agency, as well as voluntary applicants (assumed to be willing and able to work), were to be given vocational training and jobs at the Vocational Center (Dom trudoliubiia), annexed physically and administratively to the Workhouse in 1895.[44]

The Vocational Center was to be the linchpin of the reformed Workhouse. The expansion of its activities, largely through the influence of Lutheran religious reformers in Germany and popularized in Russia in the 1880s by Baron O. O. Buksgeveden (Buxhoeveden), reflected an increased emphasis on job training. Studies of indigence repeatedly pointed to various economic or "providential" causes of poverty and mendicancy: inefficient farming or unproductive land, high taxes, lack of nonagricultural skills or wage income, death of a working member of the family, bad harvest, physical handicap, fire, and death of livestock.[45] Giving the needy muzhik job training and the skills necessary to function

44. *Vremennoe polozhenie*, 1–7; P. V. Krotkov, "Doma trudoliubiia v Rossii," *Sbornik statei*, 4 (1897): 68–69. Additional studies of Russia's vocational centers are A. Gorovtsev, "O rabotakh v domakh trudoliubiia," *Trudovaia pomoshch'*, 3, no. 7 (September 1900): 140–71, and "Tsel' i naznachenie domov trudoliubiia," *Vestnik Evropy*, 35, no. 6 (June 1900): 497–547; V. Ger'e, "Chto takoe Dom trudoliubiia?" *Trudovaia pomoshch'*, 1, no. 1 (November 1897): 1–43; E. Maksimov, "Zametki o vnutrennem ustroistve domov trudoliubiia," *Trudovaia pomoshch'*, 3, no. 9 (November 1900): 341–59, and no. 10 (December 1900): 467–86. By 1904, for instance, 14,000 were handed over to the Workhouse by the police and 12,000 registered voluntarily. (TsGIA, f. 1290, op. 5, d. 195, ll. 1–15).

45. Two such studies were an investigation of pauperism by a commission of the Ministry of Internal Affairs in 1877 and an investigation of mendicancy and vagrancy by a commission of the Ministry of Justice in 1899. See also *Blagotvoritel'nost' v Rossii*, 1:vi; K. I. Odynets, *Dom Trudoliubiia i ego zadachi kak organ "Obshchestva uluchsheniia narodnogo truda"* (St. Petersburg, 1887), 2:14; Linev, *Prichiny russkogo nishchenstva*, 193; Kurbanovskii, *Nishchenstvo i blagotvoritel'nost'*, 2; Maksimov, *Proiskhozhdenie*, 25; Levenstim, *Professional'noe nishchenstvo*, 2, 26; V. A. Gol'tsev, "Novye issledovaniia o pauperizme," *Russkaia mysl'*, 4, no. 1 (January 1883): 131; Raevskii, "K voprosu o nishchenstve," 83. In Moscow itself similar causes of pauperism were noted. (TsGAM, f. 184, op. 2 d. 852, ll. 60–61; Sharov, "Kharakteristika," passim.)

in an urban industrialized society, and short-term relief after calamities such as the famine of 1892, were the essential components of a new concept called "work assistance" or "work relief" (*trudovaia pomoshch'*) that quickly gained in popularity.

The emphasis on work relief and the important role of Russia's workhouses in this form of welfare found institutional expression in the Guardianship of Workhouses and Vocational Centers (Popechitel'stvo o Domakh trudoliubiia i Rabotnykh domakh), later renamed the Guardianship of Work Assistance (Popechitel'stvo o trudovoi pomoshchi), established in 1895 under the patronage of Empress Aleksandra Fedorovna. The Guardianship coordinated the work-relief measures of hundreds of private charities, marketed wares, disseminated new techniques, instruments, and tools, opened training and demonstration workshops, and ran work stations (*trudovye punkty*) where needy peasants and craftsmen could use tools and sewing machines. The chief organ of the Guardianship was a journal entitled *Trudovaia pomoshch'* (Work Assistance) published ten times a year from 1897 to 1917.[46] The Dickensian image of the Workhouse, which was reinforced by a Russian translation of E. Münsterberg's dark picture of English workhouses, was criticized on the pages of *Trudovaia pomoshch'*. Labor must not be viewed by the poor as a form of punishment or repression, or even as the equivalent of a certain amount of value produced; labor, it was argued, along with the values of self-reliance and industriousness, must be made an absolute good in and of itself. Proponents of "work relief" claimed that the labor principle (*trudovoe nachalo*) could be extended from the modest field of philanthropy to broader areas of social policy and, with the agencies of systematic state management and administration, toward a general increase in labor productivity.[47]

Although the Guardianship of Work Assistance, as well as most vocational centers themselves, functioned in small-town or rural settings, the Moscow Vocational Center, by organizing workshops and reimbursing the laborer for his work, sought to aid the city's unem-

---

46. The relevant laws governing the Guardianship of Work Assistance are found in *PSZ*, 3d ser., 26 (1906), pt. 1, no. 27814. See also Shvittau, *Trudovaia pomoshch'*, 1:vii–viii, 8–9, 10, 149; 2:242 ff; and *Kratkie svedeniia*, 2–6; D. Fleksor, "Kustarnaia promyshlennost' i trudovaia pomoshch'," *Trudovaia pomoshch'*, 3, no. 2 (February 1900): 129–71.

47. E. Münsterburg, *Prizrenie bednykh. Rukovodstvo k prakticheskoi deiatel'nosti v oblasti popecheniia o bednykh* (St. Petersburg, 1900). For more on labor assistance, see E. Maksimov, "Chto takoe trudovaia pomoshch'?" *Trudovaia pomoshch'*, 3, no. 7 (September 1900): 125–39; and P. Obninskii, "Trudovaia pomoshch' kak obshchestvennyi korrektiv," *Trudovaia pomoshch'*, 1, no. 5 (March 1898): 409–20.

ployed artisans, common laborers, and domestics.[48] The Inspector of
the Workhouse was responsible for keeping track of the work, payment, income, and expenses of the Vocational Center. An overseer,
through a group representative (*starosta*) selected from among the
lodgers themselves, passed out daily work assignments, tools, and raw
materials. Most work orders came from the city council itself or from
other large institutions; for example, the Gorbov Vocational Center
for Women, established at the Workhouse in 1896, filled sewing
orders, such as linen and robes for hospitals, aprons for the Foundling
Home, and uniforms, epaulets, blankets, and burlap bags for the
army.[49] The Vocational Center was so highly regarded by reformers
that the city council prepared an exhibit of its activities for the Paris
World Exposition in 1900.[50]

Work had a more immediate practical benefit for the institution:
the sale of wares or payment for jobs completed was meant to defray
the cost of upkeep of the wards. At the Gorbov Center, for example,
the average daily earnings of 25–37 kopeks during the period 1899 to
1908 compared favorably with the wages of casual female laborers
such as washerwomen and ragpickers, who made 30–35 kopeks per
day.[51] Several measures were taken to improve working conditions:
work was not to be done in the sleeping quarters, and if possible it
was to be done outside (and welfare reformers already had visions of
garden settlements and agricultural colonies—no doubt just what
Moscow's immigrant peasants wanted).[52]

48. Shvittau, *Trudovaia pomoshch'*, 2:195.

49. The Workhouse was run by an inspector (*smotritel'*), a warden (*nadziratel'*),
and a manager and four assistants responsible for the administration of work. For more
details on the organization, internal structure, supervision, financing, and vocational
training in the reformed Workhouse, as well as on the separate Vocational Center for
Women which opened in 1896, see the annual reports (Moskovskoe gorodskoe obshchestvennoe upravlenie, *Otchet o deiatel'nosti Moskovskogo Gorodskogo Rabotnogo
Doma* and the *Otchet zhenskogo doma trudoliubiia im. M. A. i S. N. Gorbovykh*) and
the two institutional histories, *Ocherk istorii i sovremennoi deiatel'nosti Moskovskogo
doma trudoliubiia* (Moscow, 1902), and *Moskovskii Gorodskoi dom trudoliubiia i
Rabotnyi dom v ego proshlom i nastoiashchem* (Moscow, 1913), written by A. Gaidamovich and S. Sharov, respectively, the two successive directors. A brief description is
available in *Sovremennoe khoziaistvo*, 161–65; and in D. P. Beloshapkin, "Moskovskii
Rabotnyi dom," *Trudovaia pomoshch'*, 6, no. 3 (March 1903): 320–37; no. 4 (April
1903): 374–96.

50. Moskovskaia gorodskaia duma, *Stenograficheskie otchety o sobraniiakh v 1900
g.* (Moscow, 1901), 332.

51. Popechitel'stvo o trudovoi pomoshchi, *Kratkie svedeniia po sostoiashchemu . . .
popechitel'stvu o domakh trudoliubiia i rabotnykh domakh* (St. Petersburg, 1898), 89–
91; Gor-ev, "K kharakteristike," 40.

52. *Kratkie svedeniia*, 89–91.

Welfare reorganization and vocational training were, of course, not ends in themselves but means of achieving another goal: character regeneration. Accordingly, jobs and job training were complemented by a daily regimen and cultural amenities. For the newcomer, the regimen began when, twice weekly (and after 1902, daily), the doors of the Workhouse were opened to those in police custody and to those waiting to get in to the Vocational Center. "With our terrible, sweaty, pale, red faces and bulging vacant eyes, we must have seemed to have come from another world," wrote one contemporary, himself a ward of the Workhouse.[53] Upon entering the office, the voluntary arrival had his passport, money, and documents taken for safekeeping and recorded for the police. He received an account book and agreed to abide by the rules and regulations read to him. These rules and regulations included a long list of dos and don'ts designed to inculcate the habits of discipline, personal responsibility, adherence to regimen, and the awareness of rewards and punishments that permeated all aspects of modern society. Liquor, gambling, noisy behavior, soiled or unkempt appearance, indecent (*nepristoinye*) songs and conversation, absence from work, desecration of property, and absence from the Center without the permission of the warden were all forbidden. Penalties for violations of the rules and regulations included reprimand, extra cleaning duty, deprivation of the right to leave the Workhouse, transfer to harder or lower-paying work, and expulsion from the Vocational Center.[54] After admission, voluntary arrivals and detainees alike were given a number, bedding, and a uniform, herded to baths, given a physical examination, and taken to the main building's sleeping quarters or herded to the Workhouse annex in Sokol'niki, on Moscow's outskirts.

Leisure-time activities were no less important than work and the institution's regimen in raising the cultural level of the needy. A library opened in 1897 and within five years had approximately four thousand books and several newspapers. As many as three hundred wards could use the library at any one time, and from two to three thousand books (mainly fiction) were checked out each month. Readings with magic-lantern shows (*tumannye kartiny*) organized by the Moscow Commission for Sunday Readings took place every Sunday beginning in 1897. Partly of religious and moral texts and partly of fiction, such readings attracted up to three hundred in the central building and nine

53. Podiachev, "Mytarstvo," 31–34.
54. *Kratkie svedeniia*, 94–96.

hundred in Sokol'niki. Vocal, instrumental, and dramatic perfor-
mances complemented the other leisure activities.[55]

After the reorganization of the Workhouse and the incorporation
into it of the Vocational Center in the 1890s, the numbers of poor
serviced at the institution climbed to over fifteen thousand per year,
approximately half of whom came of their own volition. The number of worker-days increased from 30,129 in 1896 to 232,241 only
four years later.[56] At the Gorbov Women's Center, for instance, the
average number of women working every day doubled from 1899
to 1901. There were, of course, other organizations with similar
aims—the Society to Encourage Industriousness and the Guardianship of Work Assistance's own "Moscow Anthill" Society, for
example[57]—but clearly the Workhouse was the city's major institution to combat pauperism, partly by vocational training which
gave the laborer the opportunity to earn wages rather than accept
the dole, and partly by total maintenance and the inculcation of
moral and religious habits and industriousness in its wards. The
Workhouse, the Vocational Center, the workshops, and the programs of vocational training, as well as the libraries, reading rooms,
public readings, picture shows, and holiday concerts, were all meant
to eradicate the debilitating effects of pauperism by restoring the
individual to self-reliance. And self-reliance led to self-improvement
and a more valuable contribution to modern urban and industrial
society or, in the words of the twenty-fifth anniversary chronicle of
the Society to Encourage Industriousness, "the creation of an intelligent, sober, literate, honest workingman . . . a goal dear to every
Russian who wants to see our industry and productivity flourish."[58]
Admittedly, the figures showing the increased numbers serviced by
the Workhouse do not, in and of themselves, demonstrate the institution's effectiveness, but it would not be too sanguine to assume
that some paupers did receive basic relief and that some of those
may have thereby even become self-reliant, industrious, and sober
citizens.

The authority on work relief in Russia, Georgii G. Shvittau, lec-
turer at the University of St. Petersburg and secretary of the journal

55. Beloshapkin, "Rabotnyi dom," 393–94.
56. *Otchet Moskovskoi gorodskoi upravy za 1899* (Moscow, 1900), 205; V. Ger'e,
"Russkaia blagotvoritel'nost' na Vsemirnoi vystavke," *Vestnik Evropy,* 35, no. 8 (August 1900): 494–95; Sharov, *Rabotnyi dom,* 67.
57. *Letopis',* 1, 141, 275–77; *SSS 1901,* 53–60, 241–42.
58. *Letopis',* 276–77.

Trudovaia pomoshch', stated in his two-volume opus that at first the concept was intended not as a new form of public assistance but as an

attempt to plan, develop and regulate that form of assistance which already exists . . . to plant and develop philanthropic activity in Russia based on work relief and especially to wipe out once and for all the current practice of irrational aid and to replace it with more expedient forms of charity and public assistance. . . . Rational organization must precede the establishment of a rational system of welfare and rational organization means combining the activities of various local organizations.[59]

Although in much of the empire the concept of work relief and the Guardianship of Work Assistance and its programs may have been perceived as the idea and organization that could unify welfare services, in Moscow this distinction went to another new organization, trumpeted by its proponents as Russia's most innovative welfare organization, the District Guardianships of the Poor.

THE GUARDIANSHIPS OF THE POOR

The concept of systematic, grass-roots welfare was not altogether new in Russia. In 1846 Count V. F. Solugub and Prince V. F. Odoevskii founded the Society for Visiting the Poor in St. Petersburg as a way to replace indiscriminate almsgiving with personal visiting to determine individual need. In the climate of the late Nicholaevan era, however, the suspicion arose that the society acted as a cover for politics: why else would members be spending their free time visiting the slums and why would the Society have the names and addresses of eight thousand poor people? In 1848 it was placed under the direction of the Imperial Philanthropic Society, a less grass-roots and therefore more respectable and trustworthy organization; seven years later it disbanded.[60] The idea of grass-roots public welfare resurfaced in the 1870s during the Russo-Turkish War when temporary district guardianships to give aid to families of soldiers were established in Moscow.[61]

In considering the proposals of the Ministry of Internal Affairs for devolution of certain welfare services, the Mamontov and Ger'e commissions were both hesitant to accept direction of the Committee to Aid and Investigate Beggars. In St. Petersburg, the city council had

59. Shvittau, *Trudovaia pomoshch'*, 2:3, 10, 149.

60. V. Il'inskii, *Blagotvoritel'nost' v Rossii: Istoriia i nastoiashchee polozhenie* (St. Petersburg, 1908), 15–16.

61. Ministerstvo vnutrennikh del, *Ministerstvo vnutrennikh del: Istoricheskii ocherk*, 2 vols. (St. Petersburg, 1901), 2:148.

decided not to take over this committee. However, the Moscow commissions recommended that in return for removing this burden from
the ministry, the city council receive permission to set up district guardianships of the poor to collect donations, give subsidies to the needy,
and regularly observe those on relief. The city council so requested on
November 12, 1891, and two months later the Council of Ministers
approved and made the approval part of the new City Statutes of that
June.[62] In 1894 a Temporary Statute was approved by the city council
and affirmed by the Ministry of Internal Affairs; it remained in force
for the remainder of the guardianships' existence, that is, until 1917.[63]

One of the major innovations of the guardianships was the decentralization of poor relief, patterned after the system in the German
town of Elberfeld admired by leading European welfare reformers
such as Octavia Hill.[64] Each district of the city had a district guardianship run by a guardian (*popechitel'*) appointed by the city council. The
guardian, in turn, appointed a district council of four to ten members,
each having the approval of the city council, which supervised the
operations of each guardianship.[65] Supported by grants from the city
council, endowment income, membership dues, an annual poor tax
and a dog tax, and special one-shot donations, the guardianships ran
almshouses, free apartments, children's shelters and nurseries, workshops for seamstresses, cafeterias, a Sunday shelter for women laborers, and employment offices.[66] Office duties of the district guardianship councils included, in addition to running the above institutions,
collecting membership dues and contributions, compiling information
on mendicants turned over by the newly formed Municipal Office to
Investigate and Aid Beggars, and determining the amount and form of
aid to be granted to each individual. The guardianships' operations
expanded steadily: during the first years of their existence their annual

62. *PSZ*, 3d ser., 12 (1892), no. 8708; *Vremennoe polozhenie*, 1–7; Moskovskoe
gorodskoe obshchestvennoe upravlenie, *Moskovskoe gorodskoe popechitel'stvo o bednykh v 1895 g.* (Moscow, 1896), 1–2; Shvittau, *Trudovaia pomoshch'*, 1:121.
63. *Popechitel'stvo v 1895 g.*, 1–2.
64. "El'berfel'dskaia sistema prizreniia bednykh," *IMGD*, 19, no. 1 (1895): 17–36.
65. *Ministerstvo vnutrennikh del: Istoricheskii ocherk*, 2:208; *Popechitel'stvo v
1895 g.*, 1–2; "Iz deiatel'nosti Moskovskikh gorodskikh uchastkovykh popechitel'stv o
bednykh," *Sbornik statei*, 4 (1897): 155–56; Moskovskoe gorodskoe obshchestvennoe
upravlenie, *Deiatel'nost' Moskovskikh gorodskikh popechitel'stv o bednykh v 1900 g.*
(Moscow, 1901), 6–8; Ger'e, "Russkaia blagotvoritel'nost'," 495–97.
66. *Deiatel'nost' Moskovskikh gorodskikh popechitel'stv o bednykh v 1900 g.*, 9–
13; *Otchet Moskovskoi gorodskoi upravy za 1901*, 259; and *za 1908*, 224; *Spravochnaia kniga po Moskovskomu gorodskomu obshchestvennomu upravleniiu* (Moscow,
1904), 439.

budget was approximately 250,000 rubles; this more than doubled during the next fifteen years.[67]

The linchpin of the system, as both proponents and critics agreed, was the volunteer caseworkers (*sotrudniki*), appointed by each district council. The volunteer caseworkers did the real legwork of the guardianships: they were charged with doing the bulk of the secretarial and office work, surveying each building in their district, making a list of all the needy, recommending the amount and form of relief in each case, dispensing the aid, studying the poor and the causes of poverty, helping the poor to help themselves, and finally, being a "good neighbor."[68] During the first three years of the guardianships' existence, approximately two thousand volunteers, about half of whom were women, served the organization. The individual volunteer caseworker would of course be guided by the advice of experts and professionals. For example, the Guardianship of the Poor in one of the city's wealthiest districts (Prechistenka), what might be called a flagship guardianship, lauded the groups of caseworkers as

key intermediaries between the individual caseworker and the Guardianship Council. No matter how capable or experienced the individual caseworker may be, the group looks at the problem from all sides and removes the personal and unpredictable element which acts in each evaluation of individual cases by the volunteer. Thus, the group brings a certain social element to the work of the volunteers, by removing the random and the subjective and by habituating them to mutual supervision (*vzaimnyi kontrol'*) and subordination of their actions to certain uniform principles.[69]

The use of volunteer caseworkers permitted a greater emphasis on "open" or "outdoor" aid, that is, relief provided outside of institutions such as the Foundling Home, the Workhouse, or almshouses. Although the use of open relief was criticized on the grounds that it permitted misuse of that relief by the poor,[70] the consensus was that open relief was the raison d'être of the organization.[71] Such outdoor relief took one or a combination of several forms: money allowances, rent and food subsidies, provision of firewood and clothes, payment

67. *Sbornik ocherkov*, 28; N. V. Nesmeianov, "Material'nye zatrudneniia," 2:447.
68. *Otchet Moskovskogo gorodskogo popechitel'stva o bednykh Prechistenskoi chasti* (Moscow, 1895), 4–12; E. Sabashnikova, "Iz deiatel'nosti moskovskikh gorodskikh uchastkovykh popechitel'stv o bednykh za 1897 g.," *IMGD*, 23, no. 1 (February 1899): 5.
69. *Otchet Moskovskogo gorodskogo popechitel'stva o bednykh Prechistenskoi chasti* (Moscow 1900), 8.
70. S. R. , "Moskovskie popechitel'stva o bednykh," *Trudovaia pomoshch'*, 2, no. 6 (June 1899): 88.
71. *Popechitel'stvo v 1895 g.*, 15; Ger'e, "Russkaia blagotvoritel'nost'," 510.

for passport, doctor's fees, hospital tax, medicine, burials, a peasant's return trip to the village, and finally, assistance in finding employment.[72] Many of the payments in kind or indirect cash payments evolved from the conviction of reformers that direct money handouts would be spent on drink or abused by "professional" beggars. Hence the guardianship dispensed indirect cash payments, such as apartment rents, doctor's fees, or clothes, as well as an early form of "food stamps" redeemable only at certain canteens. Despite the preference for payments in kind rather than in cash, records of the guardianships show that in the early years three-quarters of the aid was in cash.[73] Likewise, despite the preference for outdoor over indoor relief, during the first four years of the guardianship, the proportion of expenditures on outdoor relief declined from 70 percent to 39 percent while the proportion of indoor relief increased from 24 percent to 56 percent.[74]

The emphasis on open relief, the use of volunteer caseworkers, and the decentralization of the guardianships were meant to end what many reformers referred to as excessively impersonal or "bureaucratic" welfare organizations. P. N. Obninskii criticized the impersonality of much private and state charity in the pages of *Russkaia mysl'*. Charity of the "lady-patrons of high society," Obninskii claimed, was usually limited to shelters, almshouses, and meetings. Such charity was characterized by decorum, custom, vanity, and calculation: Obninskii called it "absentee (*zaochnaia*) charity—impersonal and colorless." A whole series of intermediaries allegedly stood between the giver and the recipient, and although an outsider could see luxurious model hospitals and shelters and societies with big names in their charters, nowhere did one see the Good Samaritan. The district guardianships, however, did offer something new: the individualization of charity.[75]

Another critic of "bureaucratic" charity was the city councilman and history professor at Moscow University, Vladimir I. Ger'e. On the pages of *Vestnik Evropy*, Ger'e argued that the well-funded institutions and large offices

of course have eagerly recruited new members and benefactors, but the immediate aim of such member-benefactors has been thereby to attain an honored

72. *Popechitel'stvo v 1895 g.*, 15–30.

73. Ger'e, "Russkaia blagotvoritel'nost'," 511.

74. "Moskovskie gorodskie popechitel'stva o bednykh v 1898," *Trudovaia pomoshch'*, 3, no. 6 (June 1900): 77; S. R., "Moskovskie popechitel'stva," 78–80, 88; Ger'e, "Russkaia blagotvoritel'nost'," 510.

75. P. N. Obninskii, "Chego nedostaet nashei blagotvoritel'nosti?" *Russkaia mysl'*, 20, no. 1, (January 1899): 87–90; *Materialy*, 18.

position in an administrative (*sluzhebnaia*) career; this has accordingly not changed the bureaucratic character of these institutions. On the other hand, such an organization has made welfare offices better able to establish permanent charitable or educational institutions than to cope tirelessly with constantly changing everyday local needs.[76]

Ger'e cited the Imperial Philanthropic Society as an example of a charitable society that had started out with the ideal of close contact with the needy but that had turned into a bureaucratic organization as council and institutional care more and more replaced persons visiting the needy.[77]

The district guardianship, on the other hand, marked the passing from the stage of indiscriminate almsgiving and institutional relief to a new stage of public concern:

Benefactors should not be invisible to the needy but should be among them and know them personally. They should bring help to where it's needed, not wait for a petitioner to knock on the office door with a written request. They must provide help not by resolutions written in a folder of petitions handed to them by secretaries but by serious consideration of actual need, guided by personal experience. . . . Being more grass-roots, the guardianships don't place paper work (*deloproizvodstvo*) above life, and they recruit people for whom charity is not an office job (*sluzhebnoe zaniatie*) but a personal and public calling.[78]

If this sounds a bit pompous or self-serving, remember the capewoman. According to Golitsynskii, the cape-woman

tries to look as poor as possible when going to the office of the charity society because she knows that the worse she looks, the more likely she is to get help. The officials are usually petty aristocrats who have no idea what need is, but who surely won't believe her if she is neat and clean in appearance. . . . If this doesn't work, a daughter, niece or grand-daughter miraculously appears and rare is the official who can turn this down![79]

Critics of impersonal or "bureaucratic" poor relief were finding fault not only with allegedly careerist charity officials. The adjective "bureaucratic" was frequently a code word, and criticism was directed against excessive state involvement in local affairs. Both Ger'e and Evgenii Maksimov, a member of the Guardianship Council of Work Assistance and another proponent of the guardianships, were on record as advocating local public control over welfare. In a long dissent-

76. Ger'e, "Russkaia blagotvoritel'nost'," 505.
77. Ibid.
78. Ibid., 518.
79. Golitsynskii, *Ulichnye tipy*, 10.

ing memorandum, Ger'e criticized the Grot Commission for placing too much emphasis on state activity in the proposals for welfare reorganization.[80] In his *Vestnik Evropy* article Ger'e reiterated that systematic struggle against need could be carried on only by public organs such as the city councils and zemstvos.[81] Maksimov likewise compared excessive central government control and the concomitant lack of initiative and flexibility with local government control and individualized aid.[82]

Such grass-roots decentralized relief, where the form and amount of aid were to be determined by experience and the individual approach rather than by "resolutions," required coordination, registration, and integration. Soon after the creation of the guardianships, the city council established with the approval of the Ministry of Internal Affairs a Council of Charities (Blagotvoritel'nyi sovet), which commenced operations in 1899. The major function of the Council of Charities was to assist and coordinate the activities of all of the city's charitable organizations and in particular to integrate the activity of the guardianships with that of other agencies. To accomplish this the council organized an Information Office to gather information on all welfare activities as well as to register the poor and maintain files on all the city's welfare cases.[83] By sending questionnaires to the guardianships and to other charitable agencies, in 1900 the Information Office had registered more than 17,000 persons, a figure that was to increase to 25,000 by 1908. Additional functions of the Council of Charities were periodically publishing statistical information on charity in Moscow, maintaining a library of books on charity, organizing conferences on welfare, and holding periodic meetings.[84]

This "correct" approach to welfare, as one of the municipality's annual reports put it,[85] was designed not only to spread information on common problems, avoid overlapping services, and publicize the guardianships, but also to discriminate between the deserving and undeserving poor in the dispensing of relief. Thus poor relief was to achieve two important objectives of welfare everywhere at the end of

80. Ger'e, "Zapiska," 55–81.
81. Ger'e, "Russkaia blagotvoritel'nost'," 512.
82. Maksimov, *Proiskhozhdenie nishchenstva*, 118.
83. *Otchet Moskovskoi gorodskoi upravy za 1899* (Moscow, 1900), 217; M. Dukhovskoi, "Vzaimodeistvie blagotvoritel'nykh uchrezhdenii v Moskve," *Trudovaia pomoshch'*, 3, no. 5 (May 1900), 462–63.
84. *Otchet Moskovskoi gorodskoi upravy za 1900*, 230–33; and *za 1908*, 258.
85. *Otchet Moskovskoi gorodskoi upravy za 1899*, 217.

the nineteenth century: systematic organization and rationalized services. Moscow's muzhiks for generations had allegedly been taking advantage of the absence of systematic charity leading ultimately, according to one author, to the propagation of the species: "Our welfare system, or rather, the absence of any system, affects the poor as rain affects mushrooms—it multiplies them."[86] Indeed, a major function of the guardianships was not so much the provision of new forms of relief as the systematization of aid; thus welfare could be controlled and no longer left to chance or to the generous but undiscriminating Muscovite. In the words of the guardianships' first annual report, "the hardest task of the guardianships is the struggle against beggars and against the habits of indiscriminant handouts of Muscovites."[87]

Such rational discrimination, in which the volunteer caseworker had a very important role to play, was intended to promote character regeneration, a benefit both to the recipient and to the donor of charity. The honest recipient, at one level, could be helped to figure out the labyrinth of charitable organizations. The dishonest potential recipient could be caught, presumably a benefit not only to society at large but to the "deserving poor."[88] But most important, rationally administered relief would help the laboring population to help itself. It was widely assumed that the poor, and indeed most of the laboring population, were improvident, weak-willed, and dishonest. Rational aid, unlike indiscriminate almsgiving, on the one hand, and impersonalized repression, on the other, would demonstrate to the needy the attitudes and behavior that were rewarded and those that were punished in modern society.[89]

The guardianships in general and the rational administration of relief and promise of character reformation in particular were also beneficial in subtle ways to the benefactors. Defenders of the guardianships claimed that this new decentralized, grass-roots organization had "enlisted widespread enthusiastic support" and had "rejuvenated

86. Odynets, *Dom trudoliubiia*, 2:28–29. See also Linev, *Prichiny russkogo nishchenstva*, 244; Levenstim, *Professional'noe nishchenstvo*, 25–30; Maksimov, *Proiskhozhdenie nishchenstva*, 19–20.

87. *Otchet Moskovskogo gorodskogo popechitel'stva o bednykh za 1895 g.* (Moscow, 1896), 53. See also S. R., "Moskovskie popechitel'stva," 90; and *Otchet Moskovskoi gorodskoi upravy za 1900*, 229.

88. S. N. Khrushchev, "Edinie blagotvoritel'nye obshchestva v Sankt-Peterburge," S"ezd po obshchestvennomu prizreniiu, *Trudy*, 239.

89. Maksimov, *Proiskhozhdenie nishchenstva*, 11, 73; N. Ezerskii, "Zadachi gorodskikh popechitel'stv," *Trudovaia pomoshch'*, 4, no. 5 (May 1901): 566; *Popechitel'stvo v 1895*, 10–14.

welfare in the city."[90] The success of the organization in Moscow was to have a demonstration effect, and Moscow was already becoming a model of welfare organization for the entire empire. Moreover, rational administration of relief was meant to assure the giver that his charity was being used properly, particularly since it was widely assumed that beggars spent their alms on drink. An account of the concept of giving food stamps for free meals instead of pocket change to the needy on the street argued that "this way the benefactor would be certain that the goal of feeding the poor by alms would be achieved and that the money he gave in Christ's name wouldn't go for drink."[91] Finally, Muscovites would benefit from the "study of poverty and the closer contact with it." Bringing rich and poor closer together would have an uplifting effect both on caseworkers and on the director of the district office, who would become a "true guardian to his poor."[92]

THE SHORTCOMINGS OF REFORM AND REGENERATION IN PRACTICE

As with reforms in the Russian economy or political system at the beginning of the twentieth century, it is very difficult to evaluate the success or failure of the efforts at individual and social reform of Moscow's muzhiks. The phrases "too little and too late," "extenuating circumstances," "the war," "Russia's traditions," so often encountered when evaluating the Stolypin reforms, economic growth, and the October Manifesto, apply equally well when evaluating slum renovation, poor relief, and the formation of a sturdy urban citizenry. As the previous chapter indicated, modest improvements were noticed at Khitrov Square, for example. Furthermore, the city, admittedly belatedly, began construction and maintenance of free lodging houses. Expenditures in medical care and welfare increased at the beginning of the twentieth century.

Yet the agencies and institutions of poor relief seem more effective on the pages of laconic annual accounts and sympathetic journals than

90. *Popechitel'stvo v 1895*, 33; I. L. Goremykin, then minister of internal affairs, in a circular of 1898, quoted in P. N. Litvinov, "O lichnom sostave gorodskikh popechitel'stv," S"ezd po obshchestvennomu prizreniiu, *Trudy*, 248. See also Ger'e, "Russkaia blagotvoritel'nost'," 509; and Nesmeianov, "Material'nye zatrudneniia," 447.

91. *Letopis'*, 73. See also *Otchet Moskovskogo gorodskogo popechitel'stva o bednykh Prechistenskoi chasti za 1895*, 22.

92. *Popechitel'stvo v 1895 g.*, 33; M. Dukhovskoi, "Gorodskie popechitel'stva o bednykh v Moskve," *Trudovaia pomoshch'*, 1, no. 1 (November 1897): 71, 74.

they were in reality. The ideas of individual and social reform were easier to express in theory than to realize in practice. Welfare in Moscow, even "reformed" welfare ca. 1900, was not without its critics, and shortcomings in the nature of the organization and institutions themselves, as well as in their relationship to broader social and economic problems, made them decidedly an "outside world" to the city's muzhiks.

Funds were, of course, a perennial problem, although it is odd that at a time when, as historians have pointed out, Moscow was in the forefront of Russian cities in the municipalization of such city services as the stockyards and the streetcars, the city council was reluctant to subsidize low-cost housing.[93] Unfortunately, as contemporaries lamented and as Michael Hamm and James Bater have argued recently, fiscal difficulties of the municipal government, such as those indicated in chapter 1, were an important constraint to ambitious projects of housing construction, slum renovation, and welfare reform.[94] Although there was a threefold increase in municipal welfare expenditures from 1894 to 1908, welfare expenditures were greatly exceeded by medical and educational expenditures. Almost one-third of the municipal welfare budget of 1,420,778 rubles in 1908, for example, went for upkeep of the Workhouse. By contrast, 82,472 rubles were spent on free apartment buildings, and less than 40,000 rubles on lodging houses.[95] The fund-eating of large institutions—schools, hospitals, the Workhouse—left little for housing and slum renovation. A lack of funds, particularly from private donations, likewise plagued the Guardianships of the Poor. After an initial spurt of private donations, a decline in contributions was noticed by 1900. The dog tax of the city council contributed little, and a poor tax, which allegedly "smacked of socialism," repeatedly met strong opposition in the city council. Finally, because fund-raising activities such as concerts were sponsored by many charitable organizations, "everyone grew tired of them."[96]

Many historians have noted that Russian city government was

93. Hanchett, "Moscow in the Late Nineteenth Century," 341–69; Bater, "Some Dimensions of Urbanization," 60–63.
94. Hamm, "Breakdown," 186, 197; Bater, "Some Dimensions of Urbanization," 60–63.
95. *Sbornik ocherkov,* 112–13; *Otchet Moskovskoi gorodskoi upravy za 1908,* 314.
96. Ezerskii, "Zadachi," 287–90; *Otchet Moskovskogo gorodskogo popechitel'stva o bednykh Prechistenskoi chasti za 1900,* 14–15.

characterized by apathy, indifference, and lack of genuine independence from the central authorities.[97] Although civic consciousness was arguably stronger in Moscow than in many other cities, apathy did hurt particularly the guardianships of the poor, which were dependent on active public support. N. I. Ezerskii claimed that by 1900 they were no longer a new and fashionable phenomenon, that they had become ignored by the press, and that few people were interested in working for them. In one of the wealthiest and best-educated districts, for example, only 1,752 out of some 50,000 residents contributed to the guardianships; most of these gave money, and only 100 were volunteer workers.[98] Ezerskii argued that the indifference faced by the guardianships was caused by the lack of discipline in Russian society, the lack of a sense of civic duty, and the low priority of public affairs.[99]

Whatever the degree of civic duty, the fact remains that the guardianships were organized so that broad public participation would be carefully controlled. Although proponents of the guardianships had criticized the excessively "bureaucratic" nature of much of Russian charity, and although the guardianships were praised because they "opened" charitable activities to the public, in fact the city council's selection of the District Guardian was as close as the "public" got to the matter. Once the city council had appointed each district's guardian, the further development of the guardianship depended on him, since he appointed the members of the district council, who in turn selected the volunteer caseworkers. The latter had no voice in running the district office.[100]

Since so much of the responsibility for the success of a district's guardianship rested on the guardian, such an appointment was crucial. A well-qualified guardian, however, was not easy to find. Given the large amount of time, the tedious work, the absence of salary or rank that came with the job, the guardian had to be already financially secure. The city council further narrowed the field of candidates by ignoring women. Neither personal satisfaction nor honor nor good conscience for fulfilling a public duty were highly regarded: "The title

97. Hamm, "Breakdown," 187; William L. Blackwell, "Modernization and Urbanization in Russia: A Comparative View," in Hamm, ed. *The City,* 313; Bater, "Some Dimensions of Urbanization," 60–63.

98. *Otchet Moskovskogo gorodskogo popechitel'stva o bednykh Prechistenskoi chasti za 1900,* 14–15; Ezerskii, "Zadachi," 295–96.

99. Ezerskii, "Zadachi," 290–91.

100. Ibid., 283.

District Guardian is worthless at the county fair of vanity."[101] Worse was the status of the volunteer caseworkers. According to the provisions of the Temporary Statute, having voting rights only in cases directly concerning them and being invited to monthly guardianship council meetings only if needed, the volunteer workers had no say in general policy. Yet they were precisely those who had the experience and expertise to make a valuable contribution.[102] This had three undesirable consequences. First, the guardianships experienced a steady loss in volunteers, from 1,706 in their first year (1895) to 1,102 fifteen years later. This loss was particularly noticeable for men. Although the loss was attributed to a combination of factors, including insufficient funds and disillusionment with the organizations's achievements, the ambiguous but largely unfavorable status of the volunteer workers was considered most influential.[103] Second, a guardianship that was understaffed or that misallocated the expertise of its caseworkers was more prone to exploitation by the "undeserving" but "cunning" poor; this defeated a major purpose of the organization.[104] Third, given the narrow field of matters in which the volunteer workers could express a voice, the guardianships, lauded as an organization that could integrate the city's charities, turned out to be atomized themselves. The lack of common interests among the volunteers or among the different district guardianships meant that "each orphanage or cafeteria run by the guardianship is a closed institution, inaccessible to outside judgment and known only by laconic annual reports."[105] This atomization, moreover, was complicated by the fact that guardianships in wealthier districts were better off than those in poor districts, a discrepancy for which the city council had no institutional means to remedy.[106]

As often happens with new organizations in traditional society, the guardianships had an image problem. The sixth annual report of one of the most active district guardianships admitted that many people did not know that the organization existed or had no idea what it did; others believed it to be another private charity not open to outsiders. These problems presumably applied to Muscovites; one wonders how

101. Ibid., 284–85.
102. Ibid., 286.
103. *Sovremennoe khoziaistvo*, 217.
104. *Otchet Moskovskogo gorodskogo popechitel'stva o bednykh Prechistenskoi chasti za 1900*, 14–15.
105. Ezerskii, "Zadachi," 291–92.
106. Ger'e, "Russkaia blagotvoritel'nost'," 512. In a similar vein, see also Kudriavtsev's critique of the Elberfeld system. (A. Kudriavtsev, *Nishchenstvo, kak predmet popecheniia tserkvi, obshchestva i gosudarstva* [Odessa, 1885], 78.)

many muzhiks knew of the existence or understood the functions of the guardianships.[107]

The Workhouse, too, had an image problem. It is doubtful that the peasants and city poor understood what the Vocational Center was, or even what the long Russian word *trudoliubie* meant. "We have heard on more than one occasion," one critic wrote, "that many call [the Vocational Center] Trudoliubov's Building, thereby taking it for a private establishment owned by a Mr. Trudoliubov."[108] Significantly, it was the newer, more reformist institution that was poorly understood; the nature and function of "Rabotnyi dom," the older, more punitive, and less reformist Workhouse, was perfectly clear in the popular mind, especially of those who had firsthand experience with the Workhouse.

One of the most intimate glimpses of life at the Workhouse came from the writer Semen P. Podiachev who, while no Dickens, left behind a fictional account of his own time in the Workhouse in 1901. Titled *Mytarstvo* (The Ordeal), the novella paints a gloomy picture of the abusive treatment, poor maintenance, and lack of work at the Workhouse. Although it might be suspected that Podiachev might not have been the most impartial observer, the Workhouse administration conceded that "in general Podiachev's sketch left an impression of indubious veracity."[109] The sleeping quarters, a huge room filled with cots with a single aisle in the middle, "made one rather melancholic. Everything was gray: gray walls, gray blankets, gray floor, gray ceiling, and even the light shining through the window somehow seemed gray."[110] One of Podiachev's fellow wards, who had been reading about the Workhouse in the Moscow papers, expressed his view of the cultural amenities:

Believe me, I was moved to tears, it was so well written! And the cleanliness, you know, and the amount of fresh air, you know, and a separate bed for everyone, eh, and first-rate dining tables, and almost a pound of meat per person, and soon even a concert hall, and they'll start showing pictures! Well, tell me for God's sake, wouldn't you go right now and look at that, eh? Will we ever see that?[111]

107. *Otchet Moskovskogo gorodskogo popechitel'stva o bednykh Prechistenskoi chasti za 1900*, 14–15.
108. A. Gorovtsev, "Tsel' i naznachenie domov trudoliubiia," 500.
109. *The Ordeal* was originally published in *Russkoe bogatstvo* in August and September 1902. The reaction to the novella may be found in Beloshapkin, "Moskovskii Rabotnyi dom," 325–26.
110. Podiachev, "Mytarstvo," 34–36.
111. Ibid., 75.

If Podiachev's description is accurate, it is hard to imagine paupers engaging in cultural activities at the Workhouse. It is also hard to imagine the indigent realizing their full potential of purposeful labor. Though vocational training and the opportunity to earn wages, trumpeted by proponents, were seemingly innocuous forms of aid, such relief was not without great difficulties. Workshops were often poorly equipped, the market was erratic, and the work, especially for those who were most in need of job training, was often not more than unskilled "outside" labor on public works projects and on construction sites, garbage and snow removal, and heavy work in freight yards. "Inside jobs" were performed at special workshops for those already skilled in certain trades (shoemaking, metalworking, carpentry) or at general workshops for the unskilled (such as gluing cartons and envelopes, sewing on hooks and buttons, weaving baskets, washing linen).[112] If there was no work available, which was not unusual, according to Podiachev, the wards idly waited in the dormitories or cafeteria:

The unskilled laborers were not mechanics, not cabinetmakers, not really craftsmen at all.... Somehow there was always work for those. But the unskilled laborers had to wait until a group of them was needed on the railroads, in the freight yards, or at some such place.[113]

Another critic called the Workhouse a "den of idleness, where sloth jeers at industriousness," and claimed that in the early days of the "reorganized" Workhouse, the wards spent only one-third of the actual workdays at work.[114] Admittedly, such proportions did increase in later annual reports, although with an impressive accounting skill in "deducting" various categories of nonworkable workdays. In addition, the annual reports reveal that even wards of the Vocational Center, which presumably provided skilled jobs or job training, spent considerable time on unskilled jobs. In 1902, for instance, only 33 percent of the workdays at the Vocational Center were spent in any of the workshops, and in most years it is hard to see a distinct work pattern at the Vocational Center.[115]

The artisan or "former artisan" population at the Vocational Center presented problems even when appropriate work was avail-

112. *Otchet Moskovskogo gorodskogo Rabotnogo doma za 1897*, 89–90; and ...
za 1898, 23–25.
113. Podiachev, "Mytarstvo," 75.
114. I. Tarasov, "Moskovskii Gorodskoi Rabotnyi dom," *Russkoe obozrenie*, 43, no. 1 (January 1896): 337, 347.
115. *Otchet Rabotnogo doma za 1902*, 24.

able. Some reformers argued that despite the recognition that work could become ennobling only when meaningful, if work were *too* attractive, the more skilled workers would lose their will to hunt for jobs on their own. Moreover, it was occasionally acknowledged that the craftsmen were the hardest to discipline and reform. In words reminiscent of Andrew Ure and many other proponents of the factory system in the early nineteenth century, A. Gorovtsev stated that craftsmen were lazy, alcoholic, insolent (*buinyi*), and poor workers.[116] Nevertheless, the independent peasant producer was clearly the occupational ideal of the Workhouse, the Vocational Center, and affiliated agencies and institutions. Aid to artisans and village craftsmen was explicit in the charter of the Guardianship of Work Assistance.[117] Given that Moscow was the empire's most important production and distribution center for consumption and luxury goods, that the village craftsman looking for work or for a market for his wares was likely to be attracted to Moscow, and that 90 percent of the province's registered master artisans, journeymen, and apprentices resided in the city, aid to the cottage industry was sensible.[118] In the long run, however, self-employment was not the wave of the future in manufacturing, retailing, or services, and the already drenched village craftsman was no more able to face the storms of the industrial cycle. In fact, it was argued that the Workhouse and Vocational Centers, subsidized for noneconomic reasons, competed with the private market and undermined the marginal artisans and craftsmen, who then became candidates for work relief, starting a vicious circle.[119]

If the sketchy data on recidivism are any indication, too many of those on relief were unable to set out on the path of self-reliance and love of work. Over a ten-year period at the Workhouse recidivism ranged from 30 to 70 percent. Officials repeatedly blamed the lack of job training or even useful labor—presumably the raison d'être of the institution—as being responsible for the fact that former wards were right back on the street after being released.[120] But this explanation,

116. Gorovtsev, "O rabotakh v domakh trudoliubiia," 141–42, 150. For Andrew Ure's opinion of the alleged difficulties encountered in training and disciplining craftsmen, see *The Philosophy of Manufactures*, 15–16, 19–21.

117. *PSZ*, 3d ser., 26 (1906), pt. 1, no. 27814.

118. TsGIA, f. 1290, op. 5, d. 195, ll. 1–15; and f. 1290, op. 5 d. 256, ll. 39–44.

119. This criticism is tempered by the fact that most orders for the Vocational Center were sent largely from other charitable institutions and hospitals. See Gorovtsev, "O rabotakh," 152.

120. Sharov, *Rabotnyi dom*, 3; Krotkov, "Doma trudoliubiia," 68–69; *Moskovskii Listok*, no. 25 (January 30, 1913), 2; Shvittau, *Trudovaia pomoshch'*, 1:122–24; Aleksandr Kraevskii, *Vopros o nishchenstve i ob organizatsii blagotvoritel'nosti v Moskve* (Moscow, 1899), 11–12; "Doklad ob ustroistve i soderzhanii kvartir," 2. Recidivism

true as far as it went, somewhat missed the point. The preponderance of unskilled laborers and unemployed artisans and domestics in the Workhouse or at Khitrov Square reflected the peasants' desperate need for supplemental income and the importance of a casual labor force in the booming metropolitan economy, not the absence of industriousness or self-reliance. Reformers may have decried the lack of craft skills, but the city economy demanded that the unskilled keep on coming.[121] Given that the demand for odd jobs in the construction and transport trades, retailing and services, carting and hauling, as well as in domestic service and manufacturing, was great but erratic, laborers entered into seemingly more casual personal and community relationships. Seventy percent of the male population of the entire city did not live with other members of their own family—not because of depravity but because of economic necessity or advantage.[122] The effectiveness of the Workhouse, the Vocational Center, and slum renovation in combatting unemployment, promoting self-reliance, or reducing the concentration of casual laborers was dependent on forces beyond the control of reformers.

Shortage of funds, among other things, limited the size of operations of even the largest welfare programs, which in turn limited the accessibility of the needy to relief in the city. For example, although many contemporary studies of the Workhouse focused on those *admitted,* in fact most people who applied for admission to the Vocational Center were *rejected.* In 1904, 1905, and 1909, for instance, 73 percent, 63 percent, and 68 percent, respectively, of those who showed up at the waiting room of the Workhouse were denied permission to stay.[123] The records of the Vocational Center provide an illustrative example of an applicant who was rejected several times before being admitted:

P. is a forty-three-year-old widowed peasant from Tula who has lived in Moscow for twenty-one years. Between 1898 and 1907 he was frequently

---

was a problem that also plagued the city's lodging houses. TsGAM, f. 179 op. 21, d. 1715, l. 60; Moskovskoe gorodskoe obshchestvennoe upravlenie, *Otchet o deiatel'nosti gorodskogo nochlezhnogo doma im. F. Ia. Ermakova* (Moscow, 1912), 4, and (Moscow, 1913), 18; Moskovskoe gorodskoe obshchestvennoe upravlenie, *Otchet o bednykh Khitrova rynka* (11 vols., Moscow, 1904–1915); and the surveys cited in chapter 7, note 110.

121. *Otchet Rabotnogo doma za 1909,* 36.
122. *PVP,* 24a, pt. 1, 4–7. See also the discussion in chapter 6.
123. *Otchet Rabotnogo doma za 1905,* 21; and *za 1909,* 25, 38. See also Sharov, "Kharakteristika," 15, 19; Sharov, *Rabotnyi dom,* 70; Raevskii, "K voprosu," 80; and *Sbornik ocherkov,* 28.

convicted of theft and was sentenced to prison five times. In 1911–12 the police turned P. over to the workhouse a few times for begging, but the Main Office didn't give him vocational training. P. came to Vocational Center voluntarily for the first time in November, 1912, but because it was full, he was not admitted.[124]

Accessibility to the city's welfare services was complicated by moral objections. Here, the attitudes of the authorities and professionals in Moscow were not unlike those of their counterparts in Europe and America, where welfare was (and still is) often regarded as promoting immoral behavior. After the 1884 sanitary inspection of lodging houses recommended construction of additional municipal units, the city council rejected a proposal of the executive board to build four new units, declaring that lodging houses sheltered

people not worthy of any special attention save for police measures concerning their ways of life and behavior. The police itself jumps on them as on wild beasts because otherwise there is no way to track down these harmful troublemakers. They either beg or go out at night looking for booty. Philanthropy from the city will just encourage drunkenness, idleness and sloth; therefore it is better to let the lodgers take care of themselves.[125]

For a long time the problems of the slum dwellers and itinerant laborers were not recognized as urgent in and of themselves. In Moscow, as in European and American cities, the catalyst to public activism was the threat to public health—both the moral and physical health of the rest of the city. It will be recalled that concern for the housing situation originated in the fear of worsening health standards and of infectious epidemics. The slum's lodging houses and overcrowded apartments were seen as breeding grounds for disease and depravity. Overcrowding per se did not horrify the police as much as did the undesirable consequences of honest laborers forced to cohabit with criminals, alcoholics, and prostitutes. Typhoid and cholera per se did not horrify the city council as much as did the spread of disease throughout the city: only after repeated outbreaks or threats of epidemics and several investigations did the city council propose extensive housing construction.

Despite the reluctant involvement of the municipality in the provision of low-cost housing as part of an effort to improve public health, accessibility to the city's welfare services was further complicated by

124. Sharov, "Kharakteristika," 1–36.
125. Quoted in Pozner, "Nochlezhnye doma," 19. See also Kishkin, "Zhilishchnyi vopros," 296.

the unending stream of immigration. The authorities feared, as was suggested in the preceding chapter, that Moscow's welfare services would be overrun by the needy from the villages and, accordingly, argued that their care was not the responsibility of the municipality. When the police proposed the provision of low-cost housing in 1863, the city council replied:

> The city is obliged to take measures to safeguard public health insofar as such measures concern the well-being of all members of the city community as a whole, and not any separate group of persons, particularly when such persons, as in the present case, are not directly linked with the city's interest; the majority of the lodgers, as is apparent from the above report, are not inhabitants of the city but belong to nonlocal associations.[126]

Although such an attitude was born in earlier, less consciously reformist times, it influenced policy at the highest levels at the beginning of the twentieth century. At the insistence of the Ministry of Internal Affairs, residency requirements were written into the Temporary Statute of the Guardianships of the Poor. At the inauguration of the guardianships in 1894, the governor-general, Prince V. A. Dolgorukov, cautioned that eligibility for relief was to be limited so that

> the care of paupers be distributed only for those born in Moscow or Moscow province and for those who have lived in the capital at least two years so that the establishment of the guardianships not serve to further the influx of paupers from other provinces into Moscow.[127]

The governor-general suggested that provincial zemstvos take responsibility for the maintenance of municipal institutions serving the nonnative population or those outside the jurisdiction of the local guardianship councils.[128] The regulation remained unchanged as late as 1914.[129] Simultaneously, the police continued to expel beggars and vagrants without a valid passport and Moscow residence permit. These regulations and practices may have been justified on the grounds that, particularly in the aftermath of Russia's worst famine, municipal lodging houses, the Workhouse, and other welfare services were already overburdened and would attract more immigrants. Shortages of low-cost housing, for example, were one reason why so many itinerant peasant

126. "Doklad ob ustroistve i soderzhanii kvartir," 6.
127. TsGAM, f. 184, op. 2, d. 852, l. 57. Additional problems presented by the residency requirements are discussed in Sergei Speranskii, "O proekte reformy obshchestvennogo prizreniia v Rossii," *Trudovaia pomoshch'*, 1, no. 7 (May 1898): 37–40.
128. TsGAM, f. 184, op. 2, d. 852, ll. 29–30.
129. *Otchet Moskovskoi gorodskoi upravy za 1908*, 219; Nesmeianov, "Material'nye zatrudneniia," 459–60.

laborers left families at home. The settlement in Moscow of yet more peasant dependents would have placed even more strain on the inadequate municipal facilities. At the same time, housing shortages contributed to the transience of residence, the tenuousness of family ties, and the concomitant cycle of disease, depravity, and demoralization, the very habits the authorities were trying to eradicate. Thus many newcomers who may have been the most in need of aid or, allegedly, of character regeneration were the least likely to receive it.

The city was not successful in wiping out the slum, for example, in part because of insufficiently vigorous efforts of the city itself. However, even assuming that moral, fiscal, political, or jurisdictional constraints had not prevented the city from being more activist, the nature of the slum community itself, and in particular the dualities examined in the previous chapter, made Khitrov market all but immune to renovation. In the first place, to a greater degree than the authorities and reformers were willing to admit, Khitrov market was a microcosm of the city as a whole. The very transience of residence and the gravitation of not only migrant laborers but presumably more settled artisans and tradesmen to the slum were dictated by the needs of the metropolitan economy itself. But the signs of alleged occupational and family dislocation which the authorities attributed to the city's indigent were in fact characteristic of almost three-quarters of Moscow's population. Since the municipal authorities and reformers had no control over the metropolitan, much less the national, economy, or over the unceasing stream of migration into Moscow, which averaged more than 100,000 persons per year between 1882 and 1902, eradication of the evils of the slum were highly unlikely.

Bonds of shared occupations and neighborhoods, values, and culture among the city's laborers further complicated the task of renovation—whether of slums or of character. Artisans, tradesmen, and even the itinerant laborers constituted more of a community than the authorities and professionals realized. Artisans and tradesmen produced and distributed goods for the larger part of the slum population, that is, for the common laborers. Proprietors of food, drinking, and lodging establishments provided essential services to all other workers. Even more disturbing from the point of view of the authorities and reformers, the slum population and indeed large numbers of the city's "lower orders" were apparently not developing a stake in the city and a commitment to the values of those who were trying to help them. Occasional glimpses of life in the slum show that the values of the authorities were frequently in conflict with those of the very people they were trying to help. For example, in January 1872 the Society to Encourage Industriousness first considered the idea of opening a soup kitchen in Khitrov Square. It was thought that the "insufficiency of hot, healthy meals among the working class brings with it epidemic diseases and alcoholism." When the first soup kitchen opened in February, not only were the local tavern keepers understandably opposed, but the residents themselves were suspicious of the new eating habits and came only reluctantly.[130]

The value system of the slum community and the suspicion of the authorities rendered enforcement of the law almost impossible. Municipal investigators and police alike were convinced that those picked up at Khitrov market for vagrancy or begging, even if expelled from the city to their place of residence, would soon be back. The underworld went about its business under the "canopy" by bribing the nearby policemen. Because proprietors of the lodging houses took in immigrants without proper city residence permits, rare was the "honest but unsuspecting laborer" who, especially if his papers were not in order, would complain to the police about crime or health conditions of the lodging houses. The city police officials hoped to reduce the number of vagrants and criminals, prevent the illicit liquor trade and gambling, and improve sanitary conditions by their ordinary rounds and periodic searches. But all measures were rendered ineffective by the Khitrov population itself. The policemen on the beat always knew when a search was coming and tipped off the building superintendents. The proprietors did their best to protect the *baryshniki* from the police. Before the police inspectors ever came, the vodka and stolen goods and tools were hidden, the women left the men's rooms, and the "illegals" hid under the stoves, on the roofs, in the garbage, or fled out the back door. Thus proprietors or sublessors were rarely fined for overcrowding, for harboring criminals or persons without residence permits, or for running an illegal workshop in the rooms of the lodging houses. Sanitary physicians and public health officials were not viewed any differently than were the police:

No sooner would someone shout that a doctor was around, than the apartments would be swept up, the windows and doors would be opened, and the pillows, blankets, and linen would be carried out and hidden in the shed.

130. *Letopis'*, 58, 64, 78.

A smelly and dirty apartment suddenly improved its appearance. If the doctor asked whether anyone was sick, all would say they were well. The sublessors would hide the sick so as to avoid fines and the inconvenience (and economic loss) of disinfecting the house with carbolic acid. The same story was repeated at the shops and taverns, where all rotten food was hidden at the slightest warning.[131]

Such accounts suggest that even if the city council had had the funds, the desire, and the power to build "crime-free" lodging houses much earlier, as the police had hoped, it is questionable that law-abiding citizens would have flocked to them. The importance of casual labor and the unceasing stream of immigrants to the metropolitan economy, the location of the major part of the city's underworld, and the multiple symbiotic relationships of members of the slum community made Khitrov market a hard nut to crack. Similarly, the Workhouse, despite its advertisement of discipline and uplifting cultural amenities, never quite reproduced the stern, prison-like English model: fictionalized accounts suggest that often idle wards were highly amused by the idea of concerts and picture shows, and police reports indicate that those released from the Workhouse were more often than not right back on the streets where they had been apprehended for vagrancy or begging. Though reformers decried improvidence, the loss of the will to work, and alcoholism, the administrators of the Guardianships of the Poor dealt largely with a transient population not likely to be very receptive to regimen, strict discipline, and character regeneration. Even if a few of the poor may have absorbed some of the values of those who tried to guide them, forces beyond the city's control prevented great strides in reform in the last decades of the old regime.

It is not difficult to find deficiencies in the city's institutions of poor relief, and the examples of shortcomings in the very inception of poor-relief measures, of unimaginative administration of programs, or of the suspiciousness of the muzhiks themselves toward the authorities and the professionals could be multiplied. And, after all, what welfare program is ever without shortcomings? More important than the success or failure of this or that program or institution was the evolution of an ethos of individual and social reform as the authorities and professionals tried to cope with the mounting problems of urban

131. Gor-ev, "K kharakteristike," 40, 49–51, 120.

growth. The varied strains of urbanization culminated in this ethos, and it is in this ethos that the relationship between Muscovite and muzhik which was the essence of urbanization can be seen most vividly. The concluding chapter will summarize the strains of urbanization and then present the resulting ethos of reform.

16. THE IAROSHENKO LODGING HOUSE, KHITROV SQUARE, EARLY
TWENTIETH CENTURY.

"After work, willing or not, they drag back to
Khitrov market: there are no lodging houses
near their jobs and they won't get turned down
at Khitrov. Thus the absence of lodging houses
near those places where the greatest concentration of day laborers work—the railroad stations,
freight yards, and lumber yards—is one of the
reasons for the accumulation of workers at the
Khitrov houses"

(TsGAM, f. 179, op. 21, d. 2009. l. 49).

17. INTERIOR OF A LODGING HOUSE, KHITROV SQUARE, LATE
NINETEENTH CENTURY. NOTICE THE PLANK BEDS (*nary*).

"These people live in impossible conditions: filth,
stench, suffocating heat. One can't stay standing for half
an hour in these apartments. They lie down together
barely a few feet apart, and there is no division between
the sexes, and adults sleep with children. The air is saturated with the most dreadfully foul language"

(S. K. Alaverdian, *Zhilishchnyi vopros v Moskve*, 46).

18. IMPERIAL FOUNDLING HOME, EARLY TWENTIETH CENTURY.

"Many a baby, over whom the Moskva would otherwise close its dark and swift waters, is saved to become a good soldier for the Tsar or a modest and
prettily dressed housemaid simply because the newborn could be put by its mother within the folds of
the foundling asylum and none be the wiser"

(John Bell Bouton, *Roundabout to Moscow,* 262–63).

"Thank God I didn't secretly give you up to the Foundling Home then. There you either would have died
long ago or they would have sent you far away and I
never would have found you"

(Daria Pavlova in S. T. Semenov's "U propasti," 22).

19. FREE CAFETERIA FOR POOR CHILDREN
RUN BY THE LEFORT DISTRICT GUARDIANSHIP
OF THE POOR, EARLY TWENTIETH CENTURY.

"The insufficiency of hot, healthy meals among the working class brings with it contagious diseases and alcoholism"

(*Letopis' pervogo dvadtsatipiatiletiia Moskovskogo Obshchestva pooshchreniia trudoliubiia*, 276–77).

Food stamps for free meals will assure the benefactor that "the goal of feeding the poor by contributions would be achieved and that the money he gave in Christ's name wouldn't go for liquor"

(ibid., 91).

"Benefactors should not be invisible to the needy but should be among them and know them personally. They should bring help to where it's needed. . . . Being more grass-roots, the guardianships don't place paper work above life, and they recruit people for whom charity is not an office job but a personal and civic calling"

(V. I. Ger'e, "Russkaia blagotvoritel'nost' na Vsemirnoi vystavke," 505).

"Each orphanage or cafeteria run by the Guardianship is a closed institution, inaccessible to outside judgment and known only by laconic annual reports"

(N. I. Ezerskii, "Zadachi gorodskikh popechitel'stv" 291– 92).

20. PRAYERS AT CHILDRENS' SHELTER RUN BY THE MESHCHANE
DISTRICT GUARDIANSHIP OF THE POOR.

"It is not enough to give the stomach food or
the hands work: one must give spiritual food,
establish mental hygiene, and freshen the sensations of man's soul with noble amusements and
moral books"

(A. R. Lednitskii, "Bor'ba s nishchenstvom," 82).

Conclusion: Urbanization and Social Reform

Symbolic of Russia's economic, political, and cultural dynamism in the late imperial period were its rapidly growing cities. Expansion and structural shifts of the economy, as well as unprecedented population growth and mobility, created a dynamic urban environment, especially in the two metropolises, St. Petersburg and Moscow. The strains of rapid urban growth—chaotic economic expansion and urban sprawl, the development of a casually employed labor force, a highly transient immigrant population, shortages of low-cost housing, and inadequate welfare, medical care, education, and public transport—were particularly acute and most thoroughly studied and publicized in the two metropolises.

Moscow was the center of a populous hinterland that constituted Russia's oldest manufacturing region. The population of this hinterland maintained a balance between agricultural and nonagricultural occupations. Though farming in Moscow's hinterland was notoriously precarious, it provided almost half of the peasant's income. Proximity to the metropolitan market actually gave farming in Moscow province a shot in the arm, and only a small proportion of peasant households had abandoned the land. Factory wages, the cottage industry, and seasonal labor away from home provided supplemental income. As a depot and distribution center and as a source of employment in a wide range of trades and crafts, Moscow maintained close economic and social ties with its hinterland. The city's gigantic calico mills lured factory laborers, and its colossal market supported city cottage industries and artisanal workshops. Moscow's peasant immigrants came from a region where rural factories, the cottage industry, long absences from home, and apparent family dislocations were facts of life. A regional economic and social system was, in part, transferred to Moscow itself.

Sectoral diversity characterized the metropolitan, as well as the regional, economy. Manufacturing, of course, was dominated by textiles, long the major industry of the region. Yet, in proportion of the labor force employed, textile manufacturing was beginning to decline, and "younger" branches of industry, such as food processing, chemicals, metalworking, printing, and machine-tools, were becoming prominent. A booming but erratic construction industry responded to the needs of urban and industrial expansion. More than one-fifth of the labor force was employed in commerce, the largest proportion of any city in the empire. Russians and foreigners alike were struck by the city's lively retail trade, particularly by its open-air markets and bazaars. As the metropolitan economy expanded and diversified, employment opportunities multiplied especially rapidly in construction, retailing, transport, services, and the professions.

The rapid growth of the metropolitan economy, when added to the continued close economic and social ties between Moscow and its hinterland and the city's long tradition as a center of small-scale production and distribution, created a dualistic economy. Large- and small-scale economic and social organizations coexisted. Although trends toward business consolidation and larger firms were in evidence, the number of businesses, as well as the number of small businessmen, continued to grow, especially during good economic years. In fact, certain informal and personal forms of manufacturing and commerce, such as small-scale production of goods for the retail market and street vending, were ideally suited to the metropolis. The tenacity of certain informal forms of economic organization and, to the dismay of reformers, the concomitant lack of regularity, habit, and time discipline, continued to distinguish Moscow even as the city's economy modernized.

The city's small-scale, consumer-goods economy suggested village life to its educated elite, and for centuries Moscow's streets, open-air markets, workshops, inns, and taverns had been populated largely by immigrants. The expanding metropolitan economy and the wide variety of employment opportunities beckoned laborers from the city's hinterland and beyond. Seven of every eight males on the labor force were immigrants, and the proportion showed no sign of significant change in the period studied. In an average year at the turn of the twentieth century, more than a hundred thousand immigrants entered the city. Although most peasant immigrants retained peasant legal status, membership in the commune, and allotment land, house, livestock, and kin in the village, communal bonds were loosening such that more peasants could come to Moscow. Indeed, census takers, municipal investigators, welfare reformers, writers of guidebooks and popular fictional sketches, and foreign visitors all witnessed the phenomenon of peasant immigration in unprecedented numbers. So great were the number of new arrivals and so small were the provincial capitals and county seats of the hinterland that Moscow's newcomers in the main had had little previous urban experience. As much as the number alone, this disturbed Muscovites. The compilers of the 1902 census summed up the attitudes of many municipal investigators and policy makers: "The tremendous influx of peasants into the capital is more and more turning Moscow into a peasant city."[1]

Although an unprecedented number of immigrants came to Moscow, there is little evidence that such moves were more likely to be permanent. For every skilled blue-collar worker or office clerk who established more or less permanent residence, seasonal or casual laborers, particularly in the construction and transport trades and domestic service, moved back and forth from village to city as the exigencies of the casual labor market dictated. The importance of seasonal labor, the erratic nature of the metropolitan economy, and frequent job turnover, when coupled with the surviving communal bonds, explain the fact that almost a hundred thousand people *left* Moscow every year. For most immigrant laborers, bringing dependents to the city remained extremely difficult; contemporary accounts demonstrate that peasant brides continued to return to the villages to bear children, or if they bore children in Moscow, they sent them back to be raised by kin in the villages. Such transient habits were reinforced by the preservation of certain customs among migratory laborers, such as the networks of fellow villagers (*zemliachestvo*) and the band of laborers (artel) that provided group cohesion during repeated trips to the city. By making it easier for immigrants to adapt to certain aspects of city life—entry in the labor force and the housing market, for instance—this group cohesion meant that a greater number of peasant laborers

1. *GDP 1902*, IV:22.

could enter the city and that, of these, more could enter without any previous urban experience than might otherwise have been the case. Ironically, from the standpoint of the authorities and reformers, although peasant ways made the city's hold on its newest residents at best tenuous, peasant ways also enabled more and more immigrants to make the move to Moscow.

Immigration of dependents, though increasing slightly, remained more difficult than immigration of the self-supporting. As a result, the metropolitan labor force constituted approximately 70 percent of the entire population at the turn of the century, a higher proportion than that of any other major European or Russian city at the time. More then two-thirds of the labor force were blue-collar, and of the blue-collar work force, two-thirds were semiskilled or menial workers. At the same time, the structure of the labor force was gradually shifting such that there were more white-collar jobs, particularly for professionals, technicians, and sales-clerical personnel, and also more skilled blue-collar jobs. Although direct evidence of individual career patterns is lacking, such structural shifts, as well as evidence that those immigrants who stayed long periods of time in the city improved their entrepreneurial skills and job prospects, suggest that both lateral and upward occupational mobility were attainable in the metropolis.

Equally attainable, and much more noticeable to the authorities were occupational stagnation and downward mobility. Nearly a hundred thousand persons left Moscow every year, and though many had no intention of staying, the job prospects of those who left were worse than of those who stayed. At the same time, an expanding yet erratic and poorly organized metropolitan economy demanded that those with poor job prospects continue to come to the city. A supply of casual laborers was essential to rapid city growth: common laborers could be hired by the job, and a myriad of street vendors, hawkers, and draymen were essential given the incomplete penetration of modern methods of retailing and distribution. In addition, the Moscow market attracted more skilled craftsmen than could find employment at any one time, making artisans also prone to downward mobility. Study after study of the city's skid row and of welfare cases showed that a disproportionate share of the group surveyed declared that they were or had been craftsmen.

To compound the hardships immigrant laborers faced, housing improvements in the main did not keep pace with the increase in population. Judged by the building materials used, the population density of apartments, the numbers of inhabitants of basement apartments, and the continued subdivision of living space, Moscow's housing stock showed little improvement at the turn of the century. A larger proportion of inhabitants lived in communal apartments than in any other Russian city, or in any European city at that time. From 1899 to 1912 the increase in the number of residents of the so-called cot-chamber subdivided tenements was double the increase in the number of such units. This was due not only to the rapid population growth but also to the fact that more and more laborers were living in privately owned housing rather than being housed by their employers. Despite the overcrowded, overly subdivided, and unhealthy private tenements, such a change in housing preferences signaled in one sense an improvement in living conditions for those whose wages, regularity of income, or working family members permitted. For the most secure in the labor force, private apartments meant a greater independence from employers and foremen and also lessened the threat of eviction from company housing.

Although an increasing number of laborers were bringing wives and chidren to Moscow and establishing more or less settled residence, the overall composition of the city's households shows that the vicissitudes of the labor and housing markets, as well as the economic and social system of the region, militated against settled nuclear families. Only half of the city's household members were related to the head of the household. Although almost three-fifths of the male population were married, less than one-third were living in Moscow with family members. To the newcomer, especially male, who rented lodgings, a cot, a chamber, a corner as a boarder with another family, a bunk in a factory barracks, or an apartment as a member of an artel, family was elsewhere, usually in the village but not infrequently in another part of Moscow itself. The housing pressure, the difficulty in finding regular employment, the transience of residence, and the difficulty in bringing dependents to Moscow meant that the proportion living communally or as lodgers, boarders, laborers, and domestics in the homes of their employers exceeded that of other major Russian and European cities. Illegal residence, as police reports indicate, compounded the housing pressure. The police themselves admitted that detention and expulsion of immigrants without proper papers were ineffectual measures to control access to scarce housing, and we may never know exactly how many immigrants ignored passport regulations and resided furtively in the city's nooks and crannies.

The composition of households and the family life of the city's muzhiks epitomized the alleged breakdown of traditional morals and family virtues in the eyes of reformers. Similarly, the existence of a highly visible casual labor force epitomized the alleged laziness and improvidence of the muzhiks, and it was not hard to assume that those who had sporadic employment were lazy and that Moscow attracted such persons from the village. By the end of the nineteenth century the spectrum of experience of the city's laborers—in particular the immigration experience and the experience in the labor and housing markets, as well as the general urban environment, the metropolitan economy and the traditions of the city—passed through the converging lens of values, perceptions, and goals of the authorities and reformers to produce a beam of reformist thought and policy. It is in this beam of reformist thought and policy that the historian can see most clearly the relationship between muzhik and Muscovite and, accordingly, the nature of urbanization itself.

Systematic reformist thought and policies were products of the late nineteenth century. Earlier in the century, reform efforts were limited to police surveillance of lodging houses; apprehension and incarceration in the Workhouse or expulsion from the city of mendicants and vagrants; confinement of the aged and infants in almshouses, orphanages, and the Imperial Foundling Home; and finally to almsgiving by generous Muscovites. Naturally, mendicancy, vagrancy, and pauperism, especially when associated with drunkenness and crime, were decried, but the individual and social disorders were not perceived as threatening. Indeed, the colorfulness of Moscow's street life, the "beloved disorder" of its commercial life, and the quixotic settlement patterns were regarded by writers of a populist bent as quintessentially representative of the Russian character and traditions. In contrast to the more orderly, harmonious appearance of St. Petersburg, a disorderly, unkempt appearance had been Moscow's trademark.[2]

The disorder of the city and its inhabitants, tolerable in the mid-nineteenth century, became abhorrent at the beginning of the twentieth. Production and distribution of most consumer goods not only were smaller in scale but suggested disorganization, erratic procedures, and volatile markets. As the metropolitan economy modernized, the informal, small-scale organizations stood out even more. The continued

2. Bater, *St. Petersburg*, 3. The "orderly" image of St. Petersburg, though, reflected the city's first century or so, not the city at the end of the nineteenth century.

backwardness and indiscipline of certain aspects of city life offended the pride of Muscovites. Ironically, even as the sobriquet "the big village" was becoming less reflective of reality in the city, it was becoming more offensive to Muscovites who regarded their city as modern and Europeanized.

To the authorities and professionals the significance of the disorder of the city and even the "big village" image went beyond architectural styles, street life, and informal forms of production and distribution. The educated elite feared that the values and ways of life of the common people not only were remote from those of the ideal inhabitant of the modern city but also posed a threat to the discipline, stability, and commitment needed to hold a city of one million together. For example, the existence of the Khitrov skid row as well as of numerous open-air markets and bazaars forced Muscovites to be aware of indigence and of a nomadic, seemingly purposeless, and dissolute way of life in the heart of the city. Simlarly, the profusion of taverns, tearooms, and communal apartments on the scruffy outskirts was testimony to the tremendous aggregation of laborers without families who had no other place to go.[3] In the eyes of reformers the immigrant casual laborer in particular was beyond the pale of modern urban civilization. His homes were the railroad freight yards, the riverfront, the construction sites, the lodging houses, the taverns, and the streets. He was male, young, and most often without family (or with family elsewhere) and the sobering influence of responsibility for the very young and the very old. He was most often in the company of his peers; loyalties and trust were reserved for his traveling companions, his artel associates, his fellow villagers. He was even less susceptible than was the skilled worker to the efforts of the authorities or the public—whether through the primary schools, Sunday schools, factory libraries, and the temperance society's tea-rooms—to inculcate respect for the social order, God, and the tsar. He was even more susceptible than was the skilled worker to the periodic campaigns against vagrancy, the vagaries of the casual labor market, and the underworld of the flophouses. Yet the Workhouse, the prison system, and the police seemed unable to reform him or keep him away from Moscow. Finally, on the eve of the revolutions of 1905 and 1917 the educated elite tended to equate the most rootless and down-and-out elements of the city's population

---

3. Chuprov, "Kharakteristika," 39.

with the laboring population as a whole in the formation of a composite image of the "dark masses."

While the economic and political threat that muzhik posed to Muscovite in times of labor strife could never be overexaggerated, the apparent homelessness, truncated family life, transience, and erratic employment of the city's commoners posed to the educated elite an even greater, and fundamentally moral, threat. Such was the threat posed by "many wild and criminal paupers who bring up children in their own image," who existed beyond the pale of urban civilization, and who allegedly would not prepare their offspring for the modern world without the intervention of Muscovites. Unfortunately, the traditional mechanisms for absorbing the city's indigent were inadequate to meet the needs of several hundred thousand needy. Moreover, traditional mechanisms lacked a reformist ideal. In the increasing involvement of the municipality and professionals in the organizations and programs described in Part Three (as well as in many other services), the components of the ethos of individual and social reform can be seen.

Those who wrote about social reform in Moscow were in the main not original thinkers and most likely held reformist ideas without being aware of the full range of implications of their assumptions and attitudes. Such assumptions frequently started with moral judgments about human nature in general and about the character of the needy muzhik in particular. In the rather dry accounts of charity and poor relief, certain alleged character traits of the needy appear again and again: idleness, improvidence, indolence, intemperance, impulsiveness, thriftlessness, apathy, laziness, fatalism, weakness of will. Although structural causes of need were increasingly recognized in Russia as elsewhere, the individual or "moral" causes continued to have powerful explanatory force. In a judicious survey of the reasons for pauperism, one of the mammoth compendia of Russian charity published by the Institutions of the Empress Maria included poor upbringing and the "lack of resistance to vice" among the personal reasons.[4] Other writers were more direct. Thus, the needy, according to one, were people who "in the great majority of cases, are to blame for their suffering."[5] Another stated that the cause of pauperism lay in disease and in "moral dissoluteness [*raspushchennost'*]. In the final analysis,

---

4. *Blagotvoritel'nost' v Rossii*, 1:vi.
5. Odynets, *Doma trudoliubiia*, 2:14.

pauperism is a result of improvidence [*nepredusmotritel'nost'*]."[6] Given these assumptions about the character of the needy, it is not difficult to identify the values that reformers wanted to inculcate into the subordinate classes: thrift, sobriety, respectability, responsibility, providence, industriousness, ambition, and strength of character. These were character traits assumed to make up the sturdy citizen and self-reliant individual. Moreover, these were values cultivated by the middle class and professionals everywhere, who regarded them as essential for an individual's productive contribution, in the broadest sense, to society.

The habits and vices of the common people could be reformed by the civilizing influence of a more disciplined, organized, and rational culture and value system. In this way, for instance, poor upbringing and socialization (such as disjointed family life, child abuse, parents possessing any of the vices of the "lower orders" listed above) could be offset. It will be remembered that the authorities were particularly concerned about the household structure of lower-class families—the presence of lodgers and other unrelated persons in the household—as well as about the mingling of households in the subdivided tenements. Renovations of deteriorating neighborhoods would help bring about renovation of deteriorating character. A similar renovation could come about by changing the amusements and leisure-time habits of the muzhiks. Most active in this field were the Society to Disseminate Useful Books and the Society to Encourage Industriousness, which organized holiday "spiritual-moral public readings and magic lantern shows" at the Belov cafeteria, and the Moscow Temperance Society, which, like temperance societies everywhere, tried to substitute rational or useful amusements for the "perverse influence of the tavern."[7] A. R. Lednitskii expressed this attitude succinctly: "It is not enough to give the stomach food or the hands work: one must give spiritual food, establish mental hygiene, freshen the sensations of man's soul with noble amusements and moral books."[8] Neither the Workhouse and other repressive measures nor material relief alone were enough: paternalistic reformers wanted to

6. V. A. Gol'tsev, "Novye issledovaniia o pauperizme," *Russkaia mysl'*, 4, no. 1 (January 1883): 131.

7. *Letopis'*, 78 and Appendix, 22–24; A. M. Korovin, "Blagotvoritel'nost' i alkogolizm," *Sbornik statei*, 2 (1901): 84–97; E. I. Voinov, "Piatiletie pervogo Moskovskogo Obshchestva trezvosti, 1896–1900," *Sbornik statei*, 2 (1901): 98–106; D. F. Suvorov, "Rogozhskoe otdelenie Obshchestva trezvosti," *Sbornik statei*, 2 (1901): 107–19.

8. A. R. Lednitskii, "Bor'ba s nishchenstvom," *Sbornik statei*, 2 (1901): 82. See also V. D. Evreinov, "K kharakteristike domov trudoliubiia," *Trudovaia pomoshch'*, 2, no. 1 (January 1899): 38–58.

transform through welfare organizations and policies the ways of lower-class culture to the ways of the new urban-industrial social order.

The desirability of stamping out certain defects of character, inculcating the corresponding virtues, and transforming the ways of the lower classes notwithstanding, no one assumed, and certainly not in Russia, that this could be accomplished overnight. The habits and vices of the common people were not the only obstacles to reform. Reformers faced equally serious obstacles in the organization of poor relief itself, in the political control over local affairs, and in the economic and social system of the metropolis.

The "correct" organization of poor relief and political control over local affairs were particularly important to reformers connected with the Guardianships of the Poor. If the lives of the common people were to be organized properly, so must the agencies and institutions meant to help them. If the elements of chance and fatalism were to be removed from the lives of the muzhiks, then the element of chance (*sluchainost'*) was to be removed from poor relief. Through the advice and services of experts and professionals, reformed welfare would impart system, rationality, technique, and supervision (*kontrol'*) to the existing agencies and institutions of poor relief.[9] This reflects a general desire to bring the elements of system, organization, technique, rationality, and above all, discipline to Russian society as a whole.

At this point, of course, ideas of individual and social reform confronted not only the ways of the lower classes but the ways of the Russian autocracy. "Local governments are the best equipped to care for local needs," Evgenii Maksimov wrote laconically in 1901,[10] but this was not self-evident to the authorities of the central government. Reformers had to struggle not only for more rational, supervised, and professional services but also for local control of these services. Here, paternalistic reformism is virtually coterminous with post-emancipation liberalism, which expressed a yearning for social duty and a commitment among Russian professionals to make society function better with the contribution of experts and local initiative in social problems. Local control, however, was frequently not that simple a matter: local authorities did not always want local control, and local control was no guarantee of successful reformism. As early as the 1860s, the police had urged the municipal authorities to provide low-cost public housing, but

9. *Otchet Gorodskogo popechitel'stva o bednykh Prechistenskoi chasti za 1900*, 8.
10. Maksimov, *Proiskhozhdenie nishchenstva*, 118.

the latter refused on the grounds that since the immigrants were not permanent city residents, the municipality was not obliged to assist them. Similarly, municipalization of several institutions, including the Workhouse, and creation of the District Guardianships of the Poor in the 1890s did not guarantee that "correct" reform programs would be carried out.

The economic ways of the new urban-industrial order, contradictory in many respects, did not make the task of reformers easier. To begin with, since the economic order created or perpetuated glaring inequalities and injustices, reformers had to stress the importance of individual rather than social change. The modern economy and social relations placed a premium on individual productivity and provided unprecedented opportunity and, for some, upward occupational mobility. Consequently, one important component of reformism was the stress on job training, self-improvement, the work ethic, and the like. At the same time, Moscow's booming metropolitan economy also demanded an unprecedented number of semiskilled and menial laborers in construction, carting and hauling, transport, and domestic and institutional service. Since these unskilled laborers were widely believed to be unruly, vagrant, weak-willed, and unambitious, another important component of reformism was the stress on thrift, sobriety, self-discipline, moral restraint, "work relief," and the like. In modern society, argued Professor Vladimir A. Gagen, the real crime is not mendicancy or vagrancy per se (against which repressive measures are ineffective anyway) but idleness, unwillingness to work, and in strikingly prescient terms, "antisocial parasitism."[11] The dualism of the city's economy meant that those who could not be integrated into its increasingly specialized, interdependent parts, or whose informal ways could not be transformed, were a threat, on the one hand, while on the other hand they satisfied a continual demand to fill unskilled, erratic, and low-paying jobs.

If the economic ways of the new urban-industrial order sent conflicting signals to the municipal authorities and reformers, the social and political ways did not. "Being a good neighbor," being a "true guardian to the poor," or "helping the poor to help themselves" may of course have been intended to uplift Muscovites and to have a civilizing effect on muzhiks. These goals were also intended to ensure or create a stable urban citizenry and thereby stave off social conflict.

11. Gagen, "Predstoiashchaia reforma," 36–37.

In this way reformist measures would move from the modest area of welfare to the larger area of social policy, which "need not be socialist," as Maksimov argued. The liberal vision of a reformed, responsible, and self-reliant Russia implicitly included a vision of a reformed, responsible, and self-reliant Russian poor. A hardworking, purposeful, modern society and a self-reliant citizenry would be freed eventually of the heavy bureaucratic restraints and tutelage that central government placed on local communities and professionals and experts, and at the same time a responsible and provident muzhik would be immune to the elemental passions of the masses and the appeal of demagogues, whether reactionaries or socialists. Only by staving off social conflict, the professionals and reformers believed, could the twin bulwarks so admired by liberals—the rule of law and respect for private property, and the rule of reason and respect for the individual—be preserved intact.

Like metropolises in Europe and America at the time, Moscow seemed to its educated elite to offer the best and the worst of the modern urban, industrial world. The city's rapid growth and modernization brought hope that civilization, discipline, industriousness, rationality, and sobriety would soon come to a poor nation. Individual initiative and enterprise could triumph over sloth and lethargy. In the great cities, Europeanized ways could now be mass-marketed and, like the watch chains and table lamps that peasants brought back to their native villages after sojourns in Moscow, could reach beyond the thin layer of the Russian elite to the common people. At the same time the city's rapid growth threatened to get out of control, and Moscow was "becoming more and more a peasant city." On the outskirts "nested wild and criminal paupers," and in the heart of the metropolis were scruffy open-air bazaars, street vendors, and the most notorious skid row in the empire. Again and again the common people were referred to as the "dark" or "ignorant" masses. Though political turmoil usually precipitated such expressions, the underlying attitude was shaped well before the revolts that ended tsarist rule. In fact, the municipal authorities and professionals tended to equate the entire laboring population with the most rootless and down-and-out elements in the city. In this simplistic equation, the educated elite's perception of the common people lagged behind the changing reality of their condition.

The strains of rapid growth, the fears of the authorities and professionals, and the attempts of the "organized minority" to reform character and to impose disciplined and rational value systems on the "unorganized majority" are the essence of urbanization. This study has analyzed urbanization in only one, albeit a very important, Russian city. Studies of other cities, particularly of cities with more variegated ethnicity, will surely show variations of the patterns of economic and spatial growth, immigration, labor force composition, and housing and welfare needs. Studies focusing on other problems of city growth and other city services—education, crime, and public health, for instance—will surely broaden our understanding of the urban environment and the integration of the common people into the modern city. Studies exploring the connection between the continuing urban instability and disorder after the Civil War and the demise of the New Economic Policy or the preoccupation of the Soviet authorities today with order and control of immigration, employment, and housing in the city will suggest the underlying continuities in the urbanization process. In this way, studies of urbanization will clarify the relationship between the common people and educated society and the tensions inherent in the modernization of late imperial and Soviet Russia.

Occupations in White-collar, Blue-collar Moscow

NOTE ON METHOD

An effort was made to adhere as closely as possible to the occupational categories used by the census compilers themselves even while rearranging them. Since the 1902 census provided a more detailed occupational breakdown than did the 1912 census, the former was used as a base. The first step involved compiling a list of occupations as found in Part 3, Section 3, pages 170–215 of the 1902 census. However, since comparison of occupation and residence was of primary concern to the census compilers here, many occupational categories were combinations of smaller divisions. The most detailed occupational listing of all was found in Part 2, Section 1, pages 46–115. Since sectoral placement of the labor force was of primary importance to the census compilers here, many jobs were repeated several times. By cross-tabulating these two parts of the census, occupational detail was produced independent from sectoral placement.

The resulting list of occupations was then compared with that found in the 1912 census (or, to be more precise, that part of the 1912 census published after the Revolution in a statistical annual of Moscow and Moscow province). This listing was not as detailed, and sometimes groupings of occupations were different from those in the 1902 census. (These will be identified in the notes on specific occupations which follow the table.) As a result, the two occupational listings are not perfectly comparable. However, both detail and similarity of categories were great enough to make the effort of comparing the two censuses seem worthwhile.

The text discusses some of the most important difficulties found in arranging the many occupational groups into a "white-collar, blue-collar" hierarchy. Additional difficulties should be pointed out here. The censuses were sufficiently vague in their indication of the size of the enterprise such that positions of ownership were very difficult to place. Consequently, many of those owners placed in the low white-collar category "small proprietors, managers, officials" could have been placed in the high white-collar category "major proprietors, managers and officials." The census compilers themselves divided owners into those who employed wage labor, those who employed only members of their own family, and those who worked alone. Since I placed many owners who employed wage labor in the category "small proprietors," there is a potential downward bias in my grouping. It does not seem, however, that employment of wage labor is sufficient cause for placement in the category "major proprietors," simply because of the tremendous distance between the industrialist employing a thousand workers and the owner of a workshop employing one journeyman.

The clergy was another category that could have been placed more highly, and this is a case where I have deviated from Edwards' (and Thernstrom's) classification system where "clergymen" are placed among the professionals. Although many of Moscow's clergy may have deserved to have been thus highly placed, the image of the Orthodox clergy runs too counter to that of "professionals" to place the group as a whole alongside engineers, lawyers, and physicians. Similarly, a rather large amorphous census category of scientists, writers, actors, musicians, and so forth, has been broken up and distributed in the categories "professionals" and "semiprofessionals." "Non-classified white-collar" are those who simply had no obvious attachment to any of the previous groups.

The text has already discussed the difficulty in placing self-employed artisans and factory workers, especially in the textile industry. The former are clearly on the border line between "small proprietors" and "skilled blue-collar," and the latter are on the border line between "skilled" and "semiskilled blue-collar." It might be added that a similar gray area exists between the "semiskilled blue-collar" and the "unskilled laborers and menial service workers." Similarly, several groups of "other workers in the transport industry" and the like have been placed in the category "semiskilled blue-collar," under the assumption that had they been skilled, their craft would have been identified. It is, of course, possible that crafts of some highly skilled blue-collar workers were not identified in the census, but it does not seem that this would have been a large number.

Job turnover and the nuances of differences among occupations cannot be reflected in this or any other classification scheme. The census asked an individual's occupation, not current job title, a problem for those who changed jobs frequently. There is a possibility for an upward bias, since many craftsmen working in trades undergoing mechanization and skill dilution may have been holding current jobs that did not set them as far apart from machine operators as the categories "skilled" and "semiskilled" suggest. Finally, it must be pointed out that the census takers did not question all one million persons in the city but questioned only heads of households, proprietors, employers, landlords, and the like. Clearly, there is room for much error in what Smirnov the landlord thought Ivanov the factory worker did for a living.

In spite of all the pitfalls discussed here and in the text, the attempt at such an occupational classification still seems worthwhile as a stepping stone to a fuller picture of labor not only in Moscow but, when complemented by other such attempts, throughout Russia.

In the classification and in more specific notes that follow, the occupations have been given a code number which simply refers to the numbers used in the census. Numbers preceded with a letter correspond to the categories and numbers used in Part 3, Section 3, of the 1902 census; numbers after the slash refer to the numbers used in the 1912 census. Those code numbers which appear in the notes are marked in the table with an asterisk (*).

WHITE-COLLAR AND BLUE-COLLAR OCCUPATIONS IN MOSCOW

Code	High White-collar Occupations	1902			1912		
		Men	Women	Total	Men	Women	Total
	Professionals						
E9 G23/182	Engineers, chemists, agronomists	1,818	—	1,818	1,365	9	1,374
G14/176*	Lawyers	859	—	859	2,551	30	2,581
G15/177	Physicians, veterinarians	1,715	114	1,829	2,428	434	2,862
G17*	Pharmacists	725	43	768	—	—	—
G21/181	Teachers	3,321	5,671	8,992	5,794	10,475	16,269
G25/184*	Scientists, writers	291	75	366	2,606	1,526	4,132
	Total professionals	8,929	5,903	14,632	14,744	12,474	27,218
	Major proprietors, managers, officials						
A2/1	Manufacturers	1,231	163	1,394	1,570	221	1,791
A8/5*	Merchants	7,748	1,221	8,969	10,052	1,857	11,909
E1/31	Directors, managers	2,478	136	2,614	3,516	256	3,772
G8 G10/168	Officers of army, navy, gendarmes, and police	1,571	0	1,571	2,167	0	2,167
G13*	Magistrates and Court officials	507	2	509	—	—	—
G27/189	Landowners	504	899	1,403	619	868	1,507
G28/190	Rentiers	1,909	5,381	7,290	5,189	12,508	17,697
	Total	15,948	7,802	23,750	23,113	15,730	38,843
	Total High White-collar	24,877	13,705	38,382	37,857	28,204	66,061

Code	Low White-collar Occupations	1902			1912		
		Men	Women	Total	Men	Women	Total
	Sales-Clerical						
E3/33	Sales clerks (*prikazchiki*)	19,742	1,034	20,776	31,478	2,407	33,885
G3 E5/32,174	Bookkeepers, accountants	3,129	183	3,312	7,542	2,030	9,572
E6*	Cashiers	497	428	925	—	—	—
E7 G4/34,175	Office clerks, secretaries (*kontorshchiki*)	12,230	1,910	14,140	18,014	4,171	22,185
E4 E8, G6/35,36	Agents, appraisers, messengers	2,685	24	2,709	6,396	35	6,431
E12 E13, G5/37,136	Telephone, telegraph, postal employees	2,560	336	2,896	6,907	1,517	8,424
G7	Inspectors	463	316	779	—	0	—
E11/131	Railroad conductors, ticket takers	2,292	0	2,292	4,900	0	4,900
	Total Sales-Clerical	43,598	4,231	47,829	75,237	10,160	85,397
	Semiprofessional						
G19/179	Clergy	1,291	646	1,937	1,485	1,717	3,202
E10	Draftsmen	398	7	405	—	—	—
E14	Railroad technicians	479	0	479	—	—	—
F85	Icon painters	739	1	740	—	—	—
G16/178*	Medical technicians	791	1,404	2,195	2,862	6,433	9,295
G18/178*	Nurses	2	1,990	1,992	—	—	—
G20/180	Lower church personnel	1,568	2,491	4,059	1,751	1,416	3,167
G25/G26/185	Artists, musicians, entertainers	3,308	1,230	4,538	3,029	1,046	4,075
	Total semiprofessional	8,576	7,769	16,345	9,127	10,612	19,739

Code	Low White-collar Occupations	1902			1912		
		Men	Women	Total	Men	Women	Total
	Small proprietors, managers, officials						
A5/2,3	Owners of nonspecified manufacturing or transport establishments	4,176	185	4,361	17,695	5,291	22,986
A3 A4*	Other small employers in manufacturing	9,536	3,639	13,175	2,637	7,891	10,528
A6/4,21	Unspecified building owners and landlords	1,606	2,759	4,365	7,881	2,884	10,765
A7 B2-7/6,10,11,17	Small merchants, landlords, lessors	3,409	1,425	4,834	13,058	2,452	15,510
C27-33 A1/18,19,20,22	Self-employed in commerce	11,405	4,276	15,681	2,343	1,490	3,833
G1/183	Minor officials	3,371	967	4,338	15,050	2,231	17,281
E15/38	Other nonspecified white-collar	8,406	789	9,195	3,071	2,036	5,107
—/28	White-collar working for head of family	4,777	1,445	6,222			
E2*	Foremen	646	35	681	—	—	—
	Total	47,332	15,520	62,852	61,735	24,275	86,010
	Total Low White-collar	99,506	27,520	127,026	146,099	45,047	191,146
	Nonclassified White-collar						
G29/192	Pensioners	1,471	3,286	4,757	2,924	6,284	9,208
G30	Supported by public or private charity	492	2,028	2,520	—	—	—
G31/193	Supported by relatives	4,850	9,998	14,848	13,279	21,289	34,568
G32/195	Students in dormitories	7,294	5,335	12,629	7,406	5,440	12,846
	Total	14,107	20,647	34,754	23,609	33,013	56,622
	Total White-collar	138,290	61,872	200,162	207,565	106,264	313,829

Code	Blue-collar Occupations	1902			1912		
		Men	*Women*	*Total*	*Men*	*Women*	*Total*
	Skilled Blue-collar						
F5/40,58	Brickmakers, potters	691	33	724	2,564	119	2,686
F6 F7 F8/41,89,90*	Silversmiths, goldsmiths, jewelers	4,088	4	4,092	4,600	85	4,685
F9 F16/46,94,144	Other metal smiths, wiremakers	4,890	175	5,065	11,476	1,786	13,262
F10 F11/42,91,143*	Mechanics, fitters (*slesari*)	10,935	0	10,935	18,471	53	18,524
C2 F12/43,92	Coppersmiths	2,536	3	2,539	2,564	89	2,653
F13	Tinsmiths	1,514	357	1,871	—	—	—
F14/44	Founders	1,710	3	1,713	1,678	0	1,678
C3 F15/45,93	Blacksmiths	3,853	0	3,853	3,359	4	3,363
F17 F18/96	Instrument makers, watchmakers	688	8	696	779	11	790
F19/95	Wheelwrights	1,133	0	1,133	643	0	643
F21/48,97	Tanners	1,398	95	1,493	1,749	56	1,805
F22/49,98	Saddlemakers	2,248	25	2,273	2,119	56	2,175
F25/99	Furriers	816	207	1,023	1,153	322	1,475
C9 F38/60,104	Cabinetmakers	8,599	1	8,600	10,118	9	10,127
F39/61,105,145*	Upholsterers	1,636	26	1,662	6,950	436	7,386
F40	Turners	2,361	8	2,369	—	—	—
F41	Patternmakers	497	33	530	—	—	—
F44 F45/62,106	Papermakers, bookbinders, etc.	5,194	648	5,842	6,537	1,317	7,854
F48 F49/64,108*	Confectioners	3,090	1,750	4,840	3,487	2,395	5,882
C12 F55/13,68,112	Tailors	8,716	12,164	20,880	11,404	22,165	33,569
F56 F57/113	Milliners, hatters	1,925	1,013	2,938	2,301	1,492	3,793
C14 F58/69,114	Shoemakers	9,791	766	10,557	11,709	1,227	12,936
F59/70,115	Glovemakers; other apparel	521	421	942	2,733	1,930	4,663
C17 F64/72,117	Carpenters	5,438	0	5,438	5,860	0	5,860
C20 F65/73,118	Painters	3,414	0	3,414	3,768	0	3,768
C18 F66	Stove fitters	1,538	0	1,538	—	—	—

Code	Blue-collar Occupations	1902			1912		
		Men	Women	Total	Men	Women	Total
F68	Plasterers	1,535	0	1,535	—	—	—
F71	Masons	695	1	696	—	—	—
74,120,146*	Stove fitters, plasterers, masons (total)	3,768	1	3,769	7,562	3	7,565
F73 F74/78,121,148	Plumbers, electricians	1,402	0	1,402	4,470	20	4,490
F80 F81/75,123	Lithographers, typesetters, other printers	5,258	235	5,493	9,696	445	10,141
F83 F86 F87/76,124	Photographers, toymakers, other industrial arts	977	80	1,057	2,666	267	2,933
F85 F89/77	Engine and boiler operators; firemen, stokers	2,974	117	3,091	1,120	24	1,144
F84	Engravers	914	2	916	—	—	—
F20/47	Workers in chemical industries	2,301	369	2,670	3,131	1,373	4,504
C1-26*	Other self-employed artisans	7,605	2,816	10,421	14,545	6,588	21,133
	Total Skilled Blue-collar	112,881	21,360	133,821	159,212	42,275	201,487

Semiskilled and Service

Code		1902			1912		
		Men	Women	Total	Men	Women	Total
F24 F25/50	Bristle and brush makers; hemp strippers; combers	1,921	2,862	4,783	1,205	2,726	3,931
F26/51,102	Winders	666	4,224	4,890	1,075	5,706	6,781
F27/52	Weavers, cotton	2,709	2,068	4,777	1,618	2,803	4,424
F28/53	Weavers, wool	5,010	2,607	7,617	2,672	2,665	5,337
F29/54	Weavers, silk	2,780	3,355	6,135	3,826	4,625	8,457
F30 F31/55,101	Weavers, other and unspecified	2,513	911	3,424	2,797	961	3,758
F32/56,100*	Stocking makers, knitters	1,659	3,879	5,538	1,940	4,927	6,867
F61 F33 F34/57	Dyers; calico-printers	3,564	391	3,955	1,817	334	2,151
F35/58	Bleachers	3,282	1,031	4,313	2,406	1,004	3,410
F36/59,103	Other textile workers	1,266	1,662	2,928	10,888	7,786	18,674
F37	Coopers	652	0	652	—	—	—
F43/147	Sawyers; other woodworkers	1,332	3	1,335	741	2	743
F46 F47/63,107*	Bakers, refiners	5,392	5	5,397	5,965	22	5,987

Code	Occupation						
F50 F103 F104/65,109,140	Other workers in food industry	5,837	173	6,010	8,875	2,132	11,007
F51/66,110*	Workers in beverage industry	1,645	466	2,111	2,067	936	3,003
F52/67	Workers in tobacco industry	1,044	1,890	2,934	265	822	1,007
F53 F54/111	Seamstresses	40	2,927	2,967	8	2,968	2,976
F62	Barbers	529	7	536	—	—	—
F70	Street pavers	300	—	300	—	—	—
F75	Lamplighters	432	—	432			
F90/80,151	Packers	4,336	1,317	5,683	2,056	872	2,928
F92 F94 F95	Other railroad, postal, telegraph workers	4,788	30	4,818	3,321	0	3,321
F96/133*	Cabdrivers	5,083	—	5,083	8,705	2	8,707
F97/134*	Draymen, teamsters	7,062	—	7,062	2,723	1	2,724
F98 F99/135	Movers, deliverymen	7,337	—	7,337	5,360	400	5,760
F102 F105 F127/141	Other workers, retail sales	5,422	213	5,635		—	—
F109	Stove stocker	1,571	18	1,589			
F114/138	Waiters	5,419	36	5,455	9,101	939	10,040
F117 G39/84,128,139,160	Cooks	2,093	33,936	36,029	4,078	28,303	32,381
F118	Dishwashers	852	298	1,150	—	—	—
F121	Unspecified journeyman	738	63	801			
F122 F123/129	Other workers, artisanal establishments	1,550	143	1,693	2,703	619	3,322
F124 F125 F126/132,153	Other workers, transport, restaurant business	2,020	5	2,025	20,526	1,820	22,346
F128 F129/85	Other workers, factory	1,844	386	2,230	5,149	2,541	7,690
F130 F131/158*	Apprentices	24,724	7,932	32,656	30,827	10,032	41,659
G9/169	Soldiers	18,024	0	18,024	21,145	0	21,145
G11/170	Policemen	2,490	0	2,490	4,991	3	4,994
G12/171,172	Firemen, night watchmen	2,386	0	2,386	3,954	46	4,000

Code	Blue-collar Occupations	1902			1912		
		Men	*Women*	*Total*	*Men*	*Women*	*Total*
G41/162,163*	Governesses	3	10,407	10,410	397	10,709	11,106
G44	Housekeepers, stewards	96	1,148	1,244	—	—	—
G45	Gasmen, gardeners	357	—	357	—	—	—
F60	Button makers; other garment workers	983	904	1,887	—	—	—
F106 F107	Peddlers	486	21	507	—	—	—
	Total semiskilled and service	142,237	85,318	227,585	175,206	97,513	272,719
	Unskilled Laborers and Menial Service Workers						
F1–4/87	Agricultural laborers	2,124	48	2,172	1,231	132	1,363
F63/71,116	Laundry workers; washerwomen	409	7,046	7,455	837	5,184	6,021
F69/119	Ditchdiggers	984	1	985	915	0	915
F67/F72 F77 F78 F79/ 79,122,149	Chimneysweeps, watercarriers, streetsweepers, ragpickers, janitors	3,613	132	3,745	4,878	156	5,034
F93 F101	Porters, freight handlers	1,706	18	1,724	6,987	3	6,990
F100 G42/81,125,150,165	Coachmen	5,758	0	5,758	25,060	107	25,167
F112 F113 F116/83,127,137	Superintendents, guards, doormen	20,753	106	20,859	1,437	12,331	13,768
F115 G38/161	Lackeys, chambermaids	2,296	13,569	15,865	—	—	—
F120	Bathhouse attendants	654	416	1,070	—	—	—
G43	Menial kitchen workers	450	855	1,305	—	—	—
G48	Menials of institutions	11,777	4,677	16,454	16,411	6,721	23,132
F76	Garbage collectors	811	0	811	—	—	—
G40 G46/164,166	Other domestic servants	1,229	14,139	15,368	2,510	43,553	46,063
F110/82,126,152,200	Day laborers, unskilled	19,099	4,167	23,266	27,170	7,464	34,634
	Total Unskilled	71,663	45,174	116,837	87,436	75,651	163,087

Unclassified Blue-collar

Code		1	2	3	4	5	6
F108/42	Artel'shchiki	1,191	1	1,192	419	0	419
24–27	Family members working for head of family	3,711	3,062	6,773	5,696	3,671	9,367
196	On poor relief	5,105	13,158	18,263	6,661	15,332	21,993
—	Other workers	1,959	2,091	4,050	8,780	6,981	15,761
—	Beggars, thieves	313	462	775	—	—	—
203	Unemployed	11,755	6,362	18,117	19,720	9,692	29,412
	Total Unclassified Blue-collar	24,034	25,136	49,170	41,276	35,676	76,952
	Total Blue-collar	350,815	176,988	527,413	463,130	251,115	714,245
	Total White- and Blue-collar	489,105	238,860	727,575	670,695	357,379	1,028,074
	Unclassified						
G34 G35	Hospital patients	5,156	3,828	8,984	7,513	6,750	14,263
G36	Prisoners	3,293	328	3,621	5,750	528	6,278
	Unspecified family members	—	—	—	610	553	1,163
	Total Unclassified	8,449	4,156	12,605	13,873	7,831	21,704
	Total Self-Supporting Population	497,554	243,016	740,570	684,568	365,210	1,049,778

Source: *PM 1902*, I, 2, i, 46–115; 3, iii, 170–215; *SEMMG*, 68–74.

*Explanations of code numbers:
G14/176. Includes magistrates and court officials in 1912.
G17. In 1912 pharmacists placed in category lower medical personnel.
G25/184. Includes artists, musicians, and actors in 1912.
A8/5. Merchants in the occupational sense of owners of commercial establishments, not in the legal sense of *kuptsy*.

G13. In 1912 grouped with lawyers.

E6. In 1912 included with bookkeepers and accountants.

G16, G18/178. In 1912 all lower medical personnel, including pharmacists, grouped together.

A3 A4. Includes small employers who subcontract work for other enterprises.

E2. Category of foreman not listed in 1912.

F6 F7 F8. Silversmiths, goldsmiths, and jewelers listed separately in 1902 but not in 1912.

F10 F11. In addition to *slesari*, includes *mekhaniki* and *montery*.

F39. Includes drapers.

F48 F49. Includes *konditery, pirozhniki, konfetchiki,* and *prianichniki*.

74. Stove fitters, plasterers, masons not listed separately in 1912.

C1-26. Self-employed artisans (*khoziaeva-odinochki*) in manufacturing, construction, and carting and hauling whose trades were not specified sufficiently in the censuses.

F32. Includes both *chulochniki* and *viazal'shchiki*.

F46 F47. Includes *pekari; bulochniki, sakharovary.*

F51. Includes *vinokury, pivovary, kvasovary.*

F96. Defined as *izvozchiki legkovye.*

F97. Defined as *izvozchiki lomovye.*

F130 F131. Apprentices not subdivided by craft. Many in this category would, of course, move into the category "skilled blue-collar" as adults.

G41. Includes the *dvorniki,* sometimes translated as "yardmen," as well as *storozha* and *shveitsary*

[Total] Various undetermined occupations account for the difference in the total labor force here, arrived at by adding the sum of its parts, and the total labor force found elsewhere in the censuses.

Birthplace and Occupation, 1902

NUMBERS AND PROPORTION OF IMMIGRANTS FROM EACH PROVINCE IN GIVEN OCCUPATION (MALES)

Occupation	All provinces	%	Moscow	%	Vladimir	%	Tver'	%	Smolensk	%	Kaluga	%	Tula	%	Riazan'	%	Iaroslavl'	%
All occupations	375,797	100	128,891	100	24,051	100	23,625	100	29,338	100	40,637	100	55,829	100	58,274	100	15,152	100
Employers	15,677	4.2	6,610	5.1	1,376	5.7	1,650	7.0	645	2.2	1,528	3.8	1,452	2.6	1,441	2.5	975	6.4
Self-employed	16,966	4.5	7,264	5.6	947	3.9	1,848	7.8	845	2.9	1,495	3.7	1,871	3.4	2,157	3.7	539	3.6
Factory clerks	2,915	0.8	1,166	0.9	359	1.5	156	0.7	200	0.7	303	0.7	291	0.5	321	0.6	119	0.8
Clerks, transport	4,500	1.2	1,241	1.0	548	2.3	335	1.4	447	1.5	323	0.8	716	1.3	697	1.2	193	1.3
Clerks, housing, restaurant	2,204	0.6	568	0.4	142	0.6	193	0.8	157	0.5	185	0.5	289	0.5	382	0.7	288	1.9
Clerks, retail	16,886	4.5	6,062	4.7	1,245	5.2	1,524	6.5	626	2.1	1,715	4.2	1,712	3.1	1,765	3.0	2,237	14.8
Workers, factory	67,633	18.0	22,612	17.5	3,433	14.3	2,162	9.2	8,564	29.2	10,874	26.8	9,190	16.5	10,064	17.3	824	5.4
Workers, other manufacturing	70,813	18.8	29,662	23.0	6,270	26.1	4,732	20.0	3,410	11.6	9,353	23.0	7,689	13.8	7,690	13.2	2,007	13.2
Workers, transport	30,718	8.2	8,009	6.2	1,157	4.8	942	4.0	2,694	9.2	2,004	4.9	7,326	13.1	8,276	14.2	310	2.0
Workers, housing, restaurant	26,121	7.0	4,015	3.1	964	4.0	1,474	6.2	2,907	9.9	1,849	4.6	6,622	11.9	6,323	10.9	1,967	13.0
Workers, retail	16,558	4.4	5,536	4.3	722	3.0	1,054	4.5	1,124	3.8	1,389	3.4	2,698	4.8	3,084	5.3	951	6.3
Apprentices	20,313	5.4	9,593	7.4	729	3.0	1,703	7.2	746	2.5	2,403	5.9	1,976	3.5	1,802	3.1	1,361	9.0
Domestics	6,068	1.6	1,057	0.8	312	1.3	197	0.8	614	2.1	423	1.0	1,734	3.1	1,620	2.8	111	0.7
Day laborers	4,874	1.3	1,121	0.9	188	0.8	378	1.6	517	1.8	502	1.2	993	1.8	1,055	1.8	120	0.8
Unemployed	7,681	2.0	2,117	1.6	566	2.4	484	2.0	674	2.3	888	2.2	1,282	2.3	1,248	2.1	422	2.8

Source: *PM 1902*, I, 2, i, 28–33.
Note: "All provinces," refers to only the eight provinces listed here.

Occupation, Age, and Birthplace, 1902

Males	All Ages			20–24				25–29				30–39				40–49			
Selected Occupations	*Total*	*M*	*%*	*Total*	*%*	*M*	*%*	*Total*	*%*	*M*	*%*	*Total*	*%*	*M*	*%*	*Total*	*%*	*M*	*%*
All Occupations	506,216	61,356	12.1	89,677	17.7	9,517	10.6	85,675	16.9	9,518	11.1	115,708	22.9	13,330	11.5	68,996	13.6	7,327	10.6
A2. Manufacturers	1,231	428	34.8	34	2.8	16	47.1	97	7.9	50	51.2	329	26.7	138	41.9	375	30.5	131	34.9
E1. Managers	2,469	627	25.4	73	3.0	34	46.6	202	8.2	150	74.3	789	32.0	203	25.7	721	29.2	147	20.4
E3. Sales clerks	19,742	3,253	16.5	3,528	17.9	622	17.6	3,649	18.5	634	17.4	5,041	25.5	832	16.5	2,768	14.0	393	14.2
E7. Office clerks	10,099	4,306	42.6	2,454	24.3	1,147	46.7	2,175	21.5	973	44.7	2,346	23.2	843	35.9	825	8.2	241	29.2
A4, B2–7. Small owners	11,904	1,781	15.0	453	3.8	92	20.3	1,431	12.0	250	17.5	3,938	33.1	645	16.4	3,257	27.4	424	13.0
C1–33. Self-employed	22,186	2,173	9.8	1,962	8.8	165	8.4	3,309	14.9	313	9.4	6,839	30.8	704	10.2	5,194	23.4	517	9.9
F6. Silversmiths	2,812	239	8.4	644	22.9	40	6.2	512	18.2	44	8.5	609	21.6	69	11.3	279	9.9	24	8.6
F11. Machinists	10,276	1,723	16.8	2,158	21.0	399	18.5	1,905	18.5	291	15.3	2,419	23.5	340	14.1	1,146	11.2	152	13.3
F38. Cabinetmakers	8,599	515	5.9	1,559	18.1	67	4.3	1,492	17.4	76	5.1	2,093	24.3	159	7.6	1,282	14.9	87	6.8
F45. Bookbinders	4,697	610	13.0	1,036	22.1	144	13.9	827	17.6	112	13.5	763	16.2	97	12.7	297	6.3	43	14.5
F58. Shoemakers	8,137	791	9.7	1,640	20.2	155	9.5	1,525	18.7	139	9.1	1,664	20.4	188	11.3	777	9.5	98	12.6
F64. Carpenters	5,343	41	0.8	819	15.3	4	0.5	1,002	18.8	10	1.0	1,572	29.4	14	0.9	965	18.1	8	0.8
F65. Painters	3,192	194	6.1	515	16.1	28	5.4	550	17.2	43	7.8	743	23.3	53	7.1	364	11.4	23	6.3
F81. Typesetters	1,852	722	39.0	418	22.6	167	40.0	326	17.6	135	41.4	374	20.1	151	40.4	159	8.6	52	32.7
F27. Weavers, cotton	2,709	36	1.3	305	11.3	5	1.6	413	15.2	10	2.4	780	28.7	7	0.9	646	23.8	2	0.3
F28. Weavers, wool	5,010	71	1.4	644	12.9	11	1.7	763	15.2	14	1.8	1,455	29.0	10	0.7	1,174	23.4	12	1.0
F33. Dyers	2,523	51	2.0	464	18.4	8	1.7	438	17.4	7	1.6	600	23.8	13	2.2	334	13.2	3	0.9
F46. Bakers	5,356	55	1.0	1,113	20.8	17	1.5	825	15.4	6	0.7	957	17.9	10	1.0	605	11.3	2	0.3
F96–98. Teamsters	14,399	173	1.2	2,993	20.8	46	1.5	3,459	24.0	46	1.3	4,519	31.4	47	1.0	2,383	16.5	27	1.1
F114. Waiters	5,419	169	3.1	883	16.3	21	2.4	831	15.3	31	3.7	1,115	20.6	43	3.9	628	11.6	32	5.1
G33. On relief	5,105	1,668	32.7	269	5.2	67	24.9	319	6.2	78	24.5	552	10.8	176	31.9	402	7.9	144	35.8
F110. Unskilled	12,256	336	2.7	2,645	21.6	58	2.2	2,514	20.5	76	3.0	2,946	24.0	73	2.5	1,420	11.6	55	3.9
F112. Superintendents	16,335	269	1.6	3,001	18.4	24	0.8	4,292	26.3	52	1.2	4,729	29.0	74	1.6	2,445	15.0	59	2.4
G48. Menials, institutions	11,777	692	5.9	1,609	13.7	66	4.1	2,364	20.1	85	3.6	3,317	28.2	171	5.2	1,939	16.5	153	7.9
— Day Laborers	6,212	695	11.2	707	11.4	68	10.0	916	14.7	100	11.0	1,845	29.7	239	13.0	1,338	21.5	143	10.7

Females Selected Occupations	All Ages			20–24				25–29				30–39				40–49			
	Total	M	%	Total	%	M	%	Total	%	M	%	Total	%	M	%	Total	%	M	%
All Occupations	249,010	45,688	18.3	35,354	14.2	5,835	16.5	33,356	13.4	4,956	14.9	51,372	20.6	7,791	15.2	36,574	14.7	5,741	15.7
E3. Sales clerks	1,046	468	44.7	273	26.1	130	47.6	206	19.7	81	39.3	264	25.2	99	37.5	118	11.3	45	38.1
E7. Office clerks	1,316	643	48.9	385	29.3	203	52.7	345	26.2	173	50.1	298	22.6	132	44.3	105	8.0	39	37.1
G18. Nurses	1,990	267	13.4	266	13.4	30	11.3	335	16.8	42	12.5	543	27.3	66	12.2	428	21.5	57	13.3
A4. Small owners	3,197	870	27.2	242	7.6	85	35.1	483	15.1	159	32.9	1,158	9.7	309	26.7	773	24.2	194	25.1
B2–7. Small owners	1,285	440	34.2	108	8.4	51	47.2	149	11.6	61	40.9	325	25.3	122	37.5	350	27.2	95	27.1
C1–33. Self-employed	12,327	3,347	27.2	1,571	12.7	562	35.8	1,815	14.7	569	31.3	3,406	27.6	920	27.0	2,310	18.7	499	21.6
F55. Tailors	6,869	2,252	32.8	1,779	25.9	578	32.5	1,071	15.6	316	29.5	1,136	16.5	326	28.7	378	5.5	109	28.8
F27. Weavers, cotton	2,068	64	3.1	400	19.3	15	3.8	415	20.1	14	3.4	569	27.5	13	2.3	304	14.7	4	1.3
F32. Stocking-knitters	3,879	627	16.2	832	21.4	117	14.1	711	18.3	86	12.1	712	18.4	118	16.6	291	7.5	65	22.3
G39. Cooks	31,390	1,013	3.2	3,827	12.2	117	3.1	4,605	14.7	111	2.4	8,893	28.3	239	2.7	7,438	23.7	267	3.6
G33. On relief	13,158	4,105	31.2	100	0.8	29	29.0	95	0.7	30	31.6	308	2.3	100	32.5	601	4.6	223	37.1
F63. Washerwomen	7,046	669	9.5	794	11.3	90	11.3	857	12.2	78	9.1	1,774	25.2	164	9.2	1,616	22.9	124	7.7
G48. Menials	4,677	574	12.3	877	18.8	93	10.6	899	19.2	71	7.9	1,151	24.6	126	10.9	665	14.2	87	13.1

Source: *PM 1902*, I, 2, i, 46–117.
Note: M denotes Moscow-born. The first percentage in each set of age groups signifies the percentage of each occupational group in the given age group; the second percentage signifies the proportion of each age group born in Moscow. Given that the occupational table in Section 3 of the 1902 census, used jointly with the table in Section 2 to compose Appendix A, did not correlate occupation with age and birthplace, the totals for most occupations in Appendix C do not equal those in Appendix A.

Bibliography

BIBLIOGRAPHICAL NOTE

Since this is a study of one city, the most important sources are those published by the city's institutions, agencies, companies, and societies. In particular, a myriad of publications of the city council and executive board present a wealth of information on all aspects of city life. Five censuses were taken at the turn of the century; the 1882 and the 1902 census, as well as two volumes of the 1897 census pertaining to Moscow, are remarkably detailed. In addition, the 1902 census was accompanied by a six-volume analysis of various aspects of city development from housing construction to literacy. Unfortunately, the final results of the 1912 census were never published, though parts are available in the Transactions of the Municipal Statistical Committee, the last prerevolutionary Statistical Yearbook, and a statistical yearbook of the city and province in 1927. In addition to publishing the city census, the executive board published statistical yearbooks, monthly bulletins, compilations of vital statistics, and censuses of commerce and manufactures, as well as surveys of public health, welfare institutions, and housing, and annual reports of institutions managed by the municipality. Several publications came out serially, and many studies appeared in the organ of the city council, *Izvestiia Moskovskoi gorodskoi dumy,* published monthly in several parts from 1877 to 1917 (with a cumulative subject index published in 1909). Through these sources the historian can learn not only about municipal services, public health, housing and working conditions, and poor relief, but also about the attitudes of the authorities and professionals to social issues of the day. Regrettably, the disorganization of and poor service at the Moscow City Archive made systematic use of unpublished documents extremely difficult; fortunately, this has not been a handicap for the present study owing to the richness of the published sources.

The city's economy and people had a close relationship with the hinterland, and studies of the Moscow provincial zemstvo as well as nationwide surveys illuminate this relationship. Particularly valuable are the statistical yearbooks and the periodic statistical studies as well as various surveys of the Ministries of Finance and of Internal Affairs and the Central Statistical Committee. I have made frequent use of Kurkin's population studies and Bulgakov's study of peasant mobility, as well as of the rich survey of Moscow's hinterland by Semenov (Tian-Shanskii).

Although statistics and municipal reports give much valuable information, they are incapable of giving an impression of the daily life of the city's muzhiks. To bring the city back to life, I have used descriptive, memoir, and fictional accounts wherever possible. Old guidebooks and handbooks provide colorful descriptions of the city, walking tours through neighborhoods, and historical sketches of the city's development. The most comprehensive was published by Sabashkin Press in 1917. Equally rich is the handsome twelve-volume chronicle, *Moskva v ee proshlom i nastoiashchem* (Moscow Past and Present), compiled by the doyen of prerevolutionary historians of the city, Ivan E. Zabelin. The memoirs of Ivan Slonov, an upwardly mobile Moscow businessman, describe the world of retailing in the 1870s and 1880s. The autobiography of Sergei T. Semenov, a peasant from Volokolamsk, gives us occasional glimpses of the interaction between the urban and rural worlds. Skilled metalworkers Semen Kanatchikov and P. Timofeev left equally valuable accounts of the workaday world. Fiction and the "journalism of the streets" complement the picture of old Moscow and the daily lives of its laboring population. Best known are Vladimir Giliarovskii's *Moskva i moskvichi* (Moscow and Muscovites) and *Trushchobnye liudi* (Slum Folk), but also worthy of mention are the sketches of A. I. Levitov and M. A. Voronov, Semenov's short stories, Podiachev's novella *Mytarstvo* (The Ordeal), and Leikin's novel *Na zarabotkakh* (Working). Although the latter is set in St. Petersburg, it provides a valuable insight into the lives of common laborers in the big city. Those prosaic aspects of city life which Muscovites took for granted often stood out in the eyes of foreigners, then as now, and accordingly I have turned occasionally to the accounts of foreign travelers.

Finally, I have used extensively several standard studies and contemporary journals. The reader will recognize the studies of Tugan-Baranovskii and Dement'ev on the factory, Svavitskii and Sher on the printers, Shestakov on the Tsindel' textile mill, Oliunina on tailors, and Schulze-Gävernitz on the Moscow and Vladimir textile industry. Among the contemporary journals, particularly valuable has been *Trudovaia pomoshch'*, a monthly devoted to welfare problems.

ARCHIVAL SOURCES

TsGAM (Tsentral'nyi gosudarstvennyi arkhiv goroda Moskvy).
F. 16 (Moskovskii General-Gubernator), op. 136, d. 175 ("Statisticheskie svedeniia o promyshlennykh predpriiatiiakh Moskovskoi gubernii za 1903").
F. 46 (Moskovskii Gradonachal'nik), op. 14, d. 1212 ("Vedomost' o fabrikakh i zavodakh v gorode Moskvy za 1910").
F. 179 (Moskovskaia gorodskaia duma i gorodskaia uprava), op. 21, d. 1715 ("Delo ob ozdorovlenii Khitrova rynka, 1910–1914").
F. 179, op. 21, d. 2009 ("Delo po voprosu ob uchastii Gorodskogo upravleniia v raspredelenii kapitalov, zaveshchannykh F. Ia. Ermakovym bednym i nuzhdaiushchim liudiam, 1910–1914").
F. 179, op. 21, d. 2457 ("O proizvodstve perepisi naseleniia, kvartir i vladenii v gorode Moskvy").
F. 179, op. 58, d. 35 ("Delo ob uchrezhdenii v Moskve gorodskikh uchastkovykh popechitel'stv o bednykh, 1894–1895").
F. 179, op. 58, d. 129 ("Mesiachnye vedomosti o kolichestve nochlezhnikov v gorodskom nochlezhnom dome za 1895 i spiski na vydachu zhalovaniia sluzhashchim nochlezhnogo doma za 1895").
F. 184 (Moskovskaia gubernskaia zemskaia uprava), op. 2, d. 852 ("Proekt doklada ob organizatsii Moskovskogo Gorodskogo Rabotnogo doma. Doklad Komissii po pereustroistvu Moskovskogo Gorodskogo Rabotnogo doma").
TsGIA SSSR (Tsentral'nyi gosudarstvennyi istoricheskii arkhiv SSSR).
F. 20 (Ministerstvo Finansov, Department torgovli i manufaktur) op. 12, dd. 127, 128, 128a, 300 ("Voprosnye listki Moskovskoi gubernii za 1879. Voprosnye listki po promyshlennym predpriiatiiam Moskovskoi gubernii za 1879, 1881").
F. 20, op. 12, dd. 119, 122, 122a, 123, 124, 125, 126, 290, 394, 395 ("Vedomosti o promyshlennykh predpriiatiiakh Moskovskoi gubernii za 1878, 1879, 1880, 1890, 1894–1895").
F. 23 (Ministerstvo Torgovli i promyshlennosti), op. 16, d. 59 ("Svedeniia o kolichestve rabochikh na predpriiatiiakh v Sankt-Peterburgskoi i Moskovskoi gubernii za 1908–1909").

F. 32 (Sovet s"ezdov predstavitelei promyshlennosti i torgovli, 1905–1918), op. 1, dd. 1708, 1709 ("Statisticheskie svedeniia za 1904–1910 o chisle predpriiatii, srednom chisle rabochikh, zastrakhovannykh rabochikh, zarplate, ubytkakh, prodolzhitel'nosti rabot v techenii goda po okrugam Moskovskomu, Kievskomu, i pr.").

F. 1284 (Ministerstvo vnutrennikh del, Departament obshchikh del), op. 194, dd. 125, 128 ("Otchet o sostoianii Moskovskoi gubernii za 1901, 1903").

F. 1284, op. 194, dd. 79, 81, 86, 87, 97, 101, 130 ("S kopii vsepoddannei-shego otcheta o sostoianii goroda Moskvy za 1902, 1904, 1907, 1908, 1909, 1910, 1911").

F. 1290 (Ministerstvo vnutrennikh del, Tsentral'nyi statisticheskii komitet), op. 2, d. 541 ("O proizvodstve v 1902 odnodnevnoi perepisi naseleniia goroda Moskvy").

F 1290, op. 5, d. 155 ("Vedomosti o chisle remeslennykh obshchestv v guberniiakh i gradonachal'stvakh, o chislennom sostave ikh, 1897").

F. 1290, op. 5 dd. 176, 180 ("Statisticheskie svedeniia o sostoianii fabrik i zavodov v 1900, 1902 gg.").

F. 1290, op. 5, dd. 195, 255 ("Statisticheskie svedeniia o kolichestve zhite-lei, promyshlennykh predpriiatiiakh i chisle rabochikh v nikh po gorodam Moskovskoi gubernii za 1904, 1909").

F. 1290, op. 5, d. 256 ("Vedomosti o chisle remeslennikov v gorodakh i posadakh v Moskovskoi gubernii za 1909").

F. 1297 (Ministerstvo vnutrennikh del, Meditsinskii department), op. 289, d. 160 ("Delo po meditsinskomu otchetu Moskovskoi gubernii").

STATISTICAL AND OTHER OFFICIAL AND SEMIOFFICIAL SOURCES

Damskoe popechitel'stvo o bednykh. *Piatidesiatiletie Damskogo popchi-tel'stva o bednykh v Moskve, 1844–94.* Moscow, 1895.

D'iakonov, et al. "O postoialykh dvorakh v Moskve." *Otchet o deiatel'nosti Moskovskoi gorodskoi upravy za 1885*, 165–78. Moscow, 1887.

Dukhovskoi, M. *Soobrazhenie po voprosu ob ustroistve Moskovskim gorod-skim upravleniem posrednicheskoi kontory dlia ukazaniia raboty v g. Moskve.* Moscow, 1895.

Duvakin, D. D. "Nochlezhnye doma." *Otchet o deiatel'nosti Moskovskoi gorodskoi upravy za 1885*, 69–82. Moscow, 1887.

Dvadtsatipiatiletie Tovarishchestva sittsenabivnoi manufaktury Emil' Tsindel' v Moskve, 1874–1899: Istoriko-statisticheskii ocherk. Moscow, 1899.

Gornostaev, I. F., ed. *Fabriki i zavody goroda Moskvy i ee prigorodov.* Moscow, 1904.

Great Britain. *Parliamentary Papers: Diplomatic and Consular Reports: Russia.* London, 1880–1910.

Ianzhul, I. I. *Fabrichnyi byt moskovskoi gubernii: Otchet za 1882–1883 g. fabrichnogo inspektora nad zaniatiiami maloletnikh rabochikh Moskov-skogo okruga.* St. Petersburg, 1884.

————. *Moskovskii fabrichnyi okrug: Otchet za 1885 g. fabrichnogo inspektora Moskovskogo okruga.* St. Petersburg, 1886.

Imperatorskoe Chelovekoliubivoe obshchestvo. *Istoricheskii ocherk Soveta Imperatorskogo Chelovekoliubivogo obshchestva i podvedomstvennykh emu blagotvoritel'nykh uchrezhdenii.* St. Petersburg, 1898.

Imperatorskoe russkoe tekhnicheskoe obshchestvo. *Doklad komissii po ozdorovleniiu Khitrova rynka.* Moscow, 1903.

Ozdorovlenie Khitrova rynka. Moscow, 1899.

"Iz deiatel'nosti Moskovskikh gorodskikh uchastkovykh popechitel'stv o bednykh." *Sbornik statei po voprosam, otnosiashchimsia k zhizni russkikh i inostrannykh gorodov,* 12 vols. (Moscow, 1895–1901), 4 (1897): 55–76; 6 (1897): 137–79; 2 (1901): 1–57.

Komarov, Nikolai A. *Voenno-statisticheskoe opisanie Moskovskoi, Vladimirskoi i Nizhegorodskoi gubernii.* Moscow, 1895.

Komissiia po peresmotru zakonov o prizrenii bednykh. *Zapiska ob istoricheskom razvitii sposobov prizreniia v inostrannykh gosudarstvakh i o teoreticheskikh nachalakh pravil'noi ego postanovki.* St. Petersburg, 1897.

Kurkin, P. I., and Chertov, A. A. *Estestvennoe dvizhenie naseleniia goroda Moskvy i Moskovskoi gubernii.* Moscow, 1927.

Materialy dlia istorii Imperatorskogo Moskovskogo vospitatel'nogo doma. 2 vols. Moscow, 1914.

Materialy k voprosu ob obshchestvennom prizrenii. Odessa, 1895.

Ministerstvo finansov, Departament torgovli i manufaktur. *Fabrichno-zavodskaia promyshlennost' i torgovlia Rossii.* St. Petersburg, 1893.

Minsterstvo finansov, Otdel promyshlennosti. *Statisticheskie svedeniia o fabrikakh i zavodakh po proizvodstvam, 1900.* St. Petersburg, 1903.

Ministerstvo torgovli i promyshlennosti. *Spisok fabrik i zavodov goroda Moskvy i Moskovskoi gubernii.* Moscow, 1916.

Svod otchetov fabrichnykh inspektorov. 16 vols. St. Petersburg, 1900–1915.

Ministerstvo torgovli i promyshlennosti, Otdel torgovli. *Remeslenniki i remeslennoe upravlenie v Rossii.* Petrograd, 1916.

Minsterstvo vnutrennikh del. *Obshchii obzor deiatel'nosti Ministerstva vnutrennikh del za vremia tsarstvovaniia Imperatora Aleksandra III.* St. Petersburg, 1901.

Ministerstvo vnutrennikh del, Glavnoe upravlenie po delam mestnogo khoziaistva. *Obshchestvennoe i chastnoe prizrenie v Rossii.* St. Petersburg, 1907.

Moskovskaia gorodskaia duma. *Sbornik obiazatel'nykh dlia zhitelei goroda Moskvy postanovlenii.* Moscow, 1914.

Stenograficheskie otchety o sobraniiakh, 1900–1913. Moscow, 1901–1914.

Zhurnaly, 1900–1913. Moscow, 1900–1914.

Moskovskaia gorodskaia duma, Komissiia po delam o pol'zakh i nuzhdakh obshchestvennykh.

Doklad ob ustroistve i soderzhanii kvartir dlia nochlezhnikov. Moscow, 1866.

Komissiia po ozdorovlenniiu Khitrova rynka. *Doklady.* Moscow, 1910–1911.

Moskovskaia gorodskaia uprava.

Dokhody i raskhody goroda Moskvy za 1899–1914. Moscow, 1915.

Doklady, 1893–1911. Moscow, 1893–1911.

Moskovskie khlebopekarni v 1895 g. Moscow, 1896.

Otchet o deiatel'nosti. Moscow, 1882–1915.

"Otchet sanitarnykh vrachei." *IMGD,* 1878–80 (various numbers).

Perepis' bol'nykh, prizrevaemykh v lechebnikh, rodovspomogatel'nykh i blagotvoritel'nykh uchrezhdeniiakh Moskovskogo gorodskogo obshchestvennogo upravleniia 11-go dekabria 1910 g. Compiled by V. P. Uspenskii. 2 vols. Moscow, 1912.

Smeta raskhodov i dokhodov goroda Moskvy. Moscow, 1910–1913.

Vedomosti nakhodiashchikhsia v Moskve torgovykh i promyshlennykh zavedenii. Moscow, 1873.

Moskovskaia gorodskaia uprava, Spravochnoe otdelenie po delam blagotvoritel'nosti. *Sbornik spravochnykh svedenii o blagotvoritel'nosti v Moskve.* Moscow, 1901.

Moskovskaia gorodskaia uprava, Statisticheskii otdel.

Ezhemesiachnyi statisticheskii biulleten' po gorodu Moskvy. Moscow, 1892–1916.

Glavneishie predvaritel'nye dannye perepisi goroda Moskvy 1902 g. 6 vols. Moscow, 1902–1907.

Glavneishie predvaritel'nye dannye perepisi goroda Moskvy 1912 g. (Trudy Statisticheskogo otdeleniia Moskovskoi gorodskoi upravy.) Vyp. 1. Moscow, 1913.

Ischislenie naseleniia goroda Moskvy v fevrale 1907 g. Moscow, 1907.

Nekotorye svedeniia o lomovom izvoze v Moskve. Moscow, 1895.

"Neskol'ko dannykh o moskovskikh koechno-kamarochnykh kvartirakh." *IMGD,* 33, no. 1 (April 1899): 95–115.

Perepis' Moskvy 1882 g. 3 vols. Moscow, 1885.

Perepis' Moskvy 1902 g. Moscow, 1904.

Sbornik statisticheskikh svedenii o blagotvoritel'nosti Moskvy za 1889 g. Moscow, 1891.

Slovar' dlia razrabotki dannykh o professional'nom sostave naseleniia. Moscow, 1913.

Smertnost' naseleniia goroda Moskvy, 1872–1889. Moscow, 1891.

Statisticheskii atlas goroda Moskvy. Moscow, 1887–1889, 1911.

Statisticheskii ezhegodnik goroda Moskvy. 4 vols. Moscow, 1906–1916.

Svodnyi biulleten' po gorodu Moskvy. Moscow, 1884–1914.

Torgovo-promyshlennye zavedeniia goroda Moskvy v 1885–1890 gg. Moscow, 1892.

Trudy. 4 vols. Moscow, 1882–1883.

Promyshlennye i torgovye zavedeniia Moskvy za 1879. (Trudy Statisticheskogo otdela Moskovskoi gorodskoi upravy), 2, 4. Moscow 1882–1883.

Moskovskaia gubernskaia zemskaia uprava.

Doklady. Moscow, 1911–1914.

Sbornik statisticheskikh svedenii po Moskovskoi gubernii. Vol. 4: *Ob-shchaia svodka po sanitarnym issledovaniiam fabrichnykh zavedenii Moskovskoi gubernii za 1879–1885 gg.* ed. F. F. Erisman and E. M. De-ment'ev, Pts. 1 and 2. Moscow, 1890–1893.

Sbornik statisticheskikh svedenii po Moskovskoi gubernii. Pt. 1: *Sanitar-noe issledovanie fabrik Bogorodskogo uezda Moskovskoi gubernii.* Compiled by A. V. Pogozhev. Moscow, 1885.

Moskovskaia gubernskaia zemskaia uprava, Otsenochnoe otdelenie. *Materialy po otsenke fabrik, zavodov i promyshlennykh zavedenii Moskovskoi gubernii.* Vyp. 1. Moscow, 1913.

Moskovskaia gubernskaia zemskaia uprava, Statisticheskoe otdelenie. *Ekono-miko-statisticheskii sbornik.* Compiled by I. M. Koz'minykh-Lanin. Moscow, 1911.

Fabrichnaia i zavodskaia promyshlennost' Moskovskoi gubernii v 1881 i 1871 gg. Moscow, 1886.

Moskovskaia guberniia po mestnomu obsledovaniiu, 1898–1900. 4 vols. in 8 parts. Moscow, 1903–1908.

Sanitarno-statisticheskie tablitsy. Compiled by P. I. Kurkin. Moscow, 1910.

Statistika dvizheniia naseleniia v Moskovskoi gubernii, 1883–1897. Compiled by P. I. Kurkin. Moscow, 1902.

Statisticheskii ezhegodnik Moskovskoi gubernii. Moscow, 1884–1904.

Moskovskii gorodskoi Rukavishnikovskii priiut, 1864–1889. Moscow, 1890.

Moskovskii sovet rabochikh, krest'ianskikh, i krasnoarmeiskikh deputatov.

Statisticheskii atlas g. Moskvy i Moskovskoi gubernii. Moscow, 1924.

Moskovskii stolichnyi i gubernskii statisticheskii komitet.

Dannye o rodivshikhsia i brakakh v gorode Moskvy. 4 vols. Moscow, 1894–1911.

Pamiatnaia knizhka Moskovskoi gubernii na 1909 god. Moscow, 1908.

Statisticheskie svedeniia o zhiteliakh goroda Moskvy po perepisi 12 deka-bria 1871 g. Moscow, 1874.

Moskovskoe gorodskoe obshchestvennoe upravlenie.

Deiatel'nost' Moskovskikh gorodskikh popechitel'stv o bednykh v 1900. Moscow, 1901.

Deiatel'nost' Moskovskoi gorodskoi upravy za 1913–16 gg. Moscow, 1916.

Doklad soveta po Rukavishnikovskomu priiutu. Moscow, 1915.

Moskovskii gorodskoi dom trudoliubiia i Rabotnyi dom v ego proshlom i nastoiashchem. Compiled by S. Sharov. Moscow, 1913.

Ocherk istorii i sovremennoi deiatel'nosti Moskovskogo doma trudoliu-biia. Compiled by A. Gaidamovich. Moscow, 1902.

Otchet detskikh priiutov za 1910–13. Moscow, 1912–1915.

Otchet domov prizreniia i besplatnykh kvartir, nakhodiashchikhsia v vede-nii Moskovskogo gorodskogo obshchestvennogo upravleniia. Moscow, 1892–1916.

Otchet gorodskogo popechitel'stva o bednykh. Moscow, 1895–1917.
Otchet gorodskogo popechitel'stva o bednykh Khitrova rynka. 11 vols.
Moscow, 1904–1914.
*Otchet gorodskogo Rukavishnikovskogo priiuta dlia maloletnikh za
1911–1913.* Moscow, 1912–1914.
Otchet o deiatel'nosti gorodskikh vrachei. Moscow, 1899.
Otchet o deiatel'nosti gorodskogo doma trudoliubiia. 3 vols. Moscow,
1912–1915.
*Otchet o deiatel'nosti gorodskogo nochlezhnogo doma im. F. Ia. Erma-
kova.* 4 vols. Moscow, 1912–1914.
*Otchet o deiatel'nosti gorodskogo sirotskogo doma im. N. Mazurina za
1914.* Moscow, 1916.
*Otchet o deiatel'nosti gorodskogo sirotskogo priiuta im. br. P., A., V.
Bakhrushinykh.* 3 vols. Moscow, 1909–1914.
Otchet o deiatel'nosti gorodskogo ubezhishcha dlia sirot. 10 vols. Mos-
cow, 1898–1916.
*Otchet o deiatel'nosti Moskovskogo Gorodskogo Rabotnogo doma,
1895–1913.* Moscow, 1896–1914.
Otchet po gorodskomu rodil'nomu domu im. S. V. Lepekhina. Moscow,
1909.
Otchet po rodil'nomu domu im A. A. Abrikosovoi. Moscow, 1909.
Otchet po zavedeniiam obshchestvennogo prizreniia za 1900. Moscow,
1900.
Otchet remeslennogo uchilishcha im. K. T. Soldatenkova. Moscow, 1910–
1917.
Otchet rodovspomogatel'nykh uchrezhdenii. Moscow, 1910.
*Otchet zhenskogo doma trudoliubiia im. M. A. i S. N. Gorbovykh, 1897–
1915.* Moscow, 1898–1916.
Popechitel'stva o bednykh goroda Moskvy v. 1895. Moscow, 1896.
*Vremennoe polozhenie o gorodskikh uchastkovykh popechitel'stvakh o
bednykh v Moskve.* Moscow, 1894.
Moskovskoe gorodskoe prisutstvie po razboru i prizreniiu nishchikh. *Doklad
rasporiaditel'nomu sobraniiu.* Moscow, 1910.
Moskovskoe gradonachal'stvo. *Obzor po gorodu Moskve za 1905–9.* Mos-
cow, 1906–1910.
Obshchestvo pooshchreniia trudoliubiia v Moskve. *Letopis' pervogo dvad-
tsatipiatiletiia.* Moscow, 1888.
Orlov, P. A., and S. G. Budagov, eds. *Ukazatel' fabrik i zavodov Evropeiskoi
Rossii.* 3d ed. St. Petersburg, 1894.
Pogozhev, A. V., ed. *Adresnaia kniga fabrichno-zavodskoi i remeslennoi pro-
myshlennosti vsei Rossii.* St. Petersburg, 1905.
———. Uchet chislennosti i sostava rabochikh v Rossii. St. Petersburg, 1906.
Polnoe sobranie zakonov Rossiiskoi imperii. 1st series: 1649 to 1825. St.
Petersburg, 1830. 2d series: 1825 to 1881. St. Petersburg, 1830–1884. 3d
series: 1881 to 1916. St. Petersburg, 1885–1916.

Popechitel'stvo o trudovoi pomoshchi.
   Kratkie svedeniia po sostoiashchemu . . . popechitel'stvu o domakh trudoliu-
   biia i rabotnykh domakh. St. Petersburg, 1898.
   Sbornik svedenii po sostoiashchemu . . . popechitel'stvu o domakh trudoliu-
   biia i rabotnykh domakh. St. Petersburg, 1901.
Prokhorovskaia Trekhgornaia manufaktura.
   Istoriko-statisticheskii ocherk. Moscow, 1900.
   Materialy k istorii Prokhorovskoi Trekhgornoi manufactury i torgovo-prom-
   yshlennoi deiatel'nosti sem'i Prokhorovykh, 1799–1915. Moscow, 1916.
Sharov, S., "Kharakteristika klientov Moskovskogo Doma trudoliubiia."
   IMGD, 38, no. 3 (March 1914): 1–42.
Sobstvennaia Ego Imperatorskogo Velichestva kantseliariia po uchrezhdeni-
   iam Imperatritsy Marii.
   Sbornik svedenii s kratkimi ocherkami blagotvoritel'nykh uchrezhdenii v
   Sankt-Peterburge i Moskve. St. Petersburg, 1899.
   Blagotvoritel'nost' v Rossii. 2 vols. St. Petersburg, 1907.
Statisticheskii ezhegodnik goroda Moskvy i moskovskoi gubernii. Moscow,
   1927.
Stranopriimnyi dom gr. Sheremeteva v Moskve, 1810–1910. Moscow, 1910.
Svod zakonov Rossiiskoi imperii. St. Petersburg, 1857–1916.
Tsentral'nyi statisticheskii komitet.
   Ezhegodnik Rossii. St. Petersburg, 1904, 1908, 1909.
   Obshchii svod po imperii rezul'tatov razrabotki dannykh pervoi vseob-
   shchei perepisi naseleniia 1897. St. Petersburg, 1905.
   Okonchatel'no ustanovlennoe pri razrabotke perepisi nalichnoe naselenie
   gorodov, 1897. St. Petersburg, 1905.
   Pervaia vseobshchaia perepis' naseleniia Rossiiskoi imperii, 1897. St. Pe-
   tersburg, 1897–1905.
   Statisticheskii vremennik Rossiiskoi imperii. St. Petersburg, 1866–90.
   Statistiki Rossiiskoi imperii. St. Petersburg, 1888–1916.
Tupitsyn, K. T. "O podval'nykh zhilykh pomeshcheniiakh v Moskve." *IMGD*,
   9, no. 1 (January 1885): 181–204.
Tverskaia gubernskaia zemskaia uprava. *Statisticheskii ezhegodnik Tverskoi*
   gubernii za 1903 i 1904 gg. Vyp. 2. Tver', 1906.
Vedomosti politseiskikh uchastkov goroda Moskvy. Moscow, 1881.

CONTEMPORARY UNOFFICIAL SOURCES

Abramov, Ia. "Iz fabrichno-zavodskogo mira." *Otechestvennye zapiski,* no. 3
   (March 1882): 1–37.
Andreev, I. V. "Filantropy i nishchie." *Delo,* no. 7 (1868): 5–38.
Anufriev, K. I. "Osnovy obiazatel'nogo prizreniia bednykh." S"ezd po ob-
   shchestvennomu prizreniiu, *Trudy,* 191–229. St. Petersburg, 1914.
Ash., Nik. "Moskovskii Uaitchepel' i proekt ego uprazdenie." *Russkoe bo-*
   gatstvo, 7 no. 1 (1899): 175–84.

Astrov, P. "Chto sdelat' v Moskve dlia Khitrova rynka?" *Trudovaia pomoshch'*, 7 no. 3 (March 1904): 363–70.

B., M. "Otkhod krest'ianskogo naseleniia na zarabotki." *Izvestiia Moskovskoi zemskoi upravy*, 3 (1911): 11–31.

B., P. "Pis'ma o Moskve." *Vestnik Evropy* (March, May, July, 1881).

Baedeker, Karl. *Russia with Teheran, Port Arthur and Peking*. London, 1914.

Bakhrushin, S. V. *Maloletnie nishchie i brodiagi v Moskve*. Moscow, 1913.

Beloshapkin, D. P. "Moskovskii Rabotnyi dom." *Trudovaia pomoshch'*, 6, no. 3 (March 1903): 320–37; no. 4 (April 1903): 374–96.

Belousov, I. A. *Ushedshaia Moskva: Zapiski po lichnym vospominaniiam s nachala 1870 g*. Moscow, 1927.

Belov, Pavel. "Kartina kustarnogo proizvodstva v sele Cherkizove, Moskovskogo uezda." *Mir Bozhii*, 6 (1900): 10–35.

Bergman, Evegenii. "Poslednie perepisi Peterburga i Moskvy." *IMGD*, 11, no. 6–7 (1887): 99–150.

Berkut, E. N. "O gorodsksikh uchastkovykh popechitel'stvakh o bednykh v Moskve (Vospominaniia sotrudnitsy)." *Trudovia pomoshch'*, 6, no. 3 (March 1903): 351–63.

Bessonov, Petr A., ed. *Kaleki perekhozhie: Sbornik stikhov i issledovanii*. 4 vols. Moscow, 1861–1864.

Bezobrazov, Vladimir P. *Narodnoe khoziaistvo Rossii*. Vol. 1: *Moskovskaia promyshlennaia oblast'*. St. Petersburg, 1882.

Bleklov, S. M. "Obrazovatel'nye uchrezhdeniia dlia rabochikh goroda Moskvy." *Russkaia mysl'*, 25, no. 5 (May 1904): 121–45.

Boborykin, P. D. *Kitai-gorod*. Moscow, 1960.

———. "Sovremennaia Moskva." In P. P. Semenov, ed., *Zhivopisnaia Rossiia*, 6:242–87. Moscow, 1898.

Bochechkarov, N. I. "O nishchenstve i raznykh vidakh blagotvoritel'nosti." *Arkhiv istorii i prakticheskikh svedenii, otnosiashchikhsia do Rossii*, 3:50–67. St. Petersburg, 1859.

Bogarov, N. P. *Moskva i Moskvichi: Istoricheskie ocherki, issledovaniia i zametki*. Moscow, 1881.

Bouton, John Bell. *Roundabout to Moscow*. New York, 1887.

Brianskii, H. G. *Moskovskie proizvoditel'no-trudovye arteli*. Petrograd, 1915.

Bulgakov, A. A. *Sovremennoe peredvizhenie krest'ianstva: Napravlenie, razmery i usloviia krest'ianskikh dvizhenii moskovskoi gubernii po novym tsifrovym dannym za desiatiletie 1894–1903 gg*. St. Petersburg, 1905.

———. "Tsifrovye dannye o vykhodakh iz krest'ianstva, peredvizheniiakh v krest'ianskoi srede i vystuplenii v krest'ianstvo Moskovskoi gubernii po arkhivym materialam Moskovskoi kazennoi palaty za desiatiletie 1894–1903 gody." *Statisticheskii ezhegodnik Moskovskoi gubernii za 1905*, 1–31. Moscow, 1906.

Buryshkin, P. A. *Moskva kupecheskaia*. New York, 1954.

Bychkov, N. *Gorodskie kazarmy v Moskve. Istoricheskaia spravka*. Moscow, 1907.

Chaslavskii, V. I. "Zemledel'cheskie otkhozhie promysly v sviazi s pereseleniem krest'ian." V. Bezobrazov, ed. *Sbornik gosudarstvennykh znanii,* 2:181–211. St. Petersburg, 1875.

Child, Theodore, et al., *The Tsar and His People.* New York, 1891.

Chuprov, A. I. *Kharakteristika Moskvy po perepisi 1882 g.* Moscow, 1884.

Dement'ev, E. M. *Fabrika: chto ona daet naseleniiu i chto ona u nego beret.* 2d ed. Moscow, 1897.

———. "Sviaz' fabrichnykh rabochikh s zemeledeliem: K voprosu ob obrazovanii fabrichnogo proletariata v Rossii." *Iuridicheskii vestnik,* 9 (1890): 399–421.

———. *Vrachebnaia pomoshch' fabrichnym rabochim v 1907 g.* St. Petersburg, 1909.

Deriuzhinskii, Vladimir F. "Obshchestvennoe prizrenie u krest'ian." *Trudovaia pomoshch',* 6 (June 1899): 1–21.

———. *Politseiskoe pravo. Posobie dlia studentov.* St. Petersburg, 1903.

———. *Zametki ob obshchestvennom prizrenii.* Moscow, 1897.

Ditiatin, I. "K istorii Gorodovogo Polozheniia 1870 g." *Iuridicheskii vestnik,* 1 (1885): 3–35; 2 (1885): 205–49; 3 (1885): 413–51.

———. "Nashi goroda za pervoe tri chetverti nastoiashchego stoletiia." *Iuridicheskii vestnik,* 2 (1880): 242–69.

———. *Ustroistvo i upravlenie gorodov Rossii.* 2 vols. St. Petersburg, 1875–1877.

Dmitriev, M. N. *Doma trudoliubiia.* St. Petersburg, 1900.

Dobson, G. *Russia.* London, 1913.

Dolgorukova, V. *Putevoditel' po Moskve.* Moscow, 1872.

Dril', Dmitrii A. *Brodiazhestvo i nishchenstvo i mery bor'by s nimi.* St. Petersburg, 1899.

———. *Maloletnie prestupniki.* 2 vols. Moscow, 1884–1888.

———. "Parizhskii kongress obshchestvennogo prizreniia i chastnoi blagotvoritel'nosti 1900 g." *Trudovaia pomoshch',* 3, no. 9 (November 1900): 382–404.

———. "Polozhenie remeslennikov i remeslennoe zakonodatel'stvo." *Iuridicheskii vestnik,* 23, no. 7, pt. 1 (January 1891): 29–59.

Dukhovskoi, N. V. "Gorodskie popechitel'stva o bednykh v Moskve." *Trudovaia pomoshch',* 1, no. 1 (November 1897): 66–79.

———. "Vzaimodeistvie blagotvoritel'nykh uchrezhdenii v Moskve." *Trudovaia pomoshch',* 3, no. 5 (May 1900): 457–71.

"El'berfel'dskaia sistema prizreniia bednykh," *IMGD,* 19, no. 1 (1895): 17–36.

Evreinov, V. D. "K kharakteristike domov trudoliubiia." *Trudovaia pomoshch',* 2, no. 1 (January 1899): 38–58.

Ezerskii, N. "Chego nedostaet moskovskim gorodskim popechitel'stvam?" *Trudovaia pomoshch',* 3, no. 8 (October 1900): 282–98.

———. "Zadachi gorodskikh popechitel'stv." *Trudovaia pomoshch',* 4, no. 5 (May 1901): 565–93.

"Fabrichnye masterskie i zhilye pomeshcheniia dlia rabochikh." *IMGD,* 8, no. 1 (1884): 12–38.

Fedorovich, L. *Zhilye pomeshcheniia rabochikh.* St. Petersburg, 1881.

Fleksor, D. "Kustarnaia promyshlennost' i trudovaia pomoshch'." *Trudovaia pomoshch'*, 3, no. 2 (February 1900): 129–71.

Fraser, John Foster. *Russia of to-day*. London, 1915.

Frankel', Z. "Neskol'ko dannykh o sanitarnom sostoianii Moskvy i Peterburga za 1909 g." *Gorodskoe Delo*, no. 20 (October 15, 1910): 1402–1409.

Gagen, V. A. *K voprosu ob organizatsii ukazaniia truda*. St. Petersburg, 1902.

———. "Predstoiashchaia reforma rabotnykh domov." *IMGD*, 32, no. 6–7 (June-July 1908): 30–39.

———. *Zemstvo i obshchestvennye raboty*. St. Petersburg, 1905.

Geinike, N. A., et al. *Po Moskve: Progulki po Moskve i ee khudozhestvennym i prosvetitel'nym uchrezhdeniiam*. Moscow, 1917.

Georgievskii, P. I. *Prizrenie bednykh i blagotvoritel'nost'*. St. Petersburg, 1894.

Ger'e, V. "Chto takoe dom trudoliubiia." *Trudovaia pomoshch'*, 1, no. 1 (November 1897): 1–43.

———. "Opyt gorodskogo popecheniia o bednykh." *Vestnik Evropy*, 31, no. 10 (October 1896): 566–85.

———. "Russkaia blagotvoritel'nost' na Vsemirnoi vystavke." *Vestnik Evropy*, 35, no. 8 (August 1900): 481–505.

———. "Vtoroi god gorodskikh popechitel'stv v Moskve." *Vestnik Evropy*, 32, no. 10 (October 1897): 584–612.

Gernet, Mikhail N., ed. *Deti-prestupniki: Sbornik statei*. Moscow, 1912.

Gertsenshtein, G. "K voprosu ob otkhozhikh promyslakh." *Russkaia mysl'*, 8, no. 9 (September 1887): 147–65.

———. "Gde i kak iutitsia peterburgskaia bednota?" *Severnyi vestnik*, no. 1, (1898): 113–33; no. 3 (1898), 139–55.

Gibshman, A. "Neskol'ko dannykh o kvartirnykh usloviiakh sluzhashchikh v Moskve." *IMGD*, 35, no. 1 (January 1911): 1–21.

Giliarovskii, V. A. *Izbrannoe*. 2 vols. Kuibyshev, 1965.

———. *Moskovskie nishchie*. Moscow, 1896.

———. *Moskva i Moskvichi*. Moscow, 1968.

Gimmer, N. "K kharakteristike Rossiiskogo proletariata." *Sovremennik*, 4 (April 1913): 321–30.

Ginzburg, N. "Prizrenie podkidyshei v Rossii." *Trudovaia pomoshch'*, 7, no. 4 (April 1904): 491–518; no. 5 (May 1904): 595–621; no. 6 (June 1904): 72–102.

Golitsynskii, A. *Ulichnye tipy*. Moscow, 1860.

Gomberg, D. "K voprosu ob uchrezhdenii Gorodskoi posrednicheskoi kontory." *IMGD*, 30, no. 17 (September 1906): 1–24.

Gorbunov, A. V. "Bor'ba s nishchenstvom i brodiazhnichestvom." *Russkaia mysl'*, 30, no. 3 (March 1909): 137–49.

———. "Obshchestvennoe prizrenie i ekonomicheskaia politika." *Mir Bozhii*, 7 (July 1898): 1–24.

Gor'kii, Maxim. *Na dne*. 3d ed. St. Petersburg, 1903.

Gornostaev, I. F., and Ia. M. Bugoslavskii. *Putevoditel' po Moskve i ee okrestnostiam*. Moscow, 1903.

Gorodskoe samoupravlenie v Rossii. Moscow, 1905.

Gorovstev, A. [Gor-ev]. "K kharakteristike ekonomicheskikh i bytovykh uslovii zhizni bezrabotnykh." *Mir Bozhii*, no. 10 (October 1899): 116–31; no. 11 (November 1899): 36–53.

———. "O rabotakh v domakh trudoliubiia." *Trudovaia pomoshch'*, 3, no. 7 (September 1900): 140–71.

———. *Trudovaia pomoshch' kak sredstvo prizreniia bednykh*. St. Petersburg, 1901.

———. "Tsel' i naznachenie domov trudoliubiia." *Vestnik Evropy*, 35, no. 6 (June 1900): 497–547.

Grigor'ev, Vasilii N. *Pereselenie krest'ian Riazanskoi gubernii*. Moscow, 1885.

Guild, Curtis. *Britons and Muscovites*. Boston, 1888.

Gvozdev, S. *Zapiski fabrichnogo inspektora*. Moscow-Leningrad, 1925.

Hapgood, Isabel F. *Russian Rambles*. Boston, 1895.

I-ov, A. "Vospitatel'nye doma v Rossii." *Vestnik Evropy*, 25, no. 6 (June 1890): 485–542.

Iakobii, A. "Blagotvoritel'nost'." *Mir Bozhii*, 3 (March 1894): 129–44; 4 (April 1894): 92–115.

Iakovlev, S. P. "Nekotorye dannye o chastnoi blagotvoritel'nosti v Moskve." *Trudovaia pomoshch'*, 1, no. 11 (November 1898): 498–509.

Ianson, Iu. "Naselenie Peterburga i ego ekonomicheskii i sotsial'nyi sostav po perepisi 1869 goda." *Vestnik Evropy*, 10, no. 5. (September-October 1875): 606–41; no. 6 (November-December 1875): 55–94.

Ianzhul, Ivan. "Fabrichnyi rabochii v srednei Rossii i Tsarstve pol'skom." *Vestnik Evropy*, 23, no. 2 (February 1888): 785–811.

———. *Iz vospominanii i perepiski fabrichnogo inspektora pervogo prizyva*. St. Petersburg, 1907.

Iasnopol'skii, L. N., ed. *Statistiko-ekonomicheskie ocherki oblastei, gubernii i gorodov Rossii*. Kiev, 1913.

Il'inskii, V. *Blagotvoritel'nost' v Rossii: Istoriia i nastoiashchee polozhenie*. St. Petersburg, 1908.

Illiustrirovannyi putevoditel' po Moskve. Moscow, 1911.

International Congress of Charities, Correction and Philanthropy, Chicago, 1893. *Report of the Proceedings*. Baltimore and London, 1894.

Isaev, A. A. *Bol'shie goroda i ikh vliianie na obshchestvennuiu zhizn'*. Iaroslavl', 1887.

Istoricheskoe opisanie Moskvy. Moscow, 1872.

Istoriia Prokhorovskoi trekhgornoi manufaktury. Moscow, 1915.

Iubileinaia Moskva, 1812–1912. Moscow, 1912.

K., N. "Iz nabliudenii sotrudnitsy gorodskogo popechitel'stva o bednykh v Moskve." *Trudovaia pomoshch'*, 4, no. 4 (April 1901): 472–78.

"K voprosu o prestupnosti Moskovskogo naseleniia," *Voprosy gorodskoi zhizni v tekushikh let*, no. 6 (1906): 198–213.

Kabo, E. O. *Ocherki rabochego byta: Opyt monograficheskogo issledovaniia rabochego byta*. Moscow, 1928.

Kadomtsev, B. P. *Professional'nyi i sotsial'nyi sostav naseleniia Evropeiskoi*

Rossii po dannym perepisi 1897 g. (*Trudy Studentov ekonomicheskogo otdeleniia Sankt-Peterburgskogo politekhnicheskogo instituta*), no. 1. St. Petersburg, 1909.

Kamenetskaia, E. N. "Blagotvoritel'naia deiatel'nost' Moskovskogo gorodskogo obshchestvennogo upravleniia." Moskovskaia gorodskaia uprava, *Sbornik ocherkov po gorodu Moskvy,* 1–17. Moscow, 1897.

Kanatchikov, S. I. *Iz istorii moego bytiia.* Moscow-Leningrad, 1929.

Kapustin, P. M. "Moskovskii ispravitel'nyi priiut." *Vestnik Evropy,* 5, no, 8 (August 1871): 607–54.

Karaffa-Korbut, K. V. "Nochlezhnye doma v bol'shikh russkikh gorodakh." *Gorodskoe delo,* no. 10 (May 15, 1912), 627–43; no. 11–12 (June 1–15, 1912), 691–712; no. 13–14 (July 1–15, 1912), 803–23.

Karyshev, N. A. "K izucheniiu nashikh otkhozhikh promyslov." *Russkoe bogatstvo,* 7 (1896): 1–24.

Kharlamov, Ia. *Khristovym imenem: Ocherki zhizni peterburgskikh nishchikh.* St. Petersburg, 1898.

Khin, M. M. "Moskovskii gorodskoi Rukavishnikovskii ispravitel'nyi priiut dlia maloletnikh prestupnikov, 1864–1886." *Iuridicheskii vestnik,* 18, no. 8 (August 1886): 581–605.

"Khitrov rynok." *Russkie vedomosti,* May 27, June 9, June 24, 1903.

Kirillov, L. A. "Gramotnost' i obrazovanie prizyvnykh Moskvy za 1874–95 gg." *Sbornik statei po voprosam, otnosiashchimsia k zhizni russkikh i inostrannykh gorodov,* 12 vols. (Moscow, 1895–1901) 10:257–75.

———. "K voprosu o vnezemledel'cheskom otkhode krest'ianskogo naseleniia." *Trudy Imperatorskogo vol'nogo ekonomicheskogo obshchestva,* 3–4 (1899): 259–99.

———. "Moskovskie domovladel'tsy v 1892 godu." *Sbornik statei po voprosam, otnosiashchimsia k zhizni russkikh i inostrannykh gorodov,* 12 vols. (Moscow, 1895–1901), 6:9–25.

Kishkin, N. M. "Zhilishchnyi vopros v Moskve i blizhaishie zadachi v razreshenii ego Gorodskoi dumoi" *Gorodskoe delo,* no. 5 (March 1, 1913), 291–300; no. 6 (March 15, 1913), 351–60.

Kleinbort, L. M. *Istoriia bezrabotitsy v Rossii, 1857–1919 gg.* Moscow, 1925.

Kokorev, I. T. *Moskva sorokovykh godov: Ocherki i povesti o Moskve XIX v.* Moscow, 1959.

Kovalenskii, M., ed. *Moskva v istorii i literature.* Moscow, 1916.

Koz'minykh-Lanin, I. M. *Artel'noe kharchevanie fabrichno-zavodskikh rabochikh Moskovskoi gubernii.* Moscow, 1915.

———. *Gramotnost' i zarabotki fabrichno-zavodskikh rabochikh Moskovskoi gubernii.* Moscow, 1912.

———. *Prodolzhitel'nost' rabochego dnia.* Moscow, 1912.

———. *Ukhod na polevye raboty fabrichno-zavodskikh rabochikh Moskovskoi gubernii.* Moscow, 1912.

———. *Vrachebnaia pomoshch' fabrichno-zavodskim rabochim v uezdakh Moskovskoi gubernii.* Moscow, 1912.

———. *Zarabotki fabrichno-zavodskikh rabochikh Moskovskoi gubernii.* Moscow, 1911.

Kraevskii, Aleksandr. *Vopros o nishchenstve i ob organizatsii blagotvoritel'nosti v Moskve.* Moscow, 1889.

Krasuskii, V. *Kratkii istoricheskii ocherk Imperatorskogo Moskovskogo vospitatel'nogo doma.* Moscow, 1878.

Krotkov, P. V. "Doma trudoliubiia v Rossii." *Sbornik statei po voprosam, otnosiashchimsia k zhizni russkikh i inostrannykh gorodov,* 12 vols. (Moscow 1895–1901), 4 (1897): 67–82.

Kudriavtsev, A. *Nishchenstvo, kak predmet popecheniia tserkvi, obshchestva i gosudarstva.* Odessa, 1885.

Kurbanovskii, Mikhail N. *Nishchenstvo i blagotvoritel'nost'.* St. Petersburg, 1860.

Kurnin, S. V. "Bezrabotnye na Khitrovom rynke v Moskve." *Russkoe bogatstvo,* no. 2 (February 1898): 165–79.

———. *O nekotorykh usloviiakh zhizni naseleniia Khitrova rynka.* Moscow, 1898.

Lebedev, V. I. "Ocherk deiatel'nosti Moskovskogo vospitatel'nogo doma." *IMGD* (July–August 1898): 1–65.

———. "Usloviia truda i zhizni v mel'kikh promyshlennykh zavedeniiakh." *Russkaia mysl',* 26, no. 2 (February 1905): 140–61.

Lednitskii, A. R. "Bor'ba s nishchenstvom." *Sbornik statei po voprosam, otnosiashchimsia k zhizni russkikh i inostrannykh gorodov,* 12 vols. (Moscow, 1895–1901), 2 (1901): 58–83.

Leikin, N. A. *Na zarabotkakh: Roman iz zhizni chernorabochikh zhenshchin.* St. Petersburg, 1891.

Lenskii, B. "Otkhozhie nezemledel'cheskie promysly v Rossii." *Otechestvennye zapiski,* 11 (November 1877): 207–58.

Leroy-Beaulieu, Anatole. *The Empire of the Tsars and the Russians.* Translated from the 3d edition by Zenaide A. Ragozin. 3 vols. New York and London, 1905.

Levenstim, A. A. *Professional'noe nishchenstvo, ego prichiny i formy: Bytovye ocherki.* St. Petersburg, 1900.

Levitov, A. I. *Sobranie sochinenii.* 2 vols. Moscow, 1884.

———. *Zhizn' moskovskikh zakoulkov: Ocherki i rasskazy.* 3d. ed. Moscow, 1875.

Liakhov, A. "Prirost naseleniia Moskvy v kontse XIX v." *IMGD,* 33, no. 1 (January 1909): 41–64.

Likhachev, A. "Nakazanie i pomoshch' nishchim." *Trudovaia pomoshch',* 2, no. 1 (January 1899): 1–24.

Linev, D. A. *Prichiny russkogo nishchenstva i neobkhodimye protiv nikh mery.* St. Petersburg, 1891.

Logan, John A. *In Joyful Russia.* New York, 1891.

Lowth, G. T. *Around the Kremlin.* London, 1868.

M. and O. "Tsifry i fakty iz perepisi Sankt-Peterburga v 1900 g." *Russkaia mysl',* 23, no. 2 (February 1902): 72–92.

Makarenko, A. "Otkhozhie i kabal'nye rabochie." *Iuridicheskii vestnik*, 4 (April 1887): 728–40.

Maksimov, E. "Chto takoe trudovaia pomoshch'?" *Trudovaia pomoshch'*, 3, no. 7 (September 1900): 125–59.

———. *Iz istorii i opyta zemskikh uchrezhdenii v Rossii.* St. Petersburg, 1913.

———. "K voprosu ob ob"edinenii blagotvoritel'nosti voobshche i trudovoi pomoshchi v chastnosti." *Trudovaia pomoshch'*, 7, no. 2 (February 1904): 215–38.

———. "Nachalo gosudarstvennogo prizreniia." *Trudovaia pomoshch'*, 3, no. 3 (March 1900): 40–58.

———. "O naloge v pol'zu bednykh." *Trudovaia pomoshch'*, 2, no. 3 (March 1899): 222–43.

———. *Ocherk zemskoi deiatel'nosti v oblasti obshchestvennogo prizreniia.* St. Petersburg, 1895.

———. "Ocherki chastnoi blagotvoritel'nosti v Rossii." *Trudovaia pomoshch'*, 1, nos. 1–8 (1897–1898).

———. "Opyt gorodskikh obshchestvennykh upravlenii v dele pomoshchi bednym." *Trudovaia pomoshch'*, 7, no. 5 (May 1904): 545–71; no. 6 (June 1904): 1–34.

———. *Proiskhozhdenie nishchenstva i mery bor'by s nim.* St. Petersburg, 1901.

———. [Filantrop] *Trudovaia pomoshch', ee osnovaniia, zadachi i vazhneishie formy.* St. Petersburg, 1899.

———. "Zametki o vnutrennem ustroistve domov trudoliubiia (Iz lichnykh nabliudenii)." *Trudovaia pomoshch'*, 3, no. 9 (November 1900): 341–59; no. 10 (December 1900): 467–86.

Maksimov, Sergei V. *Brodiachaia Rus' Khrista-radi.* St. Petersburg, 1877.

Manuilov, A. "Ocherk nashego fabrichnogo byta." *Iuridicheskii vestnik*, 3 (March 1887): 543–54.

Martynov, A. *Nazvaniia moskovskikh ulits i pereulkov.* Moscow, 1888.

Mashkov, I. P., ed. *Putevoditel' po Moskve.* Moscow, 1913.

Maslov, P. *Agrarnyi vopros v Rossii.* 3d ed. St. Petersburg, 1906.

Massal'skii, Vladimir. "Odnodnevnaia perepis' goroda Moskvy." *Narodnoe khoziaistvo*, 3, no. 7 (September–October 1902): 68–111.

Mikhailovskii, A. "Gorodskie popechitel'stva o bednykh v Moskve za sem' let svoego sushchestvovanniia." *IMGD*, 27, nos. 11–13 (June–July 1903): 1–46.

Mikhailovskii, V. G. "Goroda Rossii po pervoi vseobshchei perepisi." *Sbornik statei po voprosam, otnosiashchimsia k zhizni russkikh i inostrannykh gorodov*, 12 vols. (Moscow, 1895–1901), 6 (1897): 1–29.

———. *Materialy k voprosu ob usilenii sredstv goroda Moskvy.* Moscow, 1911.

———. "Predstoiashchee razvitie Moskvy." *IMGD*, 26, no. 9 (September 1902): 1–17.

Miunsterburg, E. *Prizrenie bednykh.* St. Petersburg, 1900.

Moskovskaia gorodskaia duma. *Sbornik statei po voprosam, otnosiashchimsia k zhizni russkikh i inostrannykh gorodov.* 12 vols. Moscow, 1895–1901.

Moskovskaia gorodskaia uprava. *Moskva: Kratkii ocherk.* Moscow, 1911.

———. *Sbornik ocherkov po gorodu Moskve.* Moscow, 1897.

———. *Sovremennoe khoziaistvo goroda Moskvy.* Moscow, 1913.

Moskovskaia promyshlennost' v ocherkakh. 2 vols. Moscow, 1899.

Moskovskie okrestnosti. Moscow, 1877.

Moskovskii Listok, 1912–1913.

"Moskovskii vospitatel'nyi dom." *IMGD,* 30, no. 5 (March 1906): 218–37.

"Moskovskie kolbasnye zavedeniia v 1896 godu." *Sbornik statei po voprosam, otnosiashchimsia k zhizni russkikh i inostrannykh gorodov,* 5 (1897): 64–92.

Moskva: Putevoditel'. Moscow, 1915.

Moskva i ee zhizn'. St. Petersburg. 1914.

Moskva na rubezhe dvukh vekov. Moscow, 1910.

Nastol'no-spravochnaia adresnaia kniga goroda Moskvy. Moscow, 1878.

"Neskol'ko dannykh o moskovskikh koechno-kamarochnykh kvartirakh." *IMGD,* 23, no. 1 (1899): 95–115.

Nesmeianov, N. "Iz zhizni moskovskogo rabotnogo doma." *IMGD,* 27, no. 1 (1903): 2–34.

Nikiforov, D. I. *Staraia Moskva.* Moscow, 1902–1904.

Nikol'skii, V. A. *Staraia Moskva: Istoriko-kul'turnyi putevoditel'.* Moscow, 1924.

"Novaia organizatsiia obshchestvennogo prizreniia v Moskve." *Vestnik Evropy,* 30, nos. 1, 4, 8 (January, April, August 1895).

"Novye vrachebno-sanitarnye meropriiatiia Moskovskogo gorodskogo obshchestvennogo upravleniia." *Sbornik statei po voprosam, otnosiashchimsia k zhizni russkikh i inostrannykh gorodov,* 5 (1897): 180–96.

Obninskii, P. N. "Chego nedostaet nashei blagotvoritel'nosti?" *Russkaia mysl',* 20, no. 1 (January 1899): 86–113.

———. "Trudovaia pomoshch' kak obshchestvennyi korrektiv." *Trudovaia pomoshch',* 1, no. 5 (March 1898): 409–20.

"Ocherk deiatel'nosti Moskovskogo vospitatel'nogo doma." *IMGD,* 22, no. 1 (July–August 1898): 1–31.

Ocherki Moskovskoi zhizni. Moscow, 1962.

"Ocherki Moskvy." *Istoricheskii vestnik,* 51 (1893): 451–80, 778–95.

Odynets, Kamilla I. *Dom Trudoliubiia i ego zadachi kak organ "Obshchestva uluchsheniia narodnogo truda."* 2 vols. St. Petersburg, 1887.

Okorokov, V. *Vozvrashchenie k chestnomu trudu padshikh devushek.* Moscow, 1888.

Oliunina, E. A. *Portnovskii promysel v Moskve i v derevniakh Moskovskoi i Riazanskoi gubernii: Materialy k istorii domashnei promyshlennosti v Rossii.* Moscow, 1914.

Opisanie goroda Moskva s vidami. Moscow, 1902.

Ostrovskii, A. N. "Bez viny vinovatye." *Polnoe sobranie sochinenii.* 16 vols., 9:149–219. Moscow, 1949–1953.

Ovsiannikov, V. "Dovoennye biudzhety russkikh rabochikh." *Voprosy truda,*
9 (September 1925): 48–60; 10 (October 1925): 55–70.
Ovtsyn, Vladimir. "K istorii i statistike gorodskogo proletariata v Rossii."
Russkaia mysl', 12 (May 1891): 60–82.
Ozerov, I. Kh. *Bol'shie goroda, ikh zadachi i sredstva upravleniia.* Moscow,
1906.
P., E. "Zadachi narodnykh domov." *Trudovaia pomoshch',* 3, no. 4 (April
1900): 394–99.
Pavlov, I. N. *Ukhodshaia Moskva.* Moscow, 1919.
Pazhitnov, K. A. *Iz istorii rabochikh artelei na zapade i v Rossii.* Leningrad,
1924.
———. "Kvartirnyi vopros v Moskve i v Peterburge." *Gorodskoe delo,* 17
(1910): 1162–1165.
———. "Moskva po dannym perepisi 1912 g." *Gorodskoe delo,* 21 (1913):
1413–1420.
———. *Polozhenie rabochego klassa v Rossii.* St. Petersburg, 1906.
Peshekhonov, A. "Krest'iane i rabochie v ikh vzaimnykh otnosheniiakh." *Rus-
skoe bogatstvo,* 8 (August 1898): 173–95; 9 (September 1898): 54–82.
Peskov, P. A. *Sanitarnoe issledovanie fabrik po obrabotke voloknistykh ve-
shchestv. (Trudy Komissii dlia osmotra fabrik i zavodov v Moskve.)* Mos-
cow, 1882.
Petrovskii, A. G. *Gorodskoi sanitarnyi nadzor v Moskve.* Moscow, 1896.
———. *Khitrov rynok, ego sanitarnoe i obshchestvennoe znachenie.* Moscow,
1898.
———. "Khitrov rynok i ego obytateli." *Vestnik Evropy,* 29, no. 6 (June
1894): 579–93.
Plekhanov, G. V. *Sochineniia.* Vol. 1. Geneva, 1905.
Podiachev, S. P. *Izbrannoe.* Moscow, 1955.
Pogozhev, A. V. "Iz zhizni fabrichnogo liuda stolitsy." *Russkaia mysl',* 6, no.
5 (May 1885): 1–17; no. 6 (June 1885): 20–34.
———. "Vozmozhna li postroika narodnogo doma v Moskve?" *Russkaia
mysl',* 19, no. 2 (February 1898): 86–97.
Pokrovskaia, Mariia I. "O zhilishchakh peterburgskikh rabochikh." *Russkoe
bogatstvo,* 6 (1897): 19–38.
"Politseiskie obiazannosti dvornikov." *IMGD,* 28, no. 3 (March 1904): 209–
12.
Poludenskii, M. "Mnenie o istreblenii v Moskve nishchikh." *Chteniia Ob-
shchestva istorii i drevnostei rossiiskikh.* Vol. 2, pt. 5 (1861): 176–83.
Pozner, M. "Nochlezhnye doma i nochlezhniki v Moskve." *IMGD,* 15, no. 6
(1891): 1–56.
Prokopovich, S. N. *Biudzhety peterburgskikh rabochikh.* St. Petersburg, 1909.
———. "Krest'ianstvo i poreformennaia fabrika." In A. K. Dzhivelegov, ed.,
Velikaia Reforma, 6:268–76. Moscow, 1911.
"Promyshlennaia kharakteristika Moskovskoi gubernii." *Vestnik promyshlen-
nosti* (April 1885).
Pryzhov, Ivan G. *Nishchie na sviatoi Rusi: Materialy dlia istorii obshchestven-
nogo i narodnogo byta v Rossii.* 2d ed. Kazan', 1913.

———. *Ocherki, stat'i, pis'ma.* Moscow, 1934.

Pyliaev, M. I. *Staraia Moskva.* St. Petersburg, 1891.

R., S. "K voprosu o bor'be s professional'nym nishchenstvom v Rossii." *Trudovaia pomoshch',* 2, no. 3 (March 1899): 244–62.

———. "Moskovskie gorodskie popechitel'stva o bednykh v 1898 g." *Trudovaia pomoshch',* 3, no. 6 (June 1900): 73–82.

———. "Moskovskie popechitel'stva o bednykh." *Trudovaia pomoshch',* 2, no. 6 (June 1899): 82–94.

"Rabochii vopros v Moskve." *Russkoe bogatstvo,* 4 (April 1899): 166–88.

Radiukin, N. "Brodiagi i nishchie." *Delo,* no. 6 (June 1867): 97–108.

Raevskii, A. A. "Gorodskoe uchastkovoe popechitel'stvo o bednykh v Moskve." *IMGD,* 19, no. 4 (April 1895): 1–20.

———. *Trudovaia pomoshch', kak zadacha gosudarstvennogo upravleniia.* Khar'kov, 1910.

Raevskii, L. D. "K voprosu o nishchenstve v Moskve." *IMGD,* 34, no. 1 (January 1910): 1–12.

Rogovin, L. M. *Ustav o pasportakh.* St. Petersburg, 1913.

S., Ia. "Gorodskoe popechitel'stvo o bednykh Khitrova rynka." *Russkie vedomosti,* no. 166 (July 21, 1907): 3.

Sabashnikova, E. "Iz deiatel'nosti moskovskikh gorodskikh uchastkovykh popechitel'stv o bednykh za 1897 g." *IMGD,* 23, no. 1 (February 1899): 1–17.

Schulze-Gävernitz, Gerhardt von. *Krupnoe proizvodstvo v Rossii (Moskovsko-Vladimirskaia khlopchatobumazhnaia promyshlennost').* Trans. B. V. Avilov. Moscow, 1899.

———. *Ocherki obshchestvennogo khoziaistva i ekonomicheskoi politiki Rossii.* Trans. B. V. Avilov. St. Petersburg, 1901.

Semenov, D. A. *Gorodskoe samoupravlenie.* St. Petersburg, 1901.

Semenov, S. T. *Dvadtsat' piat' let v derevne.* Petrograd, 1915.

———. *Krest'ianskie p'esy.* Moscow, 1912.

———. *U propasti i drugie rasskazy.* 2d ed. Moscow, 1904.

———. *V rodnoi derevne.* Moscow, 1962.

Semenov, V. P. (Tian-Shanksii). *Gorod i derevnia v Evropeiskoi Rossii.* St. Petersburg, 1910.

———. *Rossiia. Polnoe geograficheskoe opisanie nashego otechestva.* Vol. 1: *Moskovskaia promyshlennaia oblast' i verkhnee povolzh'e.* St. Petersburg, 1899.

S"ezd po obshchestvennomu prizreniiu, sozvannyi Ministerstvom vnutrennikh del. *Trudy.* Petrograd, 1914.

Sh-r, N. "Deiatel'nost' gorodskogo Blagotvoritel'nogo Soveta pri Moskovskom gorodskom upravlenii, 1898–1903." *IMGD,* 28, nos. 11–13 (June–July 1904): 1–18.

Shchekotov, M. "Blizhaishie zadachi moskovskogo obshchestvennogo upravleniia po blagoustroistvu goroda i sredstva k ikh osushchestvleniiu." *Russkaia mysl',* 20, no. 4 (April 1899): 163–78.

Shchepkin, M. P. "O traktirnom promysle v Moskve." *IMGD,* 5, no. 1 (January 1881): 37–50.

————. *Obshchestvennoe khoziaistvo goroda Moskvy v 1863–92 gg: Istoriko-statisticheskoe opisanie.* Moscow, 1895.

Sher, V. "Fabrichno-zavodskoi rabochii Moskovskoi gubernii." *Vestnik Evropy*, 49, no. 4 (April 1914): 312–31.

Shestakov, P. M. "Materialy dlia kharakteristiki fabrichnykh rabochikh v Moskve." *Russkaia mysl'*, 21, no. 1 (January 1900): 157–84.

————. *Rabochie na manufakture T-va Tsindel' v Moskve.* Moscow, 1900.

Shreider, G. I. "Gorodskaia kontra-reforma 11-go iiunia 1892 g." In *Istoriia Rossii v XIX v.*, 5:181–228. St. Petersburg, 1907–1911.

————. *Nashe gorodskoe obshchestvennoe upravlenie: Etiudy, ocherki i zametki.* St. Petersburg, 1902.

Shvittau, G. G. *Trudovaia pomoshch' v Rossii.* 2 vols. Petrograd, 1915.

Sinatsyn, P. *Preobrazhenskoe i okruzhaiushchie ego mesta; ikh proshloe i nastoiashchee.* Moscow, 1895.

Sinitskii, L. D., and L. N. Raevskii. *K voprosu o nishchenstve v Moskve.* Moscow, 1895.

Skvortsov, N. A. *Arkheologiia i topografiia Moskvy,* Moscow, 1913.

Slonov, I. A. *Iz zhizni torgovoi Moskvy.* Moscow, 1914.

Slukhovskii, I. "Bezrabotnye v Moskve." *Russkaia mysl'*, 29, no. 10 (October 1908): 192–211.

Speranskii, Sergei. "Besplatnoe ukazanie raboty v Moskve." *Sbornik statei po voprosam, otnosiashchimsia k zhizni russkikh i inostrannykh gorodov,* 5 (1897): 197–215.

————. "K istorii nishchenstva v Rossii." *Vestnik blagotvoritel'nosti,* 1–3 (1897).

————. "O proekte reformy obshchestvennogo prizreniia v Rossii." *Trudovaia pomoshch'*, 1, no. 7 (May 1898): 26–44.

Sputnik Moskvicha. Moscow, 1890.

Staraia Moskva. 2 vols. Moscow, 1912, 1914.

Staraia Moskva (Trudy obshchestva izucheniia moskovskoi oblasti). Moscow, 1929.

Stavrovskii, V. "Sanitarnoe sostoianie fabrik odnoi iz iugovostochnykh okrain Moskvy." *IMGD*, 33, no. 6-7 (1909): 40–49.

Svavitskii, A., and V. Sher. *Ocherk polozheniia rabochikh pechatnogo dela v Moskve.* St. Petersburg, 1909.

Sviatlovskii, V. V. *Zhilishchnyi vopros s ekonomicheskoi tochki zreniia.* 5 vols. St. Petersburg, 1902.

Svirskii, A. I. *Pogibshie liudi.* 3 vols. St. Petersburg, 1898.

Tabel' domov goroda Moskvy. St. Petersburg, 1868.

Tarasov, I. "Moskovskii Gorodskoi Rabotnyi dom." *Russkoe obozrenie,* 43, no. 1 (January 1896): 337–48.

Tarnovskii, E. "K voprosu o brodiazhestve." *Iuridicheskii vestnik,* no. 12 (December 1886): 766–87.

————. "Rezul'taty moskovskoi perepisi 1882 goda." *Iuridicheskii vestnik,* 4 (1887): 655–81.

————. "Ugolovno-nakazuemoe nishchenstvo v Rossii." *Trudovaia pomoshch'*, 3, no. 1 (January 1900): 17–39.

Timofeev, P. "Ocherki zavodskoi zhizni." *Russkoe bogatstvo*, no. 9 (September 1905): 19–34; no. 10 (October 1905): 71–91.

———. "Zavodskie budni." *Russkoe bogatstvo*, no. 8 (August 1903), 30–53; no. 9 (September 1903), 175–99.

Tolstoi, L. N. "O perepisi v Moskve." *Polnoe sobranie sochinenii*, 13:5–13. Moscow, 1913.

———. "Tak chto zhe nam delat'?" *Polnoe sobranie sochinenii*, 13:14–239. Moscow, 1913.

Tsentral'nyi statisticheskii komitet. *Iubileinyi sbornik*. St. Petersburg, 1913.

Tugan-Baranovskii, M. *Russkaia fabrika v proshlom i nastoiashchem*. 3d ed. St. Petersburg, 1907.

Vasilevskaia, M. B. "Novaia organizatsiia gorodskoi blagotvoritel'nosti v Moskve." *IMGD*, 19, no. 4 (April 1895): 1–23.

Vasilich, G. "Ulitsy i liudi." In I. E. Zabelin, ed., *Moskva v ee proshlom i nastoiashchem*, 12:1–17. Moscow, 1910–12.

Verner, I. "Zhilishcha bedneishego naseleniia Moskvy." *IMGD*, 26, no. 19 (1902): 1–27.

Vert, O. "Obshchestvennye raboty kak trudovaia pomoshch' nuzhdaiushchimsia." *Trudovaia pomoshch'*, 1, no. 3 (January 1898): 218–39.

Veselovskii, Boris B. *Istoriia zemstva za 40 let*. 4 vols. St. Petersburg, 1909–1911.

Vesin, L. P. "Rol' Moskvy v torgovo-promyshlennom otnoshenii." In P. P. Semenov, ed., *Zhivopisnaia Rossia*, 6:242–87. Moscow, 1898.

———. "Znachenie otkhozhikh promyslov v zhizni russkogo krest'ianstva." *Delo*, 19, no. 7 (November 1886): 127–55; 20, no. 2 (February 1887): 102–124.

"Vidy na zhitel'stvo, vydannye krest'ianskomu naseleniiu moskovskoi gubernii v 1880 i 1885 gg." *Statisticheskii ezhegodnik Moskovskoi gubernii za 1886*. Moscow, 1886.

Villiam, G. *Khitrovskii Al'bom*. Moscow, 1909.

Vonliarliarskii, V. "Gorodskie popechitel'stva o bednykh v Moskve." *Russkaia mysl'*, 17, no. 6 (June 1896): 80–91.

Voronov, M. A., and A. I. Levitov. *Moskovskie nory i trushchoby*. St. Petersburg, 1866.

Voronstov, V. P. *Ocherki kustarnoi promyshlennosti v Rossii*. St. Petersburg, 1886.

"Vospitatel'nye doma v Rossii i zapadnoi Evrope." *IMGD*, 13, no. 3 (1889): 13–41.

Vserossiiskii s"ezd deiatelei po obshchestvennomu i chastnomu prizreniiu. *Trudy*. St. Petersburg, 1910.

Vserossiiskii torgovo-promyshlennyi s"ezd 1896 g. v Nizhnem-Novgorode. *Trudy*. St. Petersburg, 1897.

Vsesviatskii, P. "Prestupnost' i zhilishchnyi vopros v Moskve." *Seminarii po ugolovnomu pravu*. Vyp. 2. Moscow, 1909.

Vsia Moskva: Adresnaia i spravochnaia kniga. Moscow, 1903, 1906, 1910, 1911.

Wz. "Pis'ma iz Moskvy." *Vestnik Evropy*, 21, no. 2 (February 1886): 897–931.

Zabelin, I. E. *Istoriia goroda Moskvy.* Moscow, 1902.

Zabelin, I.E., ed. *Moskva v ee proshlom i nastoiashchem.* 12 vols. Moscow, 1909–1912.

"Zadachi trudovoi pomoshchi." *Trudovaia pomoshch'*, 1, no. 1 (November 1897): 44–56.

Zakharov, M. P. *Putevoditel' po Moskve.* 3d ed. Moscow, 1868.

Zharinov, D. A., and N. M. Nikol'skii. *Byloe vokrug nas.* Moscow, 1922.

Zhbankov, Dmitrii N. *Bab'ia storona: Statistiko-etnograficheskii ocherk.* Kostroma, 1891.

———. "O gorodskikh otkhozhikh zarabotkakh v Soligalicheskom uezde, Kostromskoi gubernii." *Iuridicheskii vestnik*, 9 (1890): 130–48.

Zhivopisnaia Rossii. Vol. 6: *Moskva i Moskovskaia promyshlennaia oblast'.* Moscow, 1899.

Zhizhilenko, A. "Vopros o nishchenstve i brodiazhestve na mezhdunarodnom kongresse v Parizhe 1895 goda." *Trudovaia pomoshch'*, 1, no. 11 (November 1898): 476–89.

OTHER SECONDARY SOURCES

Akademiia Nauk SSSR, Institut istorii. *Istoriia Moskvy.* 6 vols. Moscow, 1952–1959.

Alaverdian, S. K. *Zhilishchnyi vopros v Moskve.* Erevan, 1961.

Anderson, Barbara. *Internal Migration during Modernization in Late Nineteenth-Century Russia.* Princeton, 1980.

———. "Who Chose the Cities? Migrants to Moscow and St. Petersburg Cities in the Late Nineteenth Century." In Donald Lee, ed., *Population Patterns in the Past.* New York, 1977.

Antonova, S. I. *Vliianie stolypinskoi agrarnoi reformy na izmeneniia v sostave rabochego klassa: Po materialam Moskovskoi gubernii, 1906–1913.* Moscow, 1951.

Bater, James H. *St. Petersburg: Industrialization and Change.* Montreal, 1976.

———. "Some Dimensions of Urbanization and the Response of Municipal Government: Moscow and St. Petersburg." *Russian History*, 5, pt. 2 (1978): 46–63.

———. "Transience, Residential Persistence and Mobility in Moscow and St. Petersburg, 1900–1914." *Slavic Review*, 39, no. 2 (June 1980): 239–54.

Berry, Lloyd E., and Robert O. Crummey, eds. *Rude and Barbarous Kingdom: Russia in the Accounts of Sixteenth-Century English Voyagers.* Madison, Wis., 1968.

Black, C. E., ed. *The Transformation of Russian Society.* Cambridge, Mass. 1960.

Blackwell, William L. *The Beginnings of Russian Industrialization.* Princeton, 1968.

Blau, Peter M., and Otis Dudley Duncan. *The American Occupational Structure.* New York, 1967.

Bogdanov, I. M. *Gramotnost' i obrazovanie v dorevoliutsionnoi Rossii i v SSSR*. Moscow, 1964.

Bogue, Donald J. *The Principles of Demography*. New York, 1969.

Bonnell, Victoria E. "Urban Working Class Life in Early Twentieth-Century Russia: Some Problems and Patterns." *Russian History*, 8, pt. 3 (1981): 360–78.

———. *Roots of Rebellion: Workers' Politics and Organizations in St. Petersburg and Moscow, 1900–1914*. Berkeley, 1984.

Bowmaker, Edward. *The Housing of the Working Classes*. London, 1895.

Bradley, Joseph. "The Moscow Workhouse and Municipal Welfare Reform in Russia." *Russian Review*, 41, no. 4 (October 1982): 427–44.

———. " 'Once You've Eaten Khitrov Soup, You'll Never Leave!': Slum Renovation in Pre-revolutionary Moscow." *Russian History*. In press.

———. "Patterns of Peasant Migration in Late Nineteenth-Century Moscow: How Much Should We Read into Literacy Rates?" *Russian History*, 6, pt. 1 (1979): 22–38.

Bremer, Robert H. *American Philanthropy*. Chicago, 1960.

Briggs, Asa. *Victorian Cities*. London, 1963.

Brower, Daniel. "L'Urbanisation russe à la fin du XIX siècle." *Annales: Économies, Sociéties, Civilisations*, 1 (February 1977): 70–86.

———. "Urban Russia on the Eve of World War I: A Social Profile." *Journal of Social History*, 13, no. 3 (Spring 1980): 424–36.

Chevalier, Louis. *Laboring Classes and Dangerous Classes in Paris During the First Half of the Nineteenth Century*. Trans. Frank Jellinek. New York, 1973.

Conk, Margo Anderson. *The United States Census and the New Jersey Occupational Structure, 1870–1940*. Ann Arbor, Mich. 1978.

Crew, David. "Definitions of Modernity: Social Mobility in a German Town, 1880–1901." *Journal of Social History*, 7, no. 1 (Fall 1973): 51–74.

Dyos, H. J. "The Growth of Cities in the 19th Century: A Review of Some Recent Writing." *Victorian Studies*, 9, no. 3 (March 1965): 225–44.

Dyos, H. J., and Michael Wolff, eds. *The Victorian City*. 2 vols. London, 1973.

Eames, Edwin, and Judith Granich Goode. *Urban Poverty in a Cross-cultural Context*. New York, 1973.

Eklof, Arthur Benoit. "Spreading the Word: Primary Education and the Zemstvo in Moscow Province, 1864–1910." Ph.D. dissertation, Princeton University, 1976.

Engelstein, Laura. *Moscow, 1905: Working-class Organization and Political Conflict*. Stanford, 1982.

Fedor, Thomas Stanley. *Patterns of Urban Growth in the Russian Empire during the Nineteenth Century*. Chicago, 1975.

Fedosiuk, Iu. A. "Moskva 100 let nazad." *Voprosy istorii*, 2 (1968): 209–16.

Fried, Albert, and R. M. Elman, eds. *Charles Booth's London: A Portrait of the Poor at the Turn of the Century Drawn from His Life and Labour of the People of London*. New York, 1963.

"From Tsar to Soviet: Moscow Province, 1880–1938." *Russian History*, 5, pt. 1 (1978).

Gerschenkron, Alexander. "Agrarian Policies and Industrialization in Russia." *Cambridge Economic History.* 2d ed. Vol. 6, pt. 2. Cambridge, 1966.

——. *Economic Backwardness in Historical Perspective.* Cambridge, Mass., 1962.

Gohstand, Robert. "The Internal Geography of Trade in Moscow from the Mid-nineteenth Century to World War I." Ph.D. dissertation, University of California, Berkeley, 1973.

Gol'denberg, M., and B. Gol'denberg. *Planirovka zhilogo kvartala Moskvy XVII, XVIII, XIX vv.* Moscow and Leningrad, 1935.

Guroff, G., and S. F. Starr. "A Note on Urban Literacy in Russia 1890–1914." *Jahrbücher für Geschichte Osteuropas,* 19, no. 4 (December 1971): 520–33.

Habbakuk, H. J. "Family Structure and Economic Change in Nineteenth-Century Europe." *Journal of Economic History,* 15, no. 1 (1955): 1–12.

Haimson, Leopold. "The Problem of Social Stability in Urban Russia, 1905–1917." Slavic Review, 23 (December 1964): 619–42; 24 (March 1965): 1–22.

Halpern, Joel. *The Changing Village Community.* Englewood Cliffs, N.J., 1967.

Hamm, Michael F., ed. *The City in Russian History.* Lexington, Ky., 1976.

——. "Khar'kov's Progressive Duma, 1910–1914: A Study in Russian Municipal Reform." *Slavic Review,* 40, no. 1 (March 1981): 17–36.

——. "The Modern Russian City: An Historiographical Analysis." *Journal of Urban History,* 4, no. 1 (November 1977): 39–76.

Hanchett, Walter S. "Moscow in the Late Nineteenth Century: A Study in Municipal Self-Government." Ph.D. dissertation, University of Chicago, 1964.

Hauser, Philip M., and Leo F. Schnore, eds. *The Study of Urbanization.* New York, 1965.

Henretta, James. "The Study of Social Mobility: Ideological Assumptions and Conceptual Bias." *Labor History,* no. 2 (Spring 1977): 165–78.

Herberstein, Baron Sigismund von. *Notes upon Russia.* Hakluyt Society edition. 2 vols. London, 1852.

Herlihy, Patricia. "Death in Odessa: A Study of Population Movements in a Nineteenth-century City." *Journal of Urban History,* 4, no. 4 (August 1978): 417–42.

Hittle, J. Michael. *The Service City: State and Townsmen in Russia, 1600–1800.* Cambridge, 1979.

Hooson, David. "The Growth of Cities in Pre-Soviet Russia." In R. P. Beckinsdale and J. M. Houston, eds., *Urbanization and Its Problems: Essays in Honour of E. W. Gilbert.* Oxford, 1970.

Huggins, Nathan Irvin. *Protestants against Poverty.* Westport, Conn., 1970.

Iakobson, A. L. *Tkatskie slobody i sela v XVII v.* Moscow and Leningrad, 1934.

Inkeles, Alex, and David Smith. *Becoming Modern.* Cambridge, Mass., 1974.

Ivanov, L. M. "K voprosu o formirovanii promyshlennogo proletariata v Rossii." *Istoria SSSR,* 4 (June–August, 1958): 27–51.

————. "O soslovno-klassovoi strukture gorodov kapitalisticheskoi Rossii." *Problemy sotsial'no-ekonomicheskoi istorii Rossii*, 312–40. Moscow, 1971.

Ivanov, L. M., ed. *Istoriia rabochego klassa Rossii, 1860–1900 gg.* Moscow, 1972.

————. *Rabochii klass i rabochee dvizhenie v Rossii, 1861–1917.* Moscow, 1966.

————. *Rossiiskii proletariat: Oblik, bor'ba, gegemoniia.* Moscow, 1970.

Ivanov, L. M., Iu. I. Kir'ianov, and Iu. I. Seryi, eds. *Rabochie Rossii v epokhu kapitalizma: Sravnitel'nyi poraionyi analiz.* Rostov-on-Don, 1972.

Jansen, Clifford J., ed. *Readings in the Sociology of Migration.* Oxford, 1970.

Johnson, Robert E. *Peasant and Proletarian: The Working Class of Moscow in the Late Nineteenth Century.* New Brunswick, N.J., 1979.

————. "Peasant Migration and the Russian Working Class: Moscow at the End of the Nineteenth Century." *Slavic Review,* 35, no. 4 (December 1976): 652–64.

Jones, Gareth Stedman. *Outcast London: A Study in the Relationship between Classes in Victorian Society.* Oxford, 1971.

Kabanov, P. I., ed., *Nekotorye voprosy istorii Moskvy i Moskovskoi gubernii v XIX-XX vv.* Moscow, 1964.

Kahan, A. "Determinants of the Incidence of Literacy in Rural Nineteenth-century Russia." In P. W. Musgrave, ed., *Sociology, History and Education: A Reader.* London, 1970.

Kazantsev, B. N. *Rabochie Moskvy i Moskovskoi gubernii v seredine XIX veka.* Moscow, 1976.

Kir'ianov, Iu. I. *Zhiznennyi uroven' rabochikh Rossii konets XIX-nachalo XX v.* Moscow, 1979.

Knights, Peter. *The Plain People of Boston: A Study in City Growth, 1830–60.* New York, 1971.

Koenker, Diane. *Moscow Workers and the 1917 Revolution.* Princeton, 1981.

Kruze, E. E. *Peterburgskie rabochie v 1912–1914 gg.* Moscow, 1961.

————. *Polozhenie rabochego klassa Rossii v 1900–1914 gg.* Leningrad, 1976.

————. *Usloviia truda i byta rabochego klassa Rossii v 1900–1914 godakh.* Leningrad, 1981.

Kurakhtanov, V. *Pervaia sittse-nabivnaia.* Moscow, 1960.

Kusmer, Kenneth. "The Functions of Organized Charity in the Progressive Era: Chicago as a Case Study." *Journal of American History,* 60, no. 3 (December 1973): 657–78.

Kut'ev, V. F. "Dokumental'nye materialy moskovskikh gosudarstvennykh arkhivov po istorii rabochego klassa goroda Moskvy v 90-e gody XIX v." Candidate's dissertation, Moscow, 1955.

Lapitskaia, S. M. *Byt rabochikh Trekhgornoi manufaktury.* Moscow, 1935.

Latysheva, G. P., and M. G. Rabinovich. *Moskva v dalekom proshlom.* Moscow, 1966.

Leasure, J. William, and Robert A. Lewis. "Internal Migration in Russia in the Late 19th century." *Slavic Review,* 27 (September 1968): 375–94.

Liashchenko, P. I. *History of the National Economy of Russia.* Trans. L. M. Herman. New York, 1949.

Lindenmeyr, Adele. "Public Poor Relief and Private Charity in Late Imperial Russia." Ph.D. dissertation, Princeton University, 1980.

Lipset, Seymour Martin, and Reinhard Bendix. *Social Mobility in Industrial Society.* Berkeley, 1959.

Lockridge, Kenneth A. *Literacy in Colonial New England.* New York, 1974.

Lubove, Roy. *The Professional Altruist: The Emergence of Social Work as a Career, 1880–1930.* Cambridge, Mass., 1965.

———. *The Progressives and the Slums: Tenement House Reform in New York City, 1890–1917.* Pittsburgh, 1962.

McGivney, Thomas. "The Lower Classes in the City of Moscow." Ph.D. dissertation, New York University, 1978.

Madison, Bernice. "The Organization of Welfare Services." In Cyril Black, ed. *The Transformation of Russian Society.* Cambridge, Mass., 1960.

Mangin, William, ed. *Peasants in Cities: Readings in the Anthropology of Urbanization.* Boston, 1970.

Mayhew, Henry. *London Labour and the London Poor.* London, 1851.

Mendel, Arthur. *Dilemmas of Progress in Tsarist Russia: Legal Marxism and Legal Populism.* Cambridge, Mass., 1961.

———. "Peasant and Worker on the Eve of the First World War." *Slavic Review*, 24, no. 1 (March 1965): 23–33.

Moskovskii sukonnyi dvor. (*Trudy istoriko-arkheograficheskogo instituta SSSR.* Vol. 13, part 5.) Leningrad, 1934.

Nifontov, A. S. "Formirovanie klassov burzhuaznogo obshchestva v russkom gorode vtoroi poloviny XIX v: Po materialam perepisei naseleniia g. Moskvy v 70–90 gg. XIX v. *Istoricheskie zapiski* no. 54 (1955): 239–50.

———. "Moskva vo vtoroi polovine XIX stoletiia." *Prepodavanie istorii v shkole*, 2. Moscow, 1947.

Novosel'skii, S. A. *Voprosy demograficheskoi i sanitarnoi statistiki.* Moscow, 1958.

Owen, Thomas C. *Capitalism and Politics in Russia: A Social History of the Moscow Merchants, 1855–1905.* Cambridge, 1981.

Pankratova, A. M. "Proletarizatsiia krest'ianstva i ee rol' v formirovanii promyshlennogo proletariata Rossii." *Istoricheskie zapiski*, 54 (1955): 194–220.

Pankratova, A. M., ed. *Istoriko-bytovye ekspiditsii, 1949–53.* 2 vols. Moscow, 1953, 1955.

Petersen, William. *Population.* 2d ed., New York, 1969.

Pinkney, David H. *Napoleon III and the Rebuilding of Paris.* Princeton, 1958.

Pintner, Walter. *Russian Economic Policy under Nicholas I.* Ithaca, N.Y., 1967.

Pipes, Richard E. *Russia Under the Old Regime.* London, 1974.

———. *Struve: Liberal on the Left, 1870–1905.* Cambridge, Mass., 1970.

Potter, Jack M., Mary N. Diaz, and George M. Foster, eds. *Peasant Society: A Reader.* Boston, 1967.

Ransel, David, ed. *The Family in Imperial Russia.* Urbana, Ill., 1978.

Rashin, A. G. "Dinamika chislennosti i protsessy formirovaniia gorodskogo naseleniia Rossii v XIX-nachale XX vv." *Istoricheskie zapiski,* 34 (1950): 32–85.

———. *Formirovanie rabochego klassa Rossii.* Moscow, 1958.

———. *Naselenie Rossii za 100 let (1811–1913): Statisticheskie ocherki.* Moscow, 1956.

Redford, Arthur. *Labour Migration in England, 1800–1850.* 3d ed. Manchester, England, 1976.

Rimlinger, Gaston V. "Expansion of the Labor Market in Capitalistic Russia." *Journal of Economic History,* 20 (June 1961): 208–15.

———. *Welfare Policy and Industrialization in Europe, America and Russia.* New York, 1971.

Robinson, Geroid T. *Rural Russia under the Old Regime.* Berkeley, 1967.

"The Role of Cities in Economic Development and Cultural Change." *Economic Development and Cultural Change,* 3 (1954–1955).

Romashova, V. I. "Formirovanie promyshlennogo proletariata Moskvy 60-e-I polovina 80-kh gg. XIX v." Candidate's dissertation, Moscow, 1963.

———. "Obrazovanie postoiannykh kadrov rabochikh v poreformennoi promyshlennosti Moskvy." *Rabochii klass i rabochee dvizhenie,* 152–162.

Rozhkova, M. K. "Fabrichnaia promyshlennost' i promysly krest'ian v 60-70-kh godakh XIX v." *Problemy sotsial'no-ekonomicheskoi istorii Rossii.* Moscow, 1971.

———. *Formirovanie kadrov promyshlennykh rabochikh v 60-kh-nachale 80-kh godov XIX v: Po materialam Moskovskoi gubernii.* Moscow, 1974.

Ryndziunskii, P. G. *Gorodskoe grazhdanstvo doreformennoi Rossii.* Moscow, 1958.

———. *Krest'ianskaia promyshlennost' v poreformennoi Rossii.* Moscow, 1966.

Sewell, William H. "Social Mobility in a Nineteenth-Century European City: Some Findings and Implications." *Journal of Interdisciplinary History,* 7, no. 2 (Autumn 1976): 217–33.

Simms, James Y., Jr. "The Crisis of Russian Agriculture at the End of the Nineteenth Century: A Different View." *Slavic Review,* 36, no. 3 (September 1977): 377–98.

Sjoberg, Gideon. *The Pre-Industrial City.* Glencoe, Ill., 1960.

Smelser, Neil, and Seymour Martin Lipset, eds. *Social Structure and Mobility in Economic Development.* Chicago, 1966.

Snegirev, V. *Moskovskie slobody.* Moscow, 1947.

Sorokin, Pitrim, and C. C. Zimmerman. *Principles of Rural-Urban Sociology.* New York, 1929.

Sorokin, Pitrim, Carle C. Zimmerman, and Charles Galpin, eds. *A Systematic Source Book in Rural Sociology,* 3 vols. Minneapolis, 1932.

Sytin, P. V. *Istoriia planirovki i zastroiki Moskvy.* 3 vols. Moscow, 1951–1972.

———. *Iz istorii moskovskikh ulits.* 3d ed. Moscow, 1958.

———. *Otkuda proizoshli nazvaniia ulits Moskvy.* Moscow, 1959.

———. *Po staroi i novoi Moskve.* Moscow, 1947.

Thernstrom, Stephan. *The Other Bostonians: Poverty and Progress in the American Metropolis, 1880–1970.* Cambridge, Mass., 1973.

Thernstrom, Stephan, and Richard Sennett, eds. *Nineteenth-Century Cities: Essays in the New Urban History.* New Haven, 1969.

Thurston, Robert. "Police and People in Moscow, 1906–1914." *Russian Review,* 39, no. 3 (July 1980): 320–38.

Tikhomirov, M. N. *Srednevekovaia Moskva v XIV–XV vekakh.* Moscow, 1957.

Tikhonov, B. V. "Osnovnye napravlenniia migratsii naseleniia Rossii." *Istoricheskie zapiski,* 88 (1971): 210–57.

———. *Pereseleniia v Rossii vo vtoroi polovine XIX v.: Po materialam perepisi 1897 g. i pasportnoi statistik.* Moscow, 1978.

"Urbanism." *Journal of Contemporary History,* July 1969.

Ure, Andrew. *The Philosophy of Manufactures.* 3d ed. London, 1835; reprinted New York, 1969.

Ushedshaia Moskva. Moscow, 1964.

Vasil'ev, B. N. "Sotsial'naia kharakteristika fabrichnykh rabochikh." *Rabochii klass i rabochee dvizhenie,* 141–51.

V'iurkov, A. *Rasskazy o staroi Moskve.* Moscow, 1960.

Vodarskii, Ia. E. *Promyshlennye seleniia tsentral'noi Rossii.* Moscow, 1972.

Von Laue, Theodore H. "Russian Labor between Field and Factory." *California Slavic Studies,* 3 (1964): 33–65.

———. "Russian Peasants in the Factory, 1892–1904." *Journal of Economic History,* 21 (March 1961): 61–80.

Walicki, A. *The Controversy over Capitalism.* Oxford, 1969.

Walkin, Jacob. *The Rise of Democracy in Pre-Revolutionary Russia.* New York, 1962.

Ward, David. *Cities and Immigrants.* New York, 1971.

Weber, Adna F. *The Growth of Cities in the Nineteenth Century.* Ithaca, N.Y., 1965.

Weber, Max. *The City.* Trans. and ed. Don Martindale and Gertrude Neuwirth. New York, 1958.

Wolfe, Albert B. *The Lodging House Question in Boston.* Boston, 1906.

Woodroofe, Kathleen. *From Charity to Social Work in England and the United States.* London, 1962.

Wrigley, E. A. *Nineteenth-Century Society.* Cambridge, 1972.

———. *Population and History.* New York, 1969.

Yaney, George L. *The Systematization of Russian Government: Social Evolution in the Domestic Administration of Imperial Russia, 1711–1905.* Urbana, Ill., 1973.

Zelnik, Reginald. *Labor and Society in Tsarist Russia: The Factory Workers of St. Petersburg, 1855–1870.* Stanford, 1971.

———. "Russian Workers and the Revolutionary Movement." *Journal of Social History* (Winter, 1972–1973): 214–36.

———. "Russian Bebels: An Introduction to the Memoirs of Semen Kanatchikov and Matvei Fisher." *Russian Review,* 35, no. 3 (July 1976): 249–89; and no. 4 (October 1976): 417–47.

Zviagintsev, E. "Vozniknovenie proletarskikh okrain v Moskve." *Istoriia proletariata SSSR*, 2 (1935): 230–44.

REFERENCE AND BIBLIOGRAPHICAL AIDS

Dal', Vladimir. *Tolkovyi slovar' zhivogo velikorusskogo iazyka.* 2d ed. 4 vols. St. Petersburg, 1880. Reprint, Moscow, 1955.

Encyclopedia of the Social Sciences. 15 vols. New York, 1930–1935.

Entsiklopedicheskii slovar', pub. F. A. Brokgauz and I. A. Efron. 41 vols. in 82. St. Petersburg, 1890–1904.

Eroshkin, N. P. *Ocherki istorii gosudarstvennykh uchrezhdenii dorevoliutsionnoi Rossii.* Moscow, 1960.

Glavnoe arkhivnoe upravlenie. *Gosudarstvennyi istoricheskii arkhiv Moskovskoi oblasti: Putevoditel'.* Moscow, 1961.

Gosudarstvennaia duma. *Katalog knig biblioteki Gosudarstvennoi dumy.* St. Petersburg, 1914.

Gul'binskii, Ignatii V. [I. V. Vladislavlev] *Gorod v proizvedeniiakh khudozhestvennoi literatury.* Moscow, 1925.

Imperatorskoe vol'noe ekonomicheskoe obshchestvo. *Bibliograficheskii ukazatel' zemskoi statisticheskoi i otsennochnoi literatury so vremeni uchrezhdeniia zemstva 1864–1903 g.* Vyp. 1. St. Petersburg, 1906.

Isaev, A. A. *Ukazatel' literatury po rynku truda i bor'be s bezrabotitsei.* Moscow, 1925.

Kaplun, S. I. *Polozhenie rabochego klassa: Bibliograficheskii ukazatel'.* Moscow, 1927.

Kir'ianov, Iu. I. *Polozhenie proletariata Rossii: Ukazatel' literatury.* 2 vols. Moscow, 1972.

Kondrat'ev, V. A., and V. I. Nevzorov. *Iz istorii fabrik i zavodov Moskvy i Moskovskoi gubernii (Konets XVIII-nachalo XX vv.): Obzor dokumentov.* Moscow, 1968.

Mezhov, Vladimir I. *Bibliograficheskii ukazatel' knig i statei, otnosiashchikhsia do blagotvoritel'nosti v Rossii i katalog knig biblioteki Imperatorskogo Chelovekoliubivogo obshchestva.* St. Petersburg, 1883.

Moskovskaia gorodskaia duma. *Ukazatel' statei, pomeshchennykh v Izvestiiakh Moskovskoi gorodskoi dumy, 1877–1909.* Moscow, 1909.

Pegov, A. M., ed. *Imena moskovskikh ulits.* Moscow, 1972.

Rogachevskii, Vasilii L. *Raboche-krest'ianskie pisateli.* Moscow, 1926.

"Ukazatel' statei pomeshchennykh v zhurnale *Trudovaia pomoshch'* za 1897–1907 gg." *Trudovaia pomoshch',* 12, no. 6 (June 1909). Reprint, St. Petersburg, 1909.

Index

Abacus, 83–84

"Active" persons, defined, 143

Age: of blue-collar and white-collar workers, 163–64; compared among estate groups, 224; distribution in the immigrant population, 134–36; and length of urban residence, 174; of lodging house residents, 278; marital, 21–22; of Moscow-born and immigrant workers, 167; and occupational mobility, 174, 177–178; patterns in Moscow, 34–36; relative to occupation and birthplace, 373–75; village ties of immigrants influenced by, 114

Agriculture, 11; decline of, 12–15; and the motivations of peasant immigrants, 129; peasant income from, 13, 14–15; by postmen, 50

Alcohol: consumption of, 49; manufacture of, 50; in skid row, 280, 281. *See also* Vodka

Alcoholism: among beggars, 254, 256; in the casual labor force, 185; at lodging houses, 207; in slums, 281

Almsgiving, 257, 350

Almshouses, 39, 42, 198, 199; church support of, 259–60; managed by district guardianships, 318; municipal, 312; number of residents in, 200

American occupational categories, 156–57

Apartments, 349; of artels, 208–9, 220; in basements, 197, 211, 214, 302, 349; communal, 208–9, 220, 225, 228, 349; "cot-chamber" type, 211–14, 220, 302, 349; low-cost or free, 283, 288, 289, 325; number of residents in, 196, 210, 273, 349; number per building, 196; private, 209–14, 349; rental costs of, 212, 234–35; social differentiation in, 235; subletting and subdivisions in, 210, 211, 213

Apprentices, number of, 96

Apprenticeship, 30; in the clothing industry, 89; literacy acquired during, 127

Arbat ward: history of, 52, 53, 54–55; residential patterns in, 54–55, 80, 229–30, 231

Artels, 27, 347; communal apartments of, 208–9, 220, 225, 228; of construction workers, 78; of migratory laborers, 27

Artisan Association, 96

Artisan production, compared with factory production, 86–87

Artisans: downward mobility of, 188–89, 348; economic status of, 158, 188–89; guild, 224; in medieval Moscow, 50–51; self-employed, 158, 160, 169n35, 189, 360; urban housing for, 55–56, 59

Associations: of craftsmen and artisans, 50–51, 96; of laborers, 71, 78, 225. *See also* Artels

Baedecker guidebooks, 60

Bakers, 163, 164, 178

Baku, 31

Banking, size of the labor force in, 78

Barracks for factory workers, 202–3

Bater, James, 86, 350n2; on municipal fiscal constraints, 325

Compositor: Huron Valley Graphics, Inc.
      Text: 10/13 Sabon
   Display: Sabon & Garamond Old Style